PERSPECTIVES
IN
NEURAL COMPUTING

Also in this series

J.G. Taylor and C.L.T. Mannion (Eds.)
Theory and Applications of Neural Networks (NCM90), 3-540-19650-1

J.G. Taylor and C.L.T. Mannion (Eds.)
Coupled Oscillating Neurons (CNO90), 3-540-19744-3

J.G. Taylor
The Promise of Neural Networks, 3-540-19773-7

J.G. Taylor (Ed.)
Neural Network Applications (NCM91), 3-540-19772-9

J.G. Taylor, E.R. Caianiello,
R.M.J. Cotterill and J.W. Clark (Eds.)

NEURAL NETWORK DYNAMICS

Proceedings of the Workshop on Complex
Dynamics in Neural Networks, June 17–21 1991 at
IIASS, Vietri, Italy

Springer-Verlag
London Berlin Heidelberg New York
Paris Tokyo Hong Kong
Barcelona Budapest

J. G. Taylor, BA, BSc, MA, PhD, FInstP
Director, Centre for Neural Networks, Department of Mathematics,
King's College, Strand, London WC2R 2LS, UK

E.R. Caianiello
Dipartimento di Fisica Teorica, Università di Salerno,
Via S. Allende, 84081 Baronissi (SA), Italy

R.M.J. Cotterill, BSc, MS, PhD, DSc, FInstP, C.Phys.
Department of Biophysics, The Technical University of Denmark,
Building 307, DK-2800 Lyngby, Denmark

J.W. Clark
Department of Physics, Washington University,
St Louis, Missouri 63130, USA

Series Editors

J. G. Taylor, BA, BSc, MA, PhD, FInstP
Director, Centre for Neural Networks, Department of Mathematics,
King's College, Strand, London WC2R 2LS, UK

C. L. T. Mannion, BSc, PhD, MInstP
Department of Electrical Engineering, University of Surrey, Guildford,
Surrey, GU2 5XH, UK

ISBN-13: 978-3-540-19771-3   e-ISBN-13: 978-1-4471-2001-8
DOI: 10.1007/978-1-4471-2001-8

British Library Cataloguing in Publication Data
A catalogue record for this book is available from the British Library

Library of Congress Cataloging-in-Publication Data
A catalog record for this book is available from the Library of Congress

Typesetting: Camera ready by author
34/3830-543210 Printed on acid-free paper

PREFACE

The papers in this volume cover a unique range of topics in which neural networks play a fundamental role. Firstly there are problems raised in the general analysis of neural network activity. Various types of network architectures and nodes are described, as are the training rules. The resultant framework of theory is important in looking at problems of application of such networks.

Secondly there is the new paradigm of oscillatory networks. These range from applications to early visual processing to higher level cognitive activity, and involve networks using correlations of neuronal activity to those which are coupled relaxation oscillators. The dynamics range from that of simple S^1 oscillators to more complex integrate-and-fire neurons with sets of ionic currents of quite general time courses. The activity in this area is part of the important bridge between neural computation (as a branch of artificial intelligence) and computational neuroscience (as a branch of neurobiology).

Thirdly there are contributions on the new paradigm of doing science by neural networks. In particular there are essays on the determination of structural properties of proteins, on nuclear phenomenology, and on resonance searches in high energy physics, as well as on the investigation of information storage. Finally there are more direct biological applications of neural networks, especially in modelling various aspects of visual cortical architecture and of visual processing.

The contributions are up-dated versions of papers given at the Workshop on Complex Dynamics in Neural Networks, June 17-21 1991 at IIASS, Vietri, Italy. We would like to thank the Director of IIASS and his staff for making the meeting possible, and for providing the beautiful environment of Vietri in which the meeting was held.

January 1992   J.G. Taylor

CONTENTS

CONTRIBUTORS

Aberger, C.
Institut für Theoretische Physik, Johannes-Kepler-Universität, A-4040 Linz, Austria

Arndt, M.
Department of Biophysics, Philipps-University Marburg, Renthof 7, D-3550 Marburg, Germany

Babloyantz, A.
Université Libre de Bruxelles, CP 231 - Campus de la Plaine, Boulevard du Triomphe, B-1050 Bruxelles, Belgium

Baird, B.
Department of Mathematics, and Department of Molecular and Cell Biology, University of California Berkeley, Berkeley, CA 94720, USA

Bohr, H.
Noyes Laboratory, and School of Chemical Sciences, University of Illinois at Urbana-Champaign, Urbana, IL 61801, USA

Borisyuk, G.N.
Research Computing Center of the USSR Academy of Sciences, Pushchino, Moscow 142292, USSR

Borisyuk, R.M.
Research Computing Center of the USSR Academy of Sciences, Pushchino, Moscow 142292, USSR

Bressloff, P.C.
GEC-Marconi Ltd, Hirst Research Centre, East Lane, Wembley, HA9 7PP, UK

Caianiello, E.R.
Dipartimento di Fisica Teorica, Università di Salerno, Via S. Allende, 84081 Baronissi (SA), Italy

Clark, J.W.
McDonnell Center for the Space Sciences, and Department of Physics, Washington University, St. Louis, MO 63130, USA

Cotterill, R.M.J.
Division of Biophysics, Technical University of Denmark, DK-2800 Lyngby, Denmark

Destexhe, A.
Université Libre de Bruxelles, CP 231 - Campus de la Plaine, Boulevard du Triomphe, B-1050 Bruxelles, Belgium

Dicke, P.
Department of Biophysics, Philipps-University Marburg, Renthof 7, D-3550 Marburg,
Germany

Eckhorn, R.
Department of Biophysics, Philipps-University Marburg, Renthof 7, D-3550 Marburg,
Germany

Engel, A.K.
Max-Planck-Institut für Hirnforschung, D-6000 Frankfurt/Main, Germany

Erb, M.
Department of Biophysics, Philipps-University Marburg, Renthof 7, D-3550 Marburg,
Germany

Folk, R.
Institut für Theoretische Physik, Johannes-Kepler-Universität, A-4040 Linz, Austria

Gazula, S.
McDonnell Center for the Space Sciences, and Department of Physics,
Washington University, St. Louis, MO 63130, USA

Gerstner, W.
Physik-Department der Technische Universität München, D-8046 Garching
bei München, Germany

Giannakopoulos, F.
Mathematisches Institut der Universität zu Köln, D-5000 Köln, Germany

Gorse, D.
Department of Computer Science, University College, Gower Street,
London, WC1E 6BT, UK

Hartmann, G.
Fachbereich 14 Elektrotechnik Universität-Gesamthochschule-Paderborn,
Pohlweg 47-49, D-4790 Paderborn, Germany

Holden, A.V.
Department of Physiology, and Centre for Nonlinear Studies, University of Leeds,
Leeds, LS2 9JT, UK

Hyde, J.
Department of Applied Mathematical Studies, and Department of Physiology,
University of Leeds, Leeds, LS2 9JT, UK

Kammen, D.M.
Department of Physics, Harvard University, Cambridge, MA 02138, USA

Khibnik, A.I.
Research Computing Center of the USSR Academy of Sciences, Pushchino,
Moscow, 142292, USSR
and
Department of Computer Science, Katholieke Universiteit Leuven, B-3001 Leuven,
Belgium

Klemmer, N.
Physik-Department der Technische Universität München, D-8046 Garching
bei München, Germany

König, P.
Max-Planck-Institut für Hirnforschung, D-6000 Frankfurt/Main, Germany

Kürten, K.E.
Institut für Theoretische Physik, Johannes-Kepler-Universität, A-4040 Linz, Austria
and
Institut für Neuroinformatik, Ruhr-Universität-Bochum, D-4630 Bochum, Germany

Littlewort, G.C.
Department of Physics, University of Arizona, Tucson, AZ 85721, USA
and
Department of Cognitive Science, University of California, San Diego, La Jolla,
CA 92093-0515, USA

Mallot, H.A.
Institut für Neuroinformatik, Ruhr-Universität-Bochum, D-4630 Bochum, Germany

Marinaro, M.
Dipartimento di Fisica Teorica, Università di Salerno, Via S. Allende,
84081 Baronissi (SA), Italy

McGuire, P.C.
Department of Physics, University of Arizona, Tucson, AZ 85721, USA

Müller, B.
Department of Physics, Duke University, Durham, NC 27706, USA

Niebur, E.
Computation and Neural Systems Program, California Institute of Technology,
Pasadena, CA 91125, USA

Nielsen, C.
Division of Biophysics, Technical University of Denmark, DK-2800 Lyngby, Denmark

Palm, G.
C.u.O. Vogt Institut für Hirnforschung, Moorenstraße 5, University of Düsseldorf,
D-4000 Düsseldorf 1, Germany

Palmer, R.G.
Department of Physics, Duke University, Durham, NC 27706, USA

Pershing, C.
Department of Physics, University of Arizona, Tucson, AZ 85721, USA

Rafelski, J.
Department of Physics, University of Arizona, Tucson, AZ 85721, USA

Rau, J.
Department of Physics, Duke University, Durham, NC 27706, USA

Reitboeck, H.J.
Department of Biophysics, Philipps-University Marburg, Renthof 7, D-3550 Marburg,
Germany

Ritz, R.
Physik-Department der Technische Universität München, D-8046 Garching
bei München, Germany

Schuster, H.G.
Institut für Theoretische Physik, Universität Kiel, D-2300 Kiel 1, Germany

Schweng, H.
Institut für Theoretische Physik, Johannes-Kepler-Universität, A-4040 Linz, Austria

Singer, W.
Max-Planck-Institut für Hirnforschung, D-6000 Frankfurt/Main, Germany

Sommer, F.T.
C.u.O. Vogt Institut für Hirnforschung, Moorenstraße 5, University of Düsseldorf,
D-4000 Düsseldorf 1, Germany

Taylor, J.G.
Director, Centre for Neural Networks, Department of Mathematics, King's College,
Strand, London, WC2R 2LS, UK

Thompson, B.C.
Department of Mathematics and Computer Sciences, University College of
Swansea, Singleton Park, Swansea, SA2 8PP, UK

Tucker, J.V.
Department of Mathematics and Computer Sciences, University College of
Swansea, Singleton Park, Swansea, SA2 8PP, UK

van Hemmen, J.L.
Institut voor Theoretische Fysica, Katholieke Universiteit Leuven, B-3001 Leuven,
Belgium
and
Physik-Department der Technische Universität München, D-8046 Garching
bei München, Germany

Withington, D.
Department of Physiology, and Centre for Nonlinear Studies, University of Leeds,
Leeds, LS2 9JT, UK

Zhang, H.
Department of Physiology, and Centre for Nonlinear Studies, University of Leeds,
Leeds, LS2 9JT, UK

FOUNDATIONS
OF NEURAL
NET DYNAMICS

Information and pattern capacities in neural associative memories with feedback for sparse memory patterns

Günther Palm and Friedrich T. Sommer

C. u. O. Vogt Institut für Hirnforschung, Moorenstr. 5
University of Düsseldorf
D-4000 Düsseldorf 1, Germany

Abstract

How to judge the performance of associative memories in applications? Using information theory, we examine the static structure of memory states and spurious states of a recurrent associative memory after learning. In this framework we consider the critical pattern capacity often used in the literature and introduce the information capacity as a more relevant performance measure for pattern completion. For two types of local learning rule, the Hebb and the clipped Hebb rule our method yields new asymptotic estimates for the information capacity.

1   Introduction

How many patterns can be stored in a large associative memory? The answer is given by the critical pattern capacity α_c (in patterns per neuron). How much information can be stored with autoassociation in a large recurrent associative memory? The answer is given by the memory capacity C (in bits per synapse). While the first question is well treated in the literature, there are no answeres at all yet to the second question. However, it is the second question, which is relevant for applications of associative memory in information retrieval.

This paper provides answers to the two questions for the case where the stored patterns are sparse (low average activity p). The number of storable patterns per neuron α_c diverges for $p \to 0$, but their information content $I(p)$ goes to zero. (p is the probability that a neuron is active in a pattern, $I(p)$ is the Shannon information.) This divergence is removed by defining the critical pattern capacity as $P := \alpha_c I(p)$. But P is still different from the memory capacity C as defined in Section 2.

The non-sparse case, typically $p = 1/2$ is more often treated in the physics literature [2, 13]. But in this case, where $I(p) = 1$ and $P = \alpha_c < \infty$, an ordinary computer memory with a suitable software is normally more efficient than an associative memory because the effort of computation and storage is at least proportional to the number of neurons n in the neural network and thus to the number of storable patterns.

Thus we restrict our attention to the sparse case, where α_c diverges and neural associative memories can in fact become more efficient than conventional computer implementations [1].

We propose a method of calculating information capacities considering the discrepancy between the set of memory states S and the set of fixed points $\mathcal{F}$ of the network dynamics, where the synaptic connectivity matrix is formed by a specified learning rule. Our method reveals the structure of these sets in the state space of the system by examining a retrieval procedure which checks the membership of each state to the set $\mathcal{F}$ and disregards the transient behaviour of states not belonging to $\mathcal{F}$. Although we concentrate on a model with parallel update the results are valid for sequential update as well, since the classification of fixed points is independent of whether the considered dynamics is sequential or parallel.

This treatment takes into account the effects of spurious states on the pattern completion property [11] of the memory which yields new asymptotic estimates for the memory capacity. These values may serve as stricter upper bounds to the information practically retrievable with more realistic iterative retrieval procedures than the critical pattern capacity values considered in the literature.

Our method also reproduces the critical pattern capacity results; in this case it is equivalent to the noise to signal treatment of Palm [3] and Nadal and Toulouse [4] for fixed activity of the memory states. As a new extension our method allows a more accurate calculation of the critical pattern capacity for memory patterns not with fixed but with low average activity (Appendix 3).

In Section 2 we give the definitions of the two types of capacity in the framework of this method mentioned at the beginning. Section 3 outlines the calculation Ansatz. Section 4 leads to the explicit results for the two learning rules considered. A detailed discussion situating our results in the relation to works using noise to signal calculations [3, 4, 5] and to works using methods of statistical physics [6, 7, 8] is given in Section 6.

The model

As storing process we consider two types of local learning rules. Let $\{0,1\}^n$ be the space of neural activity states. We choose a set of randomly generated memory states with fixed activity $\mathcal{S} := \{\xi^\mu \in \mathcal{M}_k : \mu = 1, ..., M\}$ with
$\mathcal{M}_k := \{x \in \{0,1\}^n : |x| = k\}$ to generate the memory matrix c_{ij} via the learning rule. As the learning rules we treat

$$\text{the Hebb rule} \qquad c_{ij} = \sum_{\mu=1}^M \xi_i^\mu \xi_j^\mu \qquad (1)$$

$$\text{and the clipped Hebb rule} \quad c_{ij} = H\left[\sum_{\mu=1}^M \xi_i^\mu \xi_j^\mu\right] \qquad (2)$$

$H[x]$ is the Heavyside function.

In the retrieval process we consider iteration of a parallel update step which is defined as the mapping $x \to x'$ with

$$x_j' = H\left[\sum_i c_{ij} x_i - \Theta\right] \quad \forall\; j\,,$$

where Θ denotes a global threshold. If we restrict the retrieval to $x \in \mathcal{M}_k$ the global threshold can be chosen fixed during the iteration process in order to preserve the mean activity.

2 Capacities and retrieval quality criteria

We focus on the channel capacity of the information channel consisting of the local storing process and a certain retrieval procedure. In this retrieval procedure the subset $\mathcal{F} := \{x \in \mathcal{M}_k : x = x'\}$ of fixed points of c_{ij} is obtained by checking for every $x \in \mathcal{M}_k$ the fixed point condition $x = x'$.

Any definition of information capacity is combined with a quality criterion restricting the errors which are tolerated in the retrieval process. The error in our retrieval procedure can be expressed as the correction information necessary to obtain $\mathcal{S}$ from the retrieved $\mathcal{F}$ and is written as

$$I(\mathcal{S} \mid \mathcal{F}) = I_{um} + I_{ss} \qquad (3)$$

I_{um} and I_{ss} are the contributions from the two types of errors which can be expressed in terms of the error probabilities :
$p_{um} := p[x \notin \mathcal{F} \mid x \in \mathcal{S}]$, the probability of an <u>u</u>nstable <u>m</u>emory state ,
$p_{ss} := p[x \in \mathcal{F} \mid x \notin \mathcal{S}]$, the probability of a <u>s</u>purious <u>s</u>tate .
The explicit expressions for I_{um} and I_{ss} are given in Section 3.
With the retrieval quality criterion which requires

$$\frac{1}{n^2} I(\mathcal{S} \mid \mathcal{F}) \to 0 \quad \text{as} \quad n \to \infty \qquad (4)$$

we define the **information capacity** as the information channel capacity measured in bits/synapse:

$$C := \frac{1}{n^2} \{I(\mathcal{S}) - I(\mathcal{S} \mid \mathcal{F})\} = I(\mathcal{S})/n^2 \tag{5}$$

where $I(\mathcal{S}) := \sharp \mathcal{M}_k I(p[x \in \mathcal{S}])$ is the information content in $\mathcal{S}$ and $I(p)$ the Shannon information (see Section 3). With $p = p[x \in \mathcal{S}] = M/\sharp \mathcal{M}_k$ we obtain

$$C = MI(p)/n \tag{6}$$

Inserting the maximal number M_1 of memory states for which the criterion (4) is fulfilled we obtain in (5) the information capacity.

The **critical pattern capacity** is usually defined in the physical literature [6, 7, 8] as $P := M_2 I(p)/n$ where now M_2 is the maximal number of memory states satisfying the so called <u>embedding condition</u> (for $\kappa = 0$). This quality criterion is equivalent to the requirement that $\mathcal{S} \subseteq \mathcal{F}$ and can be expressed in our terms as

$$\frac{1}{n^2} I_{um} \to 0 \quad \text{as} \quad n \to \infty \tag{7}$$

Because (4) is more restrictive than (7) the information capacity should remain below the critical pattern capacity . The critical pattern capacity is no channel capacity for any storage and retrieval procedure. It is a measure of the information content of $\mathcal{S}$ and its quality criterion does not guarantee at all that this information is accessible with autoassociative retrieval.

3 Explicit quality criteria

For the prescribed retrieval procedure we derive explicit expressions for the two contributions in formula (3) describing the information loss due to the occurance of spurious states and to unstable memory states respectively.

Defining the Shannon information as usual as
$I(p) = -p \, \mathrm{ld}[p] - (1 - p) \, \mathrm{ld}[1 - p]$ one can formulate explicitly the conditions on the error probabilities defined in Section 2 which are necessary for the fullfillment of the quality criteria (4) and (7).

The quality criterion (7) demanded by the definition of the critical pattern capacity considers only:

$$I_{um} = \sharp \{\mathcal{S} \setminus \mathcal{F}\} I \left(\frac{\sharp \{\mathcal{S} \setminus \mathcal{F}\}}{\sharp \{\mathcal{M}_k \setminus \mathcal{F}\}} \right) = \binom{n}{k} p[x \notin \mathcal{F} \cap x \in \mathcal{S}] \, \mathrm{ld} \left[\frac{p[x \notin \mathcal{F}]}{p[x \notin \mathcal{F} \cap x \in \mathcal{S}]} \right]$$

Using the fact that $\sharp \mathcal{S}, \sharp \mathcal{F} << \sharp \mathcal{M}_k$ we arrive at

$$I_{um}/n^2 = M p_{um} \, \mathrm{ld} \left[\frac{\binom{n}{k}}{M p_{um}} \right] /n^2$$

Thus criterion (7) holds if the error probability p_{um} fulfills

$$\frac{k \, ld\,[n]\, M}{n^2} p_{um} \to 0 \quad \text{as} \quad n \to \infty \tag{8}$$

Furthermore, the stronger quality criterion (4) requires the vanishing of the following term per synapse:

$$I_{\bullet\bullet} = \sharp\mathcal{F}\, I\left(\frac{\sharp\{\mathcal{F}\setminus S\}}{\sharp\mathcal{F}}\right) = \binom{n}{k}\left\{p[x\in\mathcal{F}\cap x\notin S]\, ld\left[\frac{p[x\in\mathcal{F}]}{p[x\in\mathcal{F}\cap x\notin S]}\right]\right.$$
$$\left.+ \; (p[x\in\mathcal{F}] - p[x\in\mathcal{F}\cap x\notin S])\, ld\left[\frac{p[x\in\mathcal{F}]}{p[x\in\mathcal{F}] - p[x\in\mathcal{F}\cap x\notin S]}\right]\right\}$$

Using $\sharp S \ll \sharp\mathcal{M}_k$ and $p[x\notin S] \simeq 1$ and $p[x\in\mathcal{F}] \simeq p[x\in\mathcal{F}\cap x\notin S] + p[x\in S]$ which is true if from (8) follows $p_{um} \to 0$ (this is the case for both rules, see Section 4), we obtain

$$I_{\bullet\bullet}/n^2 = \binom{n}{k}\frac{p_{\bullet\bullet}}{n^2}\, ld\left[1 + \frac{M}{\binom{n}{k}p_{\bullet\bullet}}\right] + \frac{M}{n^2}\, ld\left[1 + \frac{\binom{n}{k}p_{\bullet\bullet}}{M}\right]$$

Since for both rules the order of M is less than n^2, with $u := \binom{n}{k}p_{\bullet\bullet}/n^2$ we can estimate

$$I_{\bullet\bullet}/n^2 \leq u \; ld[1 + 1/u] + ld[1 + u]$$

which vanishes only for $u \to 0$ as $n \to \infty$. Thus the quality criterion (4) holds if p_{um} satisfies (8) and

$$u \simeq \binom{n}{k}p_{\bullet\bullet} \to 0 \quad \text{as} \quad n \to \infty \tag{9}$$

4 Calculation of pattern and information capacities

In Section 3 we derived conditions on the error probabilities (8) and (9) which are necessary for satisfaction of the quality criteria. These conditions will be used in this Section to yield the upper capacity bounds for the two examined learning rules.

First we calculate the error probabilities for the described retrieval process in general. We have to assume asymptotic statistical independence of different synaptical values c_{ij}. In the case of the clipped Hebb rule the asymptotic independence is shown in Appendix 1.

Since in one retrieval step it is decided whether any input state $x \in \mathcal{M}_k$ is a fixed point or not we obtain the defined error probabilities from the treatment of the one-step retrieval process. In the one-step case, if a memory state is entered as input, e_{01} and e_{10} are defined as the error probabilities for a single off output neuron and on output neuron respectively. Without loss of generality we may assume that $x = (1, 1, ..., 0, 0, ...)$. Let us define the probabilities that an input x activates all of its on output neurons

$$\text{for spurious states} \quad Q_{ss} := p\left[\sum_{i=1}^{k} c_{ij} \geq \Theta \text{ for } j = 1, ..., k \mid x \notin S\right] \quad (10)$$

$$\text{for memory states} \quad Q_{ms} := p\left[\sum_{i=1}^{k} c_{ij} \geq \Theta \text{ for } j = 1, ..., k \mid x \in S\right] \quad (11)$$

Because for local learning rules c_{ij} is symmetric there are statistical dependencies of the threshold problems of the first k columns and the single neuron error probabilities only yield lower bounds $Q_{ss} \geq e_{01}^{k}$ and $Q_{ms} \geq (1 - e_{10})^{k}$.

For the error probabilities we obtain

$$p_{ss} = Q_{ss} \, p\left[\sum_{i=1}^{k} c_{ij} < \Theta \text{ for } j = k+1, ..., n \mid x \notin S\right] \simeq Q_{ss} (1 - e_{01})^{n-k} \quad (12)$$

because the threshold problems for the columns $j = k+1, ..., n$ can be regarded as independent and
$p\left[\sum_{i=1}^{k} c_{ij} x_j \geq \Theta \mid x \notin S\right] \simeq p\left[\sum_{i=1}^{k} c_{ij} \xi_j^l \geq \Theta \mid j \in \{j : \xi_j^l = 0\}\right]$.

Similarly

$$\begin{aligned} p_{um} &= 1 - Q_{ms} p\left[\sum_{i=1}^{k} c_{ij} < \Theta \text{ for } j = k+1, ..., n \mid x \in S\right] \\ &\simeq 1 - Q_{ms} (1 - e_{01})^{n-k} \end{aligned} \quad (13)$$

4.1   The clipped Hebb rule

The memory matrix is generated by (2). For this rule which is treated in the one-step retrieval case [10, 11] we know: $p := k/n$, $c_{ij} \in \{0, 1\}$,
$p(c_{ij} = 1) = 1 - (1 - p^2)^M =: q$. In [16] it is shown that for $q = 1/2$ the channel capacity of the learning process reaches its optimum. If the threshold is set equal to $\Theta = k$ the error probabilities are $e_{01} = 2^{-k}$, $e_{10} = 0$, and the number of memory states:

$$M = \frac{n^2}{k^2} \ln[2] \quad (14)$$

It is straightforward to see that $Q_{ss} = 2^{-k^2/2}$ and $Q_{ms} = 1$. To achieve high capacity one has to use sparse coded patterns, i.e.

$$k = a \, \ln[n] \quad (15)$$

with a a positive constant.

Critical pattern capacity

If we put (14) and (15) into (8) the following condition results

$$\frac{\ln[2]}{k} \operatorname{ld}[n] p_{um} = p_{um}/a \to 0 \quad \text{as} \quad n \to \infty$$

With (13) we obtain as necessary condition for the quality criterion (7)

$$n \, e_{01} \to 0 \quad \text{as} \quad n \to \infty \tag{16}$$

which is equivalent with a low noise to signal criterion in the one-step retrieval process called in [9] the <u>hifi condition</u>. If we put the error behaviour for the clipped rule in (16) the requirement: $a > 1/\ln[2]$ on the constant a in (15) is demanded. Using this constraint on a in the equation (6) with (14) we obtain the critical pattern capacity

$$P = \ln[2] \tag{17}$$

Information capacity

In this range of sparseness from (12) the error probability can be written as

$$p_{ss} \simeq \exp\left[-\frac{\ln[2]}{2} \left(a \ln[n] \right)^2 \right]$$

To fulfill the second quality criterion this is inserted into (9). In this condition the leading exponent is $\quad a(\ln[n])^2 \left[1 - a\ln[2]\,/2 \right]$. Negative exponent requires the stronger condition on the constant in (15) $\quad a > 2/\ln[2]$. With this constraint as in (17) we find for the information capacity

$$C = \frac{\ln[2]}{2} \tag{18}$$

4.2 The unclipped Hebb rule

In this case the matrix c_{ij} is generated in the storing process according to (1). For the unclipped Hebb rule the error probabilities for one step retrieval are approximately [4, 12, 16]

$$e_{01} \simeq G\left(-\frac{\vartheta n}{\sqrt{kM}} \right) \quad , \quad e_{10} \simeq G\left(-\frac{(1-\vartheta)n}{\sqrt{kM}} \right)$$

($G(x)$ being the Gauss integral, $0 \leq \vartheta \leq 1$ the normalized threshold, see [16].) Low errors can only be expected in the range of high signal to noise ratio: $r := n/\sqrt{kM} \to \infty$. Then the large n behaviour of the error probabilities is given

$$e_{01} \propto \exp\left[-\frac{\vartheta^2}{2kM} n^2 \right] \quad , \quad e_{10} \propto \exp\left[-\frac{(1-\vartheta)^2}{2kM} n^2 \right]$$

see Proposition 1 in Appendix 2.

Critical pattern capacity
If we put

$$M = b \ n^2/(k \ln[n]) \tag{19}$$

with b a positive constant the condition (8) reduces to $p_{um} \rightarrow 0$ as in the clipped case. Again the condition (16) has to be satisfied. If we insert the error behaviour of the unclipped Hebb rule we obtain the condition on the constant in (19) $b < \vartheta^2/2$. Using this in (6) it leads with $\vartheta \rightarrow 1$ to the critical pattern capacity

$$P = \frac{1}{2\ln[2]} \tag{20}$$

Information capacity
In Proposition 2 of Appendix 2 we show that the error probability p_{ss} behaves like

$$p_{ss} \propto \exp\left[-\frac{\vartheta^2}{4M} n^2\right] \quad \text{as} \quad n \rightarrow \infty$$

Inserting this into (9) we obtain as the leading exponent: $k \ln[n] - \frac{\vartheta^2}{4M} n^2 \rightarrow 0$ which becomes negative for $b < \vartheta^2/4$. This yields memory capacity

$$C = \frac{1}{4\ln[2]} \tag{21}$$

5 Discussion

Our iterative retrieval procedure just extracts the set $\mathcal{F}$ of fixed points of the system. The capacity of the information channel consisting of the storing process and our retrieval process (the information capacity) can be treated using noise to signal calculations for one-step retrieval. The quality criterion of the information capacity is that the learned patterns are recognized as known and all other patterns are classified as unknown.

In our framework it is also possible to define another quality criterion yielding the critical pattern capacity (see Section 2) that has been investigated in the literature before by several methods. In the quality criterion connected to critical pattern capacity one only requires that the learned patterns are recognized; the requirement that unlearned patterns should be classified as unknown is dropped. The two quality criteria fix a range of the memory load M in which the mean number of spurious states vary between the maximum ($p_{ss} \rightarrow 1$) for the critical pattern capacity and zero ($p_{ss} \rightarrow 0$) for the information capacity.

5.1 Critical pattern capacity results

Our evaluation is essentially equivalent to the calculation in the work of Palm [9] and Nadal and Toulouse [4] (in their so called "low error regime") albeit they both consider the case of hetero association. The new aspect of our results is the extension of the treatment to memory states that are not restricted to $\mathcal{M}_k$ but have a low average density $p = k/n$ of ones (see Appendix 3) which keeps the results unchanged. Therefore we can compare our results to works treating memory states with low average activity with methods of statistical physics.

Our value for the Hebb rule (20) is a confirmation of the result of Tsodyks and Feigelman [6] calculated with mean field theory à la Amit et al [13]. They use a learning rule which approaches the Hebb rule for vanishing p. The result also coincides with the Gardner bound [7] also obtained applying techniques of statistical physics. It is an upper bound on the pattern capacity for any storing processes. Already in [4] it is mentioned that in the sparse case the Gardner limit [7], which is calculated without assumption of a local learning rule, can be reached by such a local learning rule. This is surprising because local learning rules necessarily generate a symmetric memory matrix. For nonsparse activities the Gardner limit cannot be reached with local rules: In [14] Gardner, Gutfreund and Yekutieli introduced a symmetry constraint in the Gardner calculation and obtained values far below the Gardner limit for symmetric learning matrices. In addition, the local learning bound see [16] and Figure 1 is far below the Gardner bound for nonsparse activity.

The fact that the critical pattern capacity for the clipped Hebbrule exceeds the Gardner bound of 0.29 calculated by Gutfreund and Stein [8] led to a discussion started in [8] and [5]. Nadal [5] explained this inconsitency with the fixed activity level in the Willshaw calculation. Our observation that the Willshaw result [4] is robust under the extension to memory states with fluctuating activity contradicts the explanation of Nadal. In his calculation Nadal requires the fulfillment of a mean hifi condition, in which the one-step error is averaged over the distribution of activities of the memories. This quality criterion yields a critical pattern capacity value below the Willshaw result. It is more restrictive than our criterion (25) which is sufficient to keep the averaged information loss due to unstable memory states negligible.

We believe that the Gutfreund and Stein value is so low, because the the error constraint in the Gardner calculation requires exactly zero error instead of asymptotically vanishing average error.

The values (20) and (17) can be reproduced in computer simulations with reasonable accuracy: see [15] and [18].

5.2   Information capacity results

For the Hebb rule our estimate of the information capacity (21) turns out to reach the local learning bound defined in [17] and displayed in Figure 1. Also for the clipped Hebb rule our result (18) coincides with the channel capacity of an optimal but nonconstructive iterative retrieval process as calculated in [11].

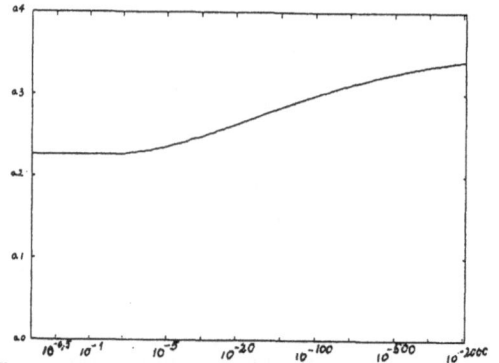

Figure 1: The local learning bound as a function of p, see [16]

Thus the retrieval procedure considered here is very idealistic and our treatment could not describe the more realistic iterative retrieval process, where one starts with an initial adress pattern and gradually updates it to find the closest fixed point. It does not regard the transient behaviour of states which are not fixed points; in real iterative retrieval there will occur effects like confusion due to irregular shapes of the basins of individual memory states and the existence of initial states whose dynamics ends outside $\mathcal{M}_k$ or in cycles. Up to now, however, no other measure can be found in the literature that considers these effects. Our information capacity value is in fact a better upper bound on the information which can effectively be retrieved with autoassociation using any realistic iterative retrieval process than the critical pattern capacity.

Since fixed point retrieval turns out to yield twice the values of one-step autoassociation, see [9], the information capacity for practical iterative retrieval procedures should be between $C/2$ and C.

5.3 Summary and perspective

The following table presents the new results of this paper together with values of the Gardner bound and the local learning bound.

	Pattern capacity P	Information capacity C
clipped Hebb rule	$\ln[2]$	$\ln[2]/2$
Hebb rule	$1/(2\ln[2])$	$1/(4\ln[2])$
Gardner bound	$1/(2\ln[2])$	
Local learning bound		$1/(4\ln[2])$

Finally we summarize the arguments for local learning rules and sparse patterns as the most promising combination for applications:

- Local learning is simple and fast: it needs two variables and one learning step.
- Sparse patterns allow economical retrieval since $\alpha_c \to \infty$ only if $p \to 0$ [7, 2, 13].

- For sparse patterns $p \to 0$ and only for sparse patterns it is possible to reach the Gardner bound using local learning rules [4].
- Within the class of local learning rules the maximum storage capacity is reached for $p \to 0$ and the Hebb rule [16], see Figure 1.
- Asymptotic information capacity values between 17% and 35% can be reached as compared to the legendary $P = 14\%$ value of the Hopfield model [2].

Thus Local learning and sparsely coded patterns naturally go together. And for technical applications of neural associative memories the combination of $\{0, 1\}$ neurons, the Hebb rule (clipped or unclipped) and sparse patterns is clearly the best.

Appendix 1

In this section we show for the clipped Hebb rule the statistical independence of two different matrix elements.

Proposition: For the binary hetero-associative (or auto-associative) storage matrix c we have

$$\frac{p[c_{1j} = 1 \text{ and } c_{2j} = 1]}{p[c_{1j} = 1] \cdot p[c_{2j} = 1]} \to 1 \text{ for } n \to \infty$$

and

$$\frac{p[c_{j1} = 1 \text{ and } c_{j2} = 1]}{p[c_{j1} = 1] \cdot p[c_{j2} = 1]} \to 1 \text{ for } n \to \infty,$$

if $p, q \to 0$ and $x := Mpq$ does not go to zero for $n \to \infty$.

Proof: $p[c_{ij} = 1] = 1 - (1 - pq)^M$.

$p[c_{1j} = 1 \text{ and } c_{2j} = 1] =$
$p[(\exists k : x_1^k = x_2^k = 1 \text{ and } y_j^k = 1) \text{ or } (\exists l, m : x_1^l, x_2^l = 0, x_1^m = 0, x_2^m, y_j^l = 1, y_j^m = 1)]$
$$= 1 - (p(E_1) + p(E_2) - p(E_1 \cap E_2)),$$

where

$$E_1 = [\forall k : \text{not } (x_1^k = x_2^k = 1 \text{ and } y_j^k = 1) \text{ and not } (x_1^k = 1, x_2^k = 0, y_j^k = 1)]$$

and

$$E_2 = [\forall k : \text{not } (x_1^k = x_2^k = 1 \text{ and } y_j^k = 1) \text{ and not } (x_1^k = 0, x_2^k = 1, y_j^k = 1)].$$

Thus $p(E_1) = p(E_2) = (1 - pq)^M$ and $p(E_1 \cap E_2) = (1 - q(2p - p^2))^M$.

Therefore

$$p[\, c_{1j} = 1 \text{ and } c_{2j} = 1] - p[c_{1j} = 1] \cdot p[c_{2j} = 1]$$
$$= (1 - 2qp + qp^2)^M - (1 - pq)^{2M} = (1 - 2qp + qp^2)^M - (1 - 2pq + p^2q^2)^M$$
$$= e^{-M(2pq - p^2q)} - e^{-M(2pq - p^2q^2)} = e^{-2pqM}(e^{Mp^2q} - e^{Mp^2q^2}).$$

We obtain

$$\frac{p[c_{1j} = 1 \text{ and } c_{2j} = 1] - p[c_{1j} = 1] \cdot p[c_{2j} = 1]}{p[c_{1j} = 1] \cdot p[c_{2j} = 1]} \quad = \quad \frac{e^{-2x}(e^{px} - e^{qpx})}{(1 - e^{-x})^2} \to 0$$

since $px \to 0$ and $pqx \to 0$.

This proposition shows the asymptotic pairwise independence of the entries c_{ij} in the memory matrix c, since entries which are not on the same row or column of the matrix, are independent anyway.

In order to show complete independence one would have to consider arbitrary finite sets of entries c_{ij}. In this strict sense the entries cannot be independent asymptotically. For example, if one considers all entries in one column of the matrix, then

$$p[c_{ij} = 0 \text{ for all } i] = (1 - q)^M \approx e^{-Mq}$$

which is in general not equal to

$$p_0^m = (1 - pq)^{Mm} \approx e^{-Mmpq}, \text{ where } p_0 = (1 - pq)^M = p[M_{ij} = 0].$$

Thus independence can at the best be shown for sets of entries of the matrix c up to a limited cardinality $L(n)$. The worst case, which is also important for our calculations of storage capacity, is again when all entries are in the same column (or row) of the matrix. This case is treated in the next proposition, which gives only a rough estimate.

Proposition:

$$\frac{p[c_{ij} = 1 \text{ for } i = 1, \ldots, l]}{p[c_{ij} = 1]^l} \to 1 \text{ for } n \to \infty$$

as long as $pl^2 \to 0$ and $x = Mpq$ does not go to zero for $n \to \infty$.

Proof:

$$
\begin{aligned}
p[c_{ij} = 1] \;\leq\; & p[c_{ij} = 1 | c_{ij} = 1 \text{ for } i = 1, \ldots, l - 1] \\
\leq\; & p[c_{ij} = 1 | \text{ there are at least } l - 1 \text{ pairs } (x^k, y^k) \text{ with } y_j^k = 1] \\
=\; & 1 - (1 - p)^{l-1}(1 - pq)^{M-l+1}.
\end{aligned}
$$

Therefore

$$
\begin{aligned}
0 \;\leq\; & \log \frac{p[c_{ij} = 1 \text{ for } i = 1, \ldots, l]}{p[c_{ij} = 1]^l} \\
\leq\; & \sum_{i=0}^{l-1} \log \frac{1 - (1 - p)^i (1 - pq)^{M-i}}{1 - (1 - pq)^M} \\
=\; & \sum_{i=0}^{l-1} \log \frac{1 - (\frac{1-p}{1-pq})^i p_0}{1 - p_0}
\end{aligned}
$$

$$\leq \sum_{i=0}^{l-1} \log \frac{1-(1-ip)p_0}{1-p_0}, \text{ since } (\frac{1-p}{1-pq})^i \geq (1-p)^i \geq 1-ip,$$

$$\leq \sum_{i=0}^{l-1} ip\frac{p_0}{1-p_0}, \text{ since } \log(1+x) \leq x,$$

$$\leq \frac{p \cdot p_0}{1-p_0} \cdot \frac{l^2}{2} \to 0 \text{ for } p \cdot l^2 \to 0,$$

$$\text{and if } p_0 = (1-pq)^M \approx e-Mpq = e-x \not\to 1.$$

Appendix 2

In the sequel we present some calculations, which are necessary for the treatment of the Hebb rule:

Proposition 1:

$$(2\pi t^2)^{-1/2}e^{-t^2/2}(1-t^2) \leq G(-t) = 1 - G(t) \leq (2\pi t^2)^{-1/2}e^{-t^2/2}$$

Proof: Since $x^2 = t^2 + (x-t)^2 + 2t(x-t)$, we have

$$\int_t^\infty e^{-x^2/2}dx = e^{-t^2/2}\int_0^\infty e^{-x^2/2}e^{-xt}dx$$

From this and with $e^{-x^2/2} \leq 1$ we obtain the second inequality directly (since $\int_0^\infty e^{-xt}dx = 1/t$) and the first one after partial integration (since $\int_0^\infty xe^{-xt}dx = 1/t$). $\Diamond$

Proposition 2:
With the definitions of Section 3 for the Hebb rule

$$Q_{ss} \propto \exp\left[\frac{-\theta^2 n^2}{4M}\right] \quad \text{as } n \to \infty \tag{22}$$

holds.
Proof:
Again $x = (1,1,...,0,0,...)$, so in the following we consider only the left upper k^2 block of c_{ij}.
i)

$$Q_{ss} \leq p[\underbrace{\sum_{i=1,j\leq i}^{k,k} c_{ij}}_{=:s} \geq \frac{k\Theta}{2}] = G\left(-\frac{n\theta}{\sqrt{2m}}\right) \leq \frac{\sqrt{2m}}{n\sqrt{2\pi}}\exp\left[-\frac{n^2\theta^2}{4M}\right]$$

since $E(s) = k^2 Mp^2/2$, $\sigma^2(s) = E(s)$ and $\Theta = kMp^2 + k\theta$, see Proposition 1.

ii) Let $\{N_{ij} : i = 1,...,k/l\}$ be a partition of each column j with $|N_{ij}| = l$. T denotes the smallest set of N_{ij} which covers the left lower triangle completely. We have

$$Q_{ss} \geq p[\underbrace{\sum_{h\in N_{ij}} c_{hj}}_{=:s'} \geq \frac{\Theta l}{k} \,\forall\, N_{ij} \in T] = p\left[s' \geq \frac{\Theta l}{k}\right]^{(1+2+...+k/l)l} \tag{23}$$

$$= G\left(-\frac{n\theta\sqrt{l}}{k\sqrt{M}}\right)^{\frac{k^2}{2l}} \simeq \left(\frac{k\sqrt{M}}{\sqrt{2\pi ln\theta}}\right)^{\frac{k^2}{2l}} \exp\left[-\frac{n^2\theta^2}{4M}\right] \qquad (24)$$

The last estimate follows from Proposition 1.

◇

Appendix 3

In this Appendix we sketch the extension of our calculation of the critical pattern capacity for memory states having a fluctuating activity with the average sparseness $p = k/n$, i.e: $\quad p[x \in S \mid |x| = l] = M p^l (1-p)^{n-l}$.

Instead of (6) we have to examine

$$I(S) = \sum_{x\in\{0,1\}^n} I(p[x \in S])$$

$$= \sum_{l=0}^{n} \binom{n}{l} I\left(p[x \in S \mid |x| = l]\right) \simeq Mnp \ \mathrm{ld}\left[\frac{p}{1-p}\right] \simeq MnI(p)$$

for $M \ll n^k$, which is true in all cases considered. Thus the information content of S is unchanged.

Considering the following information term

$$I_{um} = \sum_{x\in\{0,1\}^n} p\,[\mathrm{no}]\, I\,(p\,[x \in S \mid \mathrm{no}])$$

$$= \sum_{l=0}^{n} \binom{n}{k} p[x \notin \mathcal{F} \cap x \in S \mid |x| = l] \ \mathrm{ld}\left[\frac{p[x \notin \mathcal{F} \mid |x| = l]}{p[x \notin \mathcal{F} \cap x \in S \mid |x| = l]}\right]$$

After some algebra with approximations similiar as in the derivation of (8), the necessary condition for the quality criterion (7) on the error probabilities $p_{um}^l := p[x \notin \mathcal{F} \mid x \in S \cap |x| = l]$ is now

$$\frac{M \ \mathrm{ld}[N]}{n^2} \sum_{l=0}^{n} \binom{n}{l} p^l (1-p)^{n-l} p_{um}^l \to 0 \quad \text{for} \quad n \to \infty \qquad (25)$$

Proposition 3: Fulfillment of (8) implies that (25) holds.
Proof:
The one-step error probabilities for the clipped Hebb rule for fluctuating activity:

$$e_{01}^l = \sum_{l'=\Theta}^{l} B(l, q, l') \ , \quad e_{10}^l = H[l - \Theta]$$

with the definition of q in Section 4, $H[x]$ in Section 1 and
$B(n, q, l) := \binom{n}{l} q^l (1-q)^{n-l}$. If we put the threshold $\Theta = ck$ with the constant $c < 1$ close to one and insert (14) we obtain for (25)

$$\frac{1}{k} \sum_{l=0}^{ck} B(n, p, l) + \frac{1}{k} \sum_{l=ck}^{n} B(n, p, l) p_{um}^l =: A + B$$

The first term on the LHS, denoted by A can be estimated using the Gauß approximation: $A \simeq G(\sqrt{k}(1-c))$, which vanishes for $\ln[n](1-c) \to \infty$. Since the binomial distribution is symetric around $l = k$ we cut the sum in the second term: $B = \sum_{l=ck}^{k(2-c)} B(n,p,l)p_{um}^l$. The error probability p_{um}^l takes its maximal value at $l = k(2-c)$. Using a Chernoff approximation for the binomial sum in e_{01}^l we can estimate the second term:
$B \leq p_{um}^{k(2-c)} = ne_{01}^{k(2-c)} = n\exp(ck\ln[q])$. Thus, if c approaches unity slowly enough to guarantee the vanishing of term A, condition (8) provides vanishing of the second term B as well, and (25) is fulfilled.
◊

For the sake of brevity we concentrated on the proof for the clipped case, mutatis mutandis it is possible to show Proposition 3 for the Hebb rule.

To compare our results with the calculations in the cited works we also choose a fixed threshold for all input patterns. Of course, in finite systems the retrieval quality can be improved by adjusting the threshold to the number of active neurons in the individual input pattern x, i.e.: $\Theta = \sharp\{i : x_i = 1\}$. However, this different threshold adjustment does not affect the asymptotic capacity values.

References

[1] G. Palm, Computing with neural networks, *Science 235, 1227 - 1228 (1987)*

[2] J. J. Hopfield, Neural networks and physical systems with emergent collective computational abilities, *Proc. Natl. Sci. 79, 2554 - 2558 (1982)*

[3] G. Palm, On the asymptotic storage capacity on neural networks, *Neural Computers, Ed. R. Eckmiller, Chr. v.d. Malsburg, Springer 1988*

[4] J.-P. Nadal, G. Toulouse, Information storage in sparsely coded memory nets, *Network 1, 61 - 74 (1990)*

[5] J.-P. Nadal, Associative memory: on the (puzzling) sparse coding limit, *J.Phys A 24, 1093 - 1101 (1991)*

[6] M. V. Tsodyks, M. V. Feigelman, The enhanced storage capacity in neural networks with low activity level, *Europhys. Lett. 6 (2), 101 - 105 (1988)*

[7] E. Gardner, The space of interactions in neural network models, *J. Phys. A 21, 257 - 270 (1988)*

[8] H. Gutfreund, Y. Stein, Capacity of neural networks with discrete synaptic couplings, *J. Phys A 23, 2613 - 2630 (1990)*

[9] G. Palm, Local learning rules and sparse coding in neural networks *in: Advanced Neural Computers Ed: R. Eckmiller Elsevier Science Publishers B.V. (North Holland) (1990)*

[10] D.J. Willshaw, O.P. Buneman, H.C. Longuet-Higgins, Nonholographic associative memory, *Nature (London) 222, 960 - 962 (1969)*

[11] G. Palm, On associative memory, *Biol. Cybern. 36, 19 - 31 (1980)*

[12] S. I. Amari, Statistical neurodynamics of associative memory, *Neural Networks 1 63 - 73 (1989)*

[13] D. J. Amit, H. Gutfreund, Statistical mechanics of neural networks near saturation, *Ann. Phys. 173, 30 - 67 (1987)*

[14] E. Gardner, H. Gutfreund, I. Yekutieli, The phase space of interactions in neural networks with definite symmetry, *J. Phys. A 22, 1995 - 2008 (1989)*

[15] H. Horner, Neural networks with low levels of activity: Ising vs. McCulloch-Pitts neurons, *Z. Phys. B 75, 133 - 136 (1989)*

[16] G. Palm, Information capacities of simple storage and retrieval procedures in neural networks, *submitted to: J. of stat. Physics (1991)*

[17] G. Palm, On the information storage capacity of local learning rules, *to be published in Neural Computation (1991)*

[18] F. Schwenker, F. Sommer, G. Palm, Simulations of recurrent networks of threshold neurons with sparse activity, *in preparation*

Associative Reinforcement Training Using Probabilistic RAM Nets

Denise Gorse

Department of Computer Science, University College
London, UK

Abstract

It is described how probabilistic RAMs may be applied to problems of associative search, using local reinforcement rules which utilise synaptic rather than threshold noise in the stochastic search procedure. Examples are given of syntactical and spatial learning tasks which successfully use these techniques.

1 Introduction

There are many learning algorithms for artificial neural nets, but none of them has proven to be easily implementable in hardware, either by digital or analog technologies. In addition it is desirable to find algorithms which are biologically plausible, and which are adaptable to on-line learning situations - neither of which criteria are met by the most frequently used training algorithm, back-error propagation. A hardware implementable stochastic model which uses probabilistic RAMs (pRAMs) has recently been developed [1], in which the output from an address $\underline{u}$ (a binary n-vector) is 1 with probability $\alpha_{\underline{u}} \in [0,1]$; this generalises the three-state model of Aleksander [2].

The pRAM has several advantages over more conventional models. It has a simple and relatively inexpensive hardware implementation [3], is biologically realistic [4], has a more sophisticated repertoire of behaviours ([5],[6]) than the binary decision neuron and its variations, and admits a range of learning algorithms, some of which are themselves wholly implementable in hardware [7]. We are particularly interested in reinforcement training algorithms, both from the point of view of biological plausibility and hardware implementation. These algorithms also lend themselves to mathematical analysis [5].

2 The pRAM model

The pRAM model has claim to be the most general associative stochastic neural auto-maton operating in the binary domain [5], where the state of the automaton A is given by the 2^N-component vector $\underline{\alpha}$, with $\underline{\alpha} \in [0,1]^{2^N}$. The output $a \in \{0,1\}$ of A is 1 with probability

$$\text{Prob}(a{=}1 \mid \underline{i}) = \sum_{\underline{u}} \alpha_u \prod_{j=1}^{N} (i_j u_j + \bar{i}_j \bar{u}_j) \tag{1}$$

(where $\bar{x} \equiv 1{-}x$) dependent on the binary input vector $\underline{i}$. It is clear that A exhibits a response which is of maximal non-linearity in the components of $\underline{i}$. In particular, in the deterministic case (when $\underline{\alpha} \in \{0,1\}^{2^N}$) it can be seen that A can compute any of the 2^{2^N} possible Boolean functions of its inputs. In the language of PDP, A is the ultimate $\Sigma{-}\Pi$ unit. A is also maximally stochastic, in that the probabilistic aspects of its behaviour are governed by the 2^N random variables α_u rather than a single stochastic threshold variable, as is usually the case (as for example in the model of Barto [8]). These stochastic features were motivated by a model of synaptically noisy neurons developed earlier by Taylor [9], which led both to the pRAM and to a theoretical analysis of noisy neurons in terms of random iterative networks [10], extending the spin glass approach to neural networks to a more realistic level. The pRAM may be regarded as a hardware realisation of this noisy neural model, in which the values α_u stored at the 2^N memory locations are assigned an appropriate neurobiological interpretation.

By assigning appropriate values to the stored probabilities α_u it is possible to con-struct pRAM nets whose stochastic behaviour closely approximates that of a network of biological neurons. This is a result of the identity theorem of Gorse and Taylor [1], which demonstrates that a pRAM with suitable parameters will evolve in time identi-cally to a net of synaptically noisy neurons. In order to illustrate this equivalence, we can consider the simplest case of a single-input pRAM/neuron, whose behaviour is governed by two memory parameters α_0, α_1. In neurophysiological language α_0 corresponds to the probability of a purely spontaneous firing event (input i=0), whereas α_1 is the firing probability associated with the arrival of an incoming pulse (input i=1). In terms of the various neurophysiological parameters the memory content values are given by

$$\alpha_0 = \int dq\, \rho_{\text{thresh}}(q)\, \rho^{(s)}(q)$$

$$\alpha_1 \;=\; \int dq \; \rho_{thresh}(q) \, \rho^{(d)}(q)$$

$\rho^{(s)}(q) \, dq$ gives the probability that the amount of neurotransmitter q received due to spontaneous leakage into the synaptic cleft $\in$ [q, q + dq]; $\rho^{(d)}(q) \, dq$ is a corresponding probability associated with the neurotransmitter emitted in response to a presynaptic firing event. $\rho_{thresh}(q)$ is the threshold function in the total amount of neurotransmitter. The spontaneous and deterministic density functions $\rho^{(s)}$, $\rho^{(d)}$ could be modelled for example by Poisson processes with different rate constants λ ($\lambda^{(d)} \gg \lambda^{(s)}$). The model may be considerably extended in the direction of greater neurobiological realism [4], incorporating details of the firing response (such as the mechanism of summation of postsynaptic effects, refractory period, pulse length, etc) and of cell spatial geometry.

The natural arena in which to investigate the behaviour of pRAM nets is that of the theory of Markov processes, and such analysis has been carried out for some simple nets [4]. However it is possible to set the discussion within the wider context of a theory of random iterated neural nets, introduced in a quenched form by Amari [11] and developed for models of the type described above (in which the "connection weights" are the amounts of neurotransmitter q_{ij} released into the $j \to i$ cleft with some probability distribution $\rho(q_{ij})$ by Bressloff and Taylor [10]. In this work the activity of the ith neuron can be described by

$$a_i(t+1) \;=\; F_i(\, \{\, q_{ij} \,\},\, s_i,\, \underline{a}(t) \,)$$

where F_i is a suitable binary function and the q_{ij} and thresholds s_i (and hence the a_i themselves) are random variables. By taking appropriate functions F_i and distributions $\rho_{ij}(q_{ij})$, $\rho_i(s_i)$ it is possible to recover a range of well known neural models. Bressloff and Taylor have usually taken ρ to be a δ-function and F_i to be a θ-function. The pRAM model is more general in that the δ-function is replaced by a distribution function ρ_i for which

$$\int_{-\infty}^{q} \rho_i(s_i) \, ds_i \;=\; \rho^{(i)}{}_{thresh}(q)$$

where $\rho^{(i)}{}_{thresh}(q)$ (with $\rho^{(i)}{}_{thresh}(\infty) = 1$) is the threshold function of the pRAM/neuron model. It is of interest to note that

$$a_i(t+1) \; = \; \theta(\sum_{j=1}^{N} q_{ij} a_j(t) - s_i)$$

and

$$\rho_{ij}(q_{ij}) = \delta(q_{ij} - <q_{ij}>), \quad \rho_i(s_i) = \beta \, e^{-\beta s_i}(1 + e^{-\beta s_i})^{-2}$$

yield the Little model; it can thus be clearly seen that the noise in this model arises solely from processes at the axon hillock, whereas it appears that for real neurons these processes are not important compared with the stochastic activity at synaptic junctions, which pRAM models are able to naturally incorporate.

2.1 pRAM reinforcement training

Reinforcement (reward-penalty) training strategies offer an attractive alternative to fully supervised learning in situations in which the information the net can obtain from its environment is limited. In reinforcement training schemes individual nodes only receive information about the quality of the performance of the network as a whole, and have to discover for themselves how to change their behaviour so as to improve this. It is possible to extend the ideas of Barto [8] to pRAM nets, adopting the update rule

$$\Delta \underline{\alpha_u}(t) = \rho((a - \underline{\alpha_u})r + \lambda(\overline{a} - \underline{\alpha_u})p)(t) \times \delta_{\underline{u}, \underline{i}} \tag{2}$$

where r, p are global success and failure signals $\in \{0,1\}$ emitted with a probability dependent both on the the binary input to pRAM A ("context" vector $\underline{i}$) and A's action in that context. The constant λ represents the ratio of punishment to reward; a non-zero value of λ is necessary in order to prevent the system converging on false minima. When r=1 (success) the probability α_u changes so as to increase the chance of emitting the same value, a, from that location in the future, whilst if p=1 (failure) the probability of emitting the other value, 1-a, when addressed increases. Note that the probabilities of reward and penalty are independent in this model; this allows the possibility of "neutral" actions which are neither punished nor rewarded but may correspond to a useful exploration of the environment. The presence of the Kronecker delta in (2) ensures that the update only occurs at the location which was accessed at time t; in the continuous-input extension to be presented below the role of the $\delta_{\underline{u}, \underline{i}}$ will be played by a more general distribution function.

Properties of the reinforcement rule (2) have been analysed in [5], within the context of a detailed study of binary-input pRAMs as "universal associative stochastic learning automata". The performance of a pRAM system utilising the learning rule (2) was compared with one using the associative reward-penalty (A_{R-P}) rule of Barto [8], and it was found that the pRAM algorithm was significantly (around 8-10) times faster. This increase in training speed may be largely due to the high degree of non-linearity in the response characteristics of pRAM nets, but we also feel that the stochastic features of the system are likely to have beneficial effects.

2.1.1 Learning sequential structure using reinforcement training

The problem we will consider here is an example of a *regular grammar*, one which can be recognised by a deterministic finite state machine. Various authors have addressed the question of using recurrent nets to recognise regular grammars (see for example [12] and references therein). Recently it has been indicated how higher order (quadratic) terms can help speed up the training process [13]; since we have terms up to order N we may hope that a pRAM net would learn this task even more efficiently [14].

We will assume that we have an alphabet of two symbols, so that the input strings are *binary*. A string of length L is thus a sequence I(1), I(2),..., I(t),..., I(L). The architecture we will use consists of N (N+1)-input pRAMs whose outputs $a_i(t)$ depend both on previous activity in the net $\underline{a}(t-1)$ and on the external (pattern) input I(t):

$$a_i(t) = \sum_{\underline{u}} \alpha_{\underline{u}}^{(i)} [\prod_{j=1}^{N} (u_j a_j(t-1) + \bar{u}_j \bar{a}_j(t-1))][u_{N+1} I(t) + \bar{u}_{N+1} \bar{I}(t)]$$

The final output of the first node, $a_1(L)$, gives the computed classification of the string, which will be compared with the desired output for that pattern, d(L). We will consider here just the learning of the *dual parity* grammar: d(L) = 1 if and only if there are an even number of both 1's and 0's in the string. This grammar is relatively simple but still complex enough to show the power of the method. The training algorithm utilizes information about the desired classification

$$d(t) = [1 - (\sum_{r=1}^{t} I(r)) \bmod 2][1 - (t - \sum_{r=1}^{t} I(r)) \bmod 2]$$

of the substring I(1), I(2),...,I(t) to provide a reinforcement signal at each time step t. The binary reinforcement signal r(t) is set to 1 (reward) if $a_1(t) = d(t)$, 0 (penalty) otherwise, and the memory contents of the N×(N+1)-pRAM net are updated according to $\alpha_{\underline{u}}^{(i)}(t) = \alpha_{\underline{u}}^{(i)}(t-1) + \Delta\alpha_{\underline{u}}^{(i)}(t)$, where

$$\Delta\alpha_{\underline{u}}^{(1)}(t) = \rho(\ (\ a_1(t) - \alpha_{\underline{u}}^{(1)}(t) \ )r(t) + \lambda(\ \bar{a}_1(t) - \alpha_{\underline{u}}^{(1)(t)} \ )\bar{r}(t) \ ) \ \times \ \delta_{\underline{u}, (a(t-1), I(t))}$$

for the "classification" node 1, and

$$\Delta\alpha_{\underline{u}}^{(i)}(t) = \rho(\ (\ a_i(t-1) - \alpha_{\underline{u}}^{(i)}(t) \ )r(t) + \lambda(\ \bar{a}_i(t-1) - \alpha_{\underline{u}}^{(i)}(t) \ )\bar{r}(t) \ ) \ \times \ \delta_{\underline{u}, (a(t-2), I(t-1))}$$

for the "hidden" nodes i = 1..N. Notice that the hidden units are reinforced not according to the present action but to the one taken at the time before. It is this feature which enables the net to develop knowledge about temporal structure.

The net was trained on strings of lengths L = 1-4 (P=30), using an initial state a(0) = (1,0,0). Although updates are made at every time step, the performance of the algorithm was assessed by counting the number of epochs (presentations of all P strings) before a convergence criterion was satisfied. This required that every pattern be correctly classified for 16 consecutive epochs. This criterion was reached (with $\rho = 0.5$, $\lambda = 0.1$) after 34 epochs.

The reinforcement algorithm compared well with a gradient descent approach to the same problem [14]. This latter resembled more closely the approach of Giles, Sun, Chen et al [13], but by using the additional non-linearity available to pRAM nodes was able to improve convergence speed by at least an order of magnitude over results quoted in [13]. However this supervised approach is computationally expensive and if implemented in hardware would require the temporal integration of spike trains. Taking into account the computational overheads associated with a software controller, and the necessity for time averaging in the supervised case, we may conclude that *in real-time terms* reinforcement training is likely to be several orders of magnitude faster than the gradient descent algorithm.

3 The integrating pRAM

It is clear that there would be useful applications for pRAM nets in the fields of robotics and adaptive control. However, many problems of adaptive control are most easily formulated in terms of real-valued inputs; quantisation of the state space (as used by Barto et al [15] in their solution of the pole balancing problem) is always possible but makes great demands on memory space and also results in a loss of accuracy in the system's internal representation of its environment. For this reason we developed an extension of the pRAM model, the i-pRAM, which maps real-valued inputs to binary outputs.

In neuronal terms working with real-valued inputs corresponds to using mean firing frequencies: a continuous input vector $\underline{x} \in [0,1]^N$ may be approximated by the time-average (over some period R) of successive binary input patterns $\underline{i} \in \{0,1\}^N$:

$$x_j \equiv \frac{1}{R} \sum_{r=1}^{R} i_j(r)$$

We can extend the output probability function (1) to describe the operation of an associative pRAM automaton with real-valued inputs x_j, $j = 1..N$, and binary output a, (defining the *integrating pRAM* or *i-pRAM*). An simple choice of output function would be

$$\text{Prob}(a=1 \mid \underline{x}) = \sum_{\underline{u}} \alpha_{\underline{u}} X_{\underline{u}}(\underline{x}) \tag{3a}$$

where

$$X_{\underline{u}}(\underline{x}) = \prod_{j=1}^{N} (x_j u_j + \overline{x}_j \overline{u}_j) \tag{3b}$$

$$\equiv \text{Prob}(\underline{u} \text{ addressed} \mid \underline{x})$$

3.1 i-pRAM reinforcement training

The reinforcement rule (2) has a natural generalisation to

$$\Delta\alpha_{\underline{u}}(t) = \rho((a - \alpha_{\underline{u}})r + \lambda(\overline{a} - \alpha_{\underline{u}})p)(t) \times X_{\underline{u}}(t) \tag{4}$$

Thus in the i-pRAM *every* location is available to be updated, with the change proportional to that address's resposibility for the i-pRAM binary output a. As for the pRAM, $\alpha_{\underline{u}}(t+1) = \alpha_{\underline{u}}(t) + \Delta\alpha_{\underline{u}}(t) \in [0,1]$, so the reinforcement rule (4) does not require any form of clipping operation and can be simply realised in hardware. Work is currently in progress to construct i-pRAM nets with inbuilt local learning rules of this type.

The i-pRAM reinforcement rule (4) may be further generalised in order to deal with situations in which reward or punishment may arrive an indefinite number of time steps after the critical action which caused the environmental response. In such delayed reinforcement tasks it is necessary to learn path-action, rather than position-action associations. This can be done by adding *eligibility traces* to each memory location. These decay exponentially where a location is not accessed, but otherwise are incremented to reflect both access frequency and the resulting i-pRAM action. The trace e_u records "access and activity", whilst f_u records "access and inactivity" (both are equally important in developing an appropriate response to a changing environment). The eligibility traces are initialised to zero at the start of a task, and subsequently updated according to

$$e_u(t) = \delta e_u(t-1) + \overline{\delta}a(t)X_u(t) \tag{5a}$$

$$f_u(t) = \delta f_u(t-1) + \overline{\delta a}(t)X_u(t) \tag{5b}$$

The necessary extension of (4), which results in the capacity to learn about temporal features of the environment, is

$$\Delta\alpha_u(t) = \rho(\; (\overline{\alpha_u}e_u - \alpha_u f_u)r + \lambda(\overline{\alpha_u f_u} - \alpha_u e_u)p \;)(t) \tag{6}$$

This rule can also be implemented in hardware. An example of a task for which reinforcement training is not fully effective without eligibility traces is described in [6]. We consider the problem of temporal prediction to be one of the most important facing neural network theorists. However we do not feel that eligibility traces offer a complete solution to this problem, since actions are rewarded purely on the basis of temporal distance from a reinforcing event. What is needed is the capacity to build a more sophisticated model of the environment, including the ability to predict future reinforcement (interesting work has been done in this area by Myers [16]). We are presently working on developments of the i-pRAM model which are able to store and predict temporal sequences, and intend to apply the results to various practical problems of adaptive control.

3.1.1 i-pRAM spatial learning

i-pRAMs have been used very successfully [6] in an associative search problem originally proposed by Barto and Sutton [17]. The task involves training a simulated "bug" to find its way to a particular spatial location, given certain (real-valued) location cues. The environment { $y: y \in [0,1]^2$ } contains four neutral landmark generators N, S, E, W and a central attractant A. The real-valued landmark signals allow the bug to locate itself within its two-dimensional environment; these signals form the context within which movement decisions are taken. The real-valued attractant signal is not an i-pRAM input; its gradient at a given point is used to generate appropriate reward and penalty signals. As Barto and Sutton [17] suggested, the landmark and attractant signals could be regarded as "odours" within the environment of a simple organism; in the work described in [6] all five "odours" fall off in a Gaussian way with distance.

The bug itself consists of a net of four movement generating i-pRAMs, M_N, M_S, M_E, M_W, each of which has inputs (n, s, e, w) from all four landmark generating i-pRAMs. Positional updates are made according to the rule

$$y_1(t+1) = (y_1 + (m_E - m_W)D)(t)$$
$$y_2(t+1) = (y_2 + (m_N - m_S)D)(t)$$

(with wraparound), where the $m_i \in \{0,1\}$ are the outputs of the four i-pRAMs, and D is the step size (1/64). The net maps a real-valued context vector $\underline{x} = (n, s, e, w) \in [0,1]^4$ to a binary output vector $\underline{m} = (m_N, m_S, m_E, m_W) \in \{0,1\}^4$. The reward and punishment signals are generated stochastically, with a probabilility depending on the increase or decrease in attractant concentration produced by the move just made.

The 4×2^4 movement generator memory contents were initially assigned random values $\in [0,1]$ - in [6] these corresponded to a central region that was initially effectively repellent. The network was then trained with the attractant in place, with $\rho = 1.0$, $\lambda = 0.4$. The bug climbs the attractant gradient, but also learns to associate landmark-coded positions with "favourable" movements. Moreover when the trained bug is replaced in a new part of its environment it is able to find its way to the central region even though the attractant itself is no longer present.

As remarked by Barto and Sutton [17], the associative search problem faced by the "bug" in this case is relatively straightforward in that the movement control information is formed by the linear superposition of the influences of the four landmark generators - it is for this reason that their net of linear associative search units is able to solve the problem. Since pRAMs are able to capture higher order information about their environment it might be expected that an i-pRAM net would be able to solve a much wider range of control problems, involving non-linear associations, than a network of more conventional nodes with the same architecture.

The i-pRAM net's ability to generalise (in this case to discover the rotational symmetry inherent in the problem) is dependent to some degree on its training history. Networks which learn too quickly, heading off on a direct line to the central region, do not perform well when replaced in an unvisited part of the environment. This behaviour can be moderated by using smaller values of ρ and λ; this results in a training path which includes more "neutral" (unreinforced) activity. In this case neutral activity corresponds to movement at a constant distance (constant attractant gradient) from the centre $\underline{y} = (\cdot 0.5, 0.5)$. The experience of such paths is precisely what is needed to discover the rotational symmetry of the problem; this is a clear example of the benefit of decoupling reward and penalty signals and allowing some degree of unreinforced exploratory behaviour during the training process.

4 Conclusions

Reinforcement training is biologically plausible in that it does not require detailed error feedback from the environment. The success/failure signal could also be generated from within the neural net automaton itself, according to the degree to which the automaton's actions were successful in achieving some preassigned goal. This combination of reinforcement training with internal goal structures would bring neural nets closer to biological reality and would offer the possibility of constructing autonomous robots which are able to develop their own problem-solving strategy in an unfamiliar environment. The use of pRAMs and i-pRAMs would make it possible for such robot controllers to be built entirely in hardware, and their non-linear and stochastic features would allow the development of flexible and effective behavioural strategies. We are presently investigating ways in which goal structures could be built into pRAM networks, and developing techniques for the construction of large nets to be used in a range of real-world applications.

References

1. Gorse D and Taylor JG. An analysis of noisy RAM and neural nets. Physica 1989; D34:90-114

2. Aleksander I. The logic of connectionist systems. In: Aleksander I (ed) Neural Computing Architectures. MIT Press, 1989, pp 133-155

3. Clarkson TG, Gorse D and Taylor JG. Hardware realisable models of neural processing. In: Proceedings of the First IEE International Conference on Artificial Neural Networks, 1989, pp 310-314

4. Gorse D and Taylor JG. A general model of stochastic neural processing. Biol. Cybern. 1990; 63:299-306

5. Gorse D and Taylor JG. Universal associative stochastic learning automata. Neural Network World 1991; 1:193-202

6. Gorse D and Taylor JG. A continuous input RAM-based stochastic neural model. Neural Networks 1991; 4:657-665

7. Clarkson TG, Gorse D and Taylor JG. From wetware to hardware: reverse engineering using probabilistic RAMs (to appear in Journal of Intelligent Systems)

8. Barto AG and Anandan P. Pattern recognising stochastic learning automata. IEEE Trans. Syst., Man, Cyb. 1985; SMC-15:360-375

9. Taylor JG. Spontaneous behaviour in neural networks. J. Theor. Biol. 1972; 36:513-528

10. Bressloff PC and Taylor JG. Random iterative networks. Phys. Rev. 1990; A41:1126-1137

11. Amari, SI. Characteristics of random nets of analog neuron-like elements. IEEE Trans. Syst., Man, Cyb. 1972; SMC-2:643-657

12. Servan-Schreiber D, Cleeremans A and McClelland JL. Encoding sequential structure in simple recurrent networks (paper presented at IEEE Conference on Neural Information Processing Systems, Denver, Colorado, 1988)

13. Giles CL, Sun GZ, Chen HH, Lee YC and Chen D. Higher order recurrent networks and grammatical inference. In: Touretzky DS (ed) Advances in Neural Information Processing Systems, vol 2. Morgan Kauffman, San Mateo Ca., 1990, pp 380-387

14. Gorse D and Taylor JG. Learning sequential structure with recurrent pRAM nets. In: Proceedings of IJCNN Seattle, 1991, pp 37-42.

15. Barto AG, Sutton RS and Anderson CW. Neuronlike adaptive elements that can solve difficult learning control problems. IEEE Trans. Syst., Man, Cyb. 1983; SMC-13:834-846

16. Barto AG and Sutton RS. Landmark learning: an illustration of associative search. Biol. Cybern. 1981; 42:1-8

17. Myers CE. Reinforcement training when results are delayed and interleaved in time. In: Proceedings of INNC-90-Paris, 1990, pp 860-863

Unlearning and Its Relevance to REM Sleep: Decorrelating Correlated Data

J.L. van Hemmen[1]

Instituut voor Theoretische Fysica, K.U.Leuven
B-3001 Leuven
Belgium

and

N. Klemmer

Physik-Department der TU München
D-8046 Garching bei München
FR Germany

Abstract

We review the performance of Hebbian unlearning in a neural network with parallel dynamics and stationary patterns. One of the main problems of Hebbian learning, and any local coding procedure, is that it *cannot* store extensively many patterns with *different* activities - the synaptic coding problem. The reason behind it is that undesirable correlations are introduced during learning. Hebbian unlearning is an unsupervised procedure whose main function is to remove these correlations. Its characteristic features are: (i) A solution of the synaptic coding problem which is so good that the storage capacity is near to or even saturating the theoretical upper bound. (ii) The existence of an optimal and a critical number of dreams at and above which, respectively, storage and retrieval are optimal (D_{opt}) or break down completely (D_c) so that all information is lost. (iii) The existence of a critical resemblance, or overlap, m_c so that for an initial overlap m_i greater than m_c the network always converges to a pattern whereas for m_i less than m_c it relaxes to a state with blinking neurons, thus signaling that it had not seen this state before. (iv) For neurons with self-interaction the convergence time, which is to be interpreted as the duration of a dream, diverges at $D_{opt} < D_c$ so that it is hard to do too much unlearning. The consequences for ordinary REM sleep are discussed.

1 Introduction

Rapid eye movement (REM) sleep [1], or dream sleep, is found in almost all mammals. After a period of deep non-REM sleep the first, short, REM period occurs and four more periods of increasing duration follow. During REM sleep the brain

---

[1]Present and permanent address: Physik-Department der TU München, D-8046 Garching bei München, FR Germany; e-mail: Leo.van.Hemmen @ Physik.TU-Muenchen.DE

seems to be very active, as is also suggested by the rapidly moving (closed) eyes. A natural question then is - and we will face this question - what REM sleep is good for. We have nothing to say about the interpretation of dreams, a venerable subject [2]. Instead we concentrate on a clarification of what might be an important mechanism in handling data during REM sleep. We first list some facts.

A deprivation of REM sleep leads to a large REM rebound. Apparently data have been gathered which now have to be worked on. There are indications, see e.g. [3], that deprivation *after* training on a task leads to retention deficits. Characteristic are also the bizarre intrusions of REM dreams, which typically consist of a *mixture* of features or objects encountered during the day before. It was already Freud's opinion [2] that in condensation the objects or events brought together always have some feature *in common*. Condensation is a central Freudian notion indicating the process that engenders the mixtures. It is known physiologically that neurons which were active during the day are usually also active during subsequent REM sleep [1,4,5]. Apparently, REM sleep has a biologically important function. The question is : which one ?

As to the explanation and modeling of REM sleep, Hobson and McCarley [6] suggested some time ago that there is a dream state generator in the *pons* that, during REM sleep, produces a series of impulses in the forebrain, the so-called PGO (ponto-geniculo-occipital) bursts. These pulses provide frequent and semi-random stimuli to the cortex and might thus function as the driving force for REM dreams. This idea was taken up by Crick and Mitchison [7], who hypothesized that during REM sleep the network, once it has been excited by a PGO wave, relaxes to a parasitic or spurious state, which then is to be weakened or, as they called it, "unlearned". Since learning is distributive and realized in the synapses, so is unlearning. The proposal of Crick and Mitchison has been implemented very nicely by Hopfield *et al.* [8] in a way the former agreed upon later on [9]. The "brain washing" of Clark *et al.* [10-11] is different, aims at non-REM sleep and, therefore, will not be discussed here.

Our own work suggests that unlearning, hence REM sleep, solves the synaptic coding problem by eliminating undesirable correlations between the patterns that are *always* present since the activity of the patterns varies. Once these correlations have been removed, a "fine-polish" follows so as to get rid of more subtle correlations and improve the signal-to-noise ratio. In a sense, the whole procedure boils down to decorrelating correlated patterns.

In Sect. 2 we sketch the underlying formalism and formulate the problem. Section 3 is devoted to our results for systems of neurons without self-interactions. We then add the self-interaction in Sect. 4 and show how it improves the performance. In Sect. 5 we indicate what happens, if a symmetric dilution is carried out. In Sect. 6 we summarize our results and evaluate their relevance to an explanation of REM sleep.

2 Formalism

Aiming at simulations, it is advantageous to take formal neurons, about half of which are active. A large population of active neurons leads to good statistics. In our simulations we could only allow a system size up to $N = 500$ so that a more realistic activity of 5 to 10 % was out of question. This naturally leads to a neural coding in terms of $S_i = \pm 1$. For the activity we aimed at, the ± 1 coding is optimal. (Low activity requires a 0/1 coding [12].) The interpretation of $S_i = \pm 1$ is in terms of a firing rate : $S_i = +1(-1)$ means neuron i fires with maximal (minimal) rate. So the S_i are Ising spins, with $1 \leq i \leq N$.

Patterns (ξ_i^μ; $1 \leq i \leq N$) with $1 \leq \mu \leq q$ are *specific* Ising spin configurations, here taken to be random. That is, the ξ_i^μ are independent, identically distributed random variables which assume the values $+1$ and -1 with probability p and $(1 - p)$, respectively. The notion $p = \text{Prob} \{\xi_i^\mu = +1\}$ will be used frequently. The activity a associated with p is defined to be the mean value $\langle \xi_i^\mu \rangle = 2p - 1 \equiv a$. Furthermore, the patterns are taken to be *stationary*, which is consistent with a firing rate interpretation of the ξ_i^μ.

For our synaptic coding we take the Hebbian learning rule [13,14]

$$\Delta J_{ij} = N^{-1} \cdot \frac{1}{T_l} \sum_{0 \leq t \leq T_l} S_i(t + \Delta t) S_j(t) \qquad (2.1)$$

that gives the change of the synaptic coupling J_{ij} (from j to i) during a learning session with duration T_l. Delays are under study but will not be considered here. In passing we note that the rule (2.1) is local, i.e., the change ΔJ_{ij} depends only on the states of the neurons at i and j.

If the patterns are stationary, i.e., $S_i(t) = \xi_i^\mu$, then we recover the Hopfield model [15]

$$J_{ij} = N^{-1} \sum_\mu \xi_i^\mu \xi_j^\mu \qquad (2.2)$$

provided $p = 0.5$ (or $a = 0$). Let $\alpha = q/N$. The storage capacity of the Hopfield model is $\alpha_c^{\text{Hopfield}} = 0.14$, which is to be contrasted with the theoretical upper bound $\alpha_c^{\text{max}} = 1$ [19]. In real-life situations, however, the activity a does not vanish and varies from pattern to pattern. Then *no* extensive storage capacity is possible : $\alpha_c = 0$. It is easy to see why. We have, using (2.2) and $h_i = \sum_j J_{ij} S_j$, that

$$h_i^\mu = \sum_j J_{ij} \xi_j^\mu = \xi_i^\mu + N^{-1} \sum_{j(\neq i)\nu(\neq \mu)} \xi_i^\nu \xi_j^\nu \xi_j^\mu \simeq \xi_i^\mu + (q - 1)a^3 . \qquad (2.3)$$

Since the dynamics is $S_i(t + \Delta t) = \text{sgn}[h_i(t)]$ we get a uniform signal, and not ξ_i^μ, as soon as $(q - 1)|a|^3 > 1$. That is, q must stay finite and $\alpha_c = 0$. This is the synaptic coding problem.

Updating a single neuron at a time, which is sequential dynamics, Hopfield *et al.* [8] implemented unlearning as a three-step procedure : (i) *Random shooting*, which gives a random initial state. (ii) *Relaxation* to a stationary state (η_i^d; $1 \leq i \leq N$), the only kind of limit point that is allowed by sequential dynamics. (iii) *Unlearning* through

$$J_{ij} \longrightarrow J_{ij} - \frac{\varepsilon}{N} \eta_i^d \eta_j^d \qquad (2.4)$$

with $0 < \varepsilon \ll 1$. Here $0 \leq d \leq D$ labels the "dreams". The authors [8] used very small samples ($N \leq 32$), uncorrelated patterns ($p = 0.5$) only, and took $\alpha \leq 0.15$. For an extensive study of (2.4) we refer to [16] and [17].

We have extended unlearning to parallel dynamics, with system sizes $N \leq 500$ and correlated patterns by taking $0.2 \leq p \leq 0.8$. Parallel dynamics means a parallel updating of all the neurons at the same time. Physiologically it seems slightly more plausible than sequential dynamics since a neuron in the state $S_i = -1$ with $h_i > 0$ now need not wait for a change until it gets updated.

Parallel dynamics can, and does, offer a new aspect : 2-cycles. These are states $\eta = (\eta^1, \eta^2)$ where some neurons blink. At blinking neurons η^1 and η^2 have opposite sign. Hebbian unlearning is performed by applying (2.1) to a 2-cycle and multiplying the result by $-\varepsilon$ so as to get

$$J_{ij} \longrightarrow J_{ij} - \frac{\varepsilon}{2N}(\eta_i^1 \eta_j^2 + \eta_i^2 \eta_j^1) \tag{2.5}$$

with $0 < \varepsilon \ll 1$. In the main text we will not specify ε. Though results do improve by taking ε smaller and smaller, it can be shown that the limit $\varepsilon \to 0$ exists. So it suffices to stick to a finite but small ε.

To plot results of a simulation, it is handy to use overlaps. The overlap with pattern μ is

$$m_\mu = N^{-1} \sum_{i=1}^{N} \xi_i^\mu S_i. \tag{2.6}$$

We have $m_\mu = 1$ if and only if $S_i = \xi_i^\mu$ and $m_\mu < 1$ in all other cases. An initial overlap, before the dynamics starts, is denoted by m_i, a final one by m_f.

3 Neural nets without self-interaction

We first study networks where a neuron cannot interact with itself so that J_{ii} has to vanish. In so doing we concentrate on the case $a = 0$ since we will reduce the case $a \neq 0$ to this one later on.

Optimal and critical number of dreams. Figure 1 shows what happens if we present a noiseless pattern $(m_i = 1)$ as a stimulus to a system equipped with plain Hebbian learning (2.2) and $\alpha = q/N = 0.4 > \alpha_c^{\text{Hopfield}} = 0.14$. Before unlearning $(D = 0)$ we end up with $m_f \simeq 0.35$, the so-called remanent magnetization m_{rem} - by no means a faithful retrieval. As D proceeds, things improve and m_f approaches 1. There are two special values of D, viz., D_{opt} that optimizes retrieval [16] through a maximization of the domain of attraction of each pattern and $D_c > D_{\text{opt}}$ above which all information is lost $(m_f = 0)$. As one sees, the transition at D_c is rather sudden; it is first-order. Including a for a moment we have for large N and small ε

$$D_{\text{opt}} = \frac{q}{2\varepsilon}(1 + \alpha + 2a^2) \tag{3.1}$$

and for $\alpha > \alpha_c^{\text{Hopfield}}$

$$D_c = \frac{q}{2\varepsilon}(3 - \alpha + 2a^2). \tag{3.2}$$

The influence of $a \neq 0$ is hard to notice as the dependence upon a is quadratic.

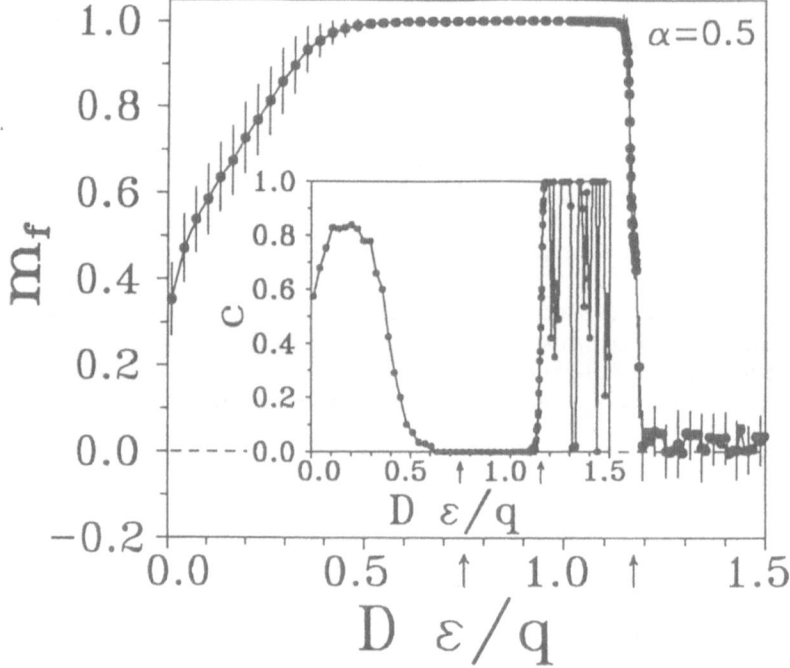

Fig. 1. Final overlap m_f as a function of $D\varepsilon/q$ for a pattern as initial stimulus. A perfect storage is equivalent to $m_f = 1$. Arrows indicate D_{opt} and D_c. Parameters : $N = 400$, $\alpha = 0.5$, $p = 0.5$ and $\varepsilon = 0.014$. The insert shows that the fraction c of patterns converging to a 2-cycle is reduced to zero as D approaches D_{opt}, i.e., as associative memory gets restored.

Phase space structure. A physical procedure to check whether associative memory is restored (despite $\alpha > \alpha_c^{\text{Hopfield}}$) is studying the energy landscape. For parallel dynamics the energy per neuron, a Lyapunov functional, is

$$E = -\frac{1}{N}\sum_{i=1}^{N}|h_i| = -\frac{1}{N}\sum_i |\sum_{j(\neq i)} J_{ij}S_j|. \tag{3.3}$$

See [18] for a general argument. We have plotted the energy as a function of the final overlap m_f in Fig. 2. As unlearning starts, there is a big cloud of attractors with $m_f \simeq 0.35$, the remanent magnetization. As D increases, the energies are raised, due to $-\varepsilon$ in (2.4) and (2.5), but the patterns get stabilized; apparently they do not rise as fast as the cloud that surrounds them. And at D_{opt} the patterns are in a fairly big energy valley (insert) so that associative memory is restored.

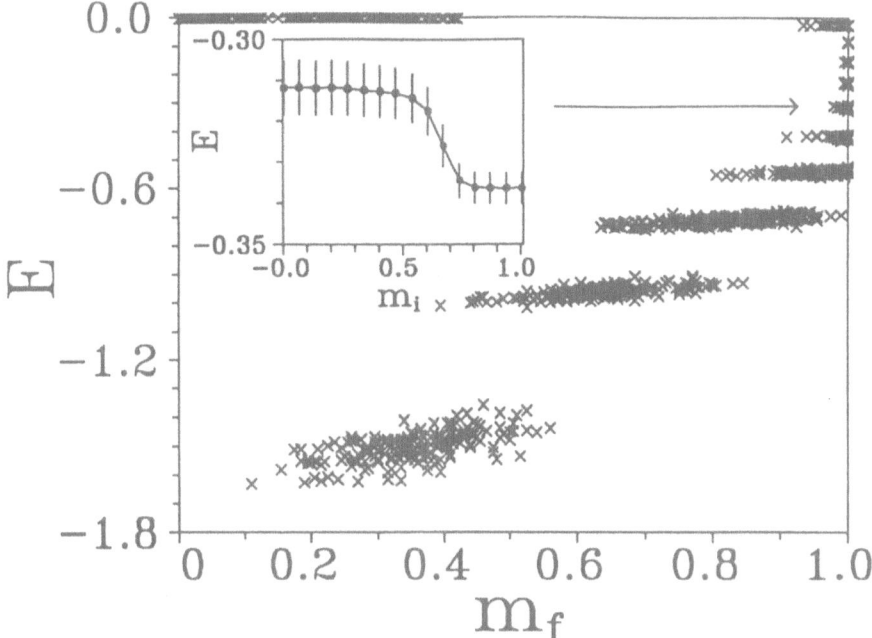

Fig. 2. Energy (3.3) as a function of the final overlap m_f for *patterns as initial stimuli* $(m_i = 1)$. Parameters : $N = 400$, $\alpha = 0.5$, $p = 0.5$ and $\varepsilon = 0.014$. The lowest set of points refers to the cloud of attractors around a pattern with overlap $m_{\text{rem}} \approx 0.35$. During unlearning m_f increases until the energy is close to zero. For the simulations, the total number of dreams started with $D = 0$ and was increased in steps of $\Delta D = 1800$. The insert shows a plot of the energy at D_{opt} (see arrow) as a function of the initial overlap m_i with a pattern. It clearly exhibits that associative memory has been restored as a "valley in energy landscape".

But what happens precisely ? It is known that, given q patterns, the Hopfield model has $\exp(\delta q)$ fixed points ($\delta > 0$). Suppose $\alpha > \alpha_c^{\text{Hopfield}}$. Is it then true that we have to eliminate exponentially many attractors so as to stabilize our q patterns ? If this were taken literally, D_{opt} should scale like $\exp(\delta q)$ instead of q.

According to Vaas [17], each pattern is surrounded by a *cloud* of attractors, which at $D = 0$ are correlated with each other more strongly than with the pattern. See the $D = 0$ curve of Fig. 3. Only the attractors in the cloud are stable beyond $\alpha_c^{\text{Hopfield}} = 0.14$. The remanent magnetization tells us, however, where they come from. Since there are q clouds, D_{opt} scales with q.

Does, then, unlearning eliminate the spurious states in the cloud ? No it does not, even though the patterns themselves become stable; cf. the insert of Fig. 2. The distribution of the intra-cloud overlaps changes as D increases, it moves to $m = 0$ but the cloud itself remains in good condition until D reaches D_c. Then all the clouds suddenly disappear and the information is gone (see Fig. 3). It is a surprising fact that during a dream $(m_i \approx 0)$ one always hits a cloud, never a pattern.

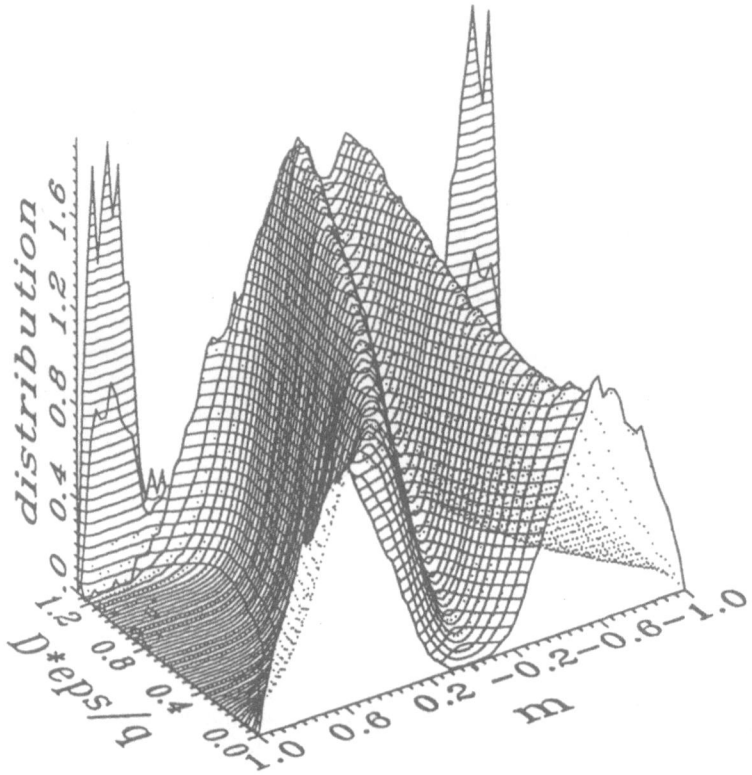

Fig. 3. Distribution of correlations (mutual overlaps) m of states *inside* a cloud for increasing $D\varepsilon/q$. The data have been averaged over all $q = \alpha N$ clouds. Parameters : $N = 100$, $\alpha = 0.4$, $p = 0.5$, and $\varepsilon = 0.01$. Up to statistical fluctuations, the distribution is symmetric with respect to $m = 0$ since $p = 0.5$. As $D\varepsilon/q$ increases it changes and the total number of attractors strongly increases until we reach $D_c\varepsilon/q \simeq 1.25$. There the clouds, each containing more than 250 attractors (so altogether more than 10^4), disappear and the system is left with only a few attractors (about 100) instead. This dramatic change is clearly visible. Attractors in *different* clouds have an overlap vanishing as $1/\sqrt{N}$, not shown here.

Critical overlap and storage capacity at D_{opt}. The value D_{opt} has been chosen so that the size of the basis of attraction of each pattern is optimal. That sounds, and is, good for associative memory. But what is the size and what are the good properties of the network after having "dreamed optimally" ?

In Fig. 4 two quantities, the retrieval rate [17] R and the fraction c of final states that are 2-cycles, have been plotted as a function of the initial overlap m_i for various system sizes, $50 \leq N \leq 400$. We expect that R vanishes for $m_i = 0$ and is 1 for $m_i = 1$. Conversely, c should vanish at $m_i = 1$ but what it does for $m_i < 1$ is a priori unclear. Looking more closely, we see that both families of curves are sigmoids which approach a 0/1 step function with a *common* discontinuity at m_c as $N \to \infty$. That is, there exists a critical m_c so that for $N \to \infty$ and $m_i > m_c$ the network relaxes to the pattern with which it was correlated whereas for $m_i < m_c$ it converges to a 2-cycle. A Hopfield net [15] always converges to a stationary state, since it is driven by sequential dynamics, and it cannot decide whether it has ever seen this state before. In the present situation the network signals it did not, if some neurons blink. This is also extremely convenient for practical applications (plainly not to be reported here). Moreover, this dichotomous behavior is consistent with what was stated before in that the net never hits a pattern during a dream ($m_i \approx 0 < m_c$).

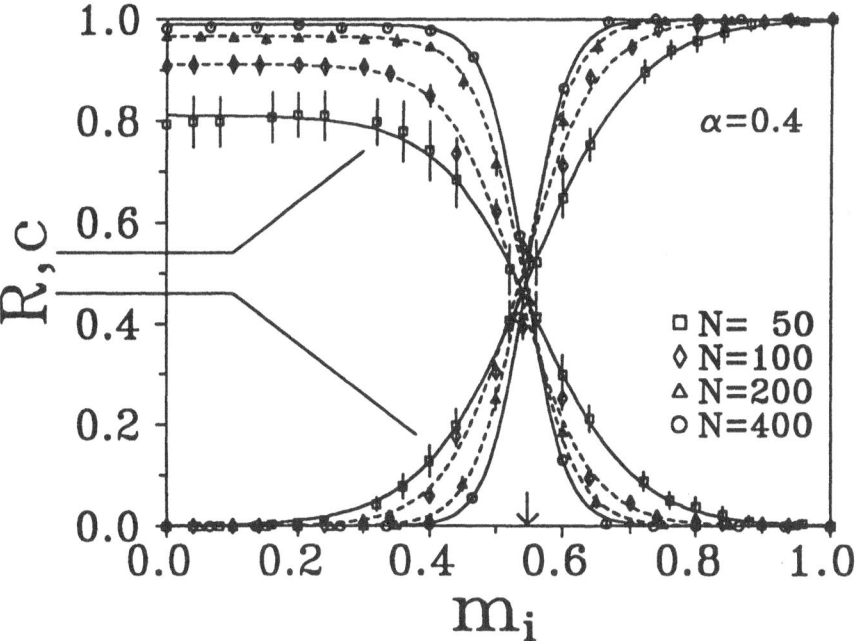

Fig. 4. Retrieval rate R and fraction c of trials converging to a 2-cycle as a function of the initial overlap m_i for various system sizes N, all at D_{opt}. Parameters : $\alpha = 0.4$, $p = 0.5$, and $\varepsilon = 0.01$. The curves cross at $m_c = 0.53$. Both the c-curves, that go downward, and the R-curves, that go upward, converge to a step function with the values 0 and 1 as $N \to \infty$.

Another important quantity is the storage capacity α_c. Let us denote its dependence upon a by writing $\alpha_c(a)$. We have

$$\alpha_c(a) = \alpha_c(0) - 2a^2 \quad \text{and} \quad \alpha_c(0) = 0.59^{+0.01}_{-0.03}. \tag{3.4}$$

It is to be noted that $\alpha_c(0) \approx 4\alpha_c^{\text{Hopfield}}$, so the improvement is substantial. Equation (3.4) also tells us that, given the ± 1 coding for the neurons, there exists a critical value $|a_c| \approx 0.54$ for $|a|$, beyond which one has to use a 0/1 coding [12].

Once we know $\alpha_c(0)$ we can also specify how many neurons blink, if $m_i < m_c$. We can write this number $c_2 N^{c_1}$ where $c_1(\alpha) = \alpha/\alpha_c$ and c_2 is of order 1.

Convergence times at D_{opt}. How long does a dream last ? It turns out that, given N, it is nearly constant as D varies between 0 and D_c whereas its size dependence is to a fair approximation given by a formula as simple as

$$t_{\mathrm{conv}} \sim \sqrt{N}. \tag{3.5}$$

For $m_i > m_c$, however, the convergence time *does not depend on* N. Both types of behavior can be checked in Fig. 5. At D_{opt} a finite t_{conv} signals pattern retrieval. Before unlearning and with $\alpha < \alpha_c^{\mathrm{Hopfield}}$ the Hopfield model exhibits a logarithmic dependence $t_{\mathrm{conv}} \sim \ln N$ for $m_i > m_c$. Of course, for $m_i < m_c$ we get (3.5).

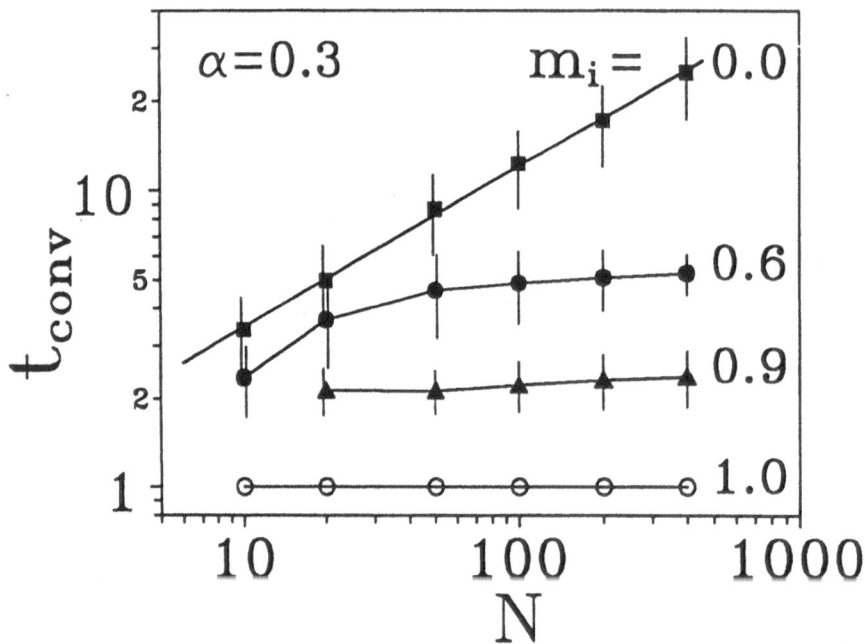

Fig. 5. Double-logarithmic plot of the convergence time t_{conv} against the system size N for various values of the initial overlap m_i, all at D_{opt}. Parameters : $\alpha = 0.3$, $p = 0.5$, and $\varepsilon = 0.01$. The straight line for $m_i = 0$ clearly confirms the relation $t_{\mathrm{conv}} \sim \sqrt{N}$. On the other hand, for $m_i > m_c = 0.43$ we find that t_{conv} *saturates* as N increases.

Biased patterns with $p \neq 0.5$. The physics of what happens if a does not vanish is simple. During the first $D_F = qa^2/\varepsilon$ dreams the network eliminates the ferromagnetic state, a global attractor that is implied by (2.2). Just note that $\langle \xi_i^\mu \xi_j^\mu \rangle = a^2$, that there are q patterns, and that we "dig in phase space" with a shovel of size ε, so that the duration scales as qa^2/ε. Indeed, as is brought out by (3.1) and (3.2), both D_{opt} and D_c may be written

$$D_\bullet(a) = D_F + D_\bullet(0).\qquad(3.6)$$

That is to say, the system first eliminates the correlations, the "mixture" states of Crick and Mitchinson [9], in about D_F dreams. Then the J_{ij} have mean zero and the network proceeds exactly as in the case $a = 0$ ($p = 0.5$). Through the unlearning the energy of the patterns themselves is raised by an amount proportional to a^2. The storage capacity ought to decrease by the same order of magnitude. That is also what (3.4) tells us. A similar dependence upon a has been found for sequential dynamics [17].

Except for D, unlearning is unsupervised. If the amount of data is more or less fixed, a network can get used to that. But with Hebbian learning it cannot cope with an activity that varies from pattern to pattern. On the other hand, unlearning easily takes care of varying activities a_μ as long as $|a_\mu| < |a_c|$. A summary of what unlearning can do is given by Fig. 6, where a small, 8×8 network had to "learn" the first 12 letters of the alphabet. A glance suffices to check that the fraction of black pixels ($\xi_i^\mu = +1$) varies from pattern to pattern. The network's mixing up the data before "dreaming", unlearning restoring them and reestablishing associative memory, it is all there.

4 Neural nets with self-interaction

Until now we had assumed the J_{ij} to vanish. A harmless looking question is what happens if we allow neural self-interactions and (un)learn the J_{ij} in a Hebbian way. Harmless as this looks, we think its neurophysiological justification should be considered carefully. The reason is that the performance of the network *greatly* improves. To see this, we check the issues of the previous section.

Whatever a, we obtain

$$D_{\text{opt}} \simeq \frac{q}{\varepsilon} \quad < \quad D_c = \frac{q}{\varepsilon}(1.14 - 0.53\log_{10}\alpha), \qquad (\alpha > \alpha_c^{\text{Hopfield}}).\qquad(4.1)$$

No dependence upon a has been found. At $D = 0$, the storage capacity is that of the Hopfield model. Since the J_{ii} have been included, the full matrix J is positive definite and it can be shown that 2-cycles do not occur. They do appear, however, as D approaches D_{opt}. Here too there is a phase separation for retrieval in the sense that as $N \to \infty$ one either ends up in ($c = 1$, $R = 0$) if $m_i < m_c$ or in ($c = 0$, $R = 1$) if $m_i > m_c$. Surprisingly, the critical overlap $m_c^{SI}(a)$ does not depend on a either as in the case $J_{ii} = 0$. Furthermore, $\alpha_c^{SI}(0) = 1.0$ and saturates the theoretical upper bound [19] for a network with symmetric J_{ij}. For $a > 0$ we obtain $\alpha_c^{SI}(a) \simeq 1 - 2a^2$.

The fact that D_{opt} and D_c scale as q can be explained as in the $J_{ii} = 0$ case. Here too there is a *cloud* of attractors around each pattern. The only difference between the two cases is that in the $J_{ii} \neq 0$ case there exists a "continuous" range of attractors overlapping down to $m_{\text{rem}} \simeq 0.35$ before unlearning starts. Figures 1 and 2 clearly show a gap around the pattern at $D = 0$. Phrased differently, the cloud now fills a "ball" with $m \gtrsim m_{\text{rem}}$ instead of a "shell" with $m \approx m_{\text{rem}}$.

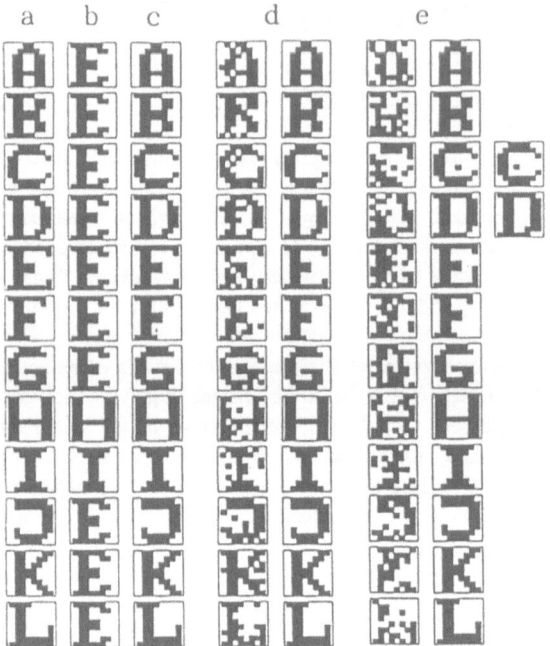

Fig. 6. Hebbian learning and unlearning for a small net consisting of $8 \times 8 = 64$ formal neurons that have been "taught" the first twelve letters A,...,L of the alphabet ($\alpha \approx 0.2$). The vertical columns refer to : (a) The patterns themselves. (b) Final states after Hebbian learning has been finished. The network has been offered the patterns themselves as stimuli but could not discern them as separate entities – thus exemplifying the synaptic coding problem. (c) Final states with the very same initial conditions but after unlearning ($D = 1.04 D_{opt}$; $\varepsilon = 3.7 \times 10^{-4}$). In (d) and (e) we show initial configurations with 12.5 and 25 % noise, respectively, and the final states toward which they converged, of course, after unlearning. The correlations which showed up in (b) have been eliminated and associative memory has been restored. The blinking C and D are finite-size effects; cf. Fig. 4.

The range between D_{opt} and D_c is rather small so that one may wonder how the system manages to avoid a collision with D_c, i.e., REM sleeping too much. That won't happen, though, as is shown in Fig. 7. If we start with a noiseless pattern ($m_i = 1$), the convergence time quickly relaxes to $t_{conv} = 1$ as D increases and diverges *only as* $D \to D_c$ from below, signalling the first-order transition at D_c. On the other hand, if we start with random shooting ($m_i \approx 0$), then t_{conv} already diverges as D approaches D_{opt}. So it is hard to dream beyond D_{opt}, let alone D_c.

5 Dilution

Of course one might argue that Hebbian (un)learning is fine but that a full connectivity is not very realistic. We have therefore performed a symmetric dilution. Let $\rho_{ij} = \rho_{ji} \in \{0,1\}$ be a stochastic variable that assumes the value 1 with probability ρ. Then $\langle \rho_{ij} \rangle = \rho$. Different pairs (i,j) are sampled independently of each other. We start with Hebbian couplings (2.2) modified according to $J_{ij} \to J_{ij}\rho_{ij}$ and assume $J_{ii} = 0$. It then turns out that, whatever ρ, the only modification in the formulae of Sect. 3 is a change of α into α/ρ. By itself, this change is reasonable since each neuron is now connected on the average to ρN instead of $(N-1)$ or N synapses, where the information is stored. In $\alpha = q/N$ we therefore have to substitute ρN for N, hence α/ρ for α. It is surprising, though, that this substitution is the only change.

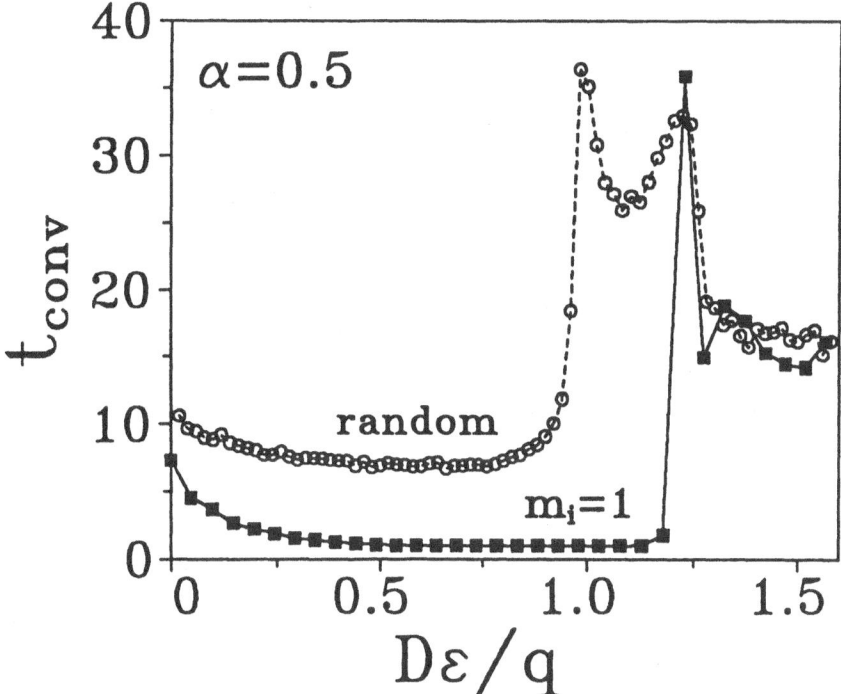

Fig. 7. Convergence time t_{conv} as a function of $D\varepsilon/q$ in a system with neural self-interaction ($J_{ii} \neq 0$) for the initial overlaps $m_i = 0$ (random) and $m_i = 1$. Parameters : $N = 500$, $\alpha = 0.5$, $p = 0.5$, and $\varepsilon = 0.02$. For $m_i = 1$, the convergence time quickly relaxes to $t_{conv} = 1$ and diverges only as D approaches D_c. This is to be contrasted with the behavior for $m_i = 0$, a dream. Then t_{conv} remains about constant as long as $D \lesssim D_{opt} = q/\varepsilon$ and diverges as D approaches D_{opt}. Due to this divergence the network cannot dream far beyond D_{opt}.

6   Conclusions

The above results apply to unlearning *per se*. If it is intrumental to REM sleep, as argued by Crick and Mitchison [7,9], what are the implications of these results ? We can (i) estimate the optimal number of dreams D_{opt}, (ii) prove that first the correlations between patterns (cf. Fig. 6) are removed before the fine-polish starts, thus explaining the character of bizarre intrusions of REM dreams, (iii) show that always a cloud, never a pattern is hit, a cloud being a set of states with *low* resemblance to the pattern, and (iv) explain in a simple way why the non-REM sleeping *Echidna*, or spiny anteater, and the *Cetacea*, whales and dolphins, have an abnormally large cortex for their body size [9]. Crick and Mitchison aptly pointed out that whales "are not the most convenient experimental animals to study", adding "More types of small *Cetacea* (such as the killer whale) could usefully be studied." Indeed, very useful, but it *is* known that both the spiny anteater and the dolphins *do not* REM sleep.

Furthermore, we would like to stress that for parallel dynamics D_{opt} depends only weakly on the activity a of the patterns. Except for D_{opt}, unlearning is unsupervised and allows storage and retrieval of patterns whose activities differ and at D_{opt} it does so most efficiently. In this way the neural network can solve the synaptic coding problem.

Much still has to be done but the results obtained so far do suggest that unlearning plays an important role in REM sleep.

Acknowledgments

The authors thank D. Albert (Heidelberg) and D. Stauffer as director of the Höchstleistungsrechenzentrum at the KFA Jülich for their help and support. J.L. van Hemmen would like to express his gratitude to the Institute for Theoretical Physics of the University of Leuven for the hospitality extended to him during his stay there, when this manuscript was written. It is also a great pleasure to thank D. Bollé (Leuven) and Z. Li (Princeton) for a critical reading of the manuscript.

References

[1] Winson, J. *The meaning of dreams*. Sci. Amer. 1990; **263**: 42-48.

[2] Freud, S. *The interpretation of dreams*. Penguin books, London and New York, 1976. Originally published 1900.

[3] Smith, C. and Kelly, G. *Paradoxical sleep deprivation applied two days after end of training retards learning*. Psych. and Behav. 1988; **43**: 213-216.

[4] Pavlides, C. and Winson, J. *Influences of hippocampal place cell firing in the awake state on the activity of these cells during subsequent sleep episodes*. J. Neurosc. 1989; **9**: 2907-2918.

[5] Hennevin, E., Hars, B., and Bloch, V. *The improvement of learning by mesencephalic reticular stimulation during postlearning paradoxical sleep*. Behav. Neural Biol. 1989; **51**: 291-306.

[6] Hobson, J.A. and McCarley, R.W. *The brain as a dream state generator: An activation-synthesis hypothesis of the dream process.* Am. J. Psychiat. 1977; **134**: 1335-1348.

[7] Crick, F. and Mitchison, G. *The function of dream sleep.* Nature 1983; **304**: 111-114.

[8] Hopfield, J.J., Feinstein, D.I., and Palmer, R.G. *"Unlearning" has a stabilizing effect in collective memories.* Nature 1983; **304**: 158-159.

[9] Crick, F. and Mitchison, G. *REM sleep and neural nets.* J. Mind and Behavior 1986; **7**: 229-250.

[10] Clark, J.W., Winston, J.V., and Rafelski, J. *Self-organization in neural networks.* Phys. Lett. A 1984; **102**: 207-211.

[11] Clark, J.W., Rafelski, J., and Winston, J.V. *Brain without mind: Computer simulation of neural networks with modifiable neuronal interactions.* Phys. Rep. 1985; **123**: 216-273.

[12] van Hemmen, J.L., Gerstner, W., Herz, A.V.M., Kühn, R., and Vaas, M. *Encoding and decoding of patterns which are correlated in space and time.* In: Dorffner, G. (ed.) *Konnektionismus in Artificial Intelligence und Kognitionsforschung.* Springer, Berlin and Heidelberg, 1990, pp. 153-162.

[13] Herz, A.V.M., Sulzer, B., Kühn, R., and van Hemmen, J.L. *The Hebb rule: Storing static and dynamic objects in an associative neural network.* Europhys. Lett. 1988; **7**: 663-669.

[14] Herz, A.V.M., Sulzer, B., Kühn, R., and van Hemmen, J.L. *Hebbian learning reconsidered: Representation of static and dynamic objects in associative neural nets.* Biol. Cybern. 1989; **60**: 457-567.

[15] Hopfield, J.J. *Neural networks and physical systems with emergent collective computational abilities.* Proc. Natl. Acad. Sci. USA 1982; **79**: 2554-2558.

[16] van Hemmen, J.L., Ioffe, L.B., Kühn, R., and Vaas, M. *Increasing the efficiency of a neural network through unlearning.* Physica A 1990; **163**: 386-392.

[17] van Hemmen, J.L. *Hebbian learning and unlearning.* In: Theumann, W.K., and Köberle, R. (eds.) *Neural networks and spin glasses.* World Scientific, Singapore, 1990, pp. 91-114.

[18] Herz, A.V.M., Li, Z., and van Hemmen, J.L. *Statistical mechanics of temporal association in neural networks with transmission delays.* Phys. Rev. Lett. 1991; **66**: 1370-1373.

[19] Gardner, E. *The space of interactions in neural network models.* J. Phys. A: Math. Gen. 1988; **21**: 257-270.

OPTIMAL ARCHITECTURES AND HIGH-ORDER NETWORKS

Karl E. Kürten

Institut für Theoretische Physik, Johannes-Kepler-Universität, A-4040 Linz, Austria
and
Institut für Neuroinformatik, Ruhr-Universität Bochum, D-4630 Bochum, FRG

ABSTRACT

Designing information-specific architectures in sparsely connected network models is a problem of high theoretical and practical interest. We propose a novel procedure which allows a system to evolve to a quasi-optimal connectivity such that information to be memorized is engraved as efficiently as possible. We self-consistently include multi-cell interactions and find a substantially improved stability of the memorized information. The problem of controlling high-order contributions can be successfully attacked with Polyà's combinatorial group-theoretical techniques.

1. INTRODUCTION

Neural network models have often been claimed to be flexible and adaptive. However, most of the currently popular models are based on fixed network architectures or even full connectivity and lack basic adaption properties present in living networks. Hence, these models cannot adapt specific structures matched to the task the network is asked to perform. In contrast, variable connectivity for each individual neuron during the learning session allows the network to undergo an optimization process, where optimal and even minimal connectivity structures might emerge. A variety of network models which capture the primary features of information processing and adaptive behaviour in living nervous systems have often been described by irreducible multi-neuron interactions of multiplicative character [1-4]. In fact, it is well known that synapses not only modify the membrane potentials of dendrites but also those of other synapses. One of the drawbacks of high-order models is the combinatorial explosion of high-order terms favoured by higher connectivity which is rarely found in nature. On the other hand, systems with lower connectivity can exhibit a larger degree of stability [5,6]. Accordingly, we intend to explore dynamical properties of *sparsely* connected networks designed for the straightforward implementation of suitable high-order interactions.

2. THE MULTI-CONNECTED NETWORK MODEL

The model network consists of a set of N interacting binary threshold units σ_i which are only capable to take the value +1 and -1 for unit i "active" or "non active", respectively. We assume that each neuron i can interact with K_i other units of the network with $1 \leq K_i \leq N-1$, while self-interactions are excluded. The state of neuron i at time t is then specified according to the deterministic threshold rule

$$\sigma_i(t+1) = \text{sgn}[h_i(t)] \qquad i = 1, ..., N \quad . \tag{2.1}$$

The net internal stimulus $h_i(t)$ is given in terms of a polynomial K_i-th order expansion of the commonly used linear superposition of the weighted input states

$$
\begin{aligned}
h_i(t) &= [c_{i0} + \sum_{(j_1)} c_{ij_1} \sigma_{j_1}(t) + ... + \sum_{(j_1)<...<(j_{K_i})} c_{ij_1...j_{K_i}} \sigma_{j_1}(t)...\sigma_{j_{K_i}}(t)] / \parallel c_i \parallel_2 \\
&= C_0 + C_1(t) + ... + C_{K_i}(t)
\end{aligned}
$$

(2.2)

with the spherical normalization

$$
\parallel c_i \parallel_2 = \{c_{i0}^2 + \sum_{(j_1)} c_{ij_1}^2 + ... + \sum_{(j_1)<...<(j_{K_i})} c_{ij_1...j_{K_i}}^2\}^{\frac{1}{2}} \ .
$$

(2.3)

The sums are only taken over those K_i neurons that are supposed to interact with neuron i.

In order to achieve faithful storage of p arbitrary patterns $\underline{S}^1, ..., \underline{S}^p \in \{-1, 1\}^N$ as stable fixed points of the dynamics (2.1) the coupling coefficients have to be determined such that the pN stability parameters κ_i^μ defined as

$$
\kappa_{i\mu} = S_i^\mu h_i(S_1^\mu, ..., S_N^\mu) \quad i = 1, ..., N \quad \mu = 1, ..., p
$$

(2.4)

be all nonnegative. Furthermore, the magnitude of the minimal stability parameter defined in (2.4) is required to be as large as possible, a necessary condition for assuring reasonably large basins of attraction for the individual patterns.

Provided that each cell chooses K distinct connections at random, a first-order network with two-cell interactions is basically able to memorize of the order of $\mathcal{O}(K)$ random unbiased patterns, where the critical capacity parameter depends strongly on the learning algorithm. Accordingly, a sparsely connected network with interactions exclusively of order s is able to store of the order of

$$
p = \mathcal{O}(\binom{K}{s}))
$$

(2.5)

uncorrelated patterns. Note that this quantity is proportional to the total number of synaptic coefficients describing the degrees of freedom of the system. Thus, the network offers an impressive storage capacity which however might become impractical due to the rapid proliferation of high-order contributions. As demonstrated in section 6 and 7 this problem can be attacked by admitting a strongly reduced pattern-specific interconnectivity or by employing suitable summation techniques for the inclusion of high-order terms.

3. CONNECTIVITY OPTIMIZATION OF A FIRST ORDER NETWORK

It has been demonstrated in refs. [5,6] that the retrieval performance as well as the storage capacity of the model can be largely improved if the connectivity is not chosen at random but adapted to the specific information the network is asked to capture.

For fixed connectivity parameters K_i the network design can be thought of as a combinatorial optimization problem, where each cell i has $\binom{N-1}{K_i}$ different ways to choose its incoming connections in order to maximize the minimal stability parameter $\kappa_{i\mu}$ in (2.4).

Since an exhaustive neighbour search is not possible for networks of respectable size one can first adopt a simple trial and error scheme [5]: Whenever a random neighbour choice fails to fulfill a minimal embedding condition after a relatively short learning session, we choose other connections picked at random in order to increase the magnitude of the smallest stability parameter.

According to various experiments which indicate that low-efficacy synapses degenerate, the strategy can be improved by substituting only those synaptic weights whose magnitudes are close to zero. They consequently hardly contribute to the stability; rather they induce synaptic noise. Hence, substantial improvement has finally been achieved by weighting the connections with the magnitudes of their synaptic efficiencies such that the probability of being exchanged increases with decreasing magnitude of the synaptic weight [6].

Note that there are two levels of optimization:

⊙ i) **Variation of the connectivity**

⊙ ii) **Variation of the synaptic weights for fixed connectivity**

The optimization of the architecture could be performed with the aid of *Trial and Error* strategies or refined *Monte Carlo* procedures, whereas the optimization of the synaptic weights could be performed with the aid of an arbitrary, not necessarily optimal learning procedure.

One of the main results of our studies suggests strongly that it is far more important to aim at optimal connectivity structures than to concentrate on optimal, time consuming learning procedures for the modification of the coupling coefficients. Hence, we first adopt Hebbian one-step learning via

$$c_{ij} = \sum_{\mu=1}^{p} S_i^\mu S_j^\mu \quad , \tag{3.1}$$

which simplifies step ii) appreciably, since the synaptic weights are given explicitly.

Another remarkable result of our studies is that networks even with an appreciable degree of dilution, but with optimized connectivity, show a quantitatively similar retrieval performance as their fully connected counterparts [5]. Moreover, due to the fact that sparsely connected networks often exhibit appreciably fewer spurious states, the fraction of perfectly recalled patterns is substantially larger than found in fully connected networks [6].

4. STABILITY IN FIRST ORDER NETWORKS

A reliable measure of the quality of memorization is usually given by the magnitude of the stability parameters $\kappa_{i\mu}$ defined in eq.(2.4). In order to gain more insight into the origin of stability we decompose $\kappa_{i\mu}$, defined for a fully connected first-order network into its individual contributions

$$\kappa_{i\mu}^{(j)} = S_i^\mu c_{ij} S_j^\mu / \parallel c_i \parallel_2 \quad j = 1, ..., N \tag{4.1}$$

and define the $p \times (N-1)$ stability matrix

$$\mathbf{K}_i = [\kappa_{i\mu}^{(j)}]_{\mu=1,...,p}^{j=1,...,N} \quad . \tag{4.2}$$

Here, the matrix element $\kappa_{i\mu}^{(j)}$ specifies the stability contribution for the i-th component of pattern μ due to the synaptic connection from j. Note that summing over an arbitrary row j gives merely

$$\sum_{(j)} \kappa_{i\mu}^{(j)} = \kappa_{i\mu} \quad , \tag{4.3}$$

whereas summing over a column μ produces

$$\sum_{\mu=1}^{p} \kappa_{i\mu}^{(j)} = c_{ij} c_{ij}^H / \parallel c_i \parallel_2 \quad . \tag{4.4}$$

The sum rule (4.4) implies that, if the actual couplings c_{ij} are chosen according to the Hebbian sign constraint

$$\text{sgn}(c_{ij}) = \text{sgn}(c_{ij}^H) \quad , \tag{4.5}$$

the arithmetic mean taken over all patterns μ is strictly positive.

Eq. (4.4) also implies that the arithmetic mean of the whole set of stability parameters $\kappa_{i\mu}^{(j)}$ taken over all patterns μ and all incoming connections j can always be written in terms of a normalized sum over the products of the actual and the Hebbian couplings

$$\bar{\kappa}_i = \frac{1}{p} \sum_{(j)} \sum_{\mu=1}^{p} \kappa_{i\mu}^{(j)} = \frac{1}{p} (\sum_{(j)} c_{ij} c_{ij}^H) / \parallel c_i \parallel_2 \quad . \tag{4.6}$$

Hence, a substantial portion of the couplings must obey the Hebbian sign constraint in order to allow for a positive mean, which can be considered as a necessary stability criterion. Note however, that an absolute stability measure of the embedded information is given by the value of the minimal $\kappa_{i\mu}$. In the case of Hebbian couplings given by eq.(3.1), expression (4.6) reduces to

$$\bar{\kappa}_i = \frac{1}{p} (\sum_{(j)} (c_{ij}^H)^2)^{\frac{1}{2}} \tag{4.7}$$

In judging the quality of memorization one might also consider the number of positive and negative entries in column j of the stability matrix $\mathbf{K}_i$ defined in (4.2), n_{ij}^+ and n_{ij}^-, respectively. These numbers obey the relations

$$n_{ij}^+ = \frac{1}{2}[p + c_{ij}^H \text{sgn}(c_{ij})] \quad \text{and} \quad n_{ij}^- = \frac{1}{2}[p - c_{ij}^H \text{sgn}(c_{ij})] \quad . \tag{4.8}$$

If the coupling c_{ij} is chosen under the Hebbian sign constraint (4.5), n_{ij}^+ assumes its minimum value $\frac{1}{2}$ for $c_{ij}^H = 0$ and reaches its maximum value p for $|c_{ij}^H| = p$, where $|c_{ij}^H|$ takes its maximal value. Hence, the fraction of positive entries in column j

$$\frac{n_{ij}^+}{p} = \frac{1}{2} + \frac{c_{ij}^H}{p} \text{sgn}(c_{ij}) \tag{4.9}$$

is a linearly increasing function of the magnitude of the Hebbian coupling c_{ij}^H as long as the actual coupling c_{ij} is chosen under the Hebbian sign constraint (4.5). Thus, the fraction of positive stability entries in an arbitrary column j is always larger than $\frac{1}{2}$. They are *all* positive if and only if $|c_{ij}| = p$. Accordingly, as is the case in biological networks, it may be inferred that large Hebbian efficiencies play a crucial role in optimized network architectures.

5. DILUTION OF THE NETWORK CONNECTIVITY

Basically, there are two completely different, though equivalent approaches for reducing the number of weights of a fully connected network without significantly degrading or even improving the performance of the network. One might start from a fully connected network and selectively delete those weights which disfavour the stabilization of the information to be engraved. This approach has the serious drawback that, before the dilution process starts, the whole set of couplings for a fully connected network has to be determined. In fact, this might be an unfeasible task, if nonlocal learning rules are taken into account. By contrast, we propose to start with a completely disconnected network and selectively add only those connections which are most effective in increasing a suitable cost function, for example the smallest stability parameter $\kappa_{i\mu}$ in (2.4). Let us first summarize a two earlier attempts, before we suggest a strategy based on selective dilution.

⊙ Random dilution

The simplest strategy for reducing the number of bonds is to delete bonds at random until the number of synapses for neuron i is reduced to K_i. The dynamics of a randomly diluted and hence asymmetric version of the Hopfield model can be solved exactly in the high-dilution limit [9], or more precisely under the condition $K \approx logN$. It has been shown that the critical number of unbiased patterns p_c the network is able to store is $p_c = \frac{2}{\pi}K$. However, for an extensive number of patterns no perfect retrieval is possible, although there exist clouds of attractors near a stored pattern. Furthermore, random dilution of a macroscopic fraction synaptic bonds can also be shown to be equivalent to adding an independent Gaussian noise to the strength of the coupling coefficients [.]. Hence, a linear decrease of the network performance according to the degree of dilution is expected.

⊙ Dilution of the smallest bonds

Just eliminating those connections with the smallest efficacies as proposed by Morgenstern [8], might be quite efficient, but hardly optimal. Eq.(4.7) reveals that for fixed K_i this choice does not optimize the minimal $\kappa_{i\mu}$ but the arithmetic mean $\bar{\kappa}_i$. The price for such a straightforward search may be a large variance, whereas a near-optimal network structure requires a subtle tradeoff between a *large* average $\bar{\kappa}_i$ and a *small* variance. Note that $\bar{\kappa}_i$ reaches its maximum value for a fully connected network. Apparently, this quantity decreases with increasing degree of dilution of the *weakest* bonds; therefore, by cutting only those, the stability cannot be improved at all.

⊙ Selective dilution

Considering the connectivity parameter K_i as fixed, the design of the network can be thought of as a combinatorial optimization problem, where each cell i has $\binom{N-1}{K_i}$ different ways to choose its interacting neighbours. Ideally, one would have to select K_i columns of the stability matrix defined in eq.(4.2) such that the minimal stability parameter defined in eq.(2.4) attains its maximum value. Once an optimal set of connections has been found for each K_i ($1 \leq K_i \leq N-1$), the quantity K_i can be used as a variational parameter in order to determine the optimal number of connections which maximize the minimal stability parameter $\kappa_{i\mu}$. The result is a network with greatest stability and minimal resources with respect to the interconnectivity structure.

6. CONSTRUCTION OF THE NETWORK ARCHITECTURE

Our focus is on sparsely connected networks, where the efficiency of information storage per synapse is usually much higher than in their fully connected counterparts. Hence, it is our intention here to build up a network connection by connection. In order to attack the combinatorial optimization problem we consult Branch-and-Bound (B&B) algorithms [11] which have been widely applied to the solution of optimization problems of high complexity.

The recipe for building our network is as follows. Since the search process is independent for each individual cell, we will describe the algorithm for a fixed cell i. We first rearrange $N-1$ possible input cells $j \neq i$ in sequential order according to the number of positive entries n_{ij}^+ in (4.2). Note that for couplings satisfying the Hebbian sign constraint (4.5) this rearrangement coincides with ordering the cells according to the magnitudes of their synaptic weights c_{ij}. This ordered set of candidates will be called our first working pool $P(1)$. The coupling with the largest n_{ij}^+ provides the very first connection j_1, while the first lower bound $b(1)$ is specified by

$$b(1) = \kappa_{min}(1) = \min_\mu(\kappa_{i\mu}) = \begin{cases} +1, & \text{for } |c_{ij_1}| = p \\ -1 & \text{for } |c_{ij_1}| \neq p \end{cases} \tag{6.1}$$

according to (4.1). The search strategy starts with a sweep through the remaining

$N-2$ connections of the working pool $P(1)$. We accept only those connections which do not decrease the first lower bound $b(1) = \kappa_{min}(1)$. Thus, the first sweep gives us n_1 connections so that the new working pool $P(2)$ consists only of $N-1-n_1$ candidates.

In the l-th step, we consider only candidates of the actual working pool $P(l)$. In analogy to the previous steps we accept first the cell with the largest n_{ij}^+ and determine the new lower bound $b(l) = \kappa_{min}(l)$. This quantity serves as acceptance criterion for adding further connections during the l-th sweep through the remaining candidates of $P(l)$. Again, only those connections are accepted which do not decrease the lower bond $b(l)$. Thus, after the l-th sweep, we can eliminate another n_l connections so that the new working pool $P(l+1)$ consists of $N-1-\sum_{i=1}^{l-1} n_i$ candidates.

This fully deterministic B&B-like procedure is repeated until the working pool is empty. It ends after at most $(N-1)$ sweeps, while the learning time is at most of the order of $\mathcal{O}(N^2)$ for each individual neuron i. Eventually, we arrive at a complete stability spectrum as a function of the connectivity and thus can determine those K_i connections which maximize the smallest stability parameter $\kappa_{i\mu}$. However, it should be stressed, that our algorithm should be considered as a working tool for finding a "good" solution in polynomial time rather than a prescription for the "optimal" solution.

7. MULTI-CELL INTERACTIONS

In principle, our optimization strategy described in the previous section could be modified to high-orders. Note however, that an s-order contribution in eq.(2.2)

$$ C_s = \sum_{(j_1)<\dots<(j_s)} c_{ij_1\dots j_s} \sigma_{j_1}(t)\dots\sigma_{j_s}(t) \quad , \tag{7.1} $$

contains $\binom{K_i}{s}$ constants. Due to this rapidly proliferating parametrization high-order networks have often been believed to be impractable for real-world applications. In fact, optimizing all high-order coupling coefficients is clearly unfeasible. However, we can assume that the optimal connectivity in first order is also a reasonable approximation for a near-optimal connectivity in low orders. Thus, we restrict multi-cell interactions to the subspace containing the optimized connectivity which evolved within the two-cell interactions such that the sums in (7.1) are performed only over those neurons which belong to the optimal set determined by the optimization procedure in first order.

For the specificatin of the high-order couplings we adopt the natural extension of the classical Hebbian learning rule to order K_i

$$ c_{ij_1\dots j_{K_i}} = \sum_{\mu=1}^{p} S_i^\mu S_{j_1}^\mu S_{j_2}^\mu \dots S_{j_{K_i}}^\mu \quad . \tag{7.2} $$

It is straightforward to evaluate a modified s-order contribution in eq.(2.2)

$$\overline{C}_s = \sum_{(j_1)\cdots(j_s)} c_{ij_1\cdots j_s}\sigma_{j_1}(t)\cdots\sigma_{j_s}(t) \quad , \tag{7.3}$$

which consists of K_i^s terms. The auxiliary quantity $\overline{C}_s$ defined in (7.3) contains "diagonal" terms specified as those of which at least two indices $j_1, \ldots, j_s$ are the same. These terms are redundant since they already appear in lower-order contributions. Inserting (7.2) in (7.3) and interchanging the order of the summations leads to the simple form

$$
\begin{aligned}
\overline{C}_s &= \sum_{(j_1)\cdots(j_s)} c_{ij_1\cdots j_s}\sigma_{j_1}\cdots\sigma_{j_s} = \sum_{(j_1)\cdots(j_s)}\sum_{\mu=1}^{p} S_i^\mu S_{j_1}^\mu \cdots S_{j_s}^\mu \sigma_{j_1}\cdots\sigma_{j_s} \\
&= \sum_{\mu=1}^{p} S_i^\mu (\sum_{(j_1)} S_{j_1}^\mu \sigma_{j_1})\cdots(\sum_{(j_s)} S_{j_s}^\mu \sigma_{j_s}) = \sum_{\mu=1}^{p} S_i^\mu [\sum_{(j_1)} S_{j_1}^\mu \sigma_{j_1}]^s \quad .
\end{aligned}
\tag{7.4}
$$

The corresponding desired s-order contribution C_s can then be evaluated via

$$C_s = \sum_{(j_1)<\cdots<(j_s)} c_{ij_1\cdots j_s}\sigma_{j_1}\cdots\sigma_{j_s} = \frac{1}{s}\overline{C}_s \operatorname*{Det}_{\alpha,\beta=1,\ldots,s}(\delta_{j_\alpha j_\beta}) \tag{7.5}$$

with $\overline{C}_s$ taken from eq. (7.3). The $s \times s$ determinant in (7.5) eliminates all "diagonal" terms with two or more indices coincident, while the statistical factor s takes care of symmetric terms. We now define "generalized" overlaps of a current net configuration $\underline{\sigma}(t)$ with one of the prescribed patterns $\underline{S}^\mu$

$$m_\alpha^\mu(t) = \sum_{(j_1)} [S_{j_1}^\mu \sigma_{j_1}(t)]^\alpha \quad , \tag{7.6}$$

where the sums in (7.6) are performed only over those neurons which belong to the optimal set determined by the optimization procedure in first order. Then, one can be easily show that the desired quantity C_s can eventually be written as

$$C_s = \sum_{\mu=1}^{p} S_i^\mu \overline{P}_s(m_1^\mu, \ldots, m_s^\mu) \tag{7.7}$$

with

$$\overline{P}_s(m_1, \ldots, m_s) = \sum_{(\underline{\alpha})} \prod_{l=1}^{s} \frac{(-1)^{\alpha_l+1}}{\alpha_l}(\frac{m_l}{l})^{\alpha_l} \quad . \tag{7.8}$$

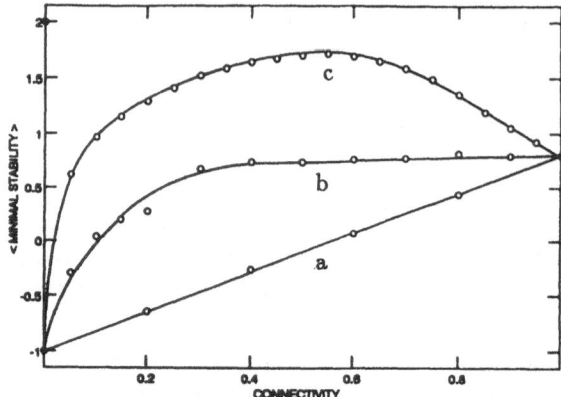

Fig.1: Average minimal stability parameter κ_{min} as a function of the dilution for a) random dilution b) dilution of the weakest bonds c) selective dilution (from below).

The sums in (7.8) are performed only over those s-dimensional vectors $\underline{\alpha} = (\alpha_1, ..., \alpha_s) \in N_0^s$ whose components are solutions of the partitioning relation

$$\sum_{l=1}^{s} l\alpha_l = s \quad . \tag{7.9}$$

The reader might verify that the function $\overline{\mathcal{P}}_s(m_1, ..., m_s)$ is a generalized Polyà polynomial [12] of the symmetric group $\mathcal{S}_s$, where the signs of the corresponding cyclic permutations $(-1)^{\alpha_l+1}$ have been included.

8. COMPUTER SIMULATIONS

8.1 Processing random patterns

In this section we demonstrate how the stability of the embedded information varies with varying connectivity for three different strategies of dilution: random dilution, dilution of the weakest bonds and *selective* dilution of the coupling coefficients as described in section 6. The simulations have been performed for $N = 100, N = 400$ and $N = 800$ cells. Though we observe some effects of size dependence at both extremes of the degree of dilution, the qualitative findings of our study are not affected.

Figure 1 shows a spline interpolation of the minimal stability parameter κ_{min}, averaged over some 50 specimen nets as a function of the degree of the connectivity. The networks consist of $N = 100$ cells, while the capacity parameter α has been chosen as $\alpha = 0.14$. Before the retrieval phase the patterns are degraded by random noise and presented as initial conditions for the network to recall. As to be expected, the simulations for *random* dilution of the couplings show a linear decrease of κ_{min}, whereas deleting bonds with the smallest efficacies only leads to a slight decrease up to almost 60% dilution.

In the case of selective dilution following the scheme of section **6**, we observe that κ_{min} is a sharply increasing function at small connectivities, reaching a maximum value slightly above 50%. With further increase of connectivity, κ_{min} shows a slow decrease until it reaches the limiting value corresponding to the stability measure for a fully connected network.

8.2 Processing artificially structured information

Storing correlated information turns out to be a serious problem for the standard Hopfield model [13], since the Hebb rule treats the individual patterns equally and considers each pattern as a new piece of information. Thus, there is a tendency to enhance overlapping features, whereas important details which distinguish the patterns are not well captured by the network. This failure as well as massive interference effects result in the appearance of attractors consisting of mixture states which degrade the network performance considerably.

In real life applications the stored information is never completely random but contains correlated structures. For example, there are large correlations among the 26 letters of the English alphabet and it is well known that the Hopfield model with the outer-product rule (3.1) is not able to treat this problem adequately in the absence of high-order interactions. However, we will demonstrate that our model is not restricted to storage and recall of random information [14]. Moreover, it also shows good performance in processing strongly structured patterns interpreted as different objects residing on a uniform background, as in figure 2 and figure 3.

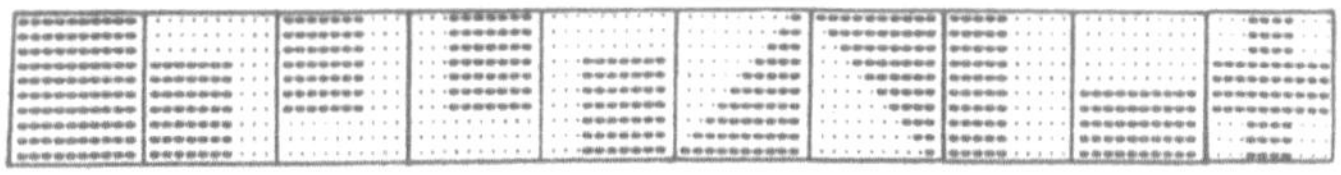

Fig.2: Samples A the network is asked to memorize

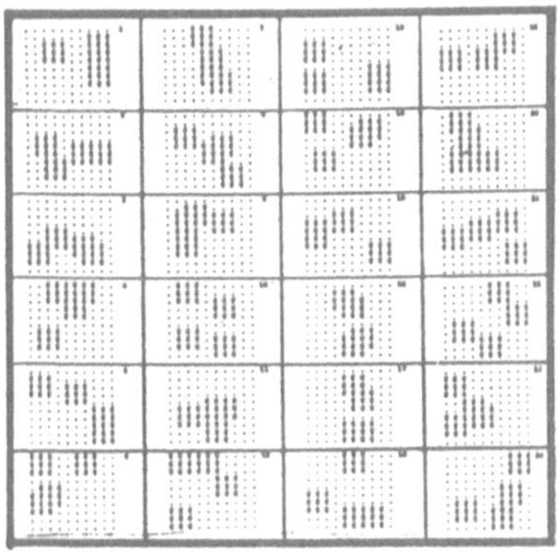

Fig.3: Samples B the network is asked to memorize

Figure 4 shows the recall performance, measured by the fraction of recognized bits, as a function of the fraction of correctly presented bits for set A. It is not

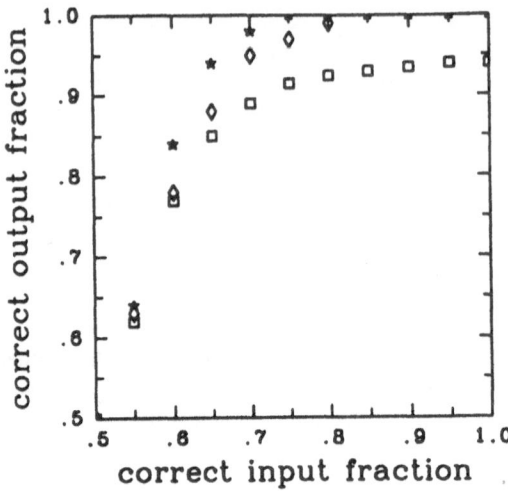

Fig.4: Recall performance of a fully connected first-order
network (squares), optimally structured first-order
network (diamonds) and an optimally structured $5-$
th order network (stars) for pattern set A.

surprising that a fully connected network (squares) is not able to stabilize this strongly
correlated training set, since the differences in the patterns cannot be well separated
by the simple learning rule and interference effects are too strong. Note that only
six out of the ten samples are fixed points of the dynamics and thus admit recall.
By contrast, the "intelligently" diluted network (diamonds), in which 40% of the
original connections have been deleted according to our strategy, can still recall the
information almost completely even if up to 20% of the pixels have been damaged. As
to be expected, working with exclusively $5-th$ order interactions (stars) according to
(7.3) improves the network performance further. Note however, that the $5-th$ order
contributions still contain redundant terms.

In order to demonstrate the efficacy of a *consistent* inclusion of high-order
terms according to (7.1) we construct 24 highly correlated quasirandom patterns seen
in figure 3. The recipe is as follows: We choose 4 bits at random on a 10×10 square
lattice such that a pattern is defined by the randomly chosen bits and their Moore
neighborhoods. Figure 5 shows convincingly that a third- order network including
"diagonal" terms is not able to store the information perfectly (stars), whereas the
third- order network, where the "diagonal" terms have been removed, is able to dis-
criminate minor differences between the patterns and does not overestimate strongly
overlapping features (triangles).

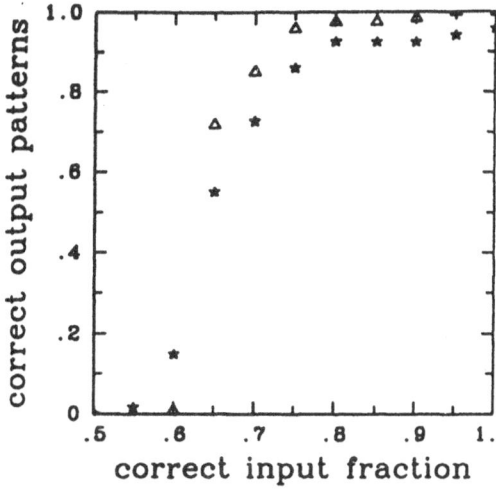

Fig.5: Recall performance of a fully connected third-order
network with (stars) and without (triangles) "diagonal" couplings for pattern set B.

9. CONCLUSIONS

We have shown that the performance of a *selectively* diluted Hebbian network
as measured by a minimal stability parameter is far better than that of the popular
fully-connected version. Moreover, high-order effects can consistently be included
with group- theoretical techniques, which increase the discrimination capability of
the network substantially.

ACKNOWLEDGEMENTS

This work benefitted from helpful discussions with E.R. Caianiello, J.W. Clark,
R. Folk and G. Senger. The author acknowledges support from the German Science
Foundation under contract number Se 251/32-1.

REFERENCES

1. P. Peretto and J.J. Niez,1986, Biol.Cybern.,**54**,53-63 *"Long term memory storage capacity of multiconnected neural networks"*

2. L. Personnaz, I. Guyon and D. Dreyfus,1987,Europhys.Lett., 4,863-867 *"High-
order neural networks: Information storage without errors"*

3. D. Psalits, C.H. Park and J.Hong,1988,Neural Networks,1, 149-163 *"Higher
order associative memories and their optical implementations"*

4. K.E. Kürten,1990, Lecture Notes in Physics,368,(Springer-Verlag) ,p.461-466,
XI Sitges Conference on Neural Networks, *"Higher-order memories in optimally
structured neural networks"*

5. K.E. Kürten,1990, J. Phys. France **51**,1585-1594 "*Quasi-optimized memoriza-tion and retrieval dynamics in sparsely connected neural network models*"

6. K.E. Kürten,1990, Parallel Processing in Neural Systems and Computers,World Scientific, ed. by R.Eckmiller, G.Hartmann and G. Hauske, 191-194 "*Dynam-ical learning in networks with sparse connectivity*"

7. S.A. Janowsky,1989, Phys.Rev.A **39**,12,6600-6603 "*Pruning versus clipping in neural networks*"

8. Y.L. Le Cun, J.S. Denker and S.A. Solla, Neural Information Processing Sys-tems, Vol.2, D. Touretzky ed. "*Optimal brain damage*"

9. B.Derrida, E.Gardner and A.Zippelius,1987, Europhys.Lett.4, 167-173. "*An exactly solvable asymmetric neural network model*"

10. I. Morgenstern,1986, Lecture Notes in Physics,12,399-427 "*Spin-glasses, opti-mization and neural networks*"

11. C. Roucairol, 1989, INRIA report 962, "*Parallel branch and bound algorithms - an overview*"

12. R. Land,1981,Mathematics of Computation,36,153,267-278, "*Computation of Polyà polynomials of primitive permutation groups*"

13. J.J. Hopfield,1982, Proc.Nat.Acad.Sci.79,2554-2558 "*Neural networks and phys-ical systems with emergent collective computational abilities*"

14. C. Aberger, R. Folk, K.E. Kürten and H. Schweng, "*Visual comparison of information storage in various neural network models*" (these proceedings)

Deterministic Networks with Ternary Neurons

Maria Marinaro

Dipartimento di Fisica Teorica

Universita' di Salerno

Abstract

The synaptic matrices for two subclasses of networks with ternary neurons are built. In the first subclass the evolution of the net is linear, in the second only a specific subset of independent states of the net evolves linearly. The possibility to use these networks as associative memories of large storage capacity is shown.

1. Introduction

The aim of this paper is to extend the study of some subclasses of boolean networks analyzed previously [1-4] to networks with ternary neurons. We shall show that many properties found for boolean nets are also valid for ternary nets. In section 2 we show that the 3^N states of the net satisfy some symmetry properties; in section 3 we specify the evolution law of the net and construct the synaptic matrices corresponding to two specific subclasses of ternary nets. In the first subclass the evolution of the net is completely linear, in the second only a subset of N independent states of the net evolves linearly. Once the evolution of this subset is assigned the evolution of all the states of the net is determined. In section 4 the complete evolution of the nets corresponding to the second subclass is analyzed for two specific choices of the subset of N independent states. In section 5, conclusive remarks are reported, in particular we show that these networks can be useful to build associative memories [5] with very large storage capacity. Some preliminary results in this direction are given.

2. Symmetry properties of a ternary network

Let us consider a network with N elements (neurons) which can assume three values. The element of the net will be denoted with the variable $X_k \equiv (0, 1, 2)$ or $\xi_k \equiv (1, 0, -1), k = 1, 2 \ldots N$.

The two notations are related by the equation

$$X_k = 1 - \xi_k \qquad (2.1)$$

In the following we use the notation ξ_k. In order to write the 3^N states of the net in a convenient form, we introduce the vector $\vec{\eta}$ with 3^N components obtained as

tensorial product of the N vectors $\begin{pmatrix} 1 \\ \xi_N \\ \xi_N^2 \end{pmatrix} \ldots \begin{pmatrix} 1 \\ \xi_1 \\ \xi_1^2 \end{pmatrix}$

$$\vec{\eta} = \begin{pmatrix} 1 \\ \xi_N \\ \xi_N^2 \end{pmatrix} \otimes \begin{pmatrix} 1 \\ \xi_{N-1} \\ \xi_{N-1}^2 \end{pmatrix} \otimes \ldots \otimes \begin{pmatrix} 1 \\ \xi_1 \\ \xi_1^2 \end{pmatrix} \qquad (2.2)$$

$\otimes$ indicates the tensor product $\begin{pmatrix} a \\ b \end{pmatrix} \otimes \begin{pmatrix} c \\ d \end{pmatrix} = \begin{pmatrix} ac \\ ad \\ bc \\ bd \end{pmatrix}$. The components of

$\vec{\eta}$ are denoted with η^α, $\alpha = 0, 1, \ldots, 3^N - 1$. The component η^α $\alpha = 3^p$ $p = (0, 1, \ldots N - 1)$ coincides with the neuron variable ξ_{p+1}. Note that each vector $\begin{pmatrix} 1 \\ \xi_k \\ \xi_k^2 \end{pmatrix}$ in (2.2) assumes the following configurations

$$\begin{pmatrix} 1 \\ 1 \\ 1 \end{pmatrix} ; \quad \begin{pmatrix} 1 \\ 0 \\ 0 \end{pmatrix} ; \quad \begin{pmatrix} 1 \\ -1 \\ 1 \end{pmatrix}$$

in corrispondence of the values

$$\xi_k = 1; 0; -1$$

In order to build all the possible states of the net it is sufficient to introduce the matrix Φ_N ($3^N \times 3^N$) as follows

$$\Phi_N = \begin{pmatrix} 1 & 1 & 1 \\ 1 & 0 & -1 \\ 1 & 0 & 1 \end{pmatrix} \otimes \begin{pmatrix} 1 & 1 & 1 \\ 1 & 0 & -1 \\ 1 & 0 & 1 \end{pmatrix} \otimes, \ldots, \otimes \begin{pmatrix} 1 & 1 & 1 \\ 1 & 0 & -1 \\ 1 & 0 & 1 \end{pmatrix}; \qquad (2.3)$$

we enumerate the rows of ϕ_N with the indices $0, 1 \ldots 3^N - 1$. The matrix which contains the 3^N states of the net is obtained from Φ_N by considering only the rows $N = 3^k$ ($k = 0, 1, 2, \ldots N - 1$). The matrix thus obtained will be denoted with $\varphi_N \equiv (N \times 3^N)$. The matrix φ_N contains all the possible states of the net at the time t. In the following we denote the column k^{th} of φ_N with the vectors $\underline{\xi}_{k-1}$ ($k = 1 \ldots 3^N - 1$). The matrix φ_N satisfies the following symmetry properties

$$\begin{cases} \varphi_{k,e} + \varphi_{k,3^{N-s+1}-e-1} = \varphi_{k,\frac{3^{N-s+1}-1}{2}} \\ \varphi_{k,e} + \varphi_{k,2\times3^{N-s}+e} = 2\varphi_{k,3^{N-s}+e} \end{cases} \qquad (2.4)$$

$$e = 0, 1, \ldots, 3^{N-s} - 1$$

$$k = 0, 1, \ldots, N - 1$$

$$s = 1, 2, \ldots, N - 1$$

The quantity 3^s gives the number of blocks in which the matrix φ_N is divided, e numbers the columns in each block. In particular by using (2.4) for $s = 1$ i.e. by dividing the matrix φ_N in three blocks, we can express all the 3^N columns of φ_N in term of the first 3^{N-1} columns (the first block). Indeed by observing that the central column of φ_N, i.e. $\varphi_k, \frac{3^N-1}{2}$ has all vanishing elements, the first equation of (2.4) becomes

$$\varphi_{k,e} = -\varphi_{k,3^N-e-1}. \qquad (2.5)$$

$$e = 0 \ldots 3^{N-1} - 1$$

Besides, keeping in mind the second equation of (2.4) and (2.5) we have

$$\varphi_{k,3^{N-1}+e} = \frac{1}{2}(\varphi_{k,e} + \varphi_{k,2\times3^{N-1}+e}) = \frac{1}{2}(\varphi_{k,e} - \varphi_{k,3^{N-1}-e-1}) \qquad (2.6)$$

The equation (2.5) gives the last 3^{N-1} columns of φ_N (third block) in term of the first 3^{N-1} (first block); the equation (2.6) gives the second block of φ_N (i.e. the columns $3^{N-1}, 3^{N-1}+1, \ldots 2 \times 3^{N-1}-1)$ in terms of the first 3^{N-1} columns of φ_N.

3. Two subclasses of ternary nets

The evolution law of a ternary net can be written as follows .

$$\underline{\xi}(t+\tau) = \sigma_3\{f[\underline{\xi}(t)]\} \tag{3.1}$$

where the N component vector $\underline{\xi}(t)$ is the generic state of the net at the time t, the ith component of $\underline{\xi}(t)$ coincides with the ith neuron at the time t; the time is a discrete variable, τ is the unity of time, the symbol $\sigma_3\{f\}$ is defined as:

$$\sigma_3\{f\} = \begin{cases} 1 & f > 0 \\ 0 & f = 0 \\ -1 & f < 0 \end{cases} \tag{3.2}$$

In this work we are interested in functions f which are linear, therefore (3.1) becomes

$$\underline{\xi}(t+\tau) = \sigma_3[A\underline{\xi}(t)] \tag{3.3}$$

where A is an $N \times N$ matrix, the synaptic matrix. To analyze the evolution of a net described by (3.3) it is convenient to define the matrix

$$W_N = A\varphi_N \tag{3.4}$$

which is obtained by the application of the matrix A to the matrix φ_n defined in section 2. We call φ_n' the matrix which contains all the states of the net after one step evolution i.e. at time $t \mid \tau$. From (3.3) and (3.4) follows:

$$\varphi_N' = \sigma_3(A\varphi_N) = \sigma_3(W_N) \tag{3.5}$$

In the literature several methods [6-9] are reported to build the synaptic matrix A, in the following the matrix A is obtained by putting some constraints on the evolution of the states. In particular we are interested in characterizing the synaptic matrix A for the two subclasses defined in the following

$$\varphi_N' = W_N \tag{3.6}$$

$$\varphi_N^{'0} = W^0 = A\varphi_N^0 \tag{3.7}$$

where φ_N^0 is a matrix $N \times N$ obtained by choosing N columns of φ_N and $\varphi_N^{'0}$ is the one step evolution of φ_N^0. The first subclass describes a net which evolves linearly. The second subclass describes a net whose evolution is linear only on a subset of N states (the states which appear in φ_N^0).

A) Synaptic matrix for the first subclass

Theorem: The synaptic matrix A for a net which evolves according to (3.6) has elements equal to $0, 1, -1$. On each row of A at most one element different from zero appears.

The proof is as follows:

From (3.6) we have for a generic element of $\varphi_N^{'}$

$$(\varphi_N^{'})_{km} = \sum_e a_{ke}(\varphi_N)_{em} = \begin{cases} 0 \\ 1 \\ -1 \end{cases} \quad k = 0, \ldots, N-1 \tag{3.8}$$

we have denoted with a_{ke} the elements of the matrix A. Since m is arbitrary and φ_N contains all the possible vectors of the three-value algebra we can choose m in such a way that

$$(\varphi)_{em} = \begin{cases} \pm 1 & \text{if } e = s, \quad s = 0, 1, \ldots, N-1 \\ 0 & \text{otherwise} \end{cases}$$

Then (3.8) becomes

$$(\varphi_A^{'})_{km} = \pm a_{ks} = \begin{cases} 0 \\ 1 \\ -1 \end{cases} \tag{3.8bis}$$

$$k = 0, \ldots, N-1$$

$$s = 0, \ldots, N-1$$

The equation (3.8bis) proves the first part of the theorem. To prove the second part, we observe that φ_N contains all the possible sequences of N elements of the three value algebra $(0, 1, -1)$, then for each row of A we can find one column of φ_N that coincides with it. To be specific let us assume that the kth row of A and the mth column of φ_N coincide, we have

$$\sum_e a_{ks}(\varphi_N)_{em} = r$$

r is the number of elements different from zero in the kth row of A

But by definition

$$\sum_{s} a_{ks} (\varphi_N)_{sm} = (\varphi'_N)_{km}$$

which implies $r = 0, 1$.

In conclusion the synaptic matrices for nets of the subclass characterized by (3.6) are very sparse matrices with at most N elements different from zero.

Some remarks on the application of this network as associative memory will be reported in sec. 5.

B) Synaptic matrix for the second subclass

The matrix A for the subclass which evolves according to the equation (3.7) can be easily built once N vectors of φ_N (the matrix φ_N^0) are choosen and their evolution is fixed (i.e. $\varphi_N'^0$ is given). It is convenient to choose the N vectors of φ_N^0 linearly independent so that any other of the 3^N vectors of φ_N can be expressed in terms of these. In this case we say that the vectors belonging to φ_N^0 form a basis.

Different choices of φ_N^0 give different nets with peculiar properties. The choice of φ_N^0 must be appropriate to the task that the net has to solve.

First, to discuss particular choices of φ_N^0 we observe that from (3.7), since φ_N^0 has all the columns linearly independent, we have:

$$A = \varphi_N'^0 (\varphi_N^0)^{-1} \tag{3.9}$$

Thus A is completely fixed by the evolution of the N vectors of the basis.

In the following we discuss two particular choices of φ_N^0; in the first the N vectors belonging to φ_N^0 are chosen orthogonal, in the second the N vectors are only independent.

The first choice is obtained by selecting the N columns of φ_N with elements all equal to zero excepting one which is equal to 1 (this basis is orthogonal) $\varphi_N^0 = I_N =$ matrix unity.

The columns of φ_N^0 are the vectors $\underline{\xi}_{p_k}$ (columns $p_k + 1$ of φ_N) with

$$p_k = \sum_{\substack{i=0 \\ i \neq k-1}}^{N-1} 3^i \quad k = (1 \ldots N)$$

It is evident that for this net

$$A = \varphi_N^{'0} \tag{3.10}$$

and if we ask the subset of the vectors of the basis to be closed under evolution, we have that the matrix A has only N elements different from zero, each column of A has one and only one element different from zero and equal to 1. The number of rows of A with non vanishing elements coincides with the number of distinct states in $\varphi_N^{'0}$.

The second choice is obtained by considering φ_N^0 as the $N \times N$ matrix whose first column has all elements equal to 1, while the ith column ($i = 2, \ldots N$) has all the elements equal to 1 excepting the $(i-1)^{th}$ element which is zero. The columns of φ_N^0 are N vectors linearly independent but not orthogonal; they correspond to the columns $3^k + 1$ of φ_N i.e. φ_0^N is the matrix whose columns are the vectors $\underline{\xi}_0, \underline{\xi}_{3^k}$ $k = 0 \ldots N-2$; for simplicity such vectors will be denoted in the following with $\underline{0}, \underline{3}^k$.

It is immediate to verify that:

$$(\varphi_N^0)^{-1} = \begin{pmatrix} 1 & 1 & 1 & \ldots & -(N-2) \\ -1 & 0 & 0 & \ldots & 1 \\ 0 & -1 & 0 & \ldots & 1 \\ 0 & 0 & -1 & \ldots & 1 \end{pmatrix} \tag{3.11}$$

Thus keeping in mind (3.9) the matrix A is easily expressed in term of the elements of the matrix $\varphi_N^{'0}$

$$a_{km} = (\varphi_N^{'0})_{k0} - (\varphi_N^{'0})_{k,m+1}$$

$$a_{kN-1} = \sum_{i=1}^{N-1} (\varphi_N^{'0})_{ki} - (N-2)(\varphi_N^{'0})_{k0} \tag{3.12}$$

$$k = 0 \ldots N-1$$

$$m = 0 \ldots N-2$$

Note that if the basis is closed under evolution and the state $\underline{0}$ is stable the matrix A has at most one element different from zero and equal to 1 in each of the first $N - 2$ columns. Then the matrix A has at most $2N - 1$ non vanishing elements. When the state $\underline{0}$ is not stable then A has at most $3N$ non vanishing elements.

4. Evolution of the nets analyzed in the previous section

Keeping in mind the structure of the matrix A for nets of the first subclass it is evident that these nets are particular additive automata whose evolution has been extensively analyzed in previous works [10]. Thus in this section we confine ourselves to the study of networks belonging to the second subclass. We discuss first the case $\varphi_N^0 = I_N$.

Let us call $\underline{Z}_1 \ldots \underline{Z}_N$ the vectors of the basis (i.e. the columns of φ_N^0). Note $\underline{Z}_i$ has all the components equal to zero except the ith which is equal to 1. We have

$$\underline{Z}_i = \underline{\xi}_{p_i}, \quad p_i = \sum_{\substack{j=0 \\ j=i-1}}^{N-1} 3^j$$

Every state can be expressed in term of the basis through the equation

$$\underline{\xi}_k = \sum_{i=1}^{N} (\underline{\xi}_k)_i \underline{Z}_i \tag{4.1}$$

where $(\underline{\xi}_k)_i$ is the ith component of $\underline{\xi}_k$

The one step evolution of $\underline{\xi}_k$ is given by

$$\underline{\xi}_k^1 = \sigma_3(A\underline{\xi}_k) = \sigma_3\left[\sum_{i=1}^{N} (\underline{\xi}_k)_i \underline{Z}_i^1\right] \tag{4.2}$$

where we have put

$$\underline{Z}_i^1 = A\underline{Z}_i$$

Some of the states $\underline{Z}_i^1$ can be coincident, we indicate with $\underline{V}_1 \ldots \underline{V}_p$ the distinct states $p \leq N$ and with $\underline{Z}_{e_1} \ldots \underline{Z}_{e_{s_e}}$ the states of the basis which are attracted by $\underline{V}_e$

Equation (4.2) becomes

$$\underline{\xi}_k^1 = \sigma_3\left[\sum_{e=1}^{p} V_e^k \underline{V}_e\right] \tag{4.3}$$

where

$$V_e^k = \sum_{m=1}^{s_e} (\underline{\xi}_k)_{e_m} \tag{4.4}$$

is the sum of all the components of $\underline{\xi}_k$ which in (4.1) multiply basis vectors attracted by $\underline{V}_e$.

Let us first consider the case in which $\underline{V}_e \epsilon \varphi_0, \underline{V}_e = \underline{Z}_{j_e}$; eq. (4.3) becomes

$$\underline{\xi}_k^1 = \sigma_3 [\sum_{e=1}^{p} V_e^k \underline{Z}_{j_e}] \tag{4.5}$$

Keeping in mind the explicit expression of the basis vectors we note that each vector in the sum contributes to a different component of $\underline{\xi}_k^1$, therefore we can write

$$\underline{\xi}_k^1 = \sum_{e=1}^{p} \sigma_3 (V_e^k) \underline{Z}_{j_e} \tag{4.6}$$

From (4.5) it is evident that $\underline{\xi}_k^1$ has at most p components different fron zero. In conclusion if $N - p$ vectors of φ_N^0 are transient any state of the net evolves in a vector which has at least $N - p$ vanishing components.

The net acts as a projector of the N-dimensional space in a p-dimensional subspace. To compute the rth component of $\underline{\xi}_k^1$ in the p-dimensional subspace we have to consider the basis vectors attracted by Z_r. Let be $\underline{Z}_{r_i} \ldots \underline{Z}_{r_m}$ the basis vectors attracted by $\underline{Z}_r$ and set

$$(\underline{\xi}_k^1)_r = \begin{cases} 0 & \sum_{i=1}^{m} (\underline{\xi}_k)_{r_i} = 0 \\ 1 & \sum_{i=1}^{m} (\underline{\xi}_k)_{r_i} > 0 \\ -1 & \sum_{i=1}^{m} (\underline{\xi}_k)_{r_i} < 0 \end{cases}$$

The results reported above can be generalized to the case in which $\underline{V}_e \not\subset \varphi_N^0$ from (4.3) by writing

$$\underline{V}_e = \sum_{i=1}^{N} (\underline{V}_e)_i \underline{Z}_i$$

we have

$$\underline{\xi}_k^1 = \sigma_3 [\sum_{e=1}^{p} V_e^k (\sum_{i=1}^{N} (V_e)_i \underline{Z}_i)] = \sigma_3 [\sum_{e=1}^{N} b_i \underline{Z}_i] = \sum_{i=1}^{N} \sigma_3 (b_i) \underline{Z}_i \tag{4.7}$$

with

$$b_i = \sum_{e=1}^{p} V_e^k (V_e)_i$$

This completes the analysis of the evolution of the network belonging to the second subclass when we have selected the matrix $\phi_N^0 = I$. Finally, we analyze the evolution of the net built by using the second choice of the matrix φ_N^0. The basis contains independent but not orthogonal vectors.

We first note that the basis vectors belong to the first $3^{N-1} - 1$ columns of φ_N (the first block), therefore to express all the states in terms of this basis we have to use the symmetry properties discussed in section 2 (see eq. 2.5 and 2.6).

By denoting with the vectors $\underline{0}, \underline{3}^k$ $k = 0 \ldots N-2$ the columns of φ_N^0 we have:

$$\underline{\xi}_e = -(r^e - 1)\underline{0} + \sum_{s=1}^{N-1} \lambda_s^e \underline{3}^{s-1} \tag{4.8}$$

first block

$$\underline{\xi}_{3^{N-1}+e} = -(r^e - N + 1)\underline{0} + \sum_{s=1}^{N-1} (\lambda_s - 1)\underline{3}^{s-1} \tag{4.9}$$

second block

$$\underline{\xi}_{3^N - e - 1} = (r^e - 1)\underline{0} - \sum_{s=1}^{N-1} \lambda_s^e \underline{3}^{s-1} \tag{4.10}$$

third block

where $e = 0, 1 \ldots 3^{N-1} - 1$

$$r^e = \sum_{s=1}^{N-1} \lambda_s^e$$

and $\lambda_s^e = 0, 1, 2$ are determined by writing e in ternary basis:

$$\lambda_s^e = 1 - (\underline{\xi}_e).$$

(see equation 2.1).

To write (4.9) and (4.10) we have used the properties of symmetry (2.5) and (2.6); explicit derivations of (4.8), (4.9) and (4.10) are given in Appendix. In order to study the evolution of the net we start with the vectors in the first block (4.8) and write the one step evolution state

$$\underline{\xi}_e^1 = \sigma_3(A\underline{\xi}_e) = \sigma_3[-(r^e-1)\underline{0}^1 + \sum_{e>1}^{N-1} \lambda_e^e \underline{Z}_e] \tag{4.11}$$

where, keeping in mind the linear evolution of φ_N^0, we have put

$$\underline{0}^1 = A\underline{0}$$

$$\underline{Z}_e = A\underline{3}^{e-1}$$

Let us first study the case in which the following equations are true

$$\underline{0}^1 \equiv \underline{0} \tag{4.12}a$$

$$\underline{Z}_e = \underline{3}^{j_e} \in \varphi_N^0 \tag{4.12}b$$

i.e. the state $\underline{0}$ is stable and the basis is closed under evolution. The eq.(4.11) becomes

$$\underline{\xi}_e^1 = \sigma[-(r^e-1)\underline{0} + \sum_{e=1}^{N-1} \lambda_e^e \underline{3}^{j_e}] \tag{4.13}$$

In general not all the states $\underline{3}^{j_e}$ are distinct, let us denote with $\underline{3}^{t_m}$ $(m=1\dots p)$ the distinct states and assume that

$$\underline{3}^{j_{m_1}} \equiv \underline{3}^{j_{m_r}} \dots \equiv \underline{3}^{j_{m_s}} \equiv \underline{3}^{t_m}$$

the equation (4.13) can be rewritten

$$\underline{\xi}_e^1 = \sigma_3[-(r^e-1)\underline{0} + \sum_{m=1}^{p} \mu_m^e \underline{3}^{t_m}] \tag{4.14}$$

where $\mu_m^e = \lambda_{m_1}^e + \lambda_{m_r}^e + \dots \lambda_{m_s}^e > 0$ note $\sum_m \mu_m^e = r^e$

It is immediately verified that eq.(3.6) is equivalent to the following equation:

$$\underline{\xi}_e^1 = -(q^e-1)\underline{0} + \sum_{m=1}^{p} b_m^e \underline{3}^{t_m} \tag{4.15}$$

where $q^e = \sum_{m=1}^{p} b_m^e$

$$b_m^e = 1 - \sigma_3(1 - \mu_m^e) \tag{4.16}$$

To verify that the two equatons (4.14) and (4.15) are equivalent it is sufficient to compare their p^{th} components.

From (4.14) we have

$$(\xi_e^1)_j = \begin{cases} \sigma[-(r^e - 1) + r^e] = 1 \text{ if } (3^{t_m})_j = 1 \forall m \\ \sigma_3(1 - \mu_n^e) \text{ if there is a value } n \text{ such that } (3_{j}^{t_*} = 0) \end{cases} \quad (4.17)$$

from (4.15) we have

$$(\varphi_e^1)_j = \begin{cases} [-(q^e - 1) + q^e] = 1 \text{ if } (3^{t_m})_j = 1 \forall m \\ [1 - b_m^e] \text{ if there is a value } n \text{ such that } (3^{t_*})_j = 0 \end{cases} \quad (4.18)$$

Keeping in mind (4.16) we see that (4.17) and (4.18) are equivalent. In conclusion, in the hypothesis (4.12) the state $\vec{\xi}_e$ where e in ternary basis is given by

$$e = \sum_{n=0} \lambda_n^e 3^n \quad (4.19)$$

evolves in the state $\underline{\xi}_e^1 = \underline{\xi}_x$ with

$$x = \sum_{m=1}^{p} b_m^e \underline{3}^{t_m} \quad (4.20)$$

where $\underline{3}^{t_m}$ are the distinct states of the basis contained in $\varphi_N^{'0}$, and $bm^e = 2$ except in the two situations

1) 3^{t_m} attracts only one state of the decomposition (4.19) with coefficient $\lambda_S = 1$, in this case $b_m^e = 1$

2) (4.19) does not contain states attracted by 3^{t_m}, in this case $b_m^e = 0$.

If the state $\underline{0}$ is not stable and is attracted by 3^μ then we have to exclude this state from (4.20) and the evolution of the state $\underline{\xi}_e$ is given by:

$$\underline{\xi}_e^1 = \underline{\xi}_x \text{ with } x = \sum_{\substack{m=1 \\ m \neq \mu}} b_m^e 3^{t_m} \quad (4.21)$$

To study the evolution of states which appear as columns of φ_N belonging to the second block we start from the equation (4.9). We observe that (4.9) can be written more conveniently as:

$$\underline{\xi}_{3^{N-1}+e} = -(r^e - N + 1)\underline{0} + \sum_{S=1}^{N-1} (\underline{\xi}_e)_S \underline{3}^{S-1} \quad (4.22)$$

where $(\underline{\xi})_s = \begin{cases} 1 \\ 0 \\ -1 \end{cases}$ is the sth component of the vectors $\underline{\xi}_e$ the $e+1$ column of φ_N. Note

$$\sum_{s=1}^{N-1} (\underline{\xi})_s \equiv N + 1 + r^e$$

After one step evolution, assuming valid (4.12), the eq. (4.22) becomes

$$\xi^1_{3_{+e}^{N-1}} = \sigma_3[-(r^e - N - 1)\underline{0} + \sum_{s=1}^{N-1} (\underline{\xi})_s \underline{3}^{j_s}] = \sigma_3[-(r^e - N - 1)\underline{0} + \sum_{m=1}^{p} V^e_m \underline{3}^{t_m}]$$

$$(4.23)$$

where, as before, we have denoted by $3^{t_m} (m = 1 \ldots p)$ the distinct states among $\underline{3}^{j_s} (s = \ldots N - 1)$ and

$$V^e_m = \sum_{i=1}^{n} (\underline{\xi}_e)_{m_i}, \quad \sum_{m=0}^{p} V^e_m = r - N + 1$$

with

$$\underline{3}^{j_{m_i}} \equiv \underline{3}^{j_{m_e}} \ldots = \underline{3}^{j_{m_n}} \equiv \underline{3}^{t_m}$$

Equation (4.23) is equivalent to the following one:

$$\xi^1_{3^{N-1}+e} = -\rho^e \underline{0} + \sum_{m=1}^{p} \sigma_3 (V^e_m)\underline{3}^{t_m}$$

$$(4.24)$$

where

$$\rho^e = \sum_m \sigma(V^e_m)$$

The equivalence of (4.23) and (4.24) can be proved by using the same procedure adopted previously. In conclusion the one step evolution of the vectors in the second block of the matrix φ_N is given by

$$\xi^1_{3_{+e}^{N-1}} = \xi_{3^{N-1}-+x}$$

$$(4.25)$$

$$x = \sum_m \sigma_3 (V^e_m)\underline{3}^{t_m} + \sum_{s=1}^{N-1} \underline{3}^{s-1}$$

if the $\underline{0}$ is stable

$$\xi^1_{3^{N-1}+e} = \varphi^1_{3^{N-1}+e}, \quad x = \sum_{m \neq \mu} \sigma_3 (V^e_m)\underline{3}^{t_m} + \sum_{s=1}^{N-1} 3^{s-1}$$

$$(4.26)$$

if the $\underline{0}$ is not stable and is attracted by 3^μ.

The evolution of the vectors in block three can be easily computed by observing that these vectors are the opposite of the ones in the first block. By using the same procedure as before we have that the one step evolution of $\underline{\xi}_{3^N - \epsilon - 1}$ is given by

$$\underline{\xi}^1_{\rho^N - \epsilon - 1} = (q^\epsilon - 1)\underline{0} - \sum_{m-1}^p b^\epsilon_m \underline{3}^{\epsilon m} \tag{4.27}$$

thus

$$\underline{\xi}^1_{3^N - \epsilon - 1} = \underline{\xi}_{3^N - x - 1} \tag{4.28}$$

with

$$x = \sum_m b^\epsilon_m \underline{3}^{\epsilon m} \; if \; \underline{0} \to \underline{0}$$

$$x = \sum_{m \neq \mu} b^\epsilon_m \underline{3}^{\epsilon m} \; if \; \underline{0} \to \underline{3}^\mu$$

b^ϵ_m are defined in (4.16).

By using the same procedure as in the previous examples (see eq.4.7), it is easy to generalize the equation (4.15) (4.23) and (4.27) to the case in which the (4.12b) is not valid. i.e. The set of basis vectors is not closed under evolution.

In conclusion, with both the choices made for φ^0_N, although in general the evolution of the networks of the second subclass is not linear for states $\underline{\xi}_* \; \varphi_0$, it is possible, by choosing appropriate bases, to express the evolution of any state of the net as a suitable linear combination of the basis vectors. [see eq. (4.6), (4.15), (4.24) and (4.27)]. The coefficients of the linear combinations of the basis vectors belong to the three value algebra. It is therefore possible to compute the evolution of these nets with a complexity of computation which is polinomial in the number of neurons. In particular, applications of these classes of networks to associative memory (i.e net which has only transient and stable states) are quite interesting. Work in this direction is in progress. Some preliminary considerations are reported in the next section.

5. Conclusion and remarks

In this section we report some particular properties of the nets under consideration.

1) The nets of the first subclass (eq.3.6) when used as associative memory are very useful to evidence the structure of the patterns to memorize. In fact, once fixed the learning algorithm from examples (see ref. [11]) the number of columns with elements different from zero of the matrix A is connected with the structure of the patterns given as examples.

Namely, let us assume that the components of the patterns, given as examples, can be divided in m sets, such that the the the signs of the n_i components belonging to the ith set $(i = 1 \ldots m)$ are correlated; then the matrix A, built by these examples, has only m columns with elements different from zero. The m columns contain rispectively $n_1, n_2, \ldots, n_m$ elements equal to ± 1.

For example, if the patterns to consider are:

$$\begin{pmatrix} 1 & -1 & 1 & -1 \\ 1 & -1 & 1 & -1 \\ -1 & -1 & 1 & 1 \\ 1 & 1 & -1 & -1 \\ 0 & 0 & 0 & 0 \end{pmatrix}$$

we have two sets of correlated components. The first set contains the components 1 and 2, the second set the components 3 and 4. The matrix A built from these patterns will have only two columns with elements different from zero. A column will have the first and second elements different from zero, the other the third and fourth ones.

2) We have seen that the nets of the second subclass, whose synaptic matrix is given by (3.10), acts as a projector of the N-dimensional space in a p-dimensional subspace. When the net is an associative memory, i.e. the evolution is such that the p states of the basis are stable and the other $N - p$ are attracted by these; it is immediate to show that the net can store 3^p patterns (the p-dimensional subspace). The amplitudes of the basins of attraction of the 3^p patterns can be changed at will [12] and varied by acting on the evolution of the N vectors of the basin.

As an application we use this net to separate n sheets whose surfaces are partially white and partially black into three classes, the first contains the sheets in which the white is predominant, the second contain the sheets in which the black is predominant and the third which contains the sheets in which black and white surface are equal. In this case it is sufficient to have only one vector of the basis stable; we divide the surface of the kth sheet in N square and represent the sheet as an N component vector $\underline{\xi}_k$. The mth component of $\underline{\xi}_k$ will be $1(-1)$ if in the mth square the white (black) is predominant, otherwise zero.

The evolution of vectors $\underline{\xi}_k$ $(k = 1 \ldots n)$ is fixed by choosing $\varphi_N'^0$ thus A as the matrix whose columns are all equal to the vector Z_i of the basis.

By using (4.6) we have

$$\underline{\xi}_k^1 = \sigma_3 [\sum (\xi_k)_i] \underline{Z}_i$$

thus ξ_k^1 is a vector whose components are all zero, but the ith which is $1\,(-1)$ if in the kth sheet the white (black) is predominant, otherwise zero.

3) Finally we want to make some considerations concerning the nets described in (3.12). Keeping in mind the eq. (4.14), (4.24) and (4.27) which give the evolution of the state in the first, second and third block, we see that, if the evolution of the net is such that only p states of the basis are stable while the others are transient, the net projects the 3^{N-1} vectors of the first (third) block in 3^{p-1} vectors which have $N - p + 1$ component equal to $1\,(-1)$. The other $p - 1$ components take value $(0, -1, 1)$; and the 3^{N-1} vectors of the second block in 3^{p-1} vectors which have $N - p + 1$ component equal to zero while $p - 1$ components take value $(0, -1, 1)$. Each block is closed under evolution, the last component of the vectors does not change under evolution, the net is an associative memory with 3^p stable states.

Acknowledgment

This work was supported by the C.N.R. "Progetto Finalizzato Sistemi Informatici e Calcolo Parallelo" under grant 90.00660.PF69 and by MURST 40%. Unita' INFM, Universita' di Salerno.

Appendix

The equation (4.8) can be written:

$$\underline{\xi}_e = \varphi_N^0 \underline{\lambda}^e \quad where \quad \underline{\lambda}^e = \begin{pmatrix} \lambda_0^e \\ \lambda_1^e \\ \vdots \\ \lambda_{N-1}^e \end{pmatrix} \qquad (A.I)$$

From $(A.I)$ we have:

$$\underline{\lambda}^e = (\varphi_N^0)^{-1} \underline{\xi}_e \qquad (A.II)$$

Keeping in mind (3.11), $(A.II)$ gives:

$$\lambda_s^e = -(\underline{\xi}_e)_s + (\underline{\xi}_e)_N \quad s = 1 \ldots N-1$$

In the first block $(\underline{\xi}_e)_N = 1$ then

$$\lambda_s^e = -(\underline{\xi}_e)_s + 1 = \begin{cases} 0 & if \ (\underline{\xi}_e)_s = 1 \\ 1 & if \ (\xi_e)_s = 0 \\ 2 & if \ (\xi_e)_s = -1 \end{cases} \qquad (A.III)$$

Finally

$$\lambda_0^e = \sum_{i=1}^{N-1} (\underline{\xi}_e)_i - (N-2)(\underline{\xi}_e)_N = -\sum_{s=1}^{N-1} \lambda_s^e + 1 = -r^e + 1 \qquad (A.IV)$$

$(A.III)$ and $(A.IV)$ prove the eq.(4.8).

To prove eq.(2.6) we write:

$$\underline{\xi}_{3^{N-1}+e} = \frac{1}{2}(\underline{\xi}_e - \underline{\xi}_{3^{N-1}-e-1}) = \frac{1}{2}\{[-(r^e-1)\underline{0} + \sum_{s=1}^{N-1} \lambda_s^e \underline{3}^{s-1}] - [r^e + 1 - 2(N-1)]$$

$$\underline{0} + \sum_{s=1}^{N-1} (2-\lambda_s^e)\underline{3}^{s-1}\} = (-r^e + N - 1)\underline{0} + \sum_{s=1}^{N-1} (\lambda_s - 1)\underline{3}^{s-1}$$

References

[1] Caianiello E.R., Marinaro M., Tagliaferri R. (1988). "The inverse problem for linear boolean nets" In R. Eckmiller and Ch. von der Marlsburg (Eds.), *Neural Computers*, NATO ASI Series, **F41**, Berlin: Springer-Verlag.

[2] Caianiello E.R., Marinaro M., Tagliaferri R. (1989). "Linear Boolean Nets Synthesizable in Polynomial Time". In R.M.J. Cotterill (Ed.), *Models of Brain Function*, Cambridge Univ. Press.

[3] Occhinegro P., Tagliaferri R., "Classes of efficiently computable linear Neural Nets", *Neural Networks*, 1990, **3**, 347.

[4] Caianiello E.R., De Benedictis A., Petrosino A., Tagliaferri R. (1991). "Neural Associative Memories with Minimum Connectivity". In press on *Neural Networks*.

[5] Kohonen T., *Associative Memory: a System Theoretical Approach*, Springer-Verlag, Berlin, 1977.

[6] Hopfield J.J., "Neuronal Networks and Phisycal Systems with Emergent Collective Computational Abilities", *Proceedings of National Accademy of Sciences USA*, 1982, **79**, 2254-2558.

[7] Amari F.," Neuronal Theory of Association and Concept Formation", *Biological Cybernetics*, 1977, **26**, 175-185.

[8] Maurani A. D., Chevallier R. C., Sirat G., "Information Retrieval in Neuronal Networks", *Rev. Phys. Appl.*, 1987, **22**, 1321-1325.

[9] Personnaz I., Guyon I., Dreyfus G., "Information Storage and Retrieval in Spin-Glass like Neuronal Networks", *Journ. Phys. Lett.*, 1985, **46**, 359-365.

[10] Caianiello E.R., Ceccarelli M., Marinaro M., "Can Spurius States be useful?". In press on *Complex Systems*.

[11] Caianiello E.R., Esposito A., Marinaro M., Tagliaferri R., "The Behaviour and Learning of a Deterministic Neural Net". Preprint I.I.A.S.S.

[12] Venkatesh S., Pancha G., Psaltis D., Sirat G. "Shaping Attraction Basins in Neuronal Networks", *Neural Networks*, 1990, **3**, 613-623.

Nets, Structure, Hierarchy

Eduardo R. Caianiello

Dipartimento di Fisica Teorica

Università di Salerno

Abstract

Remarks are made on some topics of current interest in NN theory, in particular: it is contended that discarding "spurious states" may be not a wise thing to do; that we have had perhaps enough of learning random patterns and might better concentrate on correlations among them; that there is evidence that general "structural laws" are at work in all systems, which ought to be not ignored when thinking about "neural computers". An example of such laws is given for hierarchical modular systems, which shows also how "complexity" can be for them exactly defined and handled.

I must confess that for several years, after my early enthusiasm for Neural Nets (aroused in 1955 by Grey Walter's "The Living Brain"), my interest in the subject relented for over a decade. I had found indeed that, with the machinery I had set up in my 1961 paper [1], I could easily answer *all* questions that were asked me by brain scientists (the word did not exist at the time) or computer people. As a physicist, though, I knew only too well that a theory that explains *everything* explains *nothing* at all: at best, it is a *language*. I wish also to confess that in the present situation, with NN's presented as a "universal answer" to all sorts of questions, claims and promises reaching to the sky, I feel uneasy again: are we being confronted with a theory, or with a language? I propose to share my feelings and views with you and to face some hard facts; this may perhaps help discriminating between dead ends and open routes.

The first fact we have to face is that we know of no decent mathematical method for extremizing functions with large numbers of variables. Yet the brain does it (we theorize) with enough accuracy for our survival; we do not entrust the formation of our synapses to an outside computer! Should we try analogical hardware? Has this something to do with our abuse of "real numbers", a devilish invention which conceals all possible traps under heaven? If we do not succeed in eliminating this "bottleneck", I see little hope for "neural computing".Another fact is, that everybody seems anxious to utilize statistical devices of all degrees of sophistication; yet NE ("neuronic equations", that describe the instantaneous working of an NN)[1] can be, and have been, exactly solved if one uses yes-or-no jump functions: one can, that is, given an arbitrary sequence of states, exactly specify the boolean net that will perform that sequence in the prescribed order ("inverse problem" [3]). This is a perfectly viable approach for "netlets" and for structures built out of them, on which (and on the preliminary questions it poses: "how to build higher structures?") we are currently working. I have no criticism against statistics and "all that"; it is unavoidable if we are after biological models, but perhaps not necessarily so if our intent is the design of a "neural computer". Of remarkable interest for the understanding of complex many-body processes is for instance, undoubtedly, the "spin-glass" approach; I am not so sure, though, that it is the best way to tackle NN problems. It is based on two premises: symmetry of connections (hardly tenable biologically) and a crusading spirit against "spurious states". Of the latter, which appears to be widely spread, I wish to speak a little more.

* * *

Spurious states are considered as a curse by people who work with linear threshold functions: you teach a net some states, and find that it stores many more you didn't want it to learn. How much effort is being spent in attempts at getting rid of them? Well, we have evidence in our group that this may be

---

[1] May I be forgiven if I keep for them the name under which they appeared in my already mentioned 1961 paper; W. McCulloch and early writers in the field used to attribute my name to them [2].

the same as throwing away the baby with the wash water; we have built very large classes of nets, for which it is easy to keep accurate control of attractors and basins [4]: for P taught patterns, 2^P turn out to be memorized. If we take each initial pattern to stand for a letter of an alphabet, then the net stores (that is, recognizes as steady states), together with them also all combinatorically possible "syllables" of P (distinct) letters: those actually used in the language we may accept as outputs. This is only the beginning of a story about which I hope to tell more in a future occasion; I show here, as an illustration, only a few figures. Fig.1 shows 7 segments memorized by our net; Fig.2 those of their combinations which we accept as legitimate "syllables"; Fig.3 the retrieval of some of those patterns (in one step), even if marred by considerable noise (eliminated in the recall process).

Figure 1.

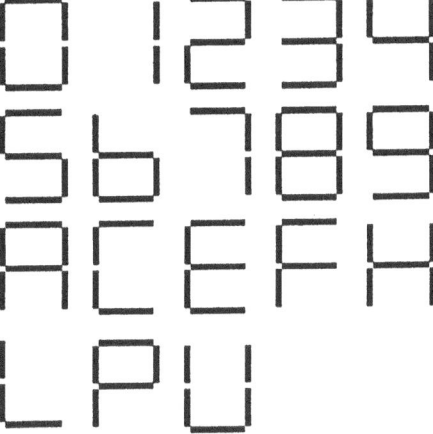

Figure 2.

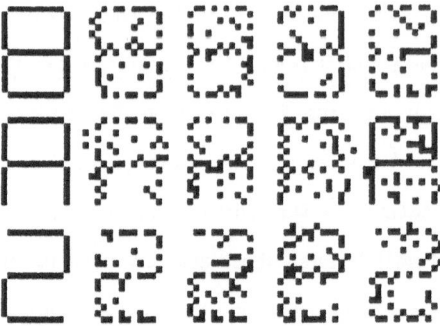

Figure 3.

The present treatment of spurious states we may thus legitimately suspect to be as unfair as the name by which they are dubbed. Another situation arises when we consider "learning" by synaptic reinforcement: I could exhibit another huge class of linear threshold nets, for which the only thing that matters is whether two elements are or not connected. Hebbian learning appears to be only a part of the game, whose relative importance has yet to be assessed.

* * *

I come now to the main topic I wish to discuss: "structure", and therefore *ipso facto* "complexity" and "hierarchy". Let me first give my physicist's definition: structure is not something that "exists" of its own, and we have only to measure, but is a "phenomenon" arising from the interaction between observer and object, and can be defined only operationally by specifying how it is measured [5]. The same I say for another concept inextricably connected to it, "complexity". Much confusion comes from different definitions: Shannon, Kolmogorov, logical depth, logical breadth... with Goedel's theorem lurking in the pit. The mistake is to assume that it suffices to name a thing for it to "exist"; as with "distance" or "time" in physics, each phenomenon is defined not by the name you give to it, but by the way you measure it. Think of "beauty".

I can find no better introduction to this subject than the words with which, seven years before the appearence of "The Origins of Species" (1859), Herbert Spencer defined evolution: "an integration of matter and a concordant dissipation of motion; during which the matter passes from an indefinite, incoherent homogeneity to a definite, coherent heterogeneity". They seem taken from some modern study on "complexity", emphasizing that "growth" requires the development of new "levels of organization": the alternance, that is, of a typically continuous with a typically discontinuous process: Nature's answer to the challenge of the second principle of Thermodynamics, to fight with the creation of new order the impending menace of thermal death. This subject is intimately tied, I believe, to progress in Neural Net studies.

No matter what we propose to do with NN's, it always amounts to a "translation" from an "input language" to an "output language", which you may associate to what you like, at the level you like (representation-interpretation, sensor-motor, syntax-semantics, speech-writing...). This is done in ways which are by now standard ("hidden neurons", understandable engineering devices for some associative memories, seem to have become another article of religion). I have recently seen a report on the use of NN's to deduce the $3 - D$ structure of proteins from their linear structure (a subject certainly of major interest); the route followed is to teach the net to associate linear chains of a given training set (given as inputs to 140 binary neurons) with the known tertiary structures (given as a "distance matrix" of 140×140 neurons) through a suitable number of hidden neurons. Then "generalization" is tested on other known proteins not included in the training set; bigger proteins demand heavier computational costs. This is exactly the same as feeding as inputs 100 of the 154 sonnets written by Shakespeare, teaching the net to give for each its correct Finnish translation, and expecting then that also the remaining 54 sonnets come out in (almost) correct Finnish. The very idea causes hilarity. This example points, however, to the correct approach to the problem: to do exactly what a human translator does; first master English and all that goes with it; then, likewise, Finnish; only after a complete mastery of the many structures and (hierarchical and heterarchical) levels of each language, may a translation be attempted.

Enough effort has been thus far given, I think, to learning as many random patterns as possible. We should now try to understand how to exploit correlations among patterns to enhance a net's learning ability, and to deduce structural laws and levels from a "text", say in English. Only after these two gigantic steps are made, we can hope to be able to associate to a text in a given language its correct translation in another language. But... is there any guarantee that we shall indeed find "structural laws" and "levels"?

* * *

This issue I took from the very first (I am referring to the early sixties) as the real crux of the matter [6]. Unsatisfied with biological data I turned to "natural language" (thought articulated), addressing what seemed to me as the main problem: parsing and building of higher order structures (syllables, words,...). This is of course an oversimplification; because a written "text" already implies the existence of an order relation; in two or more dimensions one would have to look at Yarbus's pioneering work to get inspiration on how to move at each step. Our procedure, called "Procrustes" after the well known bandit killed by Theseus on the Corinthian hystm (he is to me the perfect archetypal theorist), computes the amount of information a given string of letters can give on the next letter. If large ("q"), it lets it grow; if negligible ("a"), it cuts there: one ends up with the elements of the next higher alphabet ("syllables", if we started with "letters"). The evaluation was made by means of the Kullback-Leibler entropy (which later came into general usage). This is just a short summary, which serves to introduce the subject which interests us here, through the empirical result that while the number of combinatorically possible strings increases exponentially, the "meaningful ones" in a given language are found to increase (roughly) as the square of the number of letters of the original alphabet.

There is, therefore, indication that some "quantitative" structural laws may be indeed at work in a language. What about other systems? Can one conceive "general structural laws" valid for all systems? Such questions came one after the other to my diffident mind; I find it still surprising that they seem to be answerable at all, in what seems to be a neat way.

* * *

A physicist confronted with the project of building up a science of mechanics much prefers, to a general hand-waving account of what such a science should be, a thorough and testable treatment of only its simplest instances, say harmonic or linear motion. I started thus my quest with the crudest possible model that displays structure at work in its barest essence: of a "hierarchical modular system", such as the decimal or binary system for counting [7]. We have a module M; the corresponding "levels" go with the powers of M; a change of M is a "structural revolution" that changes all levels ("evolution" we may term a change of the occupation numbers of the levels, with M staying fixed). Levels are distinguished by the values of the powers of M. A feature typical of our approach is that we are not concerned with the "dynamical causes" of structural change, but only wish to see whether, irrespective of the mechanism, there happen to be preferred final configurations (the analogy may be with geometrical constraints that limit possible motions). The "rationale" for this drastic assumption comes from the observation that the cosmos is composed of an immense number of systems, each with its own dynamics, that yet live and co-evolve together; the harmonious balance among them all could hardly be maintained if each went its own way, like Kipling's cat.

The simplest way to relate our HMS to the "universe" in which it lives is to assume that the "average value" of a system's element (depends somehow on this universe and) stays constant under a 'modular transformation", which changes the module and thereby the number of levels:

$$M \to M^{1/p}, \quad L+1 \to pL+1$$

($L+1$ is the number of levels, counted from 0 to L; for simplicity we only consider integers; rounding off of a number to nearest integer in the same scale is assumed).

It is apparent that a modular "refinement" ($p \geq 2$) retains all old levels (as it actually happens). We have thus: a new quantity, the "value" of a level, with which we may promote information theory to a (quasi) thermodynamics; a class of "modular transformations"; a quantity, the "average value" among levels, which is wanted to stay invariant under such transformations. Enough to play physics. Calling N the total number of elements and V the total value of the HMS:

$$N = \sum_{h=0}^{L} n_h; \quad V = \sum_{h=0}^{L} n_h v_h$$

we demand that their ratio $V/N =< V >$

be the same for all p:

$$\frac{\sum_{h=0}^{L} n_h^{(1)} M^h}{\sum_{h=0}^{L} n_h^{(1)}} = \frac{\sum_{h=0}^{pL} n_h^{(p)} M^{h/p}}{\sum_{h=0}^{pL} n_h^{(p)}} =< V >$$

This equation is solved by

$$n_h = n_{h-1}/\sqrt{M}; \quad n_h = n_0 M^{-h/2}$$

(replacing M with $M^{1/p}$ changes $n_h \equiv n_h^{(1)}$ into $n_h^{(p)}$: no memory!), from which setting

$$A_h = n_h v_h = n_0 M^{h/2} = n_0 \sqrt{v_h}$$

$$\log A_h = \log n_0 + \frac{1}{2} \log v_h$$

we obtain a typical plot for the "total value A_h... at the $h - th$ level" against the order of the level. Comparison with experimental data will consist in testing both the values and the total values at each level. We see that the "universe" fixes the interaction with a whole class of HMS's, within which, at constant interaction, the system is free to evolve: we have, as should be apparent from the few formulae here reported, a new approach to fractals, as well as the renormalization group formalism fully displayed.

We show in Appendix how the issue of complexity is thoroughly met by HMS's, and report some significant examples: monetary and linguistic systems, population distributions, a variety of social hierarchies.

* * *

Can we, in conclusion, learn a few things from the sort of considerations just made? The main thing is, I believe, that we may better realize that great importance should be given to the use of NN's for "structural analysis", which they can do, rather than for brute-force input-output translation, which faces combinatorical explosion. Exact solutions for "netlets" may be at least as useful as statistical estimates, when planning higher architectures; the planning of a "neural computer" might prove sheer nonsense, if we do not first realize that there are some structural laws at work at all levels, which we may not ignore. I have spoken only of HMS's, but it should be clear that, just as it happens with harmonic motion in relation to general motion, many more systems can be described by convolutions of HMS's: one can find thus hypergeometric distributions (such as fit the distribution of species into ecological niches), and also, as will be shown in the near future, the more general negative binomial distributions, which can describe all physical phenomena, from hadron jets to galaxy distributions.

APPENDIX

HMS's and Complexity

All elements in a same level are identical (Bose-Einstein counting); level h contains n_h elements, with which $W_h = n_h + 1$ different states can be formed; levels 1 and 2 can yield $(n_1 + 1)(n_2 + 1)$ different states, etc. Hence capacity (maximum Shannon entropy) of system, taken as $S = klnW$, is $S = kln(n_1 + 1) + kln(n_2 + 1) + \ldots > kln(n_1 + n_2 + \ldots + 1)$, and its growth becomes nearly linear

84

because of modularity (the more so, the smaller $M > 1$.

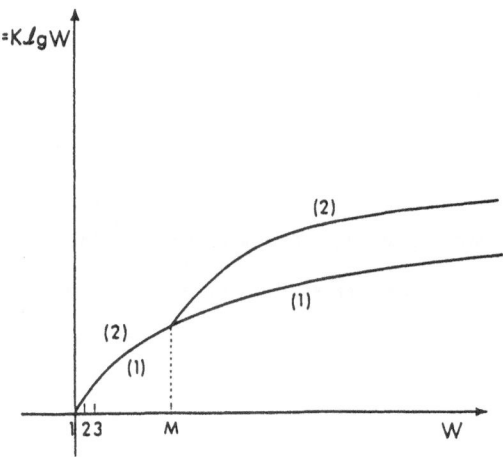

Figure 4: Gain in capacity growth (from logarithmic to nearly linear) caused by modularity: "handling of complexity".

Example: Monetary systems

The use of decimal counting system demands that some power of module M be 10. Observe that the powers of $10^{1/3}$ are:

$$1, 2.15, 4.64, 10, 21.5, 46.4, 100, \ldots$$

which round off to

$$1, 2, 5, 10, 20, 50, 50, 100, \ldots$$

We report only the Swiss and Japanese systems:

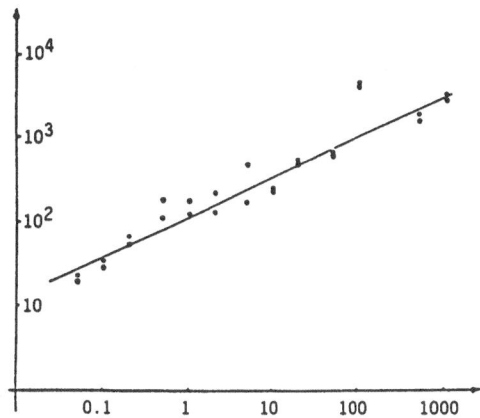

Figure 5: * Switzerland 31.12.69, x Switzerland 31.12.71.

Ordinates are in million franc.

Two important effects may be seen. The absence of 200 franc coins is the cause of a marked increase in circulation of 100 franc coins. Moreover, as soon as an external perturbation ceases the monetary circulation tends towards the canonical distribution (compare the data for coins of $0.5, 1, 2$ and 5 francs, which were in silver in 1969, and hence hoarding, but not so anymore in 1971).

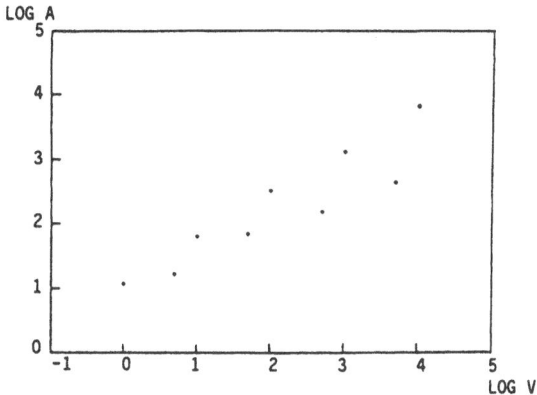

Figure 6: Japan 31.12.72. The typical zig-zag is due to the lack of values $2, 20, 200, \ldots$ in yen.

Populations

A variety of anthropological and echistic studies lead to estimating the *value* v_h of an aggregate of n_h inhabitants as proportional to n_h^2; we report only values for Europe and World (1960).

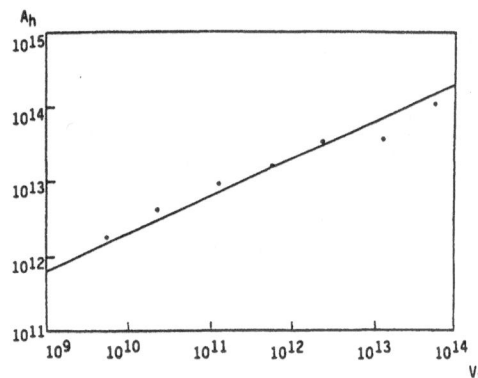

Figure 7: Europe 1960.

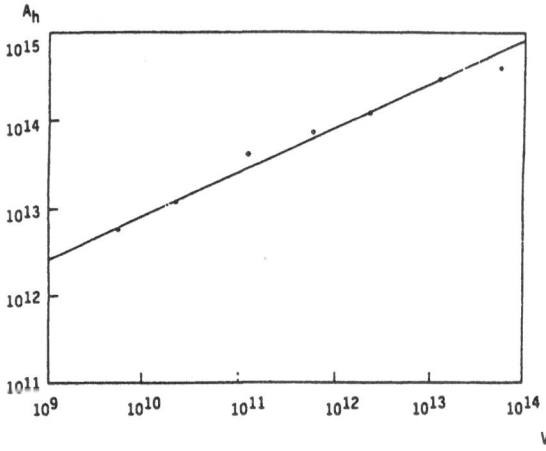

Figure 8: World 1960.

Various hierarchies (Italian Carabinieri, Administration, Finance Police, Internal Revenue)

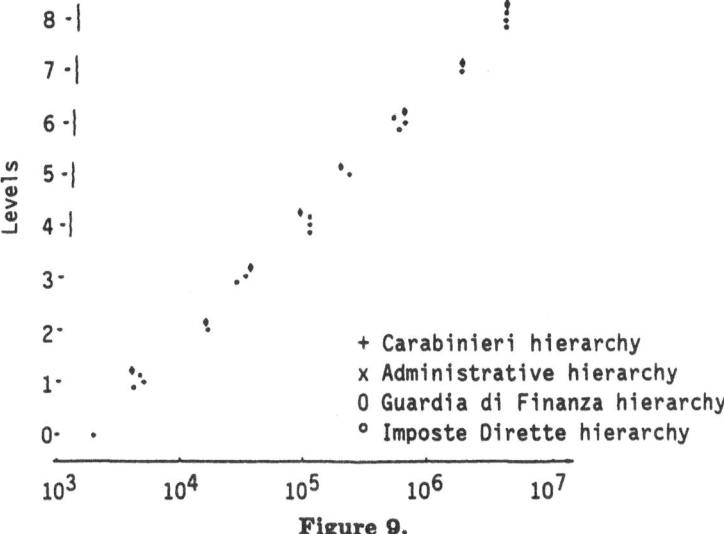

Figure 9.

Natural Languages (examples taken from 14 articles in an Italian newspaper) (We note that Zipf's law holds for all HMS's):

Levels	h	Nh	Vh	x=log(Vh)	y=log(NhVh)
Character	0	49751	1	0.00	10.81
Letter	1	22215	6	1.79	11.80
Syllable	2	8819	38	3.69	12.72
Word	3	3922	233	5.45	13.73
Predicate	4	1199	1431	7.27	14.36
Sentence	5	524	8801	9.08	15.34
Compound sentence	6	310	54128	10.90	16.64
Paragraph	7	98	332908	12.72	17.30
Subheading	8	39	2047515	14.53	18.20
Article	9	14	12593040	16.35	18.99

88

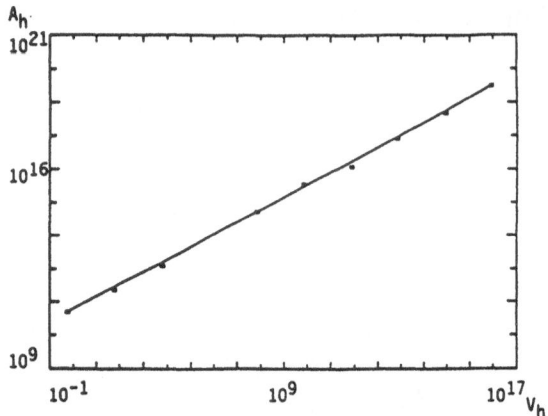

Figure 10: The magnitude of the module tells immediately whether the article is a technical report, a sports report, a generic one or a speech by a politician or a trade-union leader!

Acknowledgment

This work was supported by the C.N.R. "Progetto Finalizzato Sistemi Informatici e Calcolo Parallelo" under Grant 90.00660.PF69 and by MURST 40%.

References

[1] - Caianiello E.R.: "Outline of a Theory of Thinking Machines and Thought Processes", *Journ. Theor. Biol.*, 1961, **2**, 204.

[2] - *Encyclopedic Dictionary of Mathematics*, pag. 908, MIT Press, 1974

[3] - Caianiello E.R.: "On Boolean Functions and Nets", *Meeting in Atti Acc. Naz. Lincei 17*, Rome, 1973, 501; "Neuronic Equations Revisited and Completely Solved", *Brain Theory*, Palm G. and Aertsen A. eds., Springer-Verlag, Heidelberg, 1984, 147.

[4] - Occhinegro P., Tagliaferri R.: "Classes of efficiently computable linear Neural Nets", *Neural Networks*, 1990, **3**, 347;

- Petrosino A., Savastano F., Tagliaferri R.: "Memorization and Deleting in Linear Neural Networks", *Cybernetics and Systems 90*, Trappl R. ed., World Scientific Publishing, Singapore, 1990;

- Caianiello E.R., De Benedictis A., Petrosino A., Tagliaferri R.: "Neural Associative Memories with Minimum Connectivity", *Neural Networks*, 1991, (In press).

[5] - Caianiello E.R. and Capocelli R.: "On Form and Language: the Procrustes Algorithm for Feature Extraction", *Kybernetik*, 1971, 8, 523.

[6] - Caianiello E.R.: "On the Analysis of Natural Languages", *Proc. 3rd All Union SSR Congress on Cybernetics*, Odessa, 1965.

[7] - Caianiello E.R.: "Some Remarks on Organization and Structure", *Biol. Cybernetics*, 1977, **26**, 3; Aizerman M. A. and Caianiello E. R. eds., *Topics in the General Theory of Structures*, Reidl, Dordrecht, 1987.

Training Random Asymmetric 'Neural' Networks Towards Chaos – A Progress Report

P. C. McGuire, G. C. Littlewort[1],
C. Pershing and J. Rafelski

Department of Physics
University of Arizona
Tucson, AZ 85721

Abstract

We explore a non-Hebbian plasticity algorithm for a random asymmetric 'neural' network in synchronous, discrete time, which causes the period of the network's inherent limit cycles to quickly diverge with the plasticity parameter. The limit cycle period has a strong peak as we increase the neural units' thresholds from normal thresholds. It is much easier to increase the limit cycle period by the plasticity algorithm, when the memory of the accumulating signal of the fields at the non-firing units is non-zero.

1 Introduction

We are primarily motivated in our ongoing numerical modelling by the belief that a neural network capable to simulate higher brain functions should exhibit the ability to correlate in both time and space, yet also offer the ability to de-correlate – so that the system can be optimally ready for further, possibly novel, stimuli. Such a network either needs to have competing plasticity algorithms, or needs to have a complex architecture, in order to maintain both the ability to correlate, and to decorrelate. In the spirit of the former choice, we investigate a non-Hebbian algorithm, which we call brainwashing [1], for the de-correlating algorithm, which might be complemented by Hebbian algorithm for the competing correlating algorithm. We present some results of simulations of random (without initial architecture) asymmetric networks, which show how strong correlations can quickly and systematically be eliminated, giving rise to extraordinary long period oscillations. We believe, as implemented here that such a network needs to be an asymmetric network, since symmetric networks have shown little interesting temporal behavior.

---

[1]Present Address: Cognitive Science, UCSD, La Jolla, CA 92093-0515

The decorrelating algorithm is a robust unsupervised unlearning procedure which produces networks with nearly chaotic behavior [2,3]. The unlearning procedure depends on local information in space and time, and only requires sufficient mean activity to operate effectively. The present report carries on the work reported earlier [4], in particular with regard to an investigation of the degree of importance of the accumulation of activity signal at non-firing elements. We also correct some systematic numerical deficiencies of our earlier computer model, which slightly change the earlier results without affecting the conclusions presented in Ref.[4].

2 The Model

A network of 'discrete time' binary threshold units is connected by a matrix of weights which undergo a period of "brainwashing" before the evolving activity of the units in the network is studied. The deterministic rules for updating the state of each unit, and for modifying the weights during self-organization, will be now described [4]:

2.1 Rules for updating

The update rule for the activity a_i (binary) of threshold unit 'i' at each time step depends on the accumulated local field c_i, the activation threshold V_i of the unit and the activation function, which is the step function $\Theta[x]$ for this model;

$$a_i(t+1) = \Theta[c_i(t+1) - sV_i^0] \tag{1}$$
$$= 0 \text{ or } 1$$
$$c_i(t+1) = \lambda c_i(t).(1 - a_i(t)) + \sum_j W_{ij}(t)a_j(t) \tag{2}$$
$$V_i^0 = \frac{1}{2}\sum_k W_{ik} \tag{3}$$

There is the usual network field arising from the activity of other units which connect into unit i via the weight matrix W_{ij}; and in addition the field is allowed to accumulate (decaying by factor $0 < \lambda < 1$ each time step) until the unit is activated, (firing, $a = 1$), at which stage the field is reset to zero. Normal thresholds, V_i^0 as defined in Eq. (3), are taken to be half the sum of the incoming weights to each unit, so that, on average, half the units with $a_i = 1$ (firing) will be just sufficient stimulus to reach threshold, provided there is no accumulated field. The threshold parameter is $s = 1$ for normal thresholds.

2.2 Plasticity algorithm

The weight matrix W is initially randomly chosen, such that there is a uniform distribution of sparse, asymmetric connection strengths. The weight matrix is subsequently adjusted using the "brainwashing" algorithm for a short time, and is then constant during the process of searching for cycles in the network. The brainwashing procedure is of the form, for all i, j:

$$W_{ij}(t+1) = \eta W_{ij}(t)[1 - ba_i^{t+1}a_j^t] \qquad (4)$$

where b is the (small, positive) brainwashing rate parameter. The normalization constant η is introduced to ensure that the total 'strength' of the connection matrix remains unchanged:

$$\eta \sim 1/(1 - b\bar{a}^t\bar{a}^{t+1}) \qquad (5)$$

In other words, only weights connecting sequentially active units are modified, and the modification seeks to decorrelate the activity of the units it links, by making the relevant weights less effective. This rule is not simply an inverse of a Hebbian learning rule, because the direction of weight change is different for inhibitory connections, and changes are not additive but are proportional to the existing weight values, so weights do not change sign. The re-normalization indirectly increases the effectiveness of those weights not linking active units.

We denote the integrated brainwashing strength as B, i.e. the time T_{bw} the net is brainwashed for, multiplied by the increment b:

$$B = bT_{bw} . \qquad (6)$$

If the network activity is initialized many times with different $\bar{a}(t = 0)$, subsequent to brainwashing, there should be several different cyclic modes (α) detected, with different cycle length (L_α), different sized basins of attraction (reflected in the frequency of occurrence of a particular mode ν_α) and different latency, or transient time before onset of periodic behavior.

3 Implementation

We have implemented and studied in detail the algorithm described above, for a network of 50 units. This is relatively small by network modeling standards, but because of the already extremely long cycles discovered by us in such small nets, the present work had to remain restricted. In the simulation results presented below, the random initial weights are chosen such that 30% of the weights are inhibitory and such that each unit has 20 incoming connections, giving a contact probability of 0.4.

The network then evolves according to the update rules Eqs.(1) to (3), with the decay parameter $\lambda = 0.5$ (i.e. if an element does not fire, half of the activity is retained until the next time step). We emphasize that $\lambda < 1$ makes the network's non-firing elements at the time t remember the state of activity at times before $t - 1$. This non-Markovian character of the network gives access to many more states than are available for a Markovian net ($\lambda = 1$), in which there is no memory retained about the field non-firing elements. The brainwashing parameter was taken b=0.02-0.05, when Eq.(4) is applied.

Another parameter of great interest is the magnitude of firing threshold. Normal thresholds, V_i^0 defined in Eq.(3) will cause elements to fire when the average activity is of the net is 0.5, provided there is no accumulated field. If fields do accumulate, then the average activity should be somewhat higher than 0.5, and this is indeed found (see below). If the thresholds are scaled globally by some factor s, such that $V_i^0 \rightarrow V_i = sV_i^0$ then lower thresholds lead to higher average activity and visa versa. By using different thresholds a whole new set of cyclic modes can be found.

4 Simulation Results

4.1 The effect of brainwashing

The remarkable result presented in Figure 1 is that the average cycle length grows rapidly and possibly exponentially with the total (time integral) of brainwashing B. We note that our previous simulations [4] systematically underestimated the period of the limit cycles by an average factor of two. However, this did not affect the exponential character of the cycle length versus B curve, for our previously chosen value of $\lambda = 0.5$.

In Figure 1 we notice that for B=0 ('virgin' net) we easily find three different accessible limit cycle attractors. We observe that for larger B ($B > 0.3$) the intermediate cycle develops into the sole easily accessible very long attractor; despite efforts made we only found the very long cycle. Thus it seems that the network has a rather large basin of attraction to an oscillating mode of exponentially growing period, with short structures contained within it being rapidly erased by the non-Hebbian algorithm applied.

4.2 The effect of firing threshold

By using various different threshold levels s, a wide variety of cycles are found. Activity is found to decrease monotonically with threshold for both unbrainwashed (Figure 2) and brainwashed nets (Figure 3). For unbrainwashed nets, the average cycle length reaches a maximum at a threshold value which produces an average activity of 0.3 to 0.5 (Figure 4). It is thus possible, by adjusting the threshold level, to find long patterns of activity even in an unbrainwashed net. For slightly brainwashed nets, (Figure 5) the cycle lengths are much longer (note log scales), but the cycle length remains dependent on the threshold parameter, however, with a slightly broader peak. That means that in brainwashed nets the range of tolerable thresholds is slightly larger, and many more states become accessible through the device of shifting thresholds.

4.3 The effect of the decay parameter

When we change the rate of field accumulation at non-firing units from $\lambda = 0.0$ (fully Markovian) to $\lambda = 1.0$ (fully non-Markovian), we see two different behaviors. First, we find for sufficiently large λ, the network is easily brainwashed, and i. e. its behavior is nearly completely characterized by the single long cycle. For small λ, the network cannot be brainwashed easily – long cycles are not found for the explored range of $B < 1$. It is possible that the low mean activity ($\alpha \approx 0.1$) of such Markovian nets prohibits effective de-correlation.

The critical value separating the two behaviors of the decay (accumulation) parameter seems to be $\lambda_c \approx 0.3$ (Figure 6), above which the net is easily brainwashed, below which the net is not so amenable to 'forgetting' its short cycles.

5 Latent Knowledge of the Net

We will next consider qualitatively if information has been stored 'accidentally' in the network. Clearly, this would be a naive explanation why many 'random' networks we and others have tried show normally rather uninteresting behavior. A good measure for this would be deviation from white noise of the correlation of activity measured at equal time. We thus compute the correlation matrix (changing notation from $a_i = 0,1$ to $b_i = 2a_i - 1 = -1,1$ for inactive and active units, respectively):

$$
\begin{aligned}
K^c_{i \neq j} &= \frac{1}{L_c} \sum_{t=1}^{L_c} (b_i^t - < b_i >_{L_c})(b_j^t - < b_j >_{L_c}) \\
&= < b_i b_j >_{L_c} - < b_i >_{L_c} < b_j >_{L_c}
\end{aligned}
\tag{7}
$$

where L is the length of a typical cycle c used in the correlation calculation. In principle $|K_{ij}| < 2$, but if we drop the $i = j$ correlations, as done above, we expect to find a distribution strongly centered around zero. The result of our study are histograms of the elements K_{ij} shown in Figure 7 obtained for $[B, L] = [(0.0, 283), (0.1, 162), (0.2, 814), (0.3, 2825)]$. If the activity of each element were independent of others, such a histogram of 2,450 correlations would be close in form to a Gaussian, and naturally we should expect very long cycles in a non-Markovian system. The appearance of short recurrent cycles in unbrainwashed nets may be therefore associated with a significant 'shoulder' seen for B=0 in Figure 7, which indicates that the elements are initially not fully independent in their activity - as is indicated by the large $\chi^2 = 5.5$ (per degree of freedom) of the Gaussian fit, (see the insert in Figure 7, for χ^2, normalization, location of the center of the Gaussian and its width parameter σ).

As we brainwash even a little, $B = 0.1$, we see in Figure 7 that this shoulder practically vanishes - instead the brainwashing algorithm generates a surplus near $K_{ij} = 0$, beyond and above what would be expected from a noisy network alone. In other words, we find that brainwashing is introducing a correlation which leads to the decorrelation of the individual units. The same result is seen for longer cycles and more brainwashing. Another interesting change is the reduction of χ^2 to a value O(2-3), which suggests that the Gaussian component in the correlation dominates the distribution.

6 Conclusions

The brainwashing algorithm was designed [1] to discourage steady states and short cycles, and to decorrelate the firing activity of the units in a recurrent network. We have demonstrated that it does this remarkably well, finding that the resultant networks acquire, for $\lambda > 0.3$, a single very long cycle which becomes rapidly (exponentially ?) longer with the total amount of modification of the connections B. We also find that a rich variety of cyclic behavior is made accessible by small changes in the firing thresholds, and this variety grows with even a very small amount of brainwashing.

Seeking understanding of why brainwashed nets show 'reliable' long cycles which we have first demonstrated in a non-Markovian system, we have considered the equal time activity correlation between units. Our expectation has been that the unsupervised learning algorithm somehow induces a strong pattern of correlations in a small portion of the network. We found, however, that while brainwashing removes accidental correlations inherent in the set up of the network, it generates strong anti-correlations between elements. We are not certain if this finding has the potential to explain how the well brainwashed nets are capable of finding the dominant long cycling motion, despite their non-Markovian and nearly chaotic character. Presence of such regularity is suggestive of a significant order in the net, which we fail to detect in the above presented equal time correlation analysis. We also found that the short cycles which dominate the behavior of freshly set up nets are easily erased from 'memory' for nets *containing* memory of signal accumulation.

It is clear that the results presented here require substantial further elaboration with regard to an understanding of the one cycle domination of brainwashed nets, its strong attraction and the origin of nearly exponential growth of the dominant cycle length. We hope to return to these questions in the near future.

Acknowledgements: We would like to thank David Harley and John W. Clark for help and interest in this work. G.C. Littlewort thanks P.A. Carruthers and the Arizona Center for Complex Systems for hospitality and support during her state at The University of Arizona. P.C. McGuire would like to thank the Santa Fe Institute for hospitality and K. Atteson, S. Kauffman, G. Sonnenberg and CADMIUM for discussions and assistance.

References

[1] Clark J.W., Rafelski J. and Winston J.V. , Phys. Rep. 1985; **123**:215-273

[2] Kürten K.E., Phys. Let. 1988; **A129**:157-160

[3] Sompolinsky H., Crisanti A. and Sommers H.J., Phys. Rev. Let. 1988; **61**:259-262

[4] McGuire P.C., Littlewort G.C., and Rafelski J., *Brainwashing Random Asymmetric 'Neural' Networks* Phys. Let. 1991; A:in press.

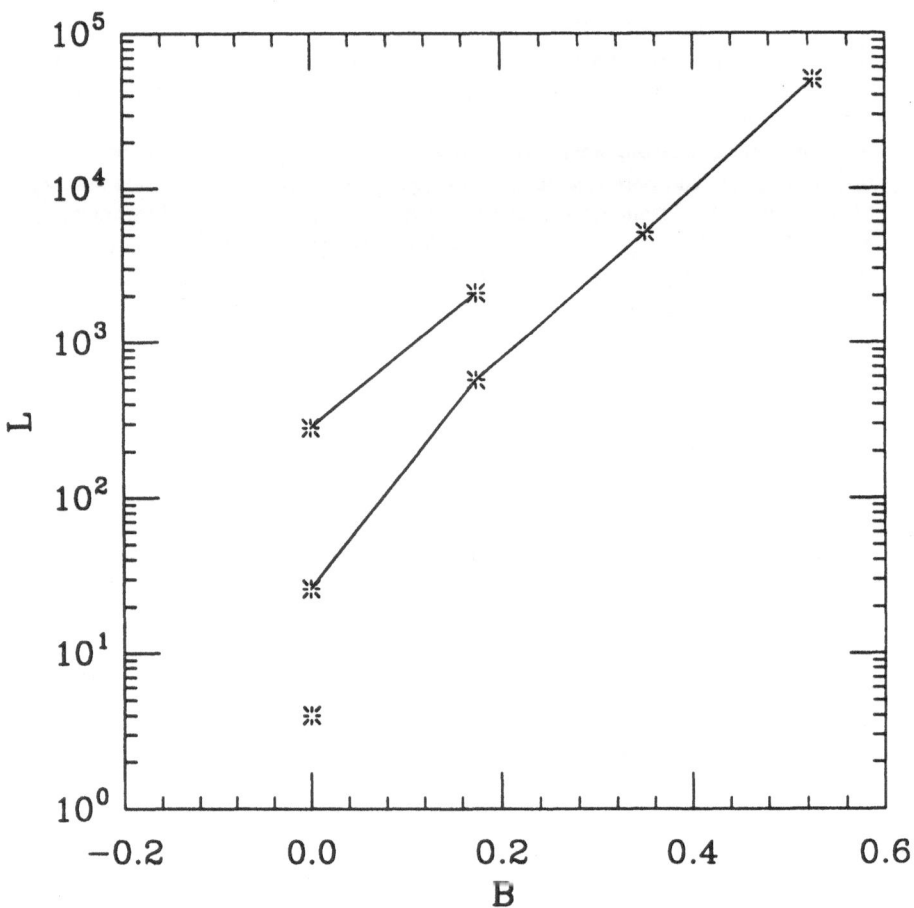

FIGURE 1

Cycle length L is shown to increase quickly as a function of total brainwashing B. This simulation had $\lambda = 0.5$ and $b = 0.035$.

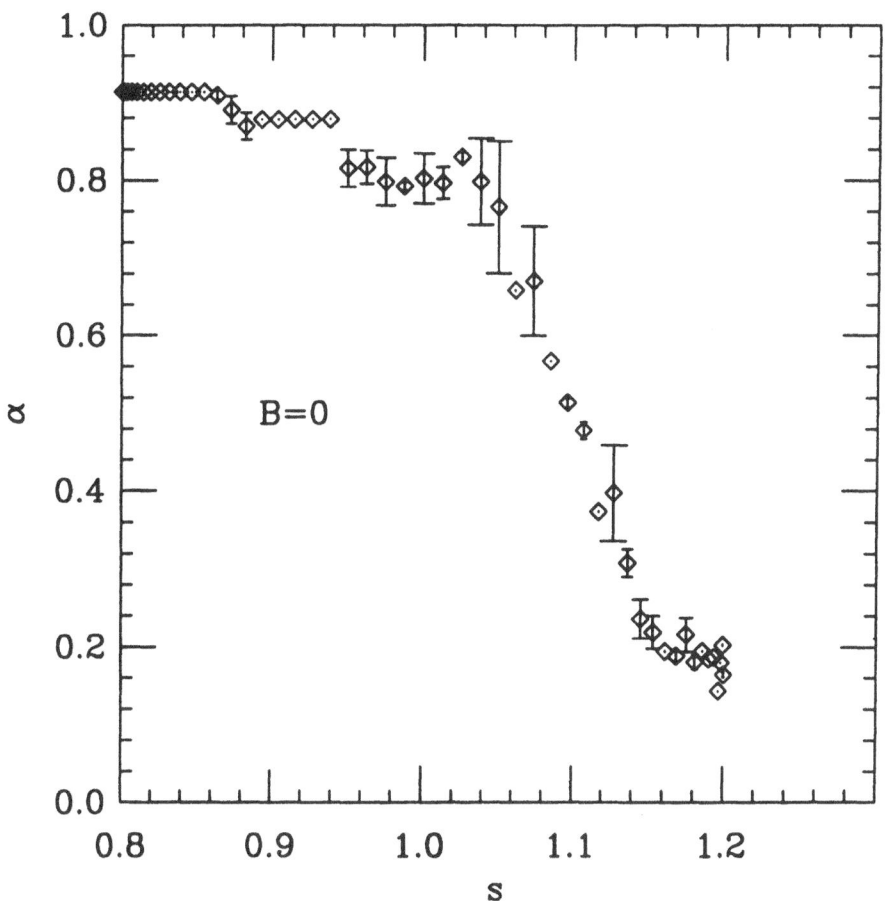

FIGURE 2

Average activity ($\alpha = \sum_{i,t} a_i^t$) is shown to decrease as a function of a threshold parameter s ($B = 0$).

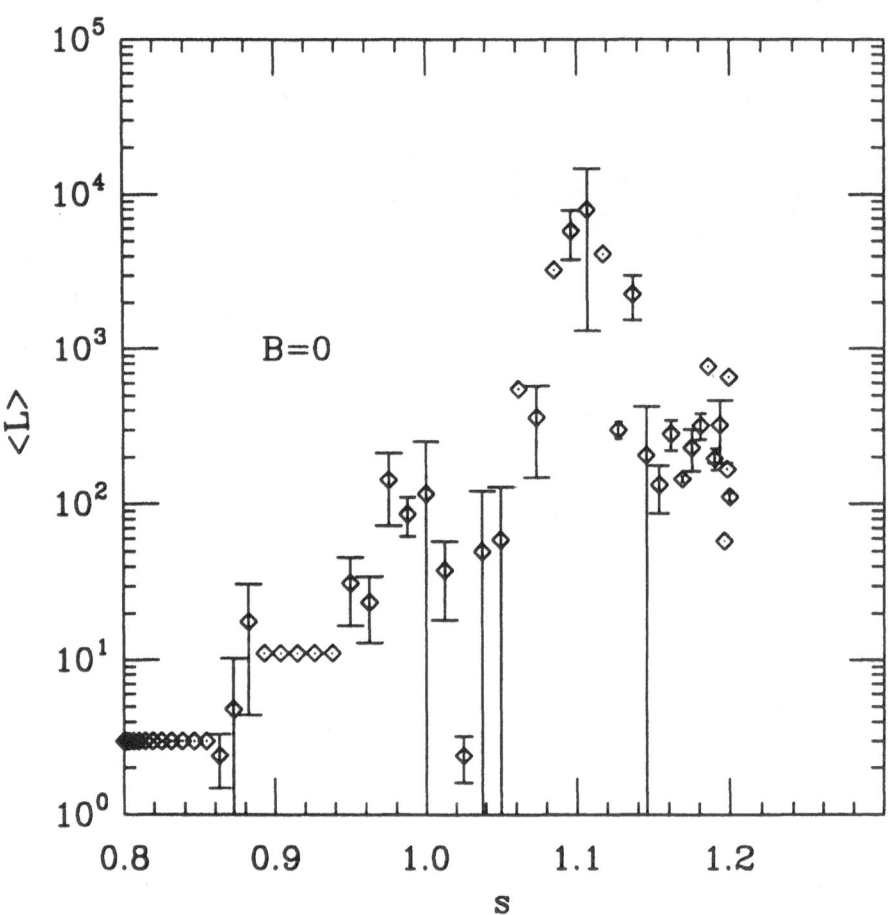

FIGURE 3
Same as Figure 2. but for a slightly brainwashed network $(B = 0.1)$.

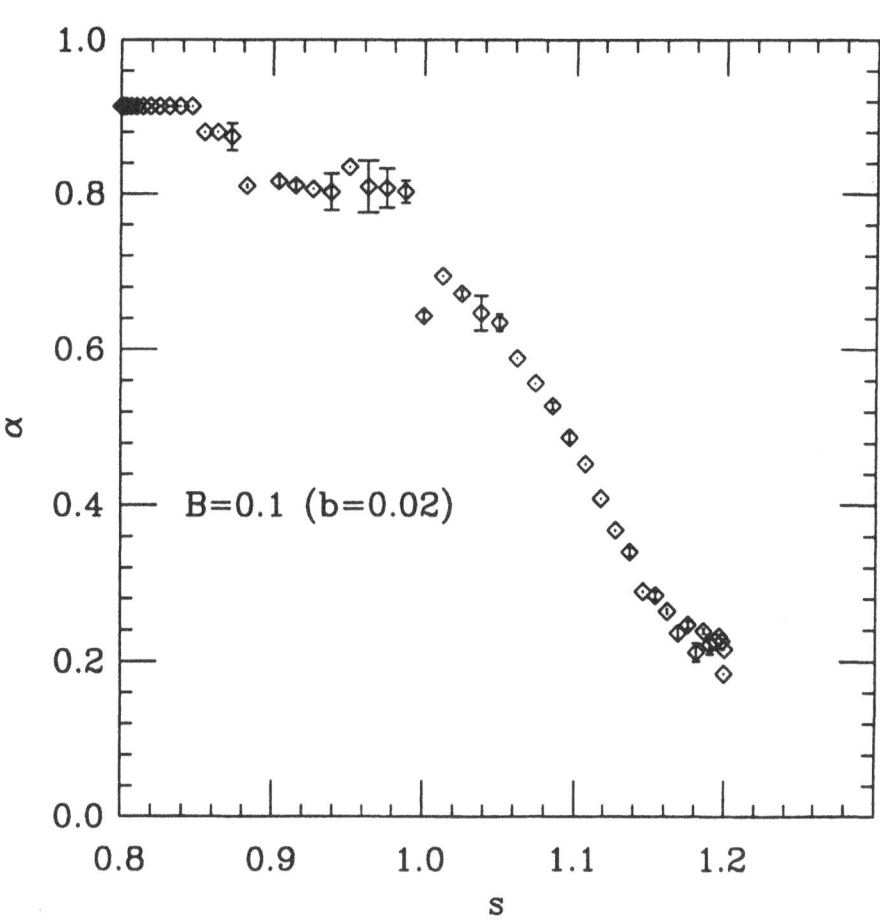

FIGURE 4

Average cycle length $< L >$ is shown as a function of threshold scaling parameter s for an unbrainwashed network ($B=0$).

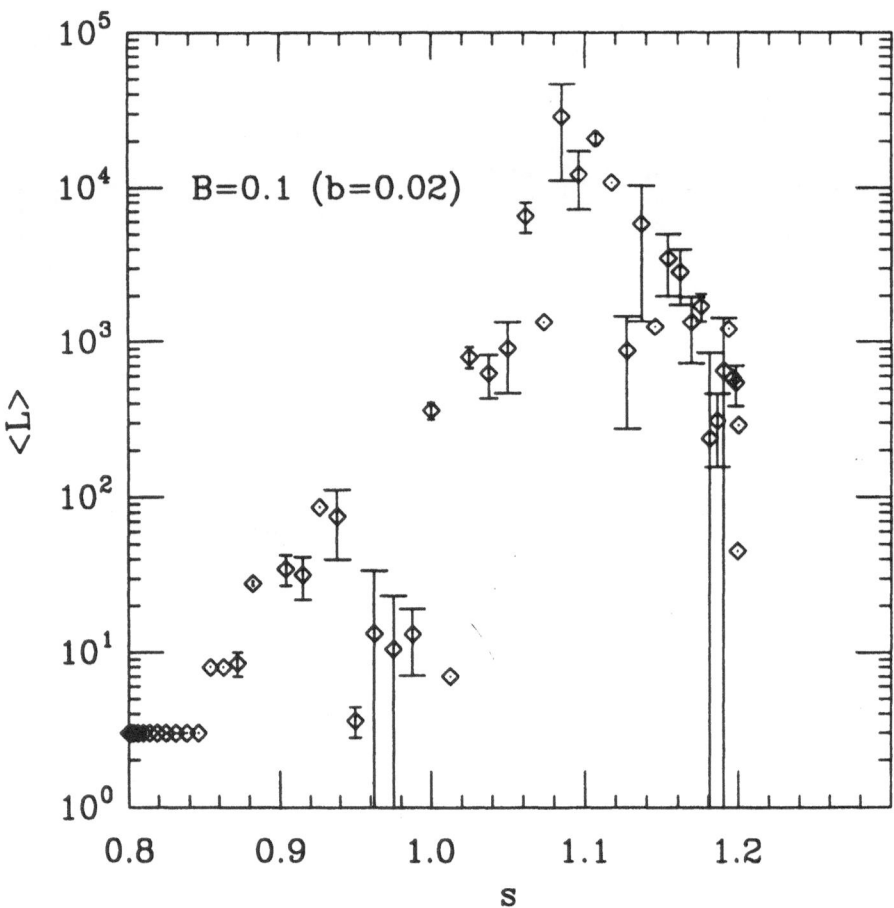

FIGURE 5
Same as Figure 4. but for a slightly brainwashed network ($B=0.1$).

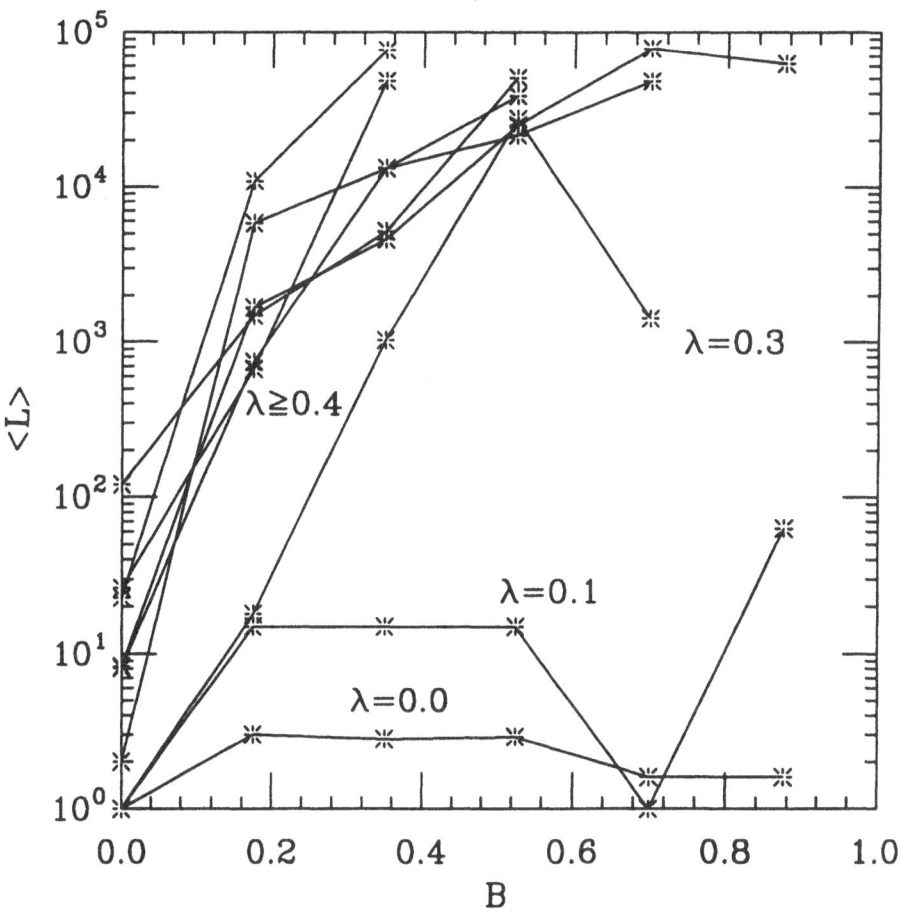

FIGURE 6

Average cycle length $< L >$ is shown as a function of total brainwashing B. The curves for various values of λ are shown. Those curves above $\lambda = 0.3$ are for $\lambda \in [0.4, 0.5, 0.6, 0.7, 0.9, 1.0]$.

102

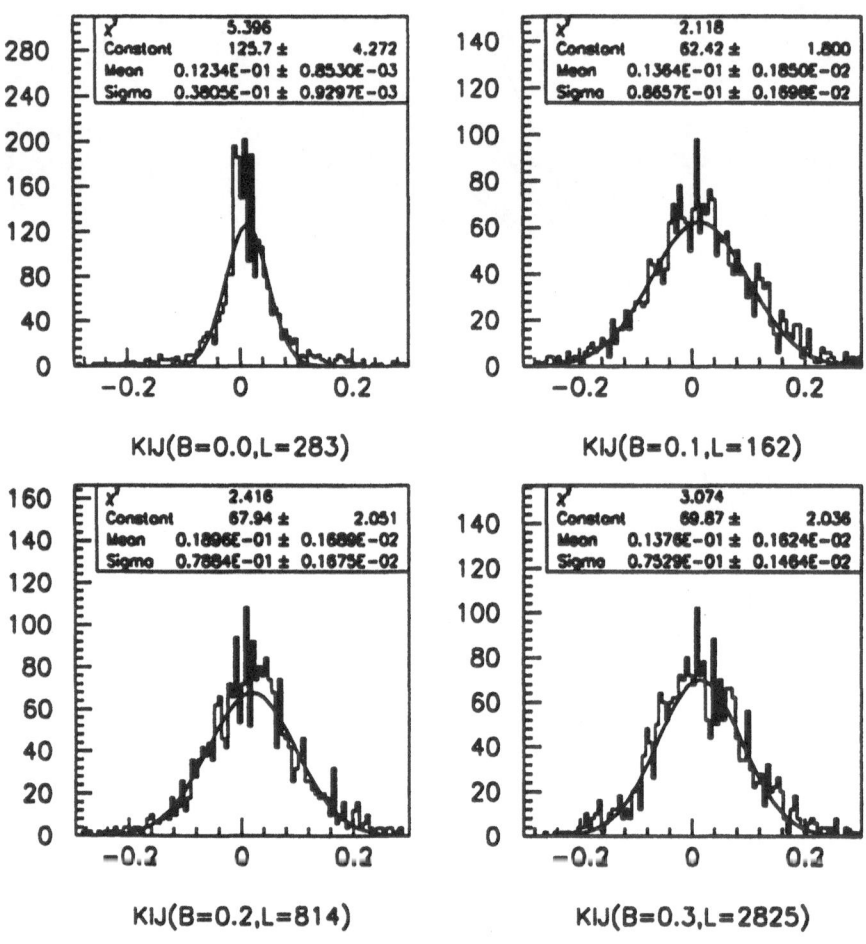

FIGURE 7

Histogram distribution of *equal time* i, j correlation of firing activity K_{ij}, along with a Gaussian fit for: $B \in [0.0, 0.1, 0.2, 0.3]$. L is the length of the dominant cycle used in evaluation of the correlation matrix.

Complex dynamics of a discrete time model of a neuron

Paul C. Bressloff

GEC-Marconi Ltd., Hirst Research Centre, East Lane,
Wembley, Middx. HA9 7PP,
United Kingdom

Abstract

The complex dynamics of a time-summating, binary-threshold neuron with inhibitory feedback is described. In the absence of noise, the dynamics is either periodic or quasiperiodic and the average firing-rate of the neuron as a function of an external input is given by a "devil's staircase". In the presence of synaptic or threshold noise the dynamics corresponds to a random iterated function system and the long-term behaviour is characterised by a probability measure with a fractal-like structure. The effects of such noise on the response characteristics of the neuron are considered.

1   Introduction: time-summating, binary-threshold neurons.

Consider a fully-connected network of N standard binary threshold neurons [1] and denote the output of neuron i, i = 1,...,N, at the mth time step by $a_i(m) \in \{0,1\}$. The binary-valued output indicates whether or not the neuron has fired an action potential. The neurons are connected by synaptic junctions of weight w_{ij}, which determine the size of the input to neuron i arising from an action potential fired by neuron j. In this simple model the membrane potential of neuron i at time m is equal to the linear sum of all the inputs received at the previous time-step,

$$V_i(m) = \sum_{j \neq i} W_{ij} a_j(m-1) + I_i \qquad (1)$$

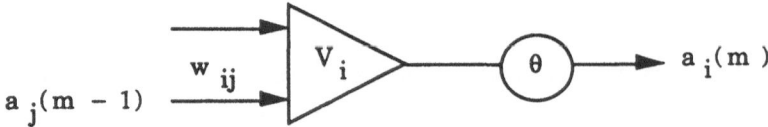

Fig. 1. A standard binary-threshold neuron.

where I_i denotes some fixed external input. Each neuron fires whenever its membrane potential exceeds a threshold h_i,

$$a_i(m) = \theta(V_i(m) - h_i) \tag{2}$$

where $\theta(x) = 1$ if $x \geq 0$ and $\theta(x) = 0$ if $x < 0$. The basic operation of this formal neuron is illustrated in fig. 1. Equations (1) and (2) determine the dynamics on the discrete space of binary outputs $\{0,1\}^N$. (We shall assume throughout that the neurons are updated synchronously).

The number of possible states of the above binary network is finite (equal to 2^N). Therefore, in the absence of noise, there is a unique transition from one state to the next and the long-term behaviour is cyclic. This follows from the fact that a finite-state system must return to a state previously visited after a finite number of time-steps ($\leq 2^N$). Moreover, the attracting cycles are simple sequences of patterns in the sense that a given pattern only occurs once per cycle. Complex sequences, on the other hand, contain repeated patterns so that there is an ambiguity as to which is the successor of each of these patterns (see fig. 2). Such ambiguities cannot be resolved by a standard binary network.

To allow the storage of complex sequences in a binary network it is necessary to introduce some memory of previous inputs which extends beyond a single time-step. A simple way to achieve this is to modify the network at the single neuron level by taking the membrane potential to be a slowly decaying function of time with decay rate $k_i < 1$, say. Thus, equation (1) becomes

$$V_i(m) = k_i V_i(m-1) + \sum_{j \neq i} w_{ij} a_j(m-1) + I_i \tag{3}$$

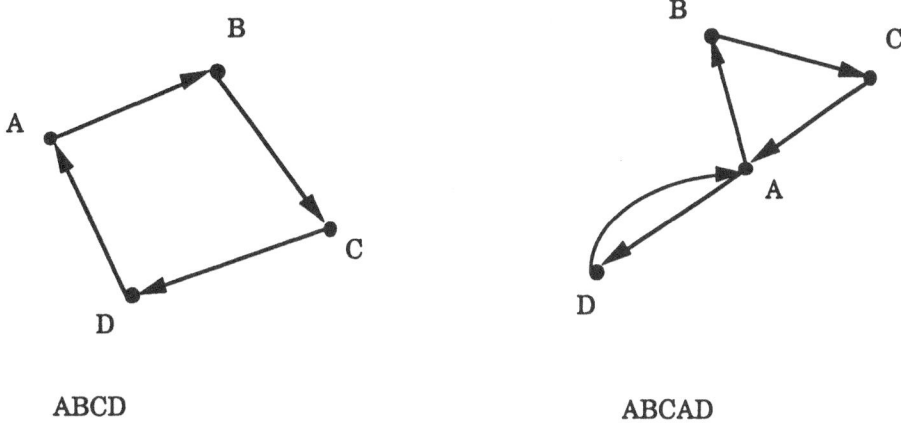

ABCD   ABCAD

Fig. 2. Example illustrating the difference between a simple sequence ABCD... and a complex sequence ABCAD...In the latter case there is an ambiguity concerning the successor of pattern A.

We shall refer to a formal neuron satisfying equations (2) and (3) as a time-summating, binary-threshold neuron. The decay term $k_iV_i(m-1)$ may be viewed as a positive feedback along a delay line of weight k_i (see fig. 3). It follows from equation (3) that the activation state depends on the previous history of inputs. Assuming $V_i(0) = 0$, we have

$$V_i(m) = \sum_{r=1}^{m} k_i^{r-1} \left[\sum_{j\neq i} w_{ij}a_j(m-r) + I_i \right] \qquad (4)$$

Such an activity trace allows a network of time-summating neurons to resolve the ambiguities arising from complex sequences, provided incoming

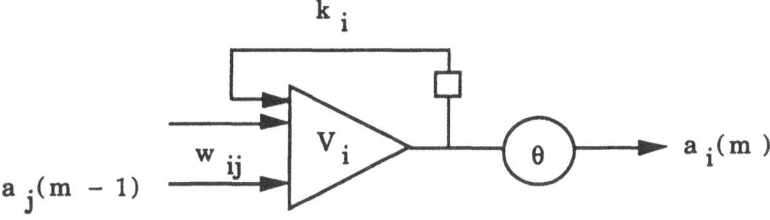

Fig. 3. A time-summating, binary-threshold neuron.

activity is held over a long enough period [2]. Moreover, using statistical-mechanical techniques it can be shown that the maximum storage capacity of a network can be enhanced in certain cases [3]. Time-summating neurons have also been incorporated into feedforward networks and allow simple on-line learning algorithms to be developed [4-6]. These deal with temporal sequences directly in the time domain so avoiding the need for a buffer to map the temporal sequences into spatial patterns of much higher dimension.

The above discussion indicates one of the reasons for studying time-summating neural networks; such networks have certain advantages over standard networks in the processing of temporal sequences. Another reason is that they incorporate, albeit in simplified form, an important temporal feature of biological neurons [7]. This concerns the leaky-integrator characteristics of the cell surface which results in the persistence of cell activity over an extended period. Thus the decay rate k_i is related to the electrical properties of the cell surface such as the effective leakage capacitance and resistance. (Recent neurophysiological evidence suggests that the associated time constant of certain cortical neurons is of the order of hundreds of milliseconds [8]). A third important aspect of time-summating neurons is that they can exhibit complex dynamics, including frequency-locking and chaos, both at the single neuron [9] and network levels [10], [11]. In the absence of noise such dynamics can be understood in terms of coupled circle maps [9]. On the other hand, in the presence of synaptic or threshold noise the dynamics is described by a random iterated function system and the long-term behaviour is characterised by a probability measure which often has a fractal-like structure [11]. In the following we shall illustrate these dynamical features by considering, for simplicity, a single time-summating neuron with inhibitory feedback.

2   Deterministic dynamics and circle maps.

Consider a single time-summating neuron with fixed external input I and inhibitory feedback whose membrane potential evolves according to the Nagumo-Sato equation [12]

$$V(m) = F(V(m-1)) = [kV(m-1) - wa(m-1) + I] \qquad (5)$$

where $a(m) = \theta(V(m)-h)$. The operation of the neuron is shown in fig. 4

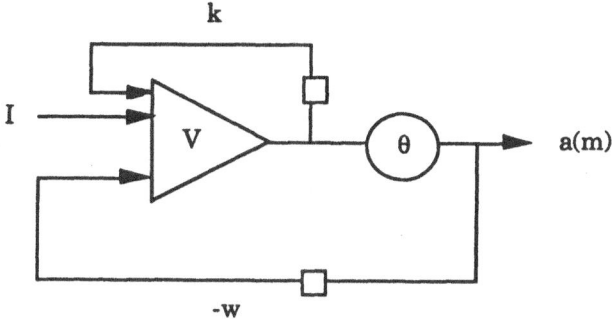

Fig. 4 A time-summating neuron with inhibitory feedback.

There are two possible interpretations of the inhibitory feedback:

1. The feedback represents the effect of relative refractory period [12]. This is the time interval beyond the absolute refractory period t_R over which a neuron is capable of firing but its likelihood of firing is suppressed. A standard way of incorporating relative refractory period in continuous time models is to take a time-dependent threshold $\kappa(\Delta t)$ where Δt is the time after emission of an action potential. Then $\kappa(\Delta t) = \infty$ for $0 \le \Delta t \le t_R$ and $\kappa(\Delta t)$ is continuous and monotonically decreasing for $\Delta t > t_R$. An alternative approach is to assume that the neuron receives a negative feedback a time t_R after firing, which then decays due to leakage. By taking t_R to be a single time-step, such feedback is given by the term $- wa(m-1)$ in equation (5).
2. An inhibitory interneuron mediates the feedback so that whenever the excitatory neuron represented by equation (5) fires, it excites the interneuron which itself fires and results in the excitatory neuron receiving a negative feedback (see fig. 5). (A more detailed model, which takes into account the dynamics of the interneuron, essentially displays the same behaviour as the simpler model).

A major difference between the two interpretations is that in the second case the inhibitory feedback involves synaptic processing and, hence, in the presence of synaptic noise the weight w becomes a random variable (see section 3). Also note that the coupling of an excitatory neuron with an inhibitory neuron using delay connections forms the basic oscillatory

Fig.5 Coupling of an excitatory neuron with an inhibitory neuron: basic oscillatory element.

element of a continuous time model used to study stimulus-induced phase synchronisation in oscillator networks [13].

The map F of equation (5) is piecewise linear with a single discontinuity at V = 0 as shown in fig. 6. Assuming that w > 0 (inhibitory feedback) and 0 < I < w, then all trajectories converge to the interval $\Sigma = [V_-, V_+]$ where $V_- = I - w$ and $V_+ = I$. The dynamics on Σ is non-trivial and has been analysed in detail elsewhere [14], [9]. In particular, the map F is equivalent to a circle map with a discontinuity at $V = V_+$. Such a circle map is obtained by imposing the equivalence relation on Σ given by $V(m) \equiv V(m) + V_+ - V_- \in S^1$. The membrane potential may then be viewed as a phase variable. To describe the behaviour on Σ it is useful to introduce the average firing-rate

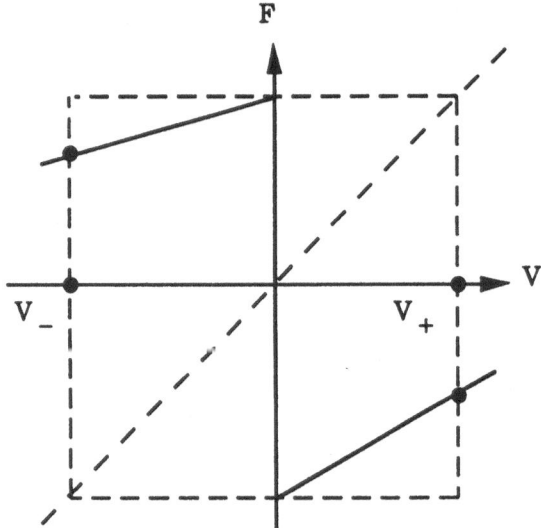

Fig. 6 Map F describing the dynamics of a time-summating neuron with inhibitory feedback; for w > 0 and 0 < I < w all trajectories converge to the bounded interval $\Sigma = [V_-, V_+]$.

$$\rho(V) = \lim_{M \to \infty} \sum_{n=0}^{M} \frac{\theta(F^n(V))}{M} \qquad (6)$$

(assuming the limit exists), where $\theta(F^n(V))$ is the output of the neuron at time n given the initial state V. In terms of the equivalent circle map description, $\rho(V)$ is a rotation number.

It can be shown that the average firing-rate is independent of the initial point V, $\rho(V) = \bar{\rho}$, and that the dynamics is either periodic or quasiperiodic depending on whether $\bar{\rho}$ is a rational or irrational number. Moreover, as a function of the external input I, $\bar{\rho}$ forms a "devil's staircase". That is, $\bar{\rho}$ is a continuous, monotonic function of I which assumes rational values on non-empty intervals of I and is irrational on a Cantor set of I (see fig. 7). If $\bar{\rho}$ is rational, $\bar{\rho} = p/q$, then there is a periodic orbit of period q which is globally attracting. On the other hand, when $\bar{\rho}$ is irrational there are no periodic

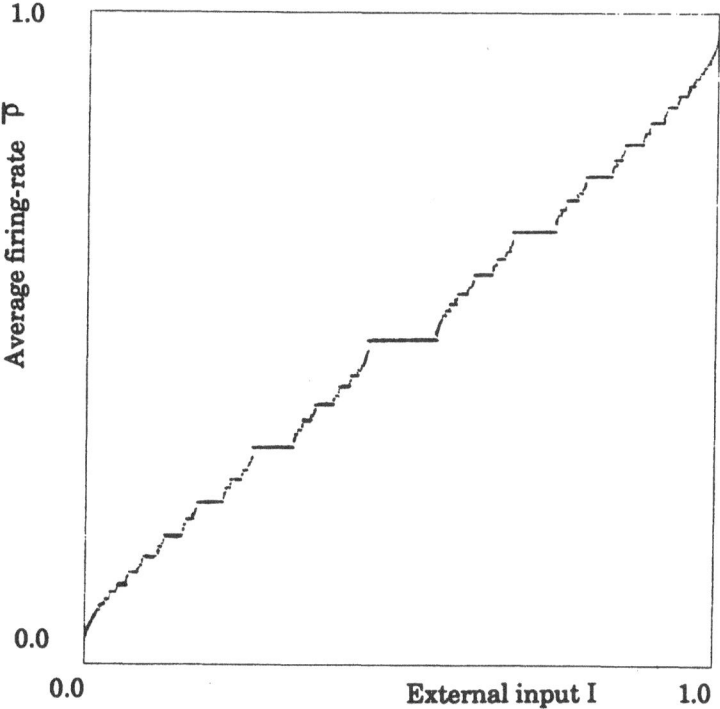

Fig. 7 Average firing-rate $\bar{\rho}$ as a function of the external input I; graph forms a "devil's staircase".

points and the attractor is a Cantor set.

Another interesting feature of the above model is that with slight modifications chaotic dynamics can occur. (This is hardly surprising since we have a discrete-time system with feedback). Two ways to achieve this are:

1. Include an extra exponential factor on the right-hand side of equation (5) so that [9]

$$V(m) \equiv F_{\omega}(V(m-1)) = \left[kV(m-1) - wa(m-1) + I\right]e^{-\omega a(m-1)} \qquad (7)$$

The exponential term is analogous to the shunting terms in continuous time leaky-integrator equations [7]. Assume as before that $w > 0$ and $0 < I < w$. so that all trajectories converge to the interval $\Sigma =[V_-,V_+]$ with $V_- = (I - w)\exp(-\omega)$ and $V_+ = I$. If, moreover, $\omega < 0$, $k \exp(-\omega) > 1$ and the overlap $\Delta = F_{\omega}(V_+) - F_{\omega}(V_-)$ is positive (see fig. 8), the dynamics on Σ is chaotic. To indicate how this occurs, consider the Liapunov exponent defined by

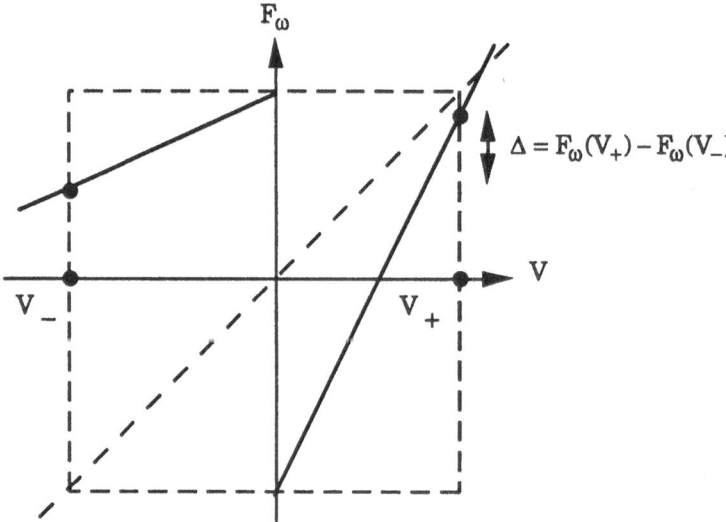

Fig. 8. Map F_{ω} for $\omega < 0$, $k \exp(-\omega) > 1$. Dynamics is chaotic when the overlap Δ is positive.

$$\lambda(V) = \lim_{M \to \infty} \frac{1}{M} \log \prod_{n=0}^{M} \left\| \frac{dF_\omega}{dV} (F_\omega^n(V)) \right\|$$

$$= \log k - \omega \lim_{M \to \infty} \frac{1}{M} \sum_{n=0}^{M} \theta(F_\omega^n(V))$$

$$= \log k - \omega \rho(V) \tag{8}$$

If $\Delta < 0$ then the behaviour of the neuron is similar to the previous case $\omega = 0$. In particular, $\bar{\rho}$ is well defined and increases monotonically from zero at $I = 0$ to the critical value $\bar{\rho}_c = |\log k/\omega|$ at $I = I_c = w(1-k)/(1-e^\omega)$, corresponding to zero Liapunov exponent, $(\bar{\lambda} = \log k - \omega\bar{\rho} = 0)$, and zero overlap. The typical behaviour is periodic. On the other hand, for $I > I_c$ so that $\Delta > 0$, the limit of equation (6) no longer exists and $\rho(V)$ is defined to be the set of limit points of the sequence $\sum_{n=0}^{M} \theta(F_\omega^n(V))/M$. It can be shown that the union of such sets over Σ is given by a closed interval $[a,b]$ where $a > \bar{\rho}_c$. It follows that the Liapunov exponent $\bar{\lambda}$ is replaced by the interval $[\lambda_a, \lambda_b]$ where $\lambda_a = \log k - \omega a > 0$ and the dynamics on Σ is chaotic in the strong sense of sensitivity to initial conditions.

2. Replace the step function by a sigmoid function [15] so that equation (5) becomes

$$V(m) = F_\beta(V(m-1)) = kV(m-1) - \frac{W}{1+e^{-\beta V(m-1)}} + I \tag{9}$$

We shall briefly discuss the dynamics of F_β as a function of the external input I. Suppose that $\kappa \equiv w\beta/2k - 1 > 1$ and $I < w$. Then F_β has two critical points at $\pm V^*$, where $\beta V^* = \log[\kappa \pm \sqrt{(\kappa^2 - 1)}]$ as shown in fig. 9. There is also a fixed point, denoted $V = V_0$, which lies in the interval $[-V^*, V^*]$. For $\beta \gg 1$ (high gain) there exists a range of values of I for which the fixed point V_0 is unstable and all trajectories converge to the interval $\Omega = [F_\beta(V^*), F_\beta(-V^*)]$ on which the dynamics is either periodic or chaotic. The possibility of chaotic dynamics arises from the fact that for $\beta \gg 1$ the negative gradient branch of the graph of F_β has an average slope of

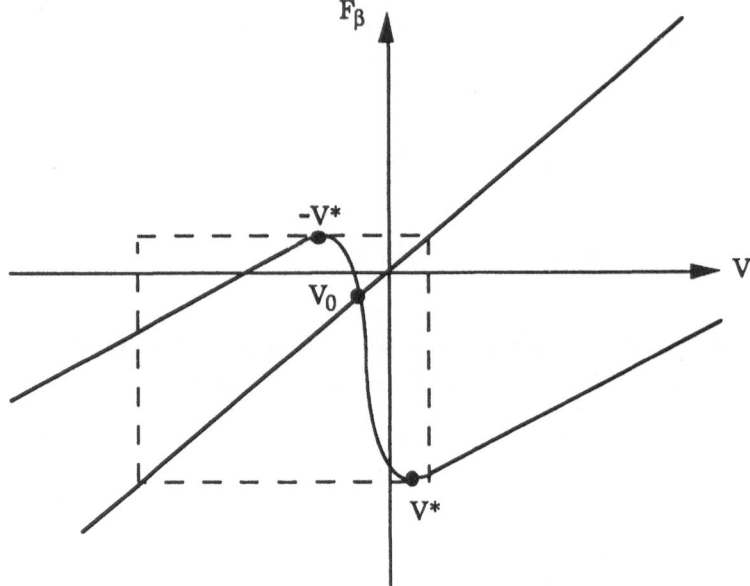

Fig. 9. The map F_β for $\beta = 25.0$ with two critical points at $V = \pm V^*$ and an unstable fixed point at $V = V_0$.

modulus greater than unit, which can lead to a positive Liapunov exponent.

It should be noted that in both cases the equivalent circle map is nonmonotonic, which is a well known scenario for chaotic dynamics [16]. The presence of chaos also leads to a break up of the devil's staircase structure, fig. 7.

3   Stochastic dynamics and random iterated functions systems.

It is well known [17] that the most significant source of intrinsic noise in real neurons arises from random fluctuations in the number of packets of chemical neurotransmitters released into the synaptic cleft on arrival of an action potential. Such multiplicative noise can be incorporated into binary networks by taking the connection weights to be independently updated at every time step according to fixed probability distributions [18, 19]. That is the connection weight at a given synapse and time m is decomposed as w(m) = $q_0 \varepsilon u(m)$ where $|q_0|$ is related to the amount of transmitter in a single packet, sign(q_0) indicates whether the synapse is excitatory or inhibitory, $\varepsilon > 0$ is a constant related to the post-synaptic efficacy, (the efficiency with which chemicals bind to receptors in the postsynaptic cell membrane), and u(m) is a random variable representing the number of packets released at time m. If an action potential arrives at the synapse at time m-1, i.e. a(m−1) = 1, then u(m) = u, where u is generated from some fixed probability distribution p, otherwise u(m) = 0. (We are assuming that the synaptic delay is equal to a single time-step) A realistic choice for p is a Binomial of size L, where L is the maximum possible number of packets that can be released. Recent evidence suggests that L = 1 for certain cortical neurons [20].

Incorporating synaptic (and threshold) noise into the excitatory neuron/inhibitory neuron system considered in section 2 (fig. 5) gives the following equation for the stochastic evolution of the excitatory neuron's membrane potential (neglecting the dynamics of the interneuron and setting $q_0 = -1$),

$$V(m) = kV(m-1) - \varepsilon u(m) + I \tag{10}$$

where u(m) = u with probability p(u) if a(m−1) ≡ θ(V(m−1) − h(m−1)) = 1 and u(m) = 0 if a(m−1) = 0. For simplicity we shall assume that u is generated according to a Binomial distribution with L = 1, i.e. $p(u) = \lambda^u (1 - \lambda)^{1-u}$ for some λ, 0 < λ < 1. Moreover, the probability distribution of the random threshold h(m) is taken to be sigmoidal, so that the probability of the neuron firing at time m, given V(m) = V, is $\psi(V) = 1/(1 + \exp(-\beta V))$ where β^{-1} is a "temperature". Equation (10) can then be formulated in terms of a system of two maps F_0, F_1 with associated probabilities Φ_0, Φ_1,

$$F_0(V) = kV + I \qquad\qquad \Phi_0(V) = 1 - \lambda\psi(V)$$

$$F_1(V) = kV - \varepsilon + I \qquad\qquad \Phi_1(V) = \lambda\psi(V) \tag{11}$$

That is, we may rewrite equation (10) as [11]

$$V(m) = F_{\alpha(m)}(V(m-1)) \tag{12}$$

114

where $F_{\alpha(m)} = F_\alpha$, $\alpha \in \{0,1\}$, with probability $\Phi_\alpha(V(m-1))$. Thus a particular trajectory of the dynamics is specified by a particular symbol sequence $\{\alpha(m); m = 1,2,... \mid \alpha(m) \in \{0,1\}\}$ together with the initial point $V(0)$.

Equations (10) and (11) describe the dynamics of a random iterated function system (IFS). A random IFS [21] consists of a finite set of continuous maps acting on some metric space and a corresponding set of probabilities for choosing one such map per iteration. (In the case of the above neuron model we can take the metric space to be $\Sigma = [V_1, V_0] \subset R$ with the Euclidean metric. Here $V_0 = I/(1 - k)$ and $V_1 = (1 - \varepsilon)/(1 - k)$ are the fixed points of the maps $F_{0,1}$). We may directly apply various results concerning the properties of random IFS's [21] to determine the limiting behaviour of the model [11]. A convenient approach is to study the evolution of probability distributions on Σ which is generated by selecting a large number of initial states and following the resulting ensemble of trajectories (see fig. 10). The stochastic dynamics is then described in terms of the sequence of probability measures $\{\mu_m \mid m = 0,1,...\}$ on Σ where

$$P(A) = \int_A \mu_m(V)dV \qquad (13)$$

is the probability of a trajectory passing through the subset $A \subset \Sigma$ at time m.

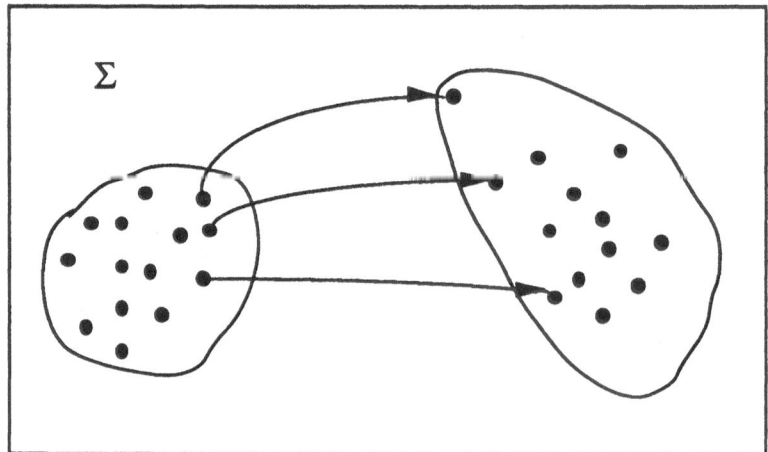

Fig. 10 Ensemble description of neuron dynamics

Note that $P(\Sigma) = 1$. It can be shown that the limiting behaviour of the system described by equations (11) and (12) is characterised by a unique invariant measure $\mu_{\mathcal{F}}$ such that for any initial distribution μ_0

$$\lim_{m \to \infty} \mu_m = \mu_{\mathcal{F}} \tag{14}$$

Moreover, $\mu_{\mathcal{F}}$ satisfies the condition [22] that for almost all trajectories, the frequency with which an orbit $\{V(m)\}$ visits a subset $B \subset \Sigma$ is given by $\mu_{\mathcal{F}}(B)$,

$$\lim_{M \to \infty} \frac{\#\{V(m) \in B | 1 \le m \le M\}}{M} = \mu_{\mathcal{F}}(B) \tag{15}$$

One of the interesting features of random IFS's is that the associated invariant measure (if it exists) often has a fractal-like structure. We shall illustrate this in the case of the invariant measure $\mu_{\mathcal{F}}$ of the single neuron model. A reasonable approximation to $\mu_{\mathcal{F}}$ may be obtained by plotting a frequency histogram displaying how often an orbit $\{V(m)\}$ visits a particular subinterval of Σ. This is a consequence of equation (15). Without loss of

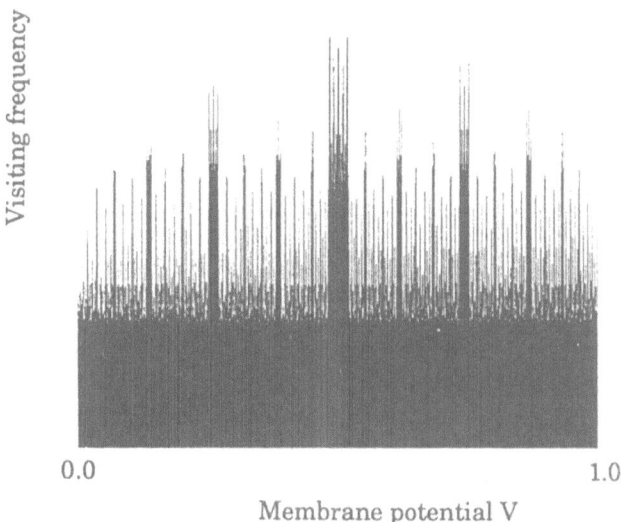

Fig. 11.The invariant measure of the random IFS consisting of the two maps F_0, F_1 with $F_0(V) = kV + 1 - k$ and $F_1(V) = kV$. The associated probabilities are $\Phi_0, \Phi_1 = 1/2$. (a) $k = 0.52$.

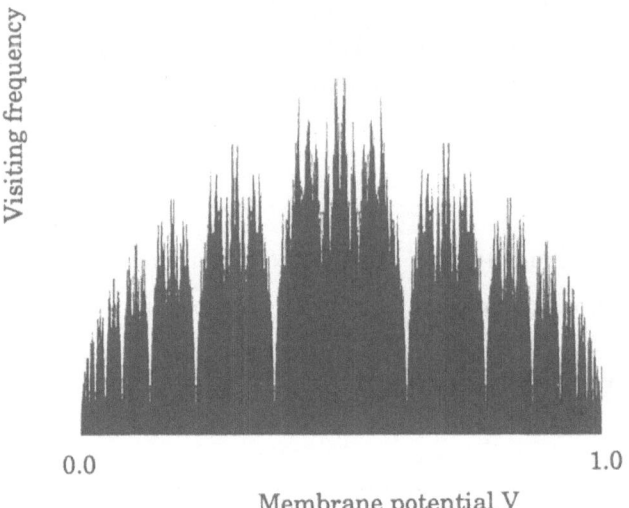

Fig. 11 continued (b) k = 0.6

generality, we consider the high temperature limit $\beta \to 0$ in which $\psi(V) \to$ 1/2 for all V and set $\varepsilon = I = 1 - k$. Equation (11) then reduces to the form

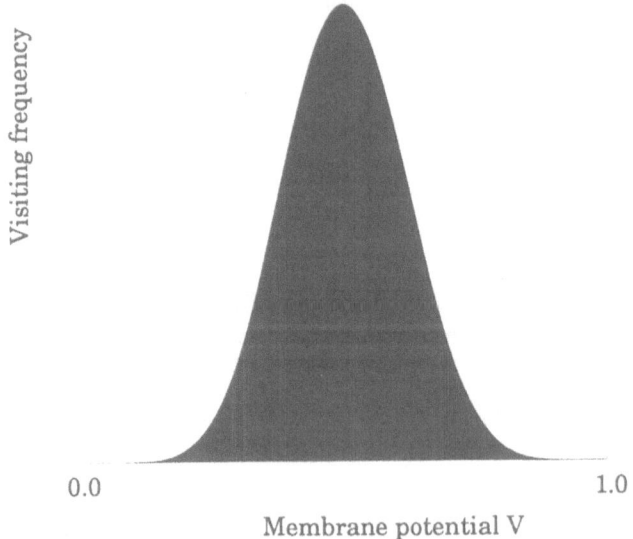

Fig. 11 continued. (c) k = 0.9.

$$F_0(V) = kV + 1 - k \qquad\qquad \Phi_0(V) = 1 - \lambda/2$$

$$F_1(V) = kV \qquad\qquad \Phi_1(V) = \lambda/2 \qquad (16)$$

with $\Sigma = [0,1]$. The invariant measure $\mu_{\mathcal{F}}$ of equation (16) in the case $\lambda = 1$ (no synaptic noise) has been an object of interest for over 50 years [23] and many of its mathematical properties are still not very well understood. For $k < 1/2$ the support of $\mu_{\mathcal{F}}$ is a Cantor set. On the other hand, for $k \geq 1/2$ the support of $\mu_{\mathcal{F}}$ is the whole unit interval and for many values of k the measure has a fractal-like structure. In fig. 11 we display the frequency histogram representation of $\mu_{\mathcal{F}}$ for $\lambda = 1$ and (a) $k = 0.52$, (b) $k = 0.6$, and (c) $k = 0.9$. It is clear that $\mu_{\mathcal{F}}$ becomes progressively smoother as $k \to 1$. (In the presence of synaptic noise, $0 < \lambda < 1$, similar behaviour occurs, but the histograms are no longer symmetric about $V = 1/2$).

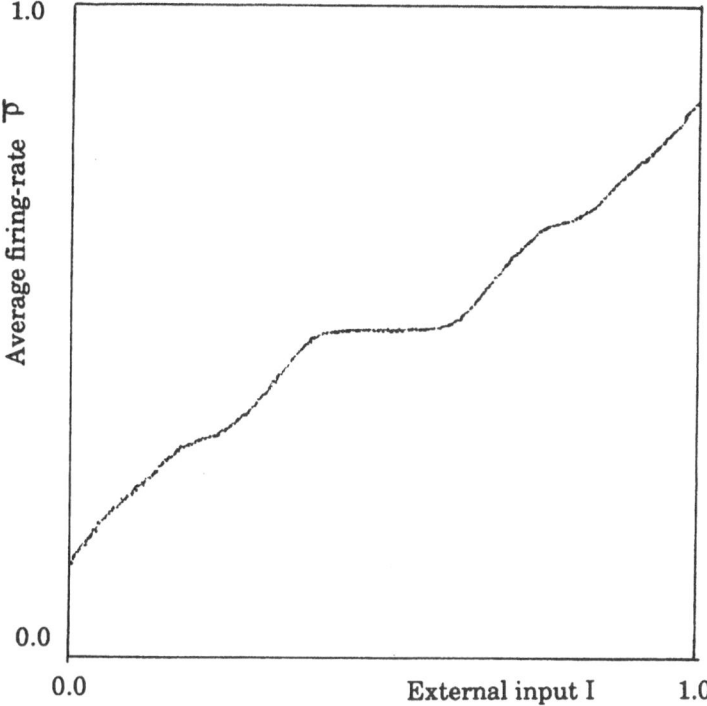

Fig. 12 Average firing-rate $\bar{p}$ as a function of the external input I for (a) T = 0.04 and $\lambda = 1.0$ (threshold noise).

118

We end this section by discussing another feature of the model, that is, the effects of synaptic and threshold noise on the response characteristics of the neuron. The average firing-rate of the neuron is defined to be

$$\rho(V) = \lim_{M \to \infty} \frac{1}{M} \sum_{m=1}^{M} \psi(F_{\alpha(m)}(V)) \tag{17}$$

(cf. equation (6)) where $\psi(F_{\alpha(m)}(V))$ is the probability of firing at time m given that the initial value of the membrane potential is V. It can be shown, using equation (15), that the average firing-rate is independent of the initial point V, $\rho(V) = \bar{\rho}$, and $\bar{\rho}$ may be rewritten in terms of an ensemble average over the invariant measure $\mu_{\mathcal{F}}$,

$$\bar{\rho} = \int_{\Sigma} \psi(V) d\mu_{\mathcal{F}}(V) \tag{18}$$

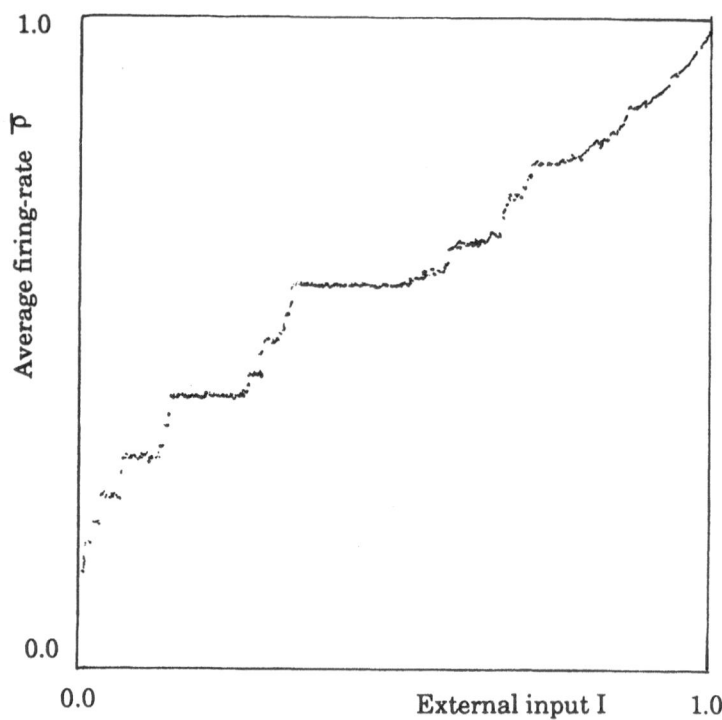

Fig. 12 continued. (b) T = 0.0, λ = 0.7 (synaptic noise).

In fig. 12 we plot the average firing-rate $\bar{\rho}$ as a function of the external input I for (a) T = 0.04, λ = 1 (threshold noise) and (b) T = 0.0, λ = 0.7 (synaptic noise). A major difference between the effects of synaptic and threshold noise is that the latter smooths the response curve of the neuron. Such behaviour can also be understood in terms of the properties of the invariant measure of a random IFS [24].

4. Conclusion

In this paper we have considered the dynamics of a simple, discrete time version of a leaky-integrator neuron. We have described how the deterministic dynamics of the model may be understood in terms of circle maps and have shown that both frequency-locking and chaos can occur. It follows that the dynamics of a network of such neurons corresponds to a system of coupled circle maps, which is analogous to a network of coupled nonlinear oscillators. Hence, this provides a discrete time framework for investigating features such as stimulus synchronisation and chaos in artificial neural networks. Also note that if some spatial structure is imposed on the network then we obtain an example of a coupled map lattice which can display a wide range of cooperative phenomena [25].

In the presence of synaptic or threshold noise we have formulated the dynamics in terms of a random iterated function system and used this to analyse the long-term stochastic behaviour of the model. Such analysis has a straightforward extension to the network level [11]. One consequence of this is that some of the techniques developed to solve the inverse problem for random IFS's may be applicable to the problem of learning in neural networks.

References.

1. McCullogh W. S. and Pitts W. Logical calculus of ideas immanent in nervous activity, Bull. Math. Biosci. 1943; 5:115-133.

2. Taylor J. G. and Reiss M. Storing temporal sequences, Neural Networks (to appear)

3. Taylor J. G. Neural Network capacity for storing temporal sequences, Int. J. Neural Syst. 1991; 2:47; Bressloff P. C. and Taylor J. G. Temporal storage capacity of time-summating binary networks, J. Phys. A (to appear)

4. Stornetta W. S., Hogg T. and Huberman B. A. A dynamical approach to temporal pattern processing. In: Anderson D. Z. (ed) Neural information processing systems. AIP, New York, 1987, pp. 750-759.

5. Mozer M. C. A focused backpropagation algorithm for temporal pattern recognition, Complex Systems, 1989; 3:349-381.

6. Watrous R. L. and Shastri L. Learning phonetic features using connectionist networks. In: Proc. IEEE first int. conf. on neural networks, San Diego, CA, June 1987, vol. IV, pp. 381-388.

7. Bressloff P. C. and Taylor J. G., Discrete time leaky-integrator networks with synaptic noise, Neural Networks, (to appear).

8. Major G. Larkman A. and Jack J. J. B. Proc. Physiol. Soc., 1990; 23.

9. Bressloff P. C. and Stark J. Neuronal dynamics in terms of discontinuous circle maps, Phys. Lett. A, 1990; 150: 187-195.

10. Bressloff P. C. Stochastic dynamics of time-summating binary neural networks, Phys. Rev. A, 1991; 44: 4005-4016.

11. Bressloff P. C. Analysis of quantal synaptic (multiplicative) noise in neural networks using iterated function systems. Submitted to Phys. Rev. A , 1991.

12. Nagumo J. and Sato S. Kybernetic, 1972; 10: 155.

13. Konig P. and Schillen T. B. Stimulus-dependent assembly formation of oscillatory responses, Neural Comp., 1991; 3:155-178.

14. Tsuda I. Self-similarity in the Belousov-Zahbotinsky reaction, Phys. Lett A, 1981; 85:4-8.

15. Aihara K., Takabe T. and Toyoda M., Chaotic neural networks, Phys. Lett. A, 1990; 144: 333-341.

16. Mackay R. S. and Tresser C. Transition to topological chaos for circle maps, Physica D, 1986; 19:206-237.

17. Katz B. The release of neural transmitter substance, Liverpool Univ., Liverpool, 1969.

18. Taylor J. G. Spontaneous behaviour in neural networks, J. Theor. Biol., 1972; 36:513-528.

19. Bressloff P. C. and Taylor J. G. Random iterative networks, Phys. Rev. A, 1990;41: 1126-1137.

20. Harrison P. J., Jack J. J. B. and Kullman D. M., J. Physiol. 1989; 412: 43.

21.Barnsley M. Fractals everywhere. Academic Press, San Diego, 1988.

22. Elton J. An ergodic theorem for iterated maps. J. of Ergod. Th. and Dynam. Syst., 1987;7:481-488.

23. Erdos P. On a family of symmetric Bernouilli convolutions, Amer. J. Math., 1939: 61: 974-976.

24. Withers W. D. Differentiabilty with respect to parameters of average values in probabilistic contracting dynamical systems, Ergod. Th. and Dynam. Syst., 1990;10:559

25. Kaneko K. Clustering, coding, switching, hierarchical ordering and control in a network of chaotic elements, Physica D, 1990; 41:137-172.

OSCILLATORY
NEURAL
NETWORKS

Correlated Neuronal Firing: a Clue to the Integrative Functions of Cortex?

Andreas K. Engel
Peter König
Wolf Singer
Max-Planck-Institut für Hirnforschung
Frankfurt/Main, F. R. Germany

Abstract

Whereas knowledge about the cellular components of cortex is rapidly accumulating, we are still largely ignorant about how distributed neuronal activity can be integrated. In particular, it is still unresolved how activites of vast numbers of neurons can be bound into cortical representations of objects and events. In this paper, we discuss evidence for the hypothesis that temporal synchrony may be the "glue" for binding. Recent cross-correlation studies show that visual cortical neurons synchronize their responses depending on coherence of features in the visual field. Furthermore, these studies indicate that neuronal responses with an oscillatory temporal structure may serve as a carrier signal for such a temporal coding mechanism. Based on these findings, we suggest that binding by a temporal code, which uses synchrony on a fast time scale, may solve the problem of integration in distributed neuronal networks.

1 Introduction: the binding problem

Conceptually, the neurobiology of the past decades has been pervaded by the idea that the relevant level for describing how nervous systems work was that of the single cell. This framework was explicitly addressed as the "single neuron doctrine" in a programatic essay by Barlow [1]. Guided by this dogma, neuroscience has made considerable progress in understanding the constituents of neuronal systems at the cellular and molecular level. In contrast, our knowledge about integrative functions of the nervous system is still poorly developed. This problem is particularly evident in cortical neurobiology where much has been learned about anatomy and physiology of single neurons and their connections, but crucial questions concerning integration of cortical activity are still unresolved. Growing evidence suggests that many cortical functions are based on distributed processes which occur in parallel at different sites. However, it is still enigmatic how relationships are established between such distributed neuronal activities, which seems required to achieve coherent perception or action. In this paper, we will discuss recent experimental evidence which may cast new light on this issue. Since most of this evidence comes from work on the visual cortex, we focus on integrative problems in this sensory modality. Based on the experimental data, we will suggest that timing of events may be the clue to the problem of cortical integration.

In recent years it has become increasingly clear that the visual system creates highly fragmented and distributed representations of objects and their relationships in a visual scene. This fragmentation results from several characteristic features of cortical organization [2,3]. Due to the structure of their receptive fields neurons in many areas of the visual cortex process information only from a limited part of the visual field. In addition, visual cortical neurons respond only to a limited range of feature constellations. To provide a basis for unified percepts, interactions are thus required between neurons with spatially separate receptive fields and, in most cases, also between cells with different feature preferences. Evidently, this is a nontrivial problem. Because of the columnar organization of many cortical areas, neurons responding to the same object are not necessarily neighbours and therefore, the interactions have to be highly selective and cannot simply rely on spatial contiguity of cortical responses. The problem of integration is further aggravated by the functional specialization of whole cortical areas. It has been argued that different features of objects, such as form, colour or motion, are analyzed rather independently by separate processing streams [2,3]. Therefore, feature integration requires the interaction of neurons not only within, but also between visual cortical areas.

Visual processing, thus, exemplifies the general problem of integrating distributed activity in the cortex, which is commonly addressed as the "binding problem" [4]. Resolving this problem seems crucial for understanding a central function of cortex, which is to represent, by patterns of neural activity, information about the environment or relevant internal states of the organism. In the visual system, the binding of features which pertain to individual objects appears as the prerequisite for figure-ground segregation and scene segmentation, i.e. for the distinction between several objects present in the visual field. Similar problems arise in other sensory modalities, and also with respect to the recall of memory [4] and the representation of motor acts.

In the classical framework of the "single neuron doctrine" it was held that the binding problem might be solved by convergence of input from the primary processing stages onto single cells with highly specific response properties [1]. Such "cardinal cells" were assumed to be located in "higher" integrative cortical areas corresponding to the presumed endstages of visual information processing. However, a number of arguments suggest that single cell representations do not provide a viable solution to the problem of integrating visual information. As discussed elsewhere in detail [e.g. 4-9], the Barlow model suffers from combinatorial problems and does not show sufficient flexibility for the rapid establishment of new representations. In addition, the model is not supported by experimental evidence. Although cells responsive to faces have been found [10], these are not selective enough to be considered as the "cardinal cells" envisioned by Barlow. Moreover, neurons selective for many other items of our visual world have not been identified.

A second classical model, suggested as an alternative to the single neuron doctrine, goes back to the work of Hebb [11]. Hebb proposed that visual scenes should be represented by assemblies of interconnected neurons rather than by the activity of single cells. Such Hebbian assemblies are assumed to consist of elementary feature detecting neurons and thus, unlike in Barlow's proposal, complex representations can be formed already in early processing stages. In the Hebb model, cells responding to features of a particular object are bound into an assembly by the concurrent elevation of their average firing rate. If the same pattern is repeatedly presented, this coactivation leads to a strengthening of synaptic coupling between the cells of the assembly which, in turn, enhances their tendency to respond together [11]. Clearly, representing objects by assemblies has distinct advantages, such as greater robustness and flexibility. However, a major drawback of the Hebb model has only recently been recognized [5,6]. The Hebb model relies on the assumption that only one assembly is activated at a time in a particular region of cortex, whereas other assemblies are suppressed. However, processing of natural scenes, where always multiple objects are present on a complex background, will require the coexistence of several assemblies. This, in turn, poses a severe problem for the Hebb model, because the coactivation of cells responding to different objects in the same cortical region makes it impossible to distinguish which cells belong to which particular assembly. Hence, false conjunctions of features become unavoidable. This dilemma has been addressed as the "superposition catastrophe" of the Hebb model [6].

To resolve this difficulty, von der Malsburg [5,6] and Abeles [7] have suggested that cell assemblies might be defined by synchronous firing of cortical neurons, rather than by mere comparison of average firing rates. Their idea was that a temporal code might solve the problems associated with Hebbian assemblies, because it would make time available as an additional dimension for organizing patterns of neural activity. This mechanism might provide the basis for integrating the responses of widely distributed neurons without the anatomical convergence of processing streams onto a single target area somewhere in the brain. In addition, using a temporal code would enable the coexistence of multiple representations in the same region of cortex. According to von der Malsburg's proposal, coactive assemblies would remain discernable because each of them would be composed of synchronously firing neurons but, with respect to each other, the assemblies would not have a fixed temporal relationship [5,6]. Thus, temporal coding might solve the superposition problem and, hence, provide an attractive mechanism for feature binding.

2 Synchrony as a "glue" for cortical representations

Recent experimental studies support the proposal that synchrony might be the glue which binds distributed neuronal activity into coherent representations [for review, see 8,9]. These studies were triggered by the discovery that neuronal responses in cat visual cortex exhibit an intrinsic temporal structure. Gray and Singer showed that, upon appropriate stimulation, these cells discharge bursts at frequencies of 30 to 70 Hz [12,13]. Because of the characteristic fluctuation of the firing probability in such burst sequences, they termed this type of response an "oscillation". Based on this finding and the subsequent demonstration of similar firing patterns in other visual areas [14,15], it was suggested that synchronization of these burst sequences, or oscillations, between spatially separate cells might physiologically instantiate the temporal code postulated by Abeles and von der Malsburg [13-17]. In line with von der Malsburg's proposal, this hypothesis emphasizes the relevance of synchrony as the code for binding, whereas the oscillations *per se* are not assumed to have a representational function. However, as will be discussed below, these firing patterns seem to have distinct advantages as carrier signals for a temporal code.

Several predictions can be derived from the hypothesis that temporal correlation is the code for assembly formation. The first is that synchronization of oscillatory responses should be found between different cells·of a visual area if they respond to coherent figures. In addition, temporal correlation should be observed between the two cerebral hemispheres. Since the visual cortex of each hemisphere processes only half of the visual field, this is required to bind features of objects which extend into both hemifields. Finally, oscillating cells should interact which are located in different visual areas. Given that different aspects of visual objects are indeed processed in separate areas [2,3], this would correspond to binding across feature domains. All three predictions have now been verified in studies of cat visual cortex [14-20].

Recordings made with multiple electrodes from area 17 have shown that oscillatory responses can synchronize across spatially separate orientation columns. This is reliably observed both in anesthetized and awake animals [14,16-18]. On the average, the recorded cells synchronize with zero phase lag, even over spatial separations of more than 7 mm. It should be noted that synchronization is not only found between cells with similar orientation preference but also between cells with dissimilar preferred orientation, in particular if the recorded cells have overlapping receptive fields [16,17]. A typical example of response synchronization is illustrated in Figure 1. Further experiments on anesthetized cats have revealed that response synchro-

---

Fig. 1. Cross-columnar synchronization of oscillatory responses in cat area 17. (**A**) Multiunit activity was recorded from two sites separated by 2 mm. (**B**) Plot of the receptive fields. Note that the cells' preferred orientations differed by 45° (indicated by the thick line drawn across each field). Nevertheless, the cells could sufficiently be coactivated by a single vertical light bar. (**C**) Peri-stimulus-time histograms of the responses. (**D**) Autocorrelograms of the two responses computed in a window of 1 s length as indicated in (**C**). The strong modulation of the correlograms with alternating peaks and throughs reflects the oscillatory structure of the recorded spike trains. (**E**) Crosscorrelogram of the two responses calculated within the same window. The correlogram modulation indicates a strong synchronization of the two oscillatory responses. (**F**) The same data as in (**E**) superimposed with a Gabor function (thick continuous line) that was fitted to the correlogram to quantify its modulation [17]. The number in the upper right corner indicates the "relative modulation amplitude", a measure of correlation strength which was determined by computing the ratio of the amplitude of the Gabor function over its offset. Abbreviations: P, posterior; L, lateral; LAT, lateral sulcus; AC, area centralis. Vertical scale bars indicate numbers of spikes. (Reproduced, with modification, from [17])

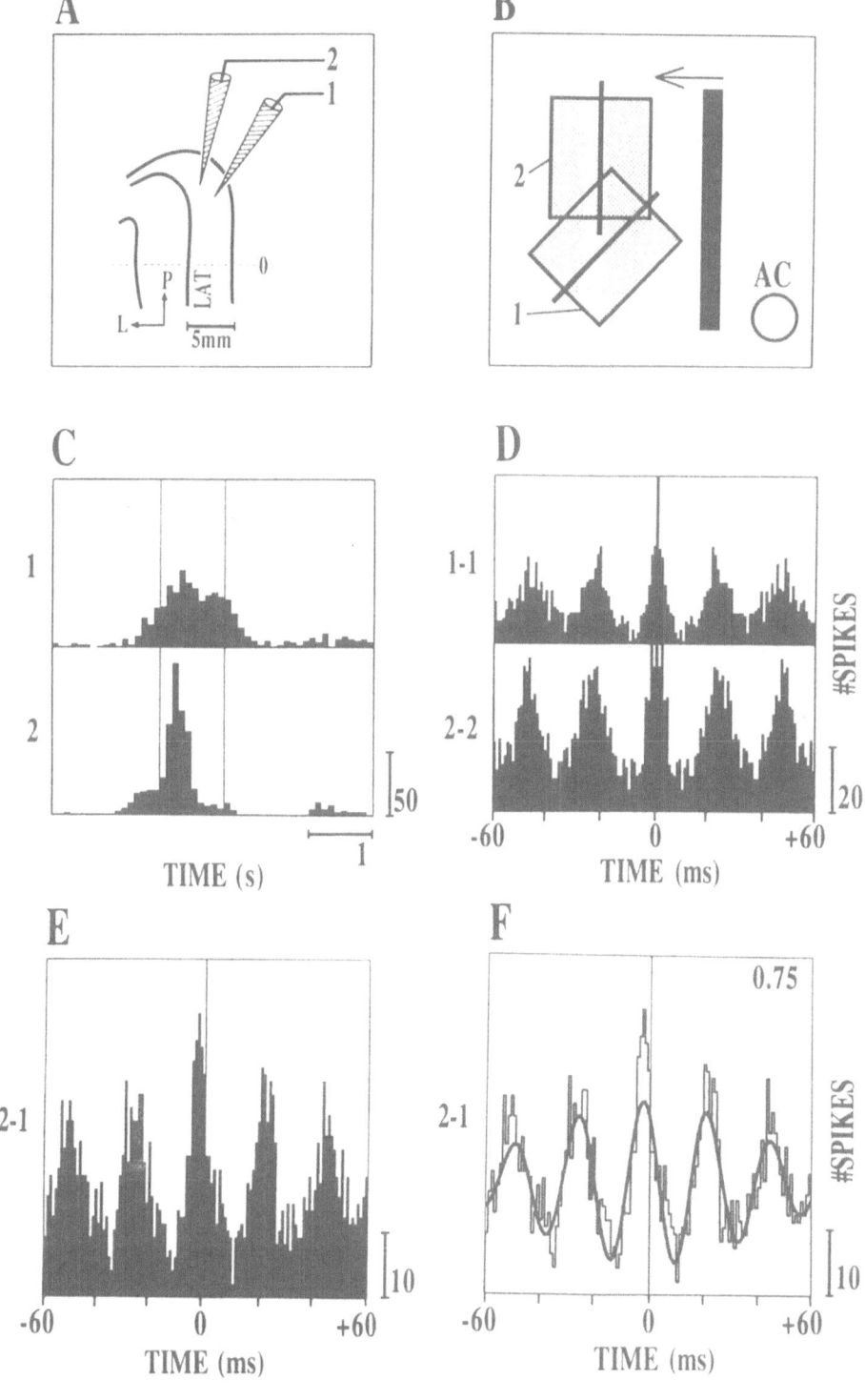

nization can well extend beyond the borders of one visual area. The possibility of interhemispheric response synchronization was discovered recently by simultaneous recording from area 17 of the left and right cerebral hemispheres [19]. With respect to their strength and average phase relationship, interactions across the hemispheres are similar to synchronization within area 17. In addition, there is now compelling evidence for interareal synchronization, which has been observed between areas 17, 18 and 19 [14,20] and between area 17 and area PMLS, a visual association area located in the suprasylvian sulcus [15].

These findings raise the question of how temporal synchrony of oscillatory responses is mediated. The data on interareal and interhemispheric synchronization suggest that temporal correlation is established at the cortical level and not triggered by common subcortical input. Since the visual projections to areas 17 and PMLS are largely relayed through different thalamic nuclei [21], reciprocal cortico-cortical connections appear as the most likely substrate for synchronization between the two areas. In the case of interhemispheric synchronization it has been shown directly that cortico-cortical connections account for the observed interaction. Since the visual afferents to the two hemispheres remain entirely segregated beyond the optic

---

Fig.2. Stimulus-dependent assembly formation by response synchronization. Multiunit activity was recorded from four different orientation columns of area 17 separated by 0.4 mm. The four recordings had overlapping receptive fields and orientation preferences of 22° (site 1), 112° (2), 157° (3) and 90° (4), as indicated by the thick line drawn across each receptive field in (A)-(D). The figure compares responses to stimulation with single moving light bars of varying orientation (left) with responses to combined presentation of two superimposed light bars (right). For each stimulus condition, the shading of the receptive fields indicates the responding cells. Stimulation with single light bars yielded a synchronization between all cells activated by the respective orientation. Thus, the cells at recording sites 1 and 3 responded synchronously to a 0° light bar (A), which occurred for the cells at sites 2 and 4 with a light bar of 112° orientation (B), and for the cells at sites 2 and 3 with a light bar of intermediate orientation (C). (D) Simultaneous presentation of two stimuli with 0° and 112° orientation activated the cells at all four sites. However, in this case the cells segregated into two distinct assemblies, depending on which stimulus was closer to their preferred orientation. Thus, responses were synchronized between sites 1 and 3, which preferred the vertical stimulus, and between 2 and 4, whose preference was close to the 112° light bar. The two assemblies were desynchronized with respect to each other. Thus, no significant synchronization occurred between sites 2 and 3. The cross-correlograms between 1-2, 1-4 and 3-4 were also flat (not shown). Note that the segregation cannot be explained by preferential anatomical wiring of cells with like orientation preference [25] because with a single light bar cells of the two assemblies can well be correlated (C). The correlograms are shown superimposed with their Gabor function (cf. Fig.1). The number to the upper right of each correlogram indicates the relative modulation amplitude. Abbreviation: n.s., not significant. Scale bars indicate the number of spikes. (Reproduced from [26])

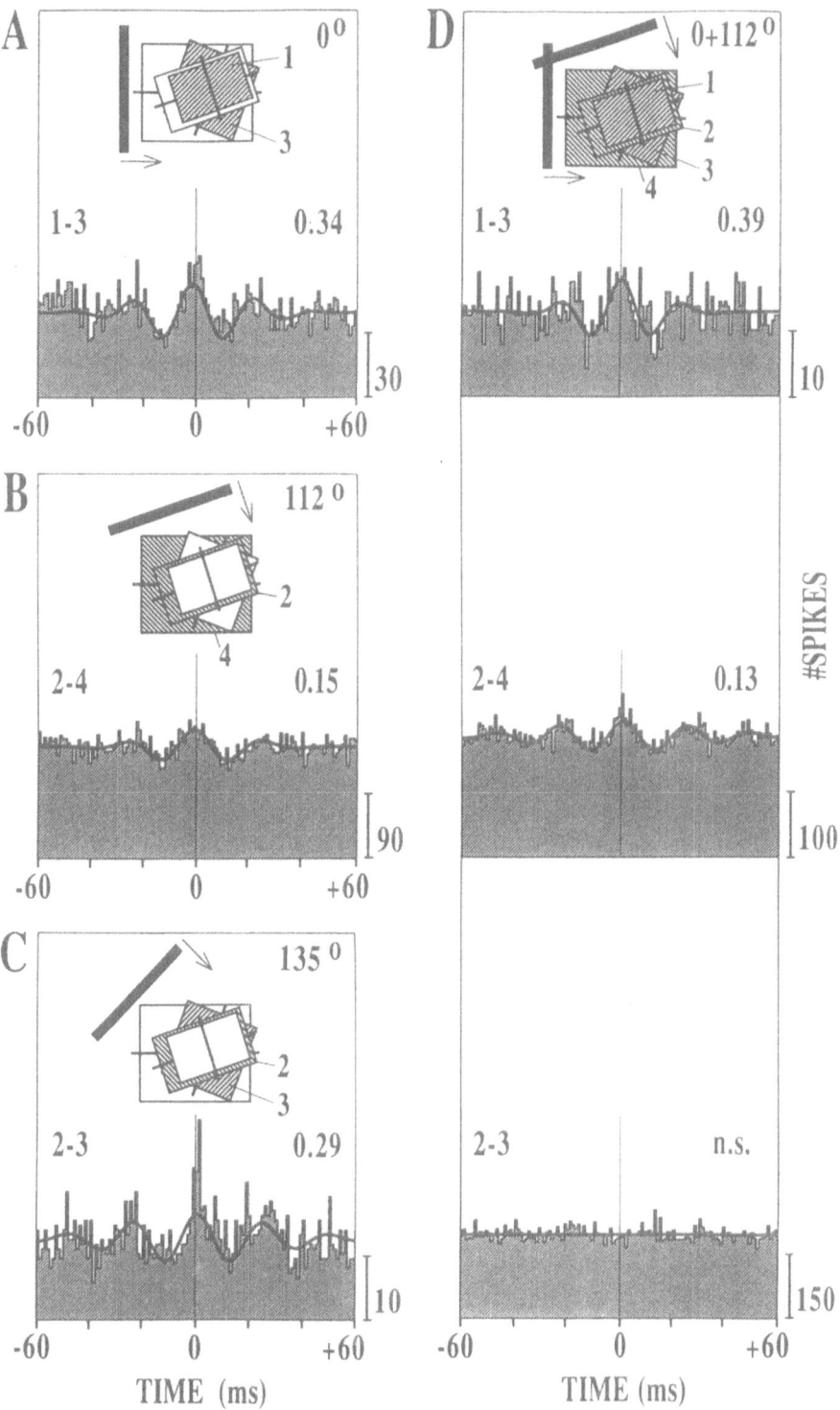

chiasm, there is no common input available and response synchronization across hemispheres can only be achieved by connections travelling through the corpus callosum [22]. The latter assumption has been tested by sectioning the corpus callosum prior to recording from the two hemispheres. Following the lesion, response synchronization between the hemispheres disappears whereas synchronization within either hemisphere is preserved [19]. Further evidence comes from recent experiments on strabismic cats. It has been shown that in area 17 of these animals only cells which are linked by horizontal intracortical connections synchronize their responses [23,24]. Altogether, the available data suggest that synchrony is mediated by reciprocal coupling at the cortical level. This conclusion has two important implications. First, the results demonstrate that reciprocal connections can establish synchrony with zero phase lag despite of finite conduction delays. In case of the callosal connections, these delays may amount to several milliseconds [22]. Previously, it was always assumed that synchronous firing without phase lag could only be achieved by common input [25]. Second, the experimental data assign a new role to reciprocal connections within and between cortical areas. Rather than contributing exclusively to receptive field properties, these connections may provide the substrate for feature binding [15,19].

Two further key predictions ensue from the idea that a temporal code is used to establish cortical representations. First, assembly formation by synchronous oscillation should occur in a stimulus-dependent manner. And second, it should be demonstrated that this mechanism permits the coexistence of different assemblies. Uniform and stereotyped synchrony of neuronal responses could hardly convey any information which might be useful for the segmentation of visual scenes. Thus, cells in the cortex should oscillate in synchrony only if they respond to the same object, but otherwise fire in an uncorrelated manner. As shown already by the Gestalt psychologists, criteria such as continuity, proximity, similarity and common fate are used for perceptual grouping of parts into wholes. If temporal correlation between cortical neurons provides a basis for object representations it should reflect these coherence criteria.

Evidence for the stimulus-dependence of synchronization in area 17 has been obtained in two recent studies [16,26]. There, it could be demonstrated that spatially separate cells fire synchronously if stimulated with a single object. However, if two independent stimuli with different orientation or direction of motion are used the same cells fire without a fixed temporal relationship. A similar stimulus-dependence has been observed for the interareal and interhemispheric synchronization [15; unpublished observations]. These experiments show that Gestalt criteria such as continuity of contours, similiarity of orientation and coherent motion are indeed important for the establishment of synchrony. Furthermore, these results suggest that synchrony can indeed be used for the stimulus-dependent definition of assemblies and, in particular, for the distinction of several representations in the same region of cortex. This is exemplified by the case illustrated in Figure 2. There, we recorded from four cell clusters with overlapping receptive fields. If stimulated with two independent objects these cells segregate into two assemblies which are spatially overlapping in area 17 but desynchronized relative to each other (Fig. 3). Just considering mean activity levels, one would in this case only know that a number of

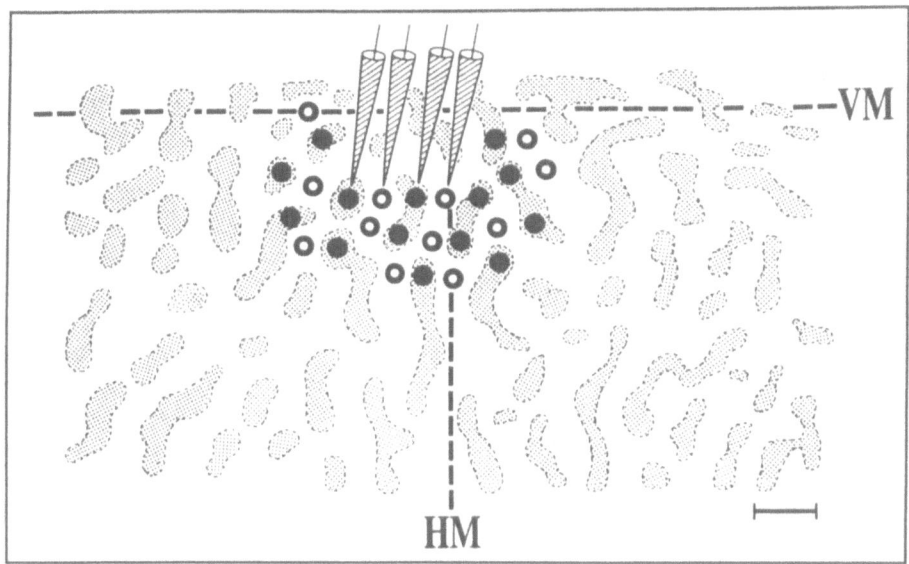

Fig.3. Cartoon of the experiment illustrated in Figure 2. The recording situation
was projected onto a map of orientation columns in area 17 generated by the 2-
deoxyglucose technique (kindly provided by Siegrid Löwel). Shaded areas represent
bands of orientation columns responding to vertical contours. Electrode symbols
indicate the recording sites. The cartoon illustrates the measurement shown in
Fig. 2D. If the cells are stimulated with two independent objects, two spatially
overlapping assemblies emerge which are desynchronized with respect to each other
(indicated by dots and circles, respectively). Abbreviations: VM, representation of
the vertical meridian; HM, representation of the horizontal meridian. Scale bar,
1mm.

different feature detectors are active, but not whether they actually respond to two
different objects or just a single one (which could, for instance, be a moving corner).
In contrast, evaluation of the temporal relationships allows to partition the whole
set of active cells into two distinct assemblies. A further advantage of the mechanism
is its high degree of flexibility and parsimony. If the input configuration is altered,
the very same cells can recombine into quite different assemblies by changing their
mutual temporal relationship.

Altogether, the results reviewed here indicate that assemblies can be formed
by response synchronization across columns, areas and even different hemispheres.
The data support the notion that a temporal coding mechanism exists in the visual
cortex which binds, in a stimulus-dependent manner, distributed neuronal activity
into coherent representations [8,9]. In particular, they suggest that such a temporal
code may provide a physiological solution to the superposition problem.

3 Oscillations: a "vehicle" for temporal codes in the brain?

So far, we have argued that synchrony may be the relevant code for binding of distributed activity into assemblies. At this point then, two important questions need to be considered. What is the relevance of oscillatory processes for synchronization? And furthermore, why should oscillations in the gamma frequency range be of particular interest? One possible assumption would be that this temporal structure encodes certain features of the visual input. However, this seems unlikely, because the oscillatory modulation of the responses varies only slightly if orientation or velocity of the stimuli are changed [27]. In addition, the mere occurrence of oscillations does not seem to reflect gross state changes of the animal. Oscillatory responses very similar to those in the anesthetized preparation have been demonstrated in awake cats [18]. Thus, it seems unlikely that the oscillations as such carry information about sensory or modulatory input to the cortex. In the following, we shall propose a different hypothesis concerning the role of oscillations. Several arguments indicate that the oscillatory modulation of neural responses may have crucial advantages for the establishment of synchrony and thus, may be instrumental as a "vehicle" for a temporal code in the cortex.

Several features of these oscillations make them well suited as carrier signals for assembly formation. One of their key features is that they represent a population phenomenon. Initially, these oscillations were observed in local field potentials, indicating the rhythmic synchronous firing of numerous cells close to the recording electrode [12,13]. Subsequent multiunit recordings from striate and extrastriate areas of cat visual cortex have confirmed that adjacent neurons indeed have a strong tendency to burst in synchrony [13,15]. This suggests that local clusters of synchronously active cells may be the fundamental processing units in the cortex. For the designation of such coherently active cell clusters, we adopt the term "neuronal group" introduced by Edelman [28], thereby extending the meaning of this notion to the temporal domain. As discussed above, assembly formation presumably requires long-range interactions within the cortex. Given this constraint, it will be much easier to build assemblies of oscillating groups of neurons than of single cells, because the temporal behaviour of groups is much better defined and more reliable [29]. In addition, due to summation effects volleys of synchronous spikes fired by such groups will be particularly effective on target neurons, whereas activity of single neurons may not be sufficient to establish synchrony over large distances. Thus, coherent bursting of local groups of adjacent cells may considerably facilitate the formation of distributed assemblies in the cortex.

The most salient feature of oscillatory responses is that these bursts occur in sequence alternately with silent intervals. Evidently, such pauses are required to define temporal relationships between bursts fired by spatially separate groups. Quantitative analysis shows very clearly that these interburst intervals do not vary stochastically but preferentially adopt values between 15 and 35 ms [13,27]. For brief episodes of 50 to 100 ms, the bursts may even occur at relatively regular intervals. Thus, the oscillation provides an intrinsic "predictor" of the next volley fired by an active population of cells. Experimental data and modelling studies indicate that this recurrence of bursts in oscillatory responses has several advantages. First, this temporal structure allows response synchronization via reciprocal connections despite of large conduction delays as it is observed, for instance, between the two cerebral hemispheres [19]. As described above, interhemispheric synchronization is mediated by callosal connections and occurs without phase lag although transcallosal activation shows delays of at least 4 to 6ms [22]. Presumably, stochastic spike trains could not be synchronized by mutual interaction under these conditions. In accordance with this hypothesis, we never observed correlograms with only one center peak in our study of interhemispheric interactions, which would indicate synchronization of non-oscillatory responses. Yet, synchronization is possible with oscillatory neuronal signals, as confirmed by recent simulation studies [30]. Due to the recurrent temporal structure of their responses, coupled neurons can mutually entrain each other and improve the synchronization from one burst to the next. Therefore, oscillatory responses may be a prerequisite for long-range synchronization in the cortex. A second advantage of oscillatory activity is that network elements which are not linked directly can be synchronized via third parties. As demonstrated in a simulated network of coupled oscillators, the temporal correlation can be established over distances which are much larger than the length of monosynaptic coupling connections [30]. Thus, widely separate sites in the cortex can, in principle, be synchronized with zero phase provided a polysynaptic reciprocal linkage exists between them. Finally, synchronization in networks of coupled oscillators is robust even if the conduction delays are not uniformly distributed but show considerable variation [30]. These considerations suggest that the recurrent nature of the burst sequences observed in visual cortex has distinct advantages for the synchronization of widely separate cell groups in the cortex.

However, it is important to notice that the oscillations are never strictly periodic, but always exhibit some jitter of their frequency [13,14,27]. Thus, if power spectra are computed over extended epochs of unit or field potential data the oscillation appears as a broad peak in the gamma frequency range above 30 Hz [13,14]. Therefore, the shorthand notion of a "40 Hz oscillation", which has been used by several authors, is clearly misleading, since it suggests a periodic process with a narrow frequency band. A certain jitter of the oscillation frequency may be desirable for at least two reasons. First, it may be easier to desynchronize cell groups if their oscillations are broad banded and, thus, to prevent the cortex from entering global states of synchrony which would be inappropriate for information processing. Second, the number of possible representations which can be coactivated in the same cortical region is increased by variation of the frequency and would presumably be lower with strictly periodic signals. Altogether, the broad banded nature of the oscillations appears as a reasonable compromise between the opposing constraints of a certain "predictability" of the firing pattern and sufficient "breakability" of synchronous states.

Further arguments support the notion that the oscillations, as a carrier signal for assembly formation, have to be in the gamma frequency range. Psychophysical studies show that segmentation of natural scenes can be accomplished within 100 to 200 ms [31]. This imposes a lower limit to the oscillation frequency, because a sufficient number of bursts must be accomodated in 200 ms to establish synchrony between cortical cell groups. Within the same time span, a reliable distinction must be performed between several assemblies representing different objects, which will also require several successive bursts. Oscillations in the alpha and beta frequency range would therefore be too slow to achieve segmentation. On the other hand, the oscillations must not be too fast to allow for synchronization over long distances. The available modelling studies indicate that reciprocally coupled oscillatory units can only be synchronized with zero phase if the coupling delays do not exceed, roughly, one third of the average period time [30,32]. For much larger delays, the oscillators assume a stable antiphase relationship [32]. Given this constraint and the known conduction delays, transcallosal synchronization, for instance, could presumably not be achieved if the oscillations were much faster than 80 or 90 Hz. Altogether, a number of reasons suggest that, at least in sensory cortices, oscillations in the gamma frequency range are well adapted for assembly formation.

The potential relevance of oscillatory signals for a temporal coding mechanism is further emphasized by their widespread occurrence. They seem to be ubiquitous in cat visual cortex [13-15,20], and have now also been found in the visual system of other species. Of particular interest is the recent demonstration of oscillatory responses in the extrastriate cortex of the awake behaving macaque [33,34] and in the striate cortex of anesthetized squirrel monkeys [35]. As in the cat, synchronous bursting of groups of cells is a prominent feature of responses in the monkey. A notable difference between the two species is that the oscillations are more irregular in the monkey and thus, even more difficult to detect with averaged auto- correlograms [33,34]. These findings are complemented by the recent observation of oscillatory activity in the optic tectum of awake pigeons [36]. Gamma oscillations have also been observed beyond the visual system. They are well known to occcur in the olfactory bulb and entorhinal cortex of various species [37]. Moreover, gamma oscillations have been reported in somatosensory and motor cortex of the monkey [38] and they are also present in the cortex of rats [39] and guinea pigs [40]. Altogether, oscillations similar to those observed in cat visual cortex have now been encountered in a wide variety of structures and species. This seems in line with the hypothesis that they may be of general relevance as as carrier signal for a temporal coding mechanism.

4 Conclusions

We have reviewed recent experimental findings which suggest a new mechanism for integration in distributed neuronal networks. A major component of the problem of cortical integration is the need to bind distributed neuronal activity into organized patterns, or assemblies, which then represent objects or events in the environment or internal states of the organism. The data reviewed above suggest that binding of neuronal activity into assemblies may be achieved by a temporal code using synchronization on a fast time scale. This renders integration possible without cardinal cells or anatomical convergence of processing streams onto an integrating "higher" cortical area. Further advantages of this mechanism are that it creates representations in a highly flexible manner and, moreover, that it permits the coexistence of several representations in the same cortical region. In the particular case of sensory systems, temporal coding may provide a solution to fundamental problems of scene segmentation and figure-ground segregation. It may be speculated that a similar mechanism might integrate distributed activity in the motor system and in association cortices.

The available evidence suggests further that oscillations are not a mere epiphenomenon of cortical activity. These firing patterns as such do not seem to have a representational function, yet they may be instrumental to a temporal coding mechanism. Salient features of oscillatory responses are the synchronous bursting of neuronal groups and the recurrence of such bursts with a certain jitter of the frequency. Signals with these properties seem to offer distinct advantages for the establishment of synchrony in the cortex, especially between groups at widely remote sites. Thus, oscillatory processes may be important as a carrier signal, or "vehicle", for temporal codes in the brain.

References

[1] Barlow HB. Single units and sensation: a neuron doctrine for perceptual psychology? Perception 1972; 1:371-394

[2] DeYoe AE, Van Essen DC. Concurrent processing streams in monkey visual cortex. Trends Neurosci 1988; 11:219-226

[3] Felleman DJ, Van Essen, DC. Distributed hierarchical processing in the primate cerebral cortex. Cerebral Cortex 1991; 1:1-47

[4] Damasio AR. Synchronous activation in multiple cortical regions: a mechanism for recall. Sem Neurosci 1990; 2:287-296

[5] von der Malsburg C. The correlation theory of brain function. Internal Report 81-2, Max-Planck-Institute for Biophysical Chemistry, Göttingen, 1981

[6] von der Malsburg C. Am I thinking assemblies? In: Palm G, Aertsen A (eds) Brain theory. Springer, Berlin, 1986, pp 161-176

[7] Abeles M. Local cortical circuits. An electrophysiological study. Springer, Berlin, 1982

[8] Engel AK, König P, Kreiter AK, Gray CM, Singer W. Temporal coding by coherent oscillations as a potential solution to the binding problem: physiological evidence. In: Schuster HG (ed) Nonlinear dynamics and neuronal networks. VCH Verlagsgesellschaft, Weinheim, 1991, pp 3-25

[9] Singer W, Artola A, Engel AK, et al. (1992) Neuronal representations and temporal codes. In: Poggio T, Glaser DA (eds) Exploring brain functions: models in neuroscience. Wiley, New York, in press

[10] Perret DI, Mistlin AJ; Chitty AJ. Visual neurones responsive to faces. Trends Neurosci 1987; 10:358-364

[11] Hebb DO. The organization of behavior. Wiley, New York, 1949

[12] Gray CM, Singer W. Stimulus-specific neuronal oscillations in the cat visual cortex: a cortical functional unit. Soc Neurosci Abstr 1987; 13:404.3

[13] Gray CM, Singer W. Stimulus-specific neuronal oscillations in orientation columns of cat visual cortex. Proc Natl Acad Sci USA 1989; 86:1698-1702

[14] Eckhorn R, Bauer R, Jordan W et al. Coherent oscillations: a mechanism for feature linking in the visual cortex? Biol Cybern 1988; 60:121-130

[15] Engel AK, Kreiter AK, König P, Singer W. Synchronization of oscillatory neuronal responses between striate and extrastriate visual cortical areas of the cat. Proc Natl Acad Sci USA 1991; 88:6048-6052

[16] Gray CM, König P, Engel AK, Singer W. Oscillatory responses in cat visual cortex exhibit inter-columnar synchronization which reflects global stimulus properties. Nature 1989; 338:334-337

[17] Engel AK, König P, Gray CM, Singer W. Stimulus-dependent neuronal oscillations in cat visual cortex: inter-columnar interaction as determined by cross-correlation analysis. Eur J Neurosci 1990; 2:588-606

[18] Gray CM, Raether A, Singer W. Stimulus-specific intercolumnar interactions of oscillatory neuronal responses in the visual cortex of alert cats. Soc Neurosci Abstr 1989; 15:320.4

[19] Engel AK, König P, Kreiter AK, Singer W. Interhemispheric synchronization of oscillatory neuronal responses in cat visual cortex. Science 1991; 252:1177-1179

[20] Kruse W, Eckhorn R, Bauer R. Stimulus-induced synchronization among three visual cortical areas of the cat. Perception 1990; 19:A55c

[21] Rosenquist AC. Connections of visual cortical areas in the cat. In: Peters A, Jones EG (eds) Cerebral cortex, vol. 3. Plenum Press, New York, 1985, pp 81-117

[22] Innocenti GM. The primary visual pathway through the corpus callosum. morphological and functional aspects in the cat. Arch Ital Biol 1980; 118:124-188

[23] König P, Engel AK, Löwel S, Singer W. Squint affects occurrence and synchronization of oscillatory responses in cat visual cortex. Soc Neurosci Abstr 1990; 16:523.2

[24] Löwel S, Singer W. Selection of intrinsic horizontal connections in the visual cortex by correlated neuronal activity. Science 1991; in press

[25] Ts'o DY, Gilbert CD, Wiesel TN. Relationships between horizontal interactions and functional architecture in cat striate cortex as revealed by cross-correlation analysis. J Neurosci 1986; 6:1160-1170

[26] Engel AK, König P, Singer W. Direct physiological evidence for scene segmentation by temporal coding. Proc Natl Acad Sci USA 1991; 88:9136-9140

[27] Gray CM, Engel AK, König P, Singer W. Stimulus- dependent neuronal oscillations in cat visual cortex: receptive field properties and feature dependence. Eur J Neurosci 1990; 2:607-619

[28] Edelman GM. The remembered present. A biological theory of consciousness. Basic Books, New York, 1989

[29] Sporns O, Tononi G, Edelman GM. Dynamic interactions of neuronal groups and the problem of cortical integration. In: Schuster HG (ed) Nonlinear dynamics and neuronal networks. VCH Verlagsgesellschaft, Weinheim, 1991, pp 205-240

[30] König P, Schillen TB. Stimulus-dependent assembly formation of oscillatory responses: I. synchronization. Neur Comput 1991; 3:155-166

[31] Biederman I. Higher-level vision. In: Osherson DN, Kosslyn SM, Hollerbach JM (eds) Visual cognition and action. MIT Press, Cambridge, 1990, pp 41-72

[32] Schuster HG, Wagner P. Mutual entrainment of two limit cycle oscillators with time delayed coupling. Progr Theor Phys 1989; 81:939-945

[33] Kreiter AK, Singer W. Oscillatory neuronal activity in the superior temporal sulcus of macaque monkeys. Soc Neurosci Abstr 1991; 17:208.1

[34] Kreiter AK, Singer W. Oscillatory neuronal responses in the visual cortex of the awake macaque monkey. Eur J Neurosci 1992; in press

[35] Livingstone MS. Visually-evoked oscillations in monkey striate cortex. Soc Neurosci Abstr 1991; 17:73.3

[36] Neuenschwander S, Varela FJ. Sensory-triggered oscillatory activity in the avian tectum. Soc Neurosci Abstr 1990; 16:47.6

[37] Freeman WJ. On the problem of anomalous dispersion in chaoto-chaotic phase transitions of neural masses, and its significance for the management of perceptual information in brains. In: Haken H, Stadler M (eds) Synergetics of cognition. Springer, Berlin, 1990, pp 126-143

[38] Murthy VN, Fetz EE. Synchronized 25-35 Hz oscillations in sensorimotor cortex of awake monkeys. Soc Neurosci Abstr 1991; 17:126.11

[39] Silva LR, Amitai Y, Connors BW. Intrinsic oscillations of neocortex generated by layer 5 pyramidal neurons. Science 1991; 251:432-435

[40] Llinás RR, Grace AA, Yarom Y. In vitro neurons in mammalian cortical layer 4 exhibit intrinsic oscillatory activity in the 10- to 50-Hz frequency range. Proc Natl Acad Sci USA 1991; 88:897-901

Two-Layered Physiology-Oriented Neuronal Network Models that Combine Dynamic Feature Linking via Synchronization with a Classical Associative Memory

M. Arndt, P. Dicke, M. Erb, R. Eckhorn and H. J. Reitboeck

Dept. of Biophysics
Philipps-University Marburg
Renthof 7, D-3550 Marburg, FRG

Abstract

A visual object 'pops out' against the background, if its local features have a high degree of perceptual coherence: the object's local features are linked by the visual system into a perceptual whole. A neuronal mechanism for such preattentive 'object definition' is likely to be based on stimulus-induced synchronized activities, as observed in the visual system of the cat [1, 2]. Based on neurophysiological evidence we developed a model neuron with the following properties [7]: 1. Convergent feeding connections can directly activate the model neurons spike discharge. 2. Modulatory action of linking inputs onto feeding inputs provides mutual enhancement and synchronization of stimulus-specific responses. The linking effect is represented by the synchronization of the spike trains of model neurons coupled by linking connections. Spatial and temporal continuity of a stimulus, thus, can produce synchronization in those neural assemblies that are activated by such stimulus. The response of a model of two identical layers is similar to that of cortical assemblies in our neurophysiological observations: Stimulated input regions that share some stimulus features induce synchronized ensemble activities via the laterally projecting recurrent linking connections, even if the stimuli are moving and are composed of spatially separated subregions. In a second type of simulation the associative property of the linking network is supported by a further layer with a classical type of associative memory [10-12]. Presenting a stimulus pattern (which is similar to stored patterns), the degree of association to one of these patterns depends on the spatial overlap of the patterns and the strength of the local linking connections in the lower layer.

1. Introduction

Stimulus-induced oscillations (35 Hz - 80 Hz) were discovered in the visual cortex of the cat [1, 2], that showed about zero mean phase difference of oscillations in the same visual cortical area and between different areas. The synchronizations are stimulus-specific indicated by high correlation if the assemblies code the same or similar visual features (location in the visual field, stimulus orientation, etc.).

These results together with theoretical proposals [3-6] support our hypothesis, that synchronization serves as a mechanism for the integration of pattern components [2, 7].

In our neural network models feature linking is realised via modulatory interactions that induce synchronizations of the spike activities of the interacting model neurons. The main advantage of this mechanism for the processing of a given stimulus in a certain feature domain is the detection of spatial and temporal continuity in a pattern of spatially variing stimulus intensities. The linking process, thus simplifies the coding of the stimulus pattern through the detection of similarities in the feature domain: similar features are linked in a current visual situation by synchronization of the activities of the corresponding neural assemblies.

2 The Model Neuron

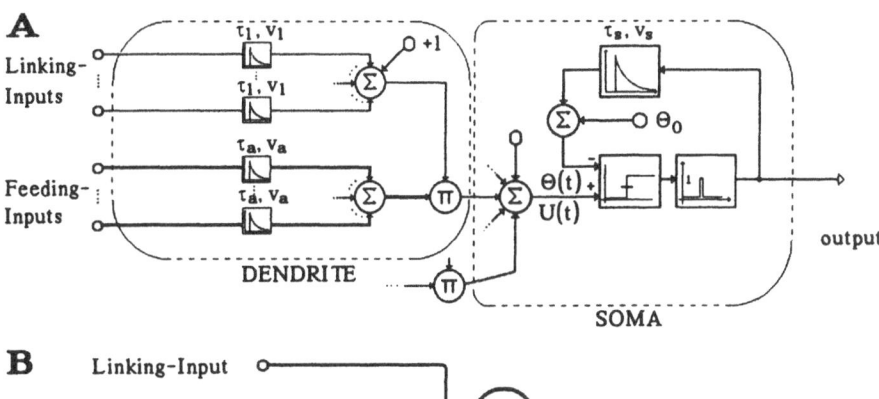

Figure 2.1: Functional diagram of the model neuron (A) and its symbol (B) (from[7])

A) Linking and feeding signals interact multiplicatively after preprocessing by leaky integrators: $U(t) = F(t) * (1 + L(t))$. The sum of the dendritic output signals, $U(t)$, is fed to the spike encoder. If $U(t)$ exceeds the dynamic threshold $\Theta(t)$ a spike is produced and fed back to the dynamic threshold mechanism via another leaky integrator.

B) Symbol of the model neuron.

In order to study the generation of synchronized neural activities, including the stimulus induced oscillations, we developed a model neuron (Fig. 2.1.A) with an input section corresponding to the dendrites of a biological neuron and an output part corresponding to the soma and axon of a neuron [7].

Inputs are either spike-trains or continous functions that simulate either receptor outputs or the average activity in a neural assembly. The model neuron has two distinct types of inputs: *FEEDING* and *LINKING* inputs. Feeding- and linking-inputs are processed by leaky integrators with different time constants and gain factors to simulate different synaptic transfer functions and the generation of postsynaptic potentials. For each type of inputs, the signals are summed separately. The sum of the feeding-inputs is subsequently multiplied by the sum of the linking-inputs plus an offset of 1. The linking inputs, therefore, have no effect without feeding inputs; they only modulate the feeding inputs. This modulating action is responsible for the synchronization of model neuron's activities.

The threshold of the spike generator is the sum of the negative feedback from the output (with a temporal decay determined by an other leaky integrator) and a threshold-offset. The output of the neuron is binary (0 or 1) representing action potentials (spikes) of equal amplitude. The threshold mechanism enables the model-neuron to fire repetitively and to act as a local nonlinear oscillator. The resulting (static) dependency of the spike frequency on the stimulus intensity is almost linear.

3. The Network

3.1 The basic linking mechanism

The linking effect in networks of our model neurons can be demonstrated in a simple simulation: two neurons are symmetrically connected via linking-synapses (Fig. 3.1A). The output of neuron 1 is connected to the linking-input of neuron 2 and vice versa. Both neurons receive an analog signal via their feeding-input, with the input of one neuron held at a constant value and the other is varied in steps.

Figure 3.1 shows phase linking in this simple network of two model neurons depending on input "contrast": for large contrasts, the output spike trains are uncorrelated. If the contrast decreases the neurons link and their outputs are strongly correlated. If the two neurons would code local receptive field properties (including disparity, color, orientation), similar local features are linked by synchronized neural spike activity. The synchronization process can be explained as follows: If the two neurons fire with about equal frequency but out of phase, the neuron which fires first increases the membrane potential of the second neuron via the linking synapse, so that the second neuron fires sooner and tends to fire in synchrony at the next discharge.

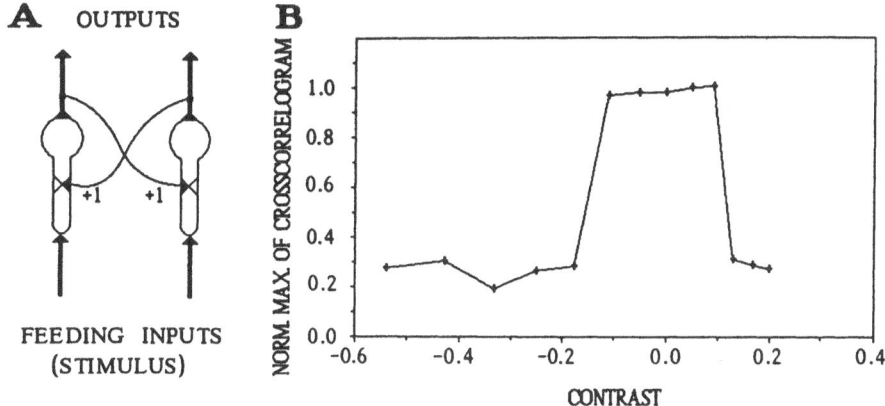

Figure 3.1 A) Elementary network of 2 model neurons, where each output is connected to the other neuron via a linking-synapse (strength +1).

B) The maxima of the short-epoch cross-correlations of spike-trains are shown as a function of the 'contrast' of the input signals. For a small input contrast the correlation strength is high while it is low for large contrasts.

3.2 Simulation with one-dimensional one-layered networks

In order to further study synchronization-linking we simulated different networks of up to 50 neurons in one layer that were interconnected as shown in Figure 3.2. Each neuron modulates the activity of its four nearest neighbors via linking-connections. The strength of the synaptic connection declines laterally with distance. A network like that simulates (in a greatly simplified manner) the lateral connections within a cortical area. All neurons are assumed to be part of the same feature map. If a stimulus is given to the network (corresponding to the activation of neurons by similar features in a visual scene) the neurons fire with a frequency depending on the similarity of the stimuli according to their local filter properties. If local stimuli are similar, the output spike activities are linked if the stimulated neurons are connected via linking synapses. Hence, only spatially continous stimuli (with interruptions of less than the lateral projection length of the network) are linked with a one layer network. The results of the simulations show that the linking-mechanism is not only able to synchronize stationary, but also moving stimuli (Fig. 3.3).

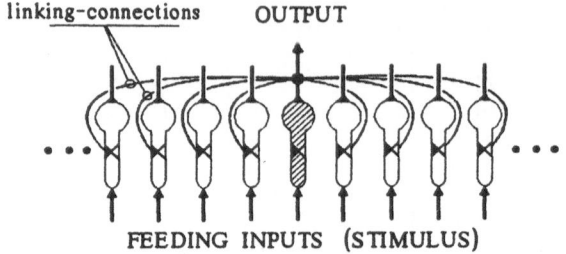

Figure 3.2 Scheme of the linking connections of each neuron in the network. The connection strength is positive and declines laterally with the distance.

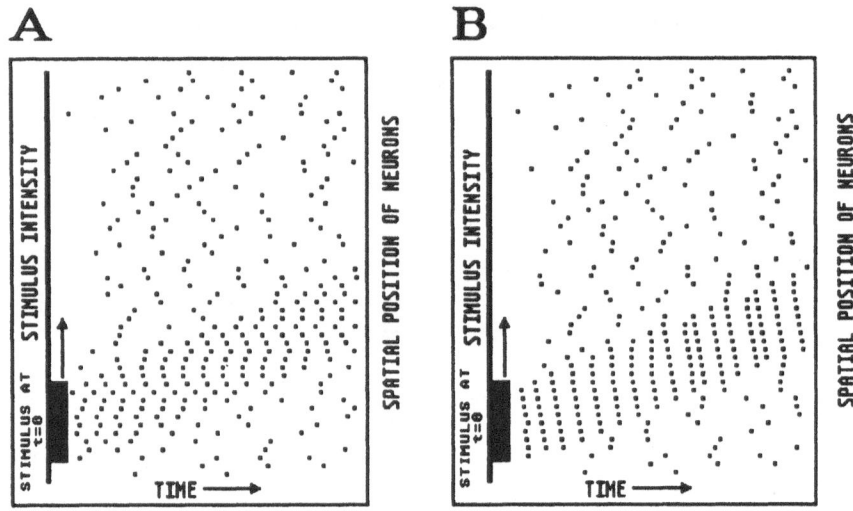

Figure 3.3 A) A moving rectangular stimulus is presented to a one-layer, one dimensional network consisting of 50 neurons, without lateral connections. The resulting spike trains are shown as a function of time for every model neuron. Spikes are marked as dots.

B) The same simulation as described in A) but with lateral linking connections. In the range of the moving stimulus activities are synchronized (Simulation: 600 bins, 1ms binwidth, uncorrelated random spike activity was added to the input of each neuron).

Figure 3.3 shows that spatio-temporal changing stimuli can be defined by synchronized assemblies of neurons. Presenting a moving 'object' to the network means that several spatially connected neurons get nearly the same input. The object therefore is defined by a continously changing assembly of synchronously firing neurons independent of the spatial position of the neurons. Neurons at the front of the stimulus join the synchronized assembly, while neurons at the end of the stimulus leave the synchronized assembly. It should, thus, be possible to separate a moving object from the background via a second neuron layer that detects synchronized activity.

3.3 Simulations of one-dimensional two-layered networks

In order to link spatially remote parts of an object via synchronized neural activity, a second layer of neurons is added. The receptive fields (RFs) of second layer (layer-2) neurons are chosen to be larger than the RFs of the first layer (layer-1) neurons (in correspondence with the increase of RF widths of 'higher' visual cortical areas). The larger RFs of layer-2 are able to bridge the gap between distant parts of an object in cooperation with the intrinsic lateral connections of each layer. The RFs of the layer-2 neurons are built by superposition of layer-1 RFs (4 converging feeding connections from layer-1 to layer-2). To provide the synchonization of distant object parts, the output activity of one layer-2 neuron was fed back to 4 layer-1 neuron via linking connections. By use of linking connections distortion of layer-1 RFs is avoided. For simplicity, the connection strength of the feed-forward feeding and the feedback linking connection was chosen to be equal for each type of connection. Each neuron, again, is connected to its four neighbors via lateral linking connections as in 3.2 (The connection strength is positive and declines with distance). Figure 3.4 shows the connection-scheme of the local network. The simulation network consists of 50 neurons in layer-1 and 23 neurons in layer-2. For the following simulations (Figs. 3.5, 3.6) two rectangular patches are applied to the feeding inputs of layer-1. The amplitudes of these stimuli differ by a factor of two and the stimuli are switched on in temporal succession.

The first simulation (Fig. 3.5A) is performed without linking connections from layer-2 to layer-1: The neural activities within the patches are synchronized, while the burst frequencies at the both stimulus positions differ markedly. Figure 3.5B shows the auto and cross-correlograms of the spike activities of the stimulus patches "a" and "b". The flat cross-correlogram indicates the desynchronization of the 'local patch activity'.

The Simulation with linking connections from layer-2 to layer-1 is depicted in Figure 3.6A. Now "interpatch" burst synchronization develops mediated by the synchronization of spike activities in layer-2 and the cross-correlogram of the corresponding spike activities at "a" and "b" (Fig. 3.6B) shows distinct maxima.

146

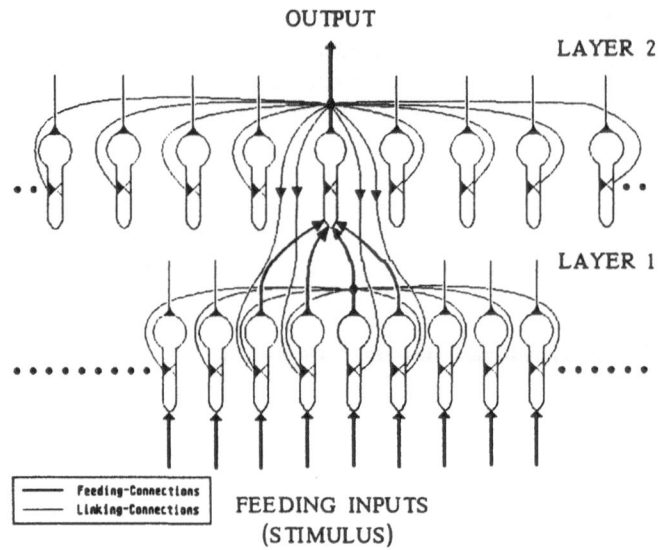

OUTPUT

LAYER 2

LAYER 1

FEEDING INPUTS
(STIMULUS)

| Feeding-Connections |
| Linking-Connections |

Figure 3.4 Scheme of the local connections in a two layer model network.

In summary: a two-layered network is able to link spatially remote parts of an object by synchronized activity. The two-layered network also has the property of the one-layered network to link moving parts of stimuli.

3.4 Negative Feedback for Stabilization of Linking-Performance

A general problem of every artificial neural network is the stabilization of its function over a broad range of input amplitudes and parameters such as the brain does. In order to stabilize the performance of our network, recurrent inhibitory connections have been introduced into the network. To the network depicted in Figure 3.4 broadly projecting negative feedback connections from layer-2 to layer-1 have been added as shown in Figure 3.7. This feedback decreases the sensitivity of the neural activity in the input layer by a negative shift of the membrane potentials after a stimulus in and around the activated region. Such a local feedback control results in highly enhanced correlation contrast between regions of synchronized stimulus-induced activities and in suppressed spontaneous activity in the surrounding region (Fig. 3.8B). Without this negative feedback loops 'the spatial' figure-ground-contrast is largely diminished (Fig. 3.8A). The simulation results show that the local negative feedback could be a neurophysiologically plausible way to ensure a stable network function.

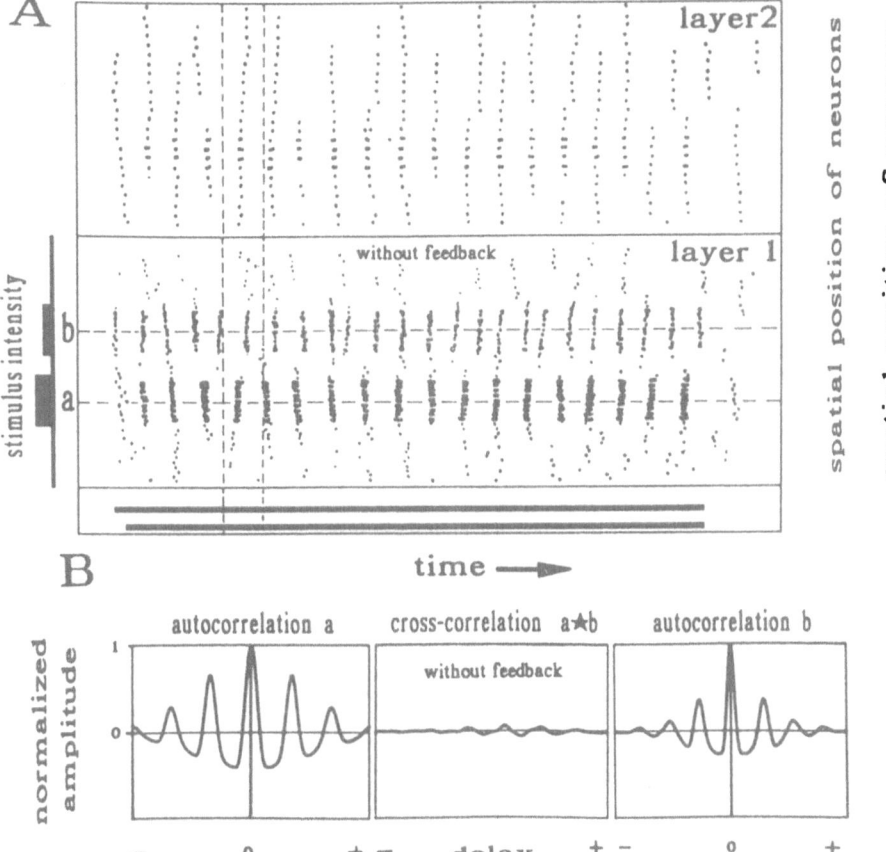

Figure 3.5 Simulation of a two-layer network. Two stimulus regions of enhanced intensity activate the feeding inputs of layer-1 To show the robustness of the model, we introduced two impediments: 1) the stimulus amplitudes at the "patches" differs by a factor of two, which causes the burst rates of the driven neurons to differ appreciably and 2) the stimuli are switched on at different times (from [7]).

A) Simulation **without linking** connections from layer-2 to layer-1: The neural activities within the patches are synchronized, while the activities of remote patches are not.

B) Auto and cross-correlograms of the spike activities of the stimulus patches at "a" and "b". The flat cross-correlogram indicates the desynchronization of the "local patch activity".

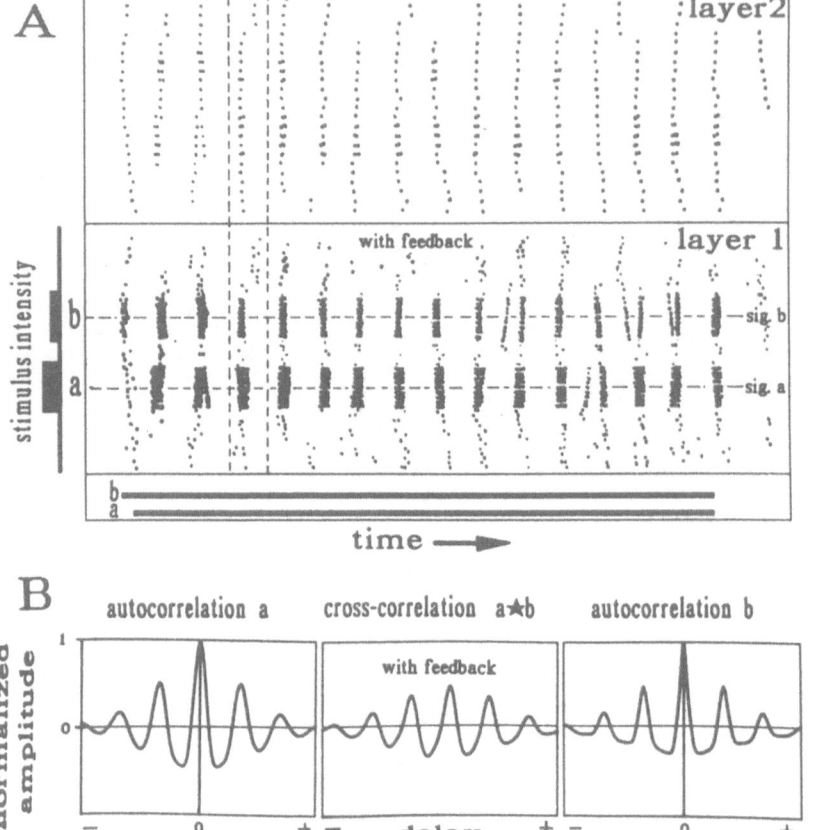

Figure 3.6 Simulation of a two–layer network. Stimulus conditions
the same as in Fig. 3.5 (from [7]).
A) Simulation **with** linking connections from layer-2 to layer-1:
The neural activities within the stimulated patches are
synchronized, as the activities of the remote patches are.
B) Auto and crosscorrelograms of the spike activities of signals at
"a" and "b". The periodic correlogram indicates their
synchronization.

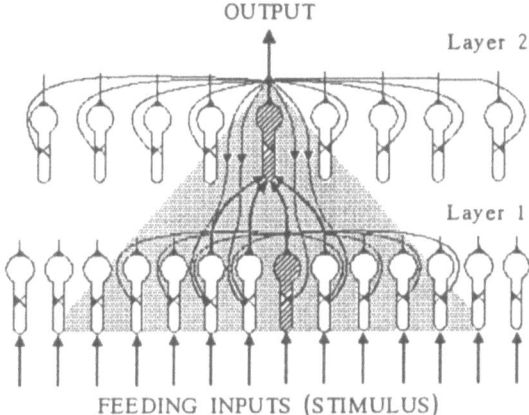

Figure 3.7 Local connection scheme of the two-layered network with additional wide-projecting inhibitory feedback connections. This scheme ensures stable performance over a wide range of stimulus amplitudes and simulation parameters. The shaded area shows the divergence range of the inhibitory projection from layer 2 to layer 1: 12 neurons of layer 1 receive weak negative feeding connections from one layer-2 neuron (from [8]).

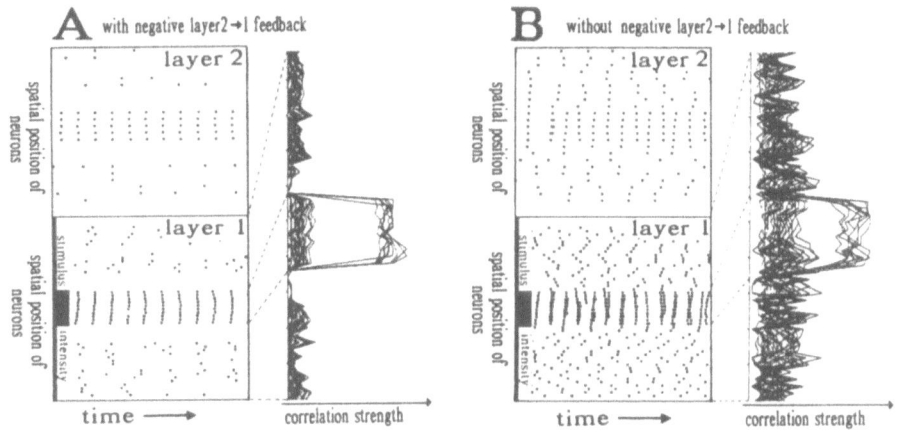

Figure 3.8 Correlation contrast is enhanced by negative feedback. To demonstrate this effect, the results of two simulations are depicted (from [8]):

A) Simulation of a two-layered network (Fig. 3.8) with negative feedback, spike-trains at left, the correlation profile at the right. The correlation profile is obtained by the spike-train crosscorrelation of each pair of neurons. The maxima of the spike-train crosscorrelations are depicted for each neuron at the neurons "location".

B) Simulation without negative feedback.

3.5 Combining the Dynamic Linking Network with an Associative Memory

In the previous simulations we modelled some properties of peripheral preprocessing in the visual cortex. In the simulation described in the following we extend the previous concept by studying the interactions of a (peripheral) lateral linking layer with (central) associative memory [9-12]. Dynamic associative memories as a fully connected layer of local oscillator circuits have already been investigated by other groups [13, 14]. These models, however, do not include a dynamic input processing layer that is able to link features via synchronization like ours (Fig. 3.9). In this simulation the strengths of the connections is modified via a global gain factor.

OUTPUT

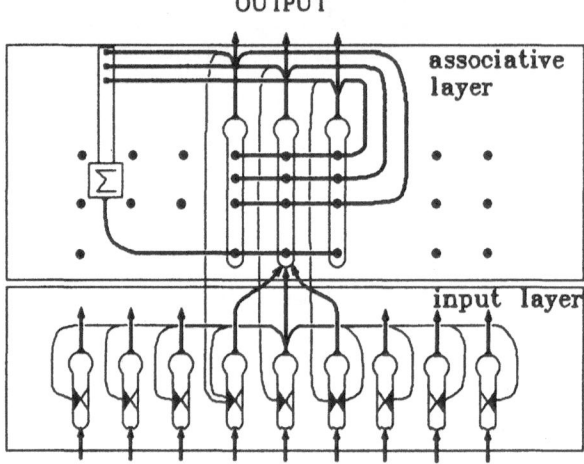

FEEDING INPUTS (STIMULUS)

Figure 3.9 The network consists of two layers (50 neurons per layer). Thin lines represent connections of the 'linking' type (lateral linking in the input layer and feedback linking from associative to input layer). Thick lines represent 'feeding' connections. A general feedback inhibition unit (upper left) regulates the activity in the associative layer. The stationary stimulus is presented to the one-dimensional input layer via feeding connections (from [9]).

The output activity of the first layer converges onto the second layer that acts as an associative memory [9]. In this layer, which is completely interconnected via feeding connections (i.e. each output is fed back to the inputs of all neurons), pattern completion and pattern competition takes place. A "winner-take-all" system is implemented via negative feedback of the global activity to all neurons of the memory layer (left in Fig. 3.9). The strength of this inhibition is determined by the total activity in this layer. Each neuron of the first layer also receives linking input signals via feedback linking connections from the corresponding neuron of the second layer. These "linkback" connections, whose strengths are also varied via a global gain factor, influence the formation of clusters of correlated activity in the input layer.

In corresponding psychophysical experiments rivalry between two inconsistent stimuli was frequently observed, with different interpretations oscillating with a period in the range of 2 s to 5 s. In order to mimic such rivalizations we presented to our model a stationary stimulus pattern which had the same degree of spatial overlap with three different patterns that were previously stored in the associative memory according to a Hebbian learning rule (Fig. 3.10: STIM, P1 – P3). Random noise was added to the stimulus. Figure 3.10 shows two examples of such simulations with different lateral linking gain factors in the input layer. For each neuron, a time segment of the spike activity is plotted. In both cases (Fig. 3.10A,B), the association switches between pattern P3 and pattern P1. The thin line at the top shows the magnitude of the global inhibition in the associative layer. The left part of each figure (Fig. 3.10A,B) shows the stimulus pattern (STIM, bottom) and the three stored patterns (P1 – P3, top). The right part shows the spikes of all 100 neurons in a time segment of 600 ms, in the lower segment the 50 neurons of the input layer and in the upper segment the 50 neurons of associative layer.

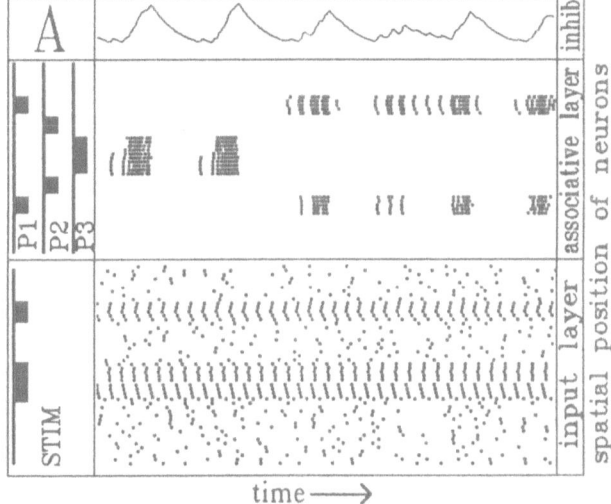

Figure 3.10 A) Simulations with weak lateral linking:
Time courses of spike activities (dots) and global inhibition (above) is shown. The activity pattern in the associative layer switches from P3 to P1.

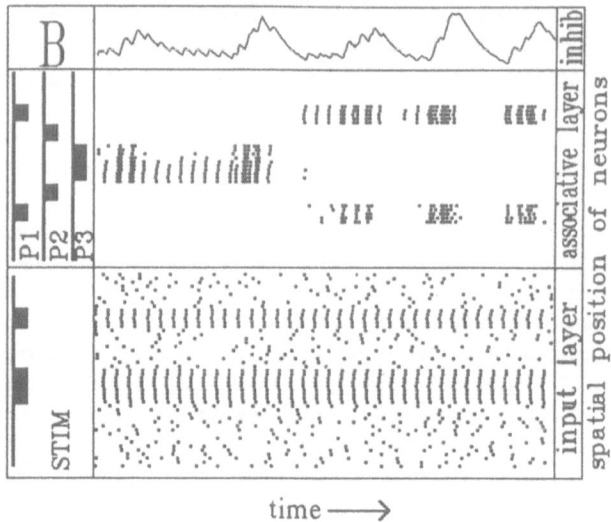

Fig. 3.10 B) Simulations with strong lateral linking:
Time courses of spike activities and global inhibition. The activity
pattern in the associative layer switches from P3 to P1.

A first result of this simulation is that the second (associative) layer performs
pattern completion according to the patterns stored via the connection strengths
within that layer. The second, and more interesting result of the simulation is that
the interpretations of the input pattern (corresponding to one of the three different
"associated" patterns) alternate in time (Fig. 3.10). The mutual interaction among
the individual neural spike activity in the associative layer and the global dynamic
inhibition results in bursting spike patterns and in rhythmic inhibition. Partly
activated patterns are thus "reconstructed" by positive feedback.

As mentioned initially, the associative layer also performs pattern competition.
If the stimulus pattern has the same degree of spatial overlap with more than one
stored pattern, it is ambiguous, which pattern should be completed. In this case
alternating interpretations (rivalry) of the same stimulus pattern are produced in
the associative layer as a result of the global inhibition mechanism in this layer.

Alternation between patterns on two different time scales are generated:
oscillations of individual neurons at about 50 Hz and the rhythmicity of global
inhibition at about 10 Hz.

The frequency of associations of patterns can be influenced by changing the
strengths of the lateral linking and feedback linking connections. With these
modifications the same network can perform different classification tasks.

For positive feedback and weak lateral linking (Fig. 3.10A) the spike activity,
evoked by the broader stimulus subregion, is divided into two regions of spike
activity, that are phase shifted relative to each other. This is caused by the

feedback from the associative layer. Because of their close neighborhood, the spike activity in this broad "stimulus block" is not so affected by noise as the spike activity evoked by the narrow block.

For strong lateral linking (Fig. 3.10B), the stimulus parts belonging to patterns P2 and P3 in the broad rectangle are synchronized. The feedback from the associative layer is not able to divide the activity block by a phase shift but can disturb the coherence in the whole block. So the synchronization in the whole block is weaker than in the phase shifted parts of the former case.

Hence those patterns stored in the associative memory that have topographical neighborhood in the stimulus domain are detected with similar frequency. This means that the coupling strength of the local neighborhood in the input layer can influence the association of patterns stored in a global connection matrix in the associative memory.

4. Discussion

We presented a series of simulations, demonstrating the effect of linking connections on the synchronization of output spike activities in differently structured networks of dynamic model neurons.

A simple two-neuron network demonstrates the basic linking mechanism of the model neurons: The output activities of the neurons are synchronized, if the difference of the input amplitude is smaller than a critical value, depending on the parameters. This means, that similarity in the input is transformed into similarity of the signal structure (i. e. synchronization of the action potentials).

Simulations of a one-dimensional one-layer network showed that synchronization of neural activity might be a fundamental mechanism to link local features together to a global "object". Even moving "objects" are represented by coherent assembly activity independent of individual neuron activity. One-layered networks with limited lateral connections are only able to link parts of an object over a limited range.

To link spatial remote parts of an object, a second layer is necessary. The activity of layer-1 neurons could be synchronized by layer-2 neurons with larger receptive fields via linking connections.

The introduction of negative feedback loops stabilizes the linking capability over a broad range of parameter variations and enhances the "correlation contrast" between object and surround.

Finally, an input layer with lateral linking connections has been combined with a second layer designed as an associative memory. This dynamic associative memory performs pattern completion and pattern competition like the models described in [13 ,14]. In contrast to these models, however, the intervals in which the neurons switch between associations can be much longer.

Switching between two different patterns is mainly achieved by the changing coincidence between parts of the activity caused by the stimulus in the input layer and the global inhibitory activity in the associative layer. The feedback linking connections generate a phase shift in the spike activities of the corresponding neurons. Patterns stored in the associative memory with topographical neighborship in the stimulus are detected with similar frequency. That means that the strength of the local neighborhood coupling in the input layer can influence the association of patterns stored in a global connection matrix in the associative memory.

5. References

[1] Gray CM, Singer W. Stimulus specific neuronal oscillations in orientation columns of cat visual cortex. Proc. Nat. Acad. Sci. USA 1989; 86: 1698-1702

[2] Eckhorn R, Bauer R, Jordan W, Brosch M, Kruse W, Munk M and Reitboeck HJ. Coherent Oscillations: A Mechanism of Feature Linking in the Visual Cortex? Mutiple Electrode and Correlation Analysis in the Cat, Biol. Cybern. 1988; 60:121-130

[3] Grossberg S. Neural Substrates of Binocular From Perception: Filtering, Matching, Diffusion and Resonance. In: Synergetics of the Brain, Basar E, Flohr H, Haken H and Mandell AJ, eds., pp. 274-298. Springer-Verlag, Berlin, 1983

[4] Reitboeck HJ. Neuronal Mechanisms of Pattern Recognition. In: Sensory Processing in the Mammalian Brain, Lund JS, ed., pp. 307-330. Oxford Univ. Press, New York, 1989

[5] Von der Malsburg C. Nervous Structures with Dynamical Links. Ber. Bunsengesell. Phys. Chem. 1985; 89: 703-710.

[6] Damasio AR. The Brain Binds Entities and Events by Multiregional Activation from Convergence Zones. Neural Comp. 1989;1:121-129.

[7] Eckhorn R, Reitboeck HJ, Arndt M and Dicke P. Feature Linking via Synchronization among Distributed Assemblies: Simulations of Results from Cat Visual Cortex, Neural Comp. 1990; 2:293-307.

[8] Dicke P, Eckhorn R. Stimulus Related Synchronizations in Model Networks: Sensitive and Stable Performance of Feature Linking is Ensured by Multiple Level Feedback. In: Synapse - Transmission - Modulation, Elsner, N., Penzlin, H (eds), Thieme, Stuttgart, 1991.

[9] Arndt M, Dicke P, Erb M, Reitboeck HJ. A multilayered physiology-oriented neuronal network model that combines feature linking with associative memory. In: Synapse - Transmission - Modulation, Elsner, N, Penzlin, H (eds), Thieme, Stuttgart, 1991.

[10] Willshaw DJ, Bunemann OP, Longuet-Higgins HC. Non-holographic associative memory, Nature 1969; 222:960-962

[11] Palm G. On Associative Memory, Biol. Cybern. 1980; 36:19-31

[12] Erb M. Simulation neuronaler Netze: Stabilität, Plastizität und Konnektivität, PhD Thesis, University of Tübingen, Tübingen, 1991.

[13] Wang DL, Buhmann J, Von der Malsburg C. Pattern Segmentation in Associative Memory, Neural Comp. 1990; 2:94-106.

[14] Gerstner W, Ritz R, Van Hemmen JL. Collective Oscillations in the Cortex: The Importance of Axonal Transmission Delays and Postsynaptic Response, Preprint, 1991

This project is sponsored by Stiftung Volkswagenwerk I/64605.

Theoretical framework for analysing the behaviour of real and simulated neural networks.

A.V.Holden [1], J.V.Tucker[2], B.C.Thompson[2], D.Withington[1] and H.Zhang[1]

[1] Department of Physiology and Centre for Nonlinear Studies, The University, Leeds LS2 9JT, UK

[2] Department of Mathematics and Computer Sciences, University College of Swansea, Singleton Park, Swansea SA2 8PP, Wales, UK

Abstract.

We outline the theory of synchronous concurrent algorithms, as it may be applied to models of neurobiological networks; and illustrate its application by an example of the behaviour of a neural network model (synchronisation and visual binding) and the formation and maintainance of a neural network (an auditory space map).

1. Introduction.

Sherrington's image of spatio-patterned activity in the nervous system as " a dissolving pattern, always a meaningful pattern though never an abiding one; a shifting harmony of subpatterns" [1] can now be assessed using multi- (or in reality pauci-) unit recordings [2], and the results of computer simulations of neuronal networks with plausible model neurones and neurobiologically motivated connectivities [3]. Neuronal activity is both irregular and patterned, and does show dependencies between the activities of different individual cells.

A common framework for describing activity in neuronal systems is that of nonlinear dynamics - a neurone may be represented by a map, or a differential (or compartmental, or partial differential) system; and a neural system by a network of such elements. Ideas from nonlinear dynamics that are current in neurobiological modelling are bifurcations, limit cycles, chaotic dynamics, transients and motion on an attractor, and basins of attraction [4,5]. Such a framework can deal with Sherrington's "harmony of subpatterns", but not with their meaning.

Even if a simulation of a neural system were to be exact, in the sense that the electrical activity in all the neurones was reproduced faithfully, it would not necessarily allow us to interpret the behaviour, and to discover what computational processes the network is performing. What is required is a general theoretical framework for simulating and analysing the computational behaviour over time of a network of processing elements.

We consider neurones as elements that compute and communicate in parallel, and propose the mathematical theory of synchronous concurrent algorithms (SCAs) as a rigorous mathematical framework that can be applied in the analysis of real and modelled neural networks [6]. An SCA is an algorithm based on a network of processing elements or modules or channels, computing and commmunicating in parallel, and synchronised by a global clock. SCAs process infinite streams of input data, and return infinite streams of output data. A general mathematical theory of SCAs has been developed using simultaneous recursive functions defined over classes of (many sorted) algebras [7]. The recursive functions represent the architecture (connectivity of a neural net) and the algebras represent the data sets (signals) and given processing elements (the functional elements of the nervous system - synapses, cells, neural assemblies, depending on the level of analysis). These tools allow very general formulations of algorithms and architectures that process any kind of data, and provide an elementary unified framework for the computational analysis of real and modelled neural networks.

This approach will be illustrated by outlining two case studies: a model for visual binding, and an approach to the formation of an auditory space map in the superior colliculus of the guinea pig.

2. Synchronous Concurrent Algorithms

2.1 Informal computational model

A *synchronous concurrent algorithm* (SCA) is an algorithm based on a network of processing elements called *modules*, connected together by *channels* that compute and communicate data in parallel and are synchronised by a global clock $T = \{0,1,2,....\}$. The SCA processes a clocked sequence $a(0)$, $a(1)$, $a(2)$, ... of data taken from a set A : this sequence is a function $a: T \rightarrow A$. Each module m is a computational device with n input channels and one output channel that implements function f_m : $A^n \rightarrow A$. Communication between modules occurs along channels that can transmit only a single datum $a \in A$ in any time cycle; channels can branch but not merge. A *source* is a module that reads data into the network: it has no input channels, and a single output. A network with n sources will process n streams a_1, a_2 , ..., a_n that form the vector-valued stream $a : T \rightarrow A^n$. A *sink* is a module from which data is read out of the network; it has a single input channel and no output channel. Two modules are *neighbours* if the output channel of one is an input channel of the other. The *architecture* is the structure of a finite network of modules connected by channels.

The terminology of this computational model can be mapped directly onto neural tissue as follows: the modules are neurones and incoming synapses, channels are axons; data are the temporal pattern of activity coming onto a synapse; sources are (sensory) inputs, sinks are (motor) outputs, and the achitecture is the structure of the neural network. Notice that in the definition of neighbour spatially adjacent neurones need not be neighbours. Thus we have a general language that can be applied to a discrete, time clocked model of a neural system to describe it in computational terms.

However, the terminology can also be applied systematically at higher levels in the nervous system. The essential point is that the modules now correspond to higher order functional units, rather than neurones. The same theoretical framework can also be applied to operations in the nervous system at any level where the operation can be specified by signal flow in a network of processing modules. The theory of SCAs thus provides a common framework for describing both the operational behaviour of the nervous system and the detailed behaviour of its elements

2.2. Formal model.

Let N be a SCA over a data set A with a clock T, and with $n > 0$ sources. The input to N is a stream $a : T \to A^n$. If N has $k > 0$ modules each with one output channel the initial state of the network is a vector $x = (x_1,..., x_k) \in A^k$, where x_i denotes the value output from the ith module at time zero. At each time $t \in T$ there is a single value output that can be determined from the t, a, and x. The *value functions* of the network are total functions

$$V_i : T \times [T \to A^n] \times A^k \to A$$

for $i = 1, ..., k$ such that $V_i(t,a,x)$ denotes the value output from the ith module at time t when the network is executed on input a and initial data x. The state of the channels is then given by *the value function* for the network

$$V_N(t,a,x) = (V_1(t,a,x),...,V_k(t,a,x)) \tag{1}$$

for each $t \in A$, $x \in A^k$.

To obtain equations for the value functions V_i of module m_i for each $t \in T$ we first need to define $V_i(0,a,x)$, and then obtain $V_i(t+1,a,x)$ from the values of $V_j(t,a,x)$ for those modules m_j which are neighbours of m_i. In the case $t = 0$:

$$V_i(0,a,x) = x_i.$$

If the ith module m_i has $n(i) > 0$ inputs and a functional specification f_i, then if at time t the input is $b_1,...,b_{n(i)}$ then the value output at time $t+1$ is $f_i(b_1,...,b_{n(i)})$. However, for $j=1,...,$ $n(i)$, the jth input channel is the output channel of either a source $\lambda \in \{1, ..., n\}$, in which case

$$b_j = a_\lambda(t), \tag{2a}$$

or a module $\mu \in \{1, ..., k\}$, in which case

$$b_j = V_\mu(t,a,x). \tag{2b}$$

Thus the equations for value functions of the network are

$$V_i(t+1, a, x) = f_i(b_1, ..., b_{n(i)}). \tag{3}$$

The indices λ and μ are independent of t, a and x and are determined by the architecture; in programming terms they are syntactic quantities.

For a specified architecture equations 2 and 3 collapse into a single system equation.

2.3. Network output.

The value function of the network V_N gives the output values for all the modules of the network; the output *from* the network are the values sent to the network's sinks. If the network N has $m > 0$ sinks, let $i_j \in \{1,...,k\}$ be the index of the module that supplies the jth sink with data (recall sinks have a single input and no output channel) then the vector of m values at the sinks at time t is;

$$F_N(t,a,x) = (V_{i_1}(t,a,x),...,V_{i_m}(t,a,x))$$

for each $t \in T$, $a : T \to A^n$ and $x \in A^k$.

Thus we have a formalisation that allows us to specify the output from a network of any architecture if we know the architecture, functionalities of the modules and initial inputs.

3. Case Studies

3.1 Synchronisation and visual binding

Sensory information processing is carried out by specialised systems of neurones that respond to different features of the sensory input, and are located at different parts of the cortex. Somehow a distributed representation of a single object gives rise to a unitary perception or triggers a behavioural response. In principle, a hierarchical convergence could unify these spatially separate representations of features, but this soon leads to a an explosion in the number of higher order cells required [8]. An alternative approach is provided by the observations of Gray, Singer *et al* [9,10,11] and Eckhorn *et al* [12,13,14] that neurones in the visual cortex that are activated by different features of the same object tend to fire in synchronised bursts. This synchronisation is seen in multiunit recordings, and as an oscillation in the extracellular field potential. This correlation in activity provides a mechanism for feature-linking, and coding global aspects of an input pattern.

3.1.1. Model

Since the process that is being modelled is synchronisation and phase locking among different neurones, it is natural to conceive of the component neurones as continuous state, continuous time elements *i.e.* differential systems. Neuronal geometry could be represented by a partial differential system, or a compartmental system. The separation of integrative (soma-dendritic electrotonic interactions) functions from information transmission functions (axonal propagation) by spike generation allows the representation of the neurone by ordinary differential systems - biophysical excitation equations [15,16], or gross simplifications such as modifications of Lapique's leaky integrator [17]. The discretisation of such continuous time models is considered in [6].

Modified leaky integrators have been used as elements in a neural network model for feature linking by Eckhorn and Reitboeck *et al.* [13]. The inputs to a model neurone are divided into two types, the *feeding* inputs that bring in the sensory information, and the *linking* inputs, which are the weighted outputs from nearby elements. The integrated linking input modulates (multiples) the integrated feeding input. Simple 1 or 2 dimensional, one or two layer networks of these elements, with the synaptic strength of the linking connections declining with distance, can simulate the experimental observations of synchronisation, and if a one to one correspondence between local neural activity and subjective sensation is assumed (equivalent to a local homunculus!) can mimic some visual illusions.

3.1.2. Model as SCA

Obviously the first aim of modelling is to simulate the experimental observations of synchronisation, and it is not all that difficult to simulate synchronisation in a system of coupled oscillatory modules. The real interest in synchronised oscillatory activity is its proposed role in generating associations and hence plausible models for higher cognitive functions such as attention.

Once we have an example of a neural network of oscillatory neurones that provides an adequate simulation of the experimental observations, the problem becomes one of relating its behaviour (or dynamics) with higher level functions. The theory of SCAs provides a framework within which a cognitive function (such as visual binding) can be specified in algorithmic terms, and the behaviour of the neural network model verified, using formally defined mathematical logics, that it fulfills this specification [18,19]

3.2 Computational maps

In the central nervous system many regions are organized in characteristic spatial patterns referred to as brain maps. In these maps there is a systematic variation in the value of a parameter across at least one dimension of the neural structure. The central nervous system contains topographic representations of sensory space in the format of maps. The structures containing topographic representations of space are composed of clusters of neurones which respond preferentially to sensory stimuli in a particular spatial location. The cell groups are arranged, within the structure, in such a way as to represent external space on a surface of the structure. Sensory space maps are either receptotopic or computational. The simple receptotopic projectional maps are typified by the visual and somatosensory systems whereas computational maps are required for the representation of auditory space.

3.2.1 Receptotopic maps

In receptotopic brain maps a spatially organized periphery (such as the retina or body surface) gives rise to central topographic representations of space via direct anatomical connections. In these two systems (visual and somatosensory) the subset of peripheral receptors activated by a stimulus is a direct function of the spatial position of that stimulus and the ordered systems of neuronal conections, which characterise primary sensory pathways, preserve neighbourhood relations and thus produce, at central neural relays, topographical replicas of the sensory periphery. In the visual and somatosensory systems these replicas constitute topographic maps of sensory space. Receptotopic maps are thought to be analogous with the continuous maps of parallel computers where some computationally relevant parameter is represented in a smooth and continuous manner [20].

3.2.2 Computational maps

In a computational map there is a systematic variation in the value of the computed parameter across at least one dimension of the neural structure. Many computational processes in the brain are not mapped, however, most of the computational maps discovered so far are involved in processing sensory information. In the auditory system, for example, many computational maps have been discovered such as maps of interaural delay and interaural intensity differences. The map of auditory space is, however, thought to represent the apex in a hierarchy of sensory processing [21]. It is this level of complexity that probably determined the relatively late neurophysiological demonstration of this brain map. Auditory space maps were first demonstrated in barn owls in 1978 [22] and in mammals in 1983 [23]. The sensory periphery of the auditory system, the cochlea, does not encode the spatial position of a stimulus. The ear performs a spectral analysis of sounds with each audible frequency transduced at a different point along the cochlea thereby producing a one dimensional 'place code' or map of this stimulus parameter. Thus the topographically ordered anatomical output from the coclea produces a template for the representation of sound frequency rather than the spatial location of a sound source. The generation of a topographic map of auditory space must involve transformations and processing that are not required in the other two sensory modalities. It is generally agreed that the coding of auditory spatial position, at least in the azimuthal axis, utilizes binaural cues of differences in stimulus intensity and time. Since a map of auditory space must involve the extraction and encoding of these binaural parameters, it is called a computational map [21] to contrast it with those spatial maps which are passive reflections of the sensory periphery. In mammals auditory space maps have been demonstrated in the midbrain structure the superior colliculus (SC) [23,24]. The SC is a multimodal structure containing not only auditory space maps but also representations of visual and somatosensory space, as well as motor maps (eg the elaboration of orientation movements of the eyes, head, pinnae and whiskers towards a novel sensory stimulus). In the SC the sensory space maps are spatially aligned with one another. The chronological appearance of the sensory maps is a reflection of the complexity surrounding their synthesis. Thus, the somatosensory and visual space maps can be demonstated soon after birth, whereas the representation of auditory space, even in a precocial species such as the guinea pig, displays a protracted developmental emergence [25].

3.2.3 Coupled maps

There is increasing evidence that the computational auditory space map relies, either for precision alignment or even for its initial construction and further maintenance, on bimodality experience

[26 - 30]. In the guinea pig the generation of an auditory space map in the SC relies heavily on sensory experience both during and immediately following its construction. In this species deprivation of visual experience during development prevents the emergence of an auditory space map in the SC [31]. The manner in which visual experience contributes to the construction of the collicular map of auditory space remains a matter for speculation. One line of thought is that visual deprivation exerts its effect through the absence of visually driven sensory input to the SC, and here it is worth reiterating that in the SC all the sensory space maps are spatially aligned. It is suggested that the normal development of the auditory space map requires coincident activation, at the colliculus, of neural activity from auditory and visual input arising from common stimuli. The topographic organization of the map results from neural mechanisms which recognize this coincident activation. They respond by arranging that input from a localized auditory stimulus is delivered selectively to the same collicular locus simultaneously receiving visual input from the same source [31].

Here we consider an equational scheme for a model of an auditory space map and then show how to derive an equational scheme for the auditory space map coupled with a visual space map.

The physiological significance of the two families of models of the two types of space maps we have discussed above in 4.2.1-2. Since we are here interested in exploring equational schemes for SCAs we will base our case study of the auditory and auditory-visual space maps on a previous specific mathematical model of binaural processing studied in Shamma, Shen and Kopalaswamy [32].

3.2.4 A model of auditory space

In [32] a neural network model is presented for binaural processing. Its architecture is given in Figure 1. Both the ipsi- and contralateral cochea give rise to n tonotopically ordered auditory nerve fibres, each of which has a frequency selectivity that can be characterised by the frequency for which it has the lowest threshold, the characteristic frequency. The ipsilateral and contralateral fibres are processed in an orderly matrix, so that at point (i,j) input x_i interacts with fibre y_j.

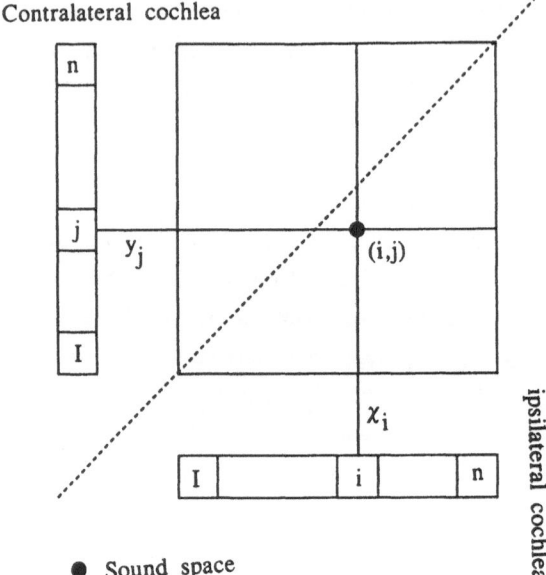

Contralateral cochlea

ipsilateral cochlea

Figure 1   ● Sound space

Auditory Space Map Equations

We will now formalize the description of the auditory space map model given above. First we will discuss the input-output behavior and then its architecture.

Input-Output

Let $F \subset \mathbb{R}$ be a set used to measure the nature of the frequencies input to the system from the cochlea.

Let $N \subset \mathbb{R}$ be a set used to measure the nature of neuronal activity at each point in the frame.

Let $T = \{0, 1, 2, \ldots\}$ be the clock used to sample input frequencies and govern the computation by the system.

The ipsi- and contra-lateral cochleas each generate n input frequencies at each time t. Thus each provide streams of input frequency data from the set $[T \to F]^n$. We use $y, x \in [T \to F]^n$ and write

$$y(t) = (y_1(t), \ldots, y_n(t))$$
$$x(t) = (x_1(t), \ldots, x_n(t))$$

where $x_i(t)$ = frequency input at cell i in the ispi cochlea

$y_j(t)$ = frequency input at cell j in the contra cochlea.

The auditory space map is modelled by a family $<v_{ij} \mid 1 \leq i, j \leq n>$ of stream transformations for the nxn frame. At each point (i,j) in the frame the transformation has the form

$$v_{i,j}: T \times [T{\to}F]^n \times [T{\to}F]^n {\to} N$$

where $v_{ij}(t,y,x)$ is the neuron activity at (i,j) at time t on processing stream of frequency data y at the ipsi cochlea and stream x at the contra cochlea.

Architecture and System

The definition of the v_{ij} proceeds in four stages as follows:

First, for each (i,j) we define a function

$$u_{ij}: T \times [T{\to}F]^n \times [T{\to}F]^n {\to} \mathbb{R}$$

which combines the frequency data of y_i, x_j at (i,j) using a function $c_{ij}: F \times F {\to} \mathbb{R}$, ie.

$$u_{i,j}(t, y, x) = c_{ij}(y_i(t), x_j(t))$$

For example, $c_{ij}(f,g) = (f+g)^2$

Secondly, at each (i,j) we generate a neighborhood or mesh $M(i,j) \subset \{1, 2, ..., n\}^n$ consisting of a set of locations in the frame. Thus, $M: \{1, 2, ..., n\}^2 {\to} P(\{1, 2, ..., n\}^2)$ and for example

$$M(i,j) = \{(i-1,j+1),(i-1,j-1),(i+1,j+1),(i+1,j-1)\}$$

The mesh $M(i,j)$ is used to sample response over a neighborhood of (i,j).

Third, we choose a threshold function $g: \mathbb{R} {\to} \mathbb{R}^+$ such as $g(r) = \max(r,0)$.

Further, we choose weights $w_{ij}(k,l) \in \mathbb{R}$.

Finally, we can combine these components to obtain the desired neuronal activity maps.

$$v_{ij}(t+1,y,x) = g(\Sigma_{(k,l) \in M(i,j)} w_{ij}(k,l) \cdot u_{ij}(t,y,x))$$

The equations for v_{ij} define the model of auditory space map and form a lateral inhibitory network.

Auditory - Visual Space Map Equations

Consider the effect of a visual map on the auditory map. Without many assumptions, either mathematical or physiological, we can define the input-output behavior of the composite system.

Input-Output

Let $R \subseteq \mathbb{R}$ be a set used to measure the nature of the stimulus received by the retina. An nxn retina receives and communicates nxn inputs at each time t. Thus, the retina provides new data streams to the auditory map of the form $e \in [T \rightarrow R]^{nxn}$ where for $t \in T$

$$e(t) = (e_{11}(t), \ldots, e_{1n}(t), \ldots, e_{n1}(t), \ldots, e_{nn}(t))$$

and $e_{ij}(t) \in R$ is the input received at point (i,j) in the retina.

The effect of the retina on the auditory space map is defined by a new family of stream transformers

$$w_{ij}: T \times [T \rightarrow F]^n \times [T \rightarrow F]^n \times [T \rightarrow R]^{nxn} \rightarrow N$$

where $w_{ij}(t, x, y, e)$ is neuronal activity at point (i,j) in the auditory map at time t on processing frequency data streams x and y through the ipsi and contra cochlea and retina input data streams e.

Architecture and System.

To define formulae for these w_{ij} requires a substantial analysis of auditory and visual maps. However, the theoretical framework easily classifies the possible forms of generalizations of the earlier auditory map equations given above.

How does the new data stream e influence the earlier model ? Clearly, each of the following characteristic components of the earlier model can depend on e:

    (i) comparison function c_{ij}

    (ii) mesh function M

    (iii) threshold function g

    (iv) weights function w_{ij}

We consider a simple case where only (i) depends on e.

A Simple Connection Between the Auditory and Visual Maps.

We suppose that the mesh selection functions, threshold and weights are characteristics of the auditory space map, and should be independent of retinal input data. We suppose visual information is used in the frame at the first stage of comparison and synthesis of signals.

Thus, we suppose for each (i,j)

$$c_{ij}: F^2 \times R \rightarrow \mathbb{R}$$

to allow the first stage of comparison $c_{ij}(r,s,e)$ to involve retina stimulus $e \in R$ and auditory stimulus $r, s \in F$.

Then we suppose a communication scheme or wiring diagram that connects in the visual and auditory maps: see figure 2.

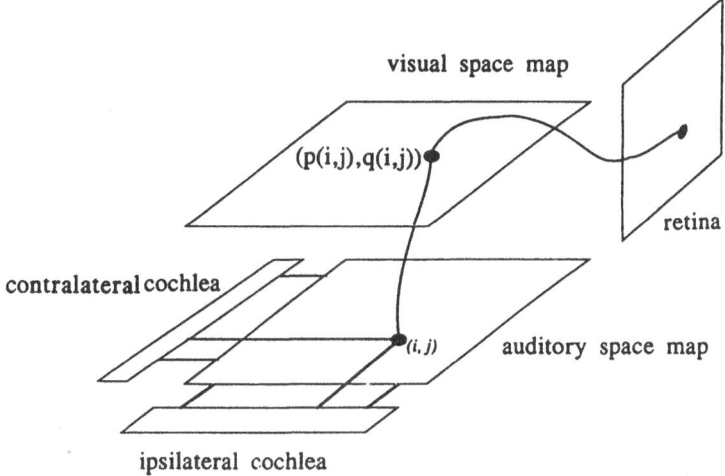

visual space map

$(p(i,j),q(i,j))$

retina

contralateral cochlea

(i,j) auditory space map

ipsilateral cochlea

Figure 2

We suppose that auditory point (i,j) is directly wired to visual point $(p(i,j),q(i,j))$. Then we redefine:

$$u_{ij}: T \times [T \to F]^n \times [T \to F]^n \times [T \to R]^{n \times n} \to \mathbb{R}$$

$$u_{ij}(t,x,y,e) = c_{ij}(x_i(t), y_j(t), e_{p(i,j),q(i,j)}(t))$$

Then the combined map

$$v_{ij}(t+1, x,y,e) = g(\textstyle\sum_{(k,l) \in M(i,j)} w_{ij}(k,l) \cdot u_{ij}(t,x,y,e))$$

4. Concluding remarks on the theory of SCAs

The representation of neural networks by formal computational models is a subtle issue, since different models characterise, or are chosen to investigate, different aspects of neural computation, and at different levels of computational abstraction. The theory of SCAs provides a framework for linking these different levels of abstraction

One important area of application of the theory of SCAs is the *specification* of architectures and behaviours of specific SCAs, and the *verification* that SCAs fulfill their specification, using formally defined mathematical logics. The issues of specification and verification are obviously important in computer science, for example, in the design and programming of hardware systems. Software tools based on the theory of SCAs have been developed [33,34]. These tools will be valuable in verifying neural network models implemented on novel,

168

parallel hardware systems.

For neurobiological applications, the theory of SCAs provides a framework within which network models for the execution of higher level operations can be rigorously validated. For example, one can specify what part of the nervous system is believed to be doing in terms of computational operations, and present a plausible network model based on the neurobiology of the system. The theory of SCAs provides a means of validating the consistency of these two algorithmic descriptions.

Acknowledgements This project is supported by UK MRC SRG 9017859

References

[1]   Sherrington, C.S. *Man and his Nature*. Cambridge Univ. Press, 1940
[2]   Holden, A.V. *Models of the stochastic activity of neurones*. Springer-Verlag, Berlin 1976
[3]   Holden, A.V. & Kryukov, V.I. (eds) *Neurocomputers and attention I neurobiology, synchronisation and chaos*. Manchester Univ. Press, 1991
[4]   Holden, A.V. (ed) *Chaos*. Manchester University Press, Manchester; Princeton University Press, Princeton 1986.
[5]   Amit, D.*Modelling brain function - the world of attractor neural networks* Cambridge University Press 1990
[6]   Holden, A.V., Tucker, J.V., & Thompson, B.C. The computational structure of neural systems. in [3]
[7]   Thompson, B.C. & Tucker, J.V. Synchronous concurrent slgorithms. Computer Science Division, University College of Swansea. Research Report 1991 (in preparation) [8]   Holden, A.V. Structural, functional and dynamical hierarchies in neural networks. In *A chaotic hierarchy* Baier, G, & Klien, M. (eds) World Scientific- Singapore (1991) 187-198
[9]   Gray,C.M., Konig, P., Engel, A.K., & Singer, W. Oscillatory responses in cat visual cortex exhibit inter-columnar synchronization which reflects global stimulus properties. *Nature* 1989 **338** 334-337
[10] Gray,C.M., Engel, A.K., Konig, P & Singer, W. Synchronization of oscillatory responses in visual cortex: a plausible mechanism for scene segmentation. In *Synergetics of Cognition*, ed. Haken, H. & Stadler, M. 1990 pp 82-98. S
[11] Engel, A.K., Konig, P.,Kreiter, A.K., Gray, C.M. & Singer, W. Temporal coding by coherent oscillations as a potential solution to the binding problem. In *Nonlinear dynamics and neural networks* ed. Schuster, H.G. VCH Weinhelm 1991 3-26
[12] Eckhorn, R., Bauer, R., Jordan, W., Brosch, M., Kruse, W., Munk, M. & Reitboeck, H.J. Coherent oscillations: a mechanism for feature linking in the visual cortex. *Biological Cybernetics* 1988 **60** 121-130
[13] Reitboeck, H.J., Eckhorn, R., Arndt, P., Dicke, P., & Stoecker, M. Neural network models for the simulation of basic visual information procesing tasks. In *Mathematical approaches to brain functioning diagnostics*. 1991 ed. Dvorak, I. & Holden, A.V. Manchester University Press 257-268
[14] Eckhorn, R., Dicke, P., Kruse, W. & Reitboeck, H.J. Stimulus-related facilitation and synchronisation among visual cortical areas: experiments and models In *Nonlinear dynamics and neural networks* ed Schsuter, H.G. 1991. VCH Weinhelm 57-75

[15] Holden, A.V. The mathematics of excitation. In *Biomathematics in 1980* ed. Ricciardi, L.M. & Scott, A.C. 1982 North Holland, Amsterdam. 15-47

[16] Holden, A.V. & Winlow, W. The nerve cell as a differential system. *I.E.E.E.Trans SMC* 1983 **13** 711-720

[17] Stein, R.B., French, A.S. & Holden, A.V. The frequency response, coherence and information capacity of two neuronal models. *Biophysical J.* 1972 **12** 295-322

[18] Hobley, K., Thompson, B.C. & Tucker, J.V. Specification and verification of synchronous concurrent algorithms - a case study of a convolution algorithm. In *The fusion of hardware design and verification.* ed Milne, G. 1989 347-374 North-Holland, Amsterdam

[19] Holden, A.V., Tucker, J.V. & Zhang, H. *in preparation.*

[20] Nelson, M.E., and J.M. Bower Brain maps and parallel computers. TINS **1990 13** 403-408.

[21] Knudsen, E.I., du Lac, S. and Esterly, S.D. Computational maps in the brain. Ann.Rev.Neurosci. 1987 **10** 41-65.

[22] Knudsen, E.I. A neural map of auditory space in the owl. Science 1987 **200** 795-797.

[23] King, A.J. & Palmer, A.R. Cells responsive to free-field auditory stimuli in guinea pig superior colliculus: distribution and response properties. *J.Physiol. 1983* **342** 361-381.

[24] King, A.J. & Hutchings, M.E. Spatial response properties of acoustically responsive neurones in the superior colliculus of the ferret: a map of auditory space. *J.Neurophysiol.* 1987 **57** 596-624.

[25] Withington-Wray, D.J., K.E. Binns, and M.J. Keating The developmental emergence of a map of auditory space in the superior colliculus of the guinea pig. *Dev.Brain Res.* 1990 **51** 225-236.

[26] Knudsen, E.I. Early blindness results in a degraded map of auditory space in the optic tectum of the barn owl. *Proc.Natl.Acad.Sci.U.S.A.* 1988 **85** 6211-6214.

[27] Knudsen, E.I., and P.F. Knudsen Sensitive and critical periods for visual calibration of sound localization by barn owls. *J.Neurosci.* 1990 **10** 222-232.

[28] King, A.J., M.E. Hutchings, D.R. Moore, and C. Blakemore Developmental plasticity in the visual and auditory representation in the mammalian superior colliculus. *Nature (Lond.)* 1988 **332** 73-76.

[29] Withington-Wray, D.J., K.E. Binns, and M.J. Keating A four-day period of bimodality auditory and visual experience is sufficient to permit normal emergence of the map of auditory space in the guinea pig superior colliculus. *Neurosci.Letts* .1990 **116** 280-286.

[30] Keating, M.J., K.E. Binns, and D.J. Withington-Wray Sensory experience and the construction and later maintenance of the superior collicular map of auditory space in the guinea pig. *Soc.Neurosci.Abstracts* **1990 16** 827.

[31] Withington-Wray, D.J., K.E. Binns, and M.J. Keating The maturation of the superior collicular map of auditory space in the guinea pig is disrupted by developmental visual deprivation. *Eur.J.Neurosci.* 1990 **2** 682-692.

[32] Shamma, S.A., Shen, N., and Gopalaswamy Stereausis: Binaural processing without neural delays. *J. Acoust. Soc. Am.* 1989 **86** 1989 989-1006.

[33] Martin, A.R. & Tucker, J.V. The concurrent asignment representation of synchronous systems. *Parallel computing* 1989 **9** 227-256

[34] Thompson, B.C. & Tucker, J.V. A parallel deterministic language and its application to synchronous concurrent algorithms. 1989 *Proc 1988 UK IT Conference* IEE 228-231

Coupled Neuronal Oscillatory Systems

Julie Hyde

Depts. of Applied Mathematical Studies and Physiology
University of Leeds
Leeds LS2 9JT
United Kingdom

Abstract

Central pattern generators can be modelled by systems of coupled oscillators. A technique of applying spatio-temporal symmetries to such models is discussed as a possible approach to classifying respiratory patternings in vertebrates.

1: Introduction

Motor output patterns of repetitive behaviours are by definition consistent and periodic. For example, during locomotion or respiration the same groups of neurones are repeatedly active. Although the motor pattern can be modified, the basic rhythm remains. Such motor behaviour possesses the feature of a nonlinear oscillatory system which may be modelled mathematically by systems of nonlinear ordinary differential equations. Here I discuss the application of symmetry and group theory to a system of coupled identical oscillators. Finally, this approach is put forward as a possible way to classifying different breathing patterns in terms of their spatio-temporal symmetries.

2: Neuronal Central Pattern Generators

Many behaviours generated by neural systems are rhythmic. eg. locomotion and breathing. Such rhythmic process may be generated by a chained reflex, or by a central pattern generator (CPG). A CPG is a network of coupled oscillatory subsystems of neurones or groups of neurones of the nervous system such that the overall behaviour of the CPG is oscillatory [1].

3: Vertebrate and invertebrate neural systems

Invertebrate neural systems provide several examples of CPG's where a detailed and almost complete description of their components, and

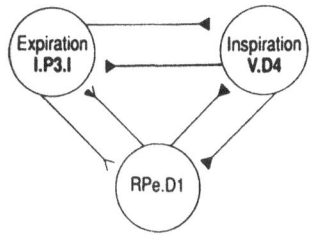

Fig 1. *Model neural network representing the CPG of the snail.*

their connections is available. One such example is the respiratory CPG of the pond snail *Lymnaea stagnalis*, which is thought to be controlled by two interneurones, labelled Input 3 (Ip.3I) interneuron and the Visceral Dorsal 4 (V.D4) interneuron. Ip.3I is primarily involved in expiration and the latter in inspiration. These respiratory neurones have reciprocal inhibitory connections with each other and synaptic interactions with appropriate motor neurones which control the opening and closing of the pneumostome [2]. (The pneumostome links the lung cavity with the external environment).

These two neurones alone are not sufficient for producing the repiratory rhythm. Adding a third cell, namely the giant dopamine cell of the right pedal ganglia (R.Pe.D1) is necessary and sufficient to reproduce the rhythm. This has recently been reproduced in an "in vitro reconstruction" of the CPG using cell culture techniques [3].

The mechanism described suggests that once R.Pe.D1 is added to the network, Ip.3I becomes excited by an inhibitory-excitatory input from R.Pe.D1.. This causes the pneumostome to open (expiration). Once Ip.3I is activated it excites R.Pe.D1 whilst inhibiting V.D4. V.D4 recovers and then fires a burst of action potentials causing the closure of the pneumostome, thus completing one cycle.

When in isolation, each of the neurones produces some repetitive pattern and so they can be thought of as oscillators, but it is only when the three are coupled with different degrees of coupling that we obtain the respiratory rhythm. The above description is illustrated in fig 1 where each of the neurones is treated as a nonlinear oscillator.

Vertebrate CPG's contain much larger numbers of component neurones, and so cannot (without access to supercomputer facilities) be simulated in detail. There is the problem of reducing a large, high order, complicated system of interacting oscillators to a simpler, lower order system. Mathematically, these systems can be suitably modelled by systems of nonlinear ordinary differential equations of the form

$$\dot{x}_i = X_i(x_i, t; \mu_i) \tag{1}$$

where x_i with $i = 1, 2 ..., N$ represents N independent variables and μ_i any varying parameters of the system. Approaches towards representing large systems of interacting oscillators by a few macroscopic variables are given by Kuramoto [4], who considers limit cycles whose shape is hardly influenced by perturbations, and so may be described by their phase alone, and by Biktashev [5], who attempts to generalise the mean field approach to explore the dynamics by a method that can be interpreted as a Galerkin procedure for the Master equation.

4: Quantitative and qualitative approaches to oscillatory systems

The parameters of the differential system in (1) may represent a biophysical variable or may simply be a mathematical parameter so that the physiological system is suitably modelled [6]. Qualitative changes in behaviour occur at critical values of certain of these parameters, a bifurcation point. If the ODE's for the system are known, the bifurcation curves may be obtained numerically. Ready made packages are available for locating equilibrium points and critical values of parameters which give rise to multiple bifurcation points of the system. [7,8].

Alternatively, if the equations to model the system are not known, then phase resetting characteristics can be studied. A mathematical representation is obtained in the form of phase transition curves or phase response curves [9]. Isochrones may also be studied experimentally. If an isochronal equation is obtained from fitting the experimental data, it is possible to obtain an equation for the dynamical system [10]. In physiological systems it is not unusual to find a certain degree of symmetry between different groups of neurones so an alternative technique which does not require numerical investigation would be to inspect the spatio-temporal symmetries from a structural model.

It is the application of symmetry to models of three and four groups of neurones that I will discuss in more detail. A basic knowledge of group theory is assumed although relevant definitions will be given.

5: Symmetry in three and four coupled oscillatory systems

It is first necessary to define three types of symmetry, namely *spatial, temporal and spatio-temporal symmetry.* *Spatial symmetry* refers to permutations of the oscillators (interpreted as neuron systems in a CPG) in a coupled system whereas *temporal symmetry* involves patterns of changing phase in the system. *Spatio-temporal symmetry* is a combination of the two types mentioned.

Definitions

Let the system of n identical oscillators be numbered $1,2,.....,n$.
At time t oscillator O_i, $1 \leq i \leq n$, is in a state $x_i(t)$. A permutation π of i is a mapping from the set $\{1,2,...,n\}$ to itself, and $\pi(i) = i'$.

The permutation π maps oscillator O_i to $O_{i'}$, and its state $x_i(t)$ to $x_{i'}(t)$. The state of the system is said to have *spatial* (or *permutational*) symmetry π if $x_i(t) = x_{i'}(t)$ for all times t and for all i. That is, after applying the permutation π, all the oscillators appear to behave as before.

To define *temporal symmetry*, it is first necessary to define *phase shift*. Let $x(t) = (x_1(t),x_2(t),...,x_n(t))$ be a time dependent vector representing the states at time t of all the n oscillators. The *phase shift* by ϕ of $x(t)$ is taken to be

$$x(t-\phi) = (x_1(t-\phi),........,x_n(t-\phi))$$

The *phase shift* ϕ is a *temporal symmetry* of $x(t)$ if for all t

$$x(t-\phi) = x(t)$$

so for our n-th order system for $i = 1,2,...,n$

$$x_i(t-\phi) = x_i(t)$$

Purely temporal symmetries arise only if $x(t)$ is periodic, so it is much more common to find mixed *spatio-temporal* symmetries. These are defined as follows:-

If π is a permutation sending each i to i' and ϕ is a phase shift, then we say that the pair $[\pi,\phi]$ is a symmetry of the state $x(t)$ if for all t for $i = 1,2,...,n$

$$x_i(t) = x_{i'}(t-\phi)$$

For consistency, the notation throughout will be for spatio-temporal symmetry. This means that if an operator on the system only requires a permutation, then it will be represented as the pair $[\pi,0]$, showing that there is no phase shift.

5:1 Three coupled oscillators

Fig 2a. *Three identically coupled oscillators with equal couplings and fig 2b is a possible model for the respiratory CPG of the snail. The solid and dashed lines represent different coupling strengths between the oscillators.*

A simple case to which knowledge of group theory can be applied is to consider three identical oscillators with the same degree of symmetric coupling between them [11].

There are two possible permutations of the oscillators. Either O_1 can be interchanged with O_2 or O_3. Let α (β) be the operation meaning each of the oscillators is interchanged with their neighbour in a clockwise (anticlockwise) direction. The permutations in cyclic notation are, $\alpha = (1\ 3\ 2)$ and $\beta = (1\ 2\ 3)$.

It is easy to see that α and β are inverses since the operation $\alpha\beta$ gives the identity element, ie. the system remains unchanged. At this stage it is necessary to define some useful notation that will appear in the symmetry table when considering the case of four coupled oscillators. Any group that involves all the possible permutations includes the symbol D_n, where n is the *order* of the element. (ie. n is the smallest number of times that any permutation has to combine with itself to give the identity). Z is used if the identity and one other permutation make up the group. A tilda ($\sim$) shows that the group involves temporal symmetry. The symbol S^1 refers to the 'circle group' of all phase shifts ϕ, taken modulo 1. The trivial case of leaving the system alone (the identity element-[I,0]) is included in the table for completeness (represented by 1).

In fig 2b, the only operation that would be feasible is to interchange O_2 and O_3. The permutation γ would be $\gamma = (1)(2\ 3)$. There exists no further suitable operations.

5:2 Four coupled oscillators

The symmetry groups for a system of four identically coupled

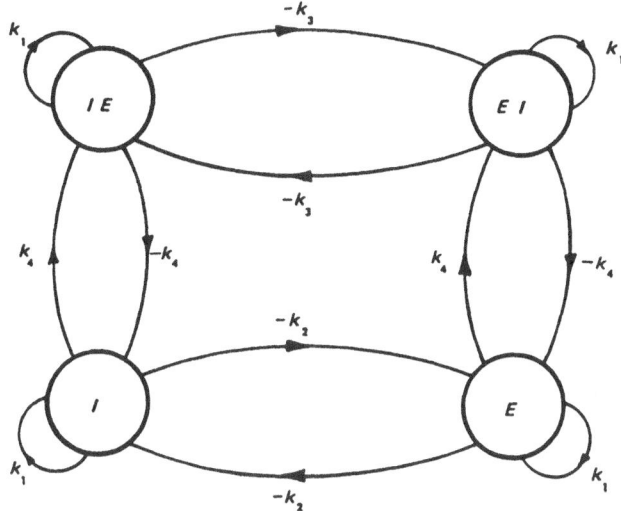

fig 3a. *The structure of the respiratory centre, showing the interconnections between the various pontine and medullar networks*
Bull math biophys, **34**, p473, 1972.

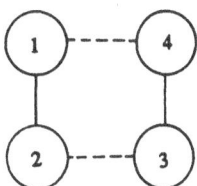

Fig 3b *A re-representation of Rubio's model. A system of four identical coupled oscillators with two distinct types of coupling.*

oscillators can be arranged in exactly the same way to that of the three coupled oscillators.

Neuronal models may not have such a high degree of symmetry. Rubio [12] gives an example of a mathematical system of equations representing the human respiratory centres. There are four centres, each of which represents a neural network, namely an inspiratory net, an expiratory net, an inspiratory-expiratory net or an expiratory-inspiratory net. The connectivity of the network is shown in fig 3a. Fig 3b shows a model representation, treating each of the networks as identical oscillators and setting two of the strengths of connectivity constants k_2 and k_3 equal to each other.

Applying group symmetry to the system 3b produces the following groups and subgroups shown in table 1 with the respective tree diagram.

Table 1. Possible symmetries of fig 3b

Let $\alpha = (1\ 2)(3\ 4)$ be front-back reflection, $\beta = (1\ 4)(2\ 3)$ be left-right reflection and $\alpha\beta = (1\ 3)(2\ 4)$ be their composite, which geometrically is an interchange across diagonals, or equivalently a rotation through 180°.

Symbol	Symmetries
$D_2 \times S^1$	$[I,\theta]\ [\alpha,\theta]\ [\beta,\theta]\ [\alpha\beta,\theta]$ for all θ
D_2	$[I,0]\ [\alpha,0],\ [\beta,0]\ [\alpha\beta,0]$
Z_2^L	$[I,0]\ [\beta,0]$
Z_2^F	$[I,0]\ [\alpha,0]$
$\tilde{Z}_2^D$	$[I,0]\ [\alpha\beta,0]$
1	$[I,0]$
$\tilde{D}_2^L$	$[I,0]\ [\alpha,\frac{1}{2}]\ [\beta,0]\ [\alpha\beta,\frac{1}{2}]$
$\tilde{D}_2^F$	$[I,0]\ [\alpha,0]\ [\beta,\frac{1}{2}]\ [\alpha\beta,\frac{1}{2}]$
$\tilde{D}_2^D$	$[I,0]\ [\alpha,\frac{1}{2}]\ [\beta,\frac{1}{2}]\ [\alpha\beta,0]$
$\tilde{Z}_2^L$	$[I,0]\ [\beta,\frac{1}{2}]$
$\tilde{Z}_2^F$	$[I,0]\ [\alpha,\frac{1}{2}]$
$\tilde{Z}_2^D$	$[I,0]\ [\alpha\beta,\frac{1}{2}]$

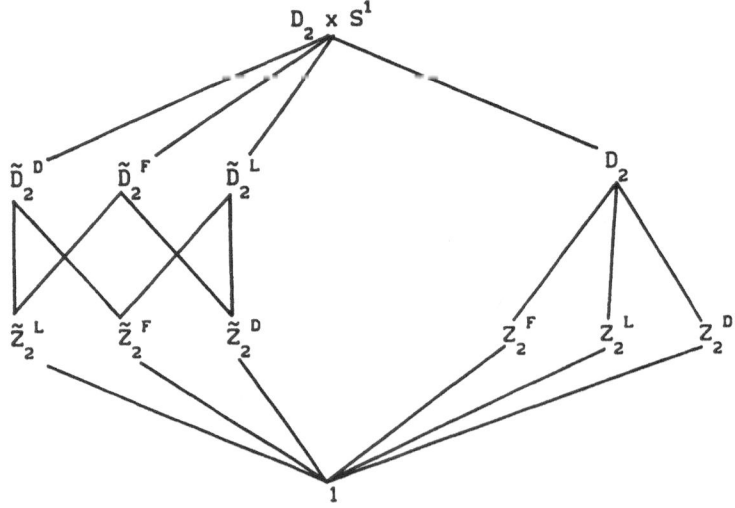

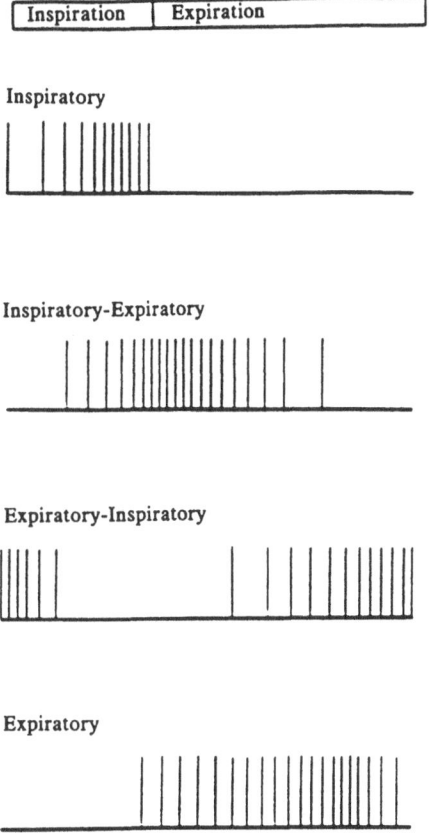

Fig 4. *The neurones firing in each of the inspiratory, expiratory, inspiratory-expiratory and expiratory-inspiratory networks.*

Different neural patterns will correspond to different ventilatory rhythms such as apneusis, panting, normal breathing, etc. Each of these behaviours can be categorized in terms of their spatio-temporal symmetries for possible different model representations of the respiratory system.

Normal breathing

Fig 4 shows when the neurones in each of the four networks are active. Inspiration is assumed to be the start of the cycle so it is set at phase 0. The phase at which neurones of other connecting networks start to fire is taken as the fraction of the period, from the start of respiration. One period is merely the time taken between successive

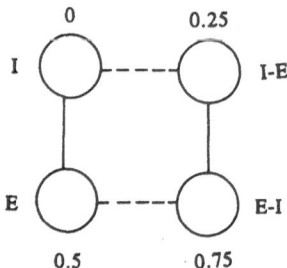

Fig 5. *Phase relations between the inspiratory (I), expiratory (E), inspiratory-expiratory (I-E) and expiratory-inspiratory (E-I) networks.*

firing of the neurones of the inspiratory network.

The neurones of the inspiratory and expiratory networks fire out of phase. That is there is a lag of half a period between the two. Similarly, there is a half a period phase lag between the firing neurones of the inspiratory-expiratory and expiratory-inspiratory networks. The neurones of the inspiratory-expiratory network start to fire, once inspiration has been active for about half of its duration, which is about a quarter of a period out of phase with the inspiratory neurones. The phase relations are shown in fig 5.

The only subgroup that can possibly represent these phase relations is $\mathbb{Z}_2^F$. ie. $[I,0]$ $[\alpha,\frac{1}{2}]$. For this model it is not possible to show any symmetries classifying the quarter of a period phase difference in the left-right symmetry. The effect of frequency on respiratory patterning has not been mentioned.

How can patternings with different symmetries arise and why do patternings change their symmetries depending on speed? Collins and Stewart (in relation to the symmetries of animal gaits) contend that such phenomena can be explained in terms of the general pattern of symmetry-breaking bifurcation in symmetric nonlinear dynamical systems, and in particular coupled oscillatory systems [13].

This could be a possible future approach once different breathing patterns for different oscillatory systems have been adequately explained and categorized in terms of their spatio-temporal symmetries.

References

[1] Selverston AI. *Are central pattern generators understandable?* The behavioural and brain sciences. 1980; 3:535-571

[2] Winlow W, Moroz LL & Syed NI. Chapter 4, *Mechanisms of behavioural*

selection in Lymnaea stagnalis. To be published.

[3] Syed NI, Bulloch AGM & Lukowiak K. *In vitro reconstruction of the respiratory central pattern generator of the mollusc Lymnaea.* Science reports 1990; **250**:282-285

[4] Kuramoto Y. *Synchronisation of pulse-coupled oscillators and excitable units.* Physica D May 1991; **50**:15-30

[5] Biktashev VM & Molchanov AM. *Macrodynamical approach to the analysis of neural networks.* Research Computing Center, Puschino. 142292, USSR. Preprint.

[6] Holden AV. *The mathematics of excitation.* In: Ricciardi LM & Scott A (eds) Biomathematics in 1980. North-Holland Amsterdam, 1982

[7] Petersen CK. *Techniques to trace curves of bifurcation points of periodic solutions.* Path User's Guide. Centre for nonlinear studies, Leeds, 1987

[8] Doedel EJ. *AUTO-Software for continuation and bifurcation problems in ordinary differential equations.* Calif Inst Tech, 1986

[9] Barbi M, Haydon PG, Holden AV & Winlow W. *On the phase response curves of repetitively active neurones.* J Theor Neurobiol 1984; **3**:15-24

[10] Hyde J & Rubio JE. *Synthesis of isochrones.* In preparation.

[11] Baesens C, Guckenheimer J, Kim S & MacKay RS. *Three coupled oscillators: mode locking, global bifurcations and toroidal chaos.* Physica D no 3, 1991; **49**:387-475

[12] Rubio JE. *A new mathematical model of the respiratory centers.* Bull math biophys 1972; **34**:467-481

[13] Golubitsky M, Stewart I & Schaeffer DG. *Singularities and groups in bifurcation theory.* Appl math sci **69**, vol 2. Springer, Berlin Heidelberg New York, 1988

Acknowledgements

I must thank I. Stewart for kindly allowing me to have a preprint of the paper "Coupled nonlinear oscillators and the symmetries of animal gaits". Without this, I would not have had the inspiration to relate their ideas to respiratory CPG's.

I am supported by a mathematical biology studentship from the Science and Engineering Research Council. This work was partially supported by UK MRC SPG 9017859 to Dr A.V. Holden.

Gamma-Band Oscillations in a Cortical Model

Rodney M.J. Cotterill and Claus Nielsen

Division of Biophysics
Technical University of Denmark
DK-2800 Lyngby, Denmark

Abstract

Computer simulation was used in a study of the dynamical behaviour of an anatomically-realistic model of the primary visual cortex. The model incorporated the inter-layer connections in a given cortical area, and also the forward and reverse projections by which adjacent areas in the visual hierarchy interact. It was found that the dynamical behaviour of a two-area model displayed oscillations at a frequency of around 50Hz, which lies in the so-called gamma band. The observed oscillations may have the same origin as those recently seen experimentally under certain conditions in the visual systems of cats.

1   Introduction

The recent reports [1, 2] of gamma-band oscillations in the multi-unit activity and local field potential recorded in the visual systems of adult cats has given rise to much excitement. These oscillations were particularly pronounced when optimally-oriented light bars were moved across the receptive fields in a coherent manner. If the movements were incoherent, the oscillations were not observed, and this led to the suggestion [3] that the oscillations are the mechanism whereby the visual system picks out coherent features from the random background. It was also suggested that these same oscillations would be the visual system's way of getting around the so-called superposition problem [4]. There have now been several reports of such experimental observations of these gamma-band oscillations, but there has until now been no theoretical study which has been able to unequivocally point to their origin. In particular, no reports of theoretical work have appeared which are able to account for the numerical value of the oscillation frequency. In the present study, such a value was produced, and it did indeed agree quite well with the observed value. As will be discussed later, however, the calculated frequency does depend upon certain assumptions regarding the characteristic times in single neurons, and to this extent the results reported here must be looked upon as being somewhat tentative.

2   Anatomical Background

The cortical model used in the present study differed rather radically from the majority of models used in cortical simulations. For a start, the interconnections between the various cortical layers were incorporated, and this is certainly a departure from the norm, in which a more simplified approach is taken. The interlayer connections have been established primarily by the experimental work of Gilbert and Wiesel [5], their data being applicable to the primary visual area in the cat. It is an interesting feature of the pattern of connections established by Gilbert and Wiesel that cells in some of the cortical layers actually receive both excitatory and inhibitory inputs. This is true of layer II + III, and also of layer IV. And because of the way things are connected up, these signals would not be received at the same time. On the contrary, the situation is that the excitatory input would invariably reach a given layer first, and this would be followed a few milliseconds later by an inhibitory input which will presumably dampen down the activity which had been provoked by the excitatory input.

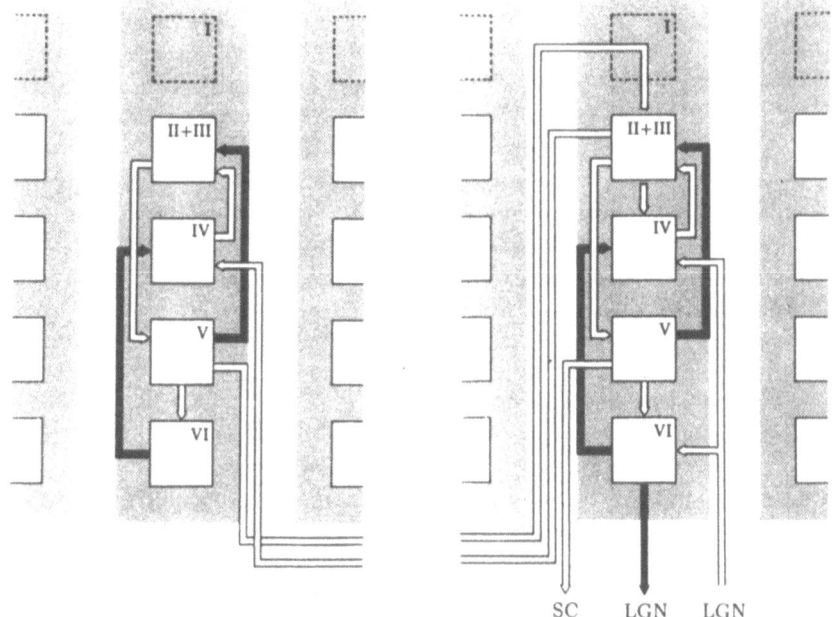

Fig. 1. Forward and reverse projections between two minicolumns (gray shading) belonging to two different cortical areas and also the intraminicolumn connections, (white, net excitatory; black, net inhibitory); the neuronal assemblies are symbolized by white rectangles. The righthand area connections were charted by Gilbert and Wiesel[5] for the striate cortex (LGN, lateral geniculate nucleus; SC, superior colliculus; neither was involved in our simulations), while the inter-area projections follow the findings of Maunsell and van Essen[6].

Equally interesting is the fact that this model, again apparently for the first time, has incorporated the pattern of forward and reverse projections that were charted primarily by the work of Maunsell and van Essen [6]. These workers discovered that the same pattern of projections are observed between successive areas, for at least five examples of pairs of areas in the visual hierarchy. As can be seen from Figure 1, the pattern is that the forward projection goes from layer II + III in one area to layer IV in the succeeding area, these connections naturally passing through the white matter. The reverse projection, on the other hand, goes from layer V in one area to layer IV in the preceding area, the route passing through the white matter and thence up through layer I, where presumably there are synaptic connections made with the distal dendrites of the layer IV neurons. This assumes that the distal dendrites of pyramidal neurons in layer IV stretch all the way up into layer I. This assumption has in fact been made in studies previously.

The other major anatomical assumption in the present work was that the cortical surface in a given area is segmented into minicolumns, the existence of which was originally postulated by Mountcastle [7]. Although the presence of such minicolumns cannot be said to have been unambiguously established, some sort of modular structure along these lines is frequently assumed to be present in the cortex. In the present model, it was assumed that all neurons lying on a given layer, within a given minicolumn, were essentially functioning as a unit, which we will here refer to as a neuronal assembly. The neurons in a given assembly were assumed to be roughly equally divided between excitatory and inhibitory sub-groups, and all neurons were treated the same, regarding the electrotonic response characteristics of their dendrites and also regarding the thresholds which determined whether action potentials would be generated. Upon injection of the activation at a given synapse, the membrane depolarization was assumed to be passed electrotonically to the somatic region, with a standard time constant, and its contribution to the somatic potential was assumed to decay thereafter in an exponential manner. This behaviour is typical of what usually goes under the name of a "leaky integrator". The dynamical simulations involved knowledge of the states of all the dendrites, somas and axons for all neurons on all layers and in all minicolumns of the entire model. The neurons were also realistic in that they were accorded a refractory period (of 8 ms), and membrane decay time (15 ms), whereas no allowance was made for the (surely very small) synaptic delay time. Within a given assembly, each of the excitatory neurons received activation from the outside and also from the other excitatory neurons, and it also received inhibition from the inhibitory neurons. Each of the inhibitory neurons, on the other hand, received only activation from the outside and from the excitatory neurons; the inhibitory neurons did not receive inhibition from each other.

3   Results

When activity is injected into such a neuronal assembly there is an initial period of about 5 ms during which nothing happens. This period of quiescence is caused by the dendritic delays, and it is followed by a rapid rise in the activity level of the excitatory cells. This rise is rather quickly brought under control, however, because the inhibitory interneurons are also quickly activated, and they send their inhibition back to the excitatory sub-group.

With the temporal response of a single neuronal assembly thus investigated, we then studied the dynamics of a system comprising two interconnected minicolumns, one in each of two different cortical areas designated ALPHA and BETA. The neuronal assemblies of particular interest were those lying in layers II + III, IV and V, and as indicated above, both the inter-layer connections within a given minicolumn and also the forward and reverse projections by which two such minicolumns are connected (via the white matter) had to be included. Thus the minicolumn in area BETA received forward projections from that in area ALPHA, and it sent reverse projections back to that area.

We followed the temporal evolution of the activity in this six-assembly system, and Fig. 2 shows the resulting pattern at 5 ms intervals. As can be seen from the figure, this pattern is in fact cyclic, and it has a frequency of approximately 40 Hz. It is encouraging that this simulated frequency is in good agreement with that observed experimentally, but, as we will discuss below, there may be good reasons for not taking this apparent agreement too seriously.

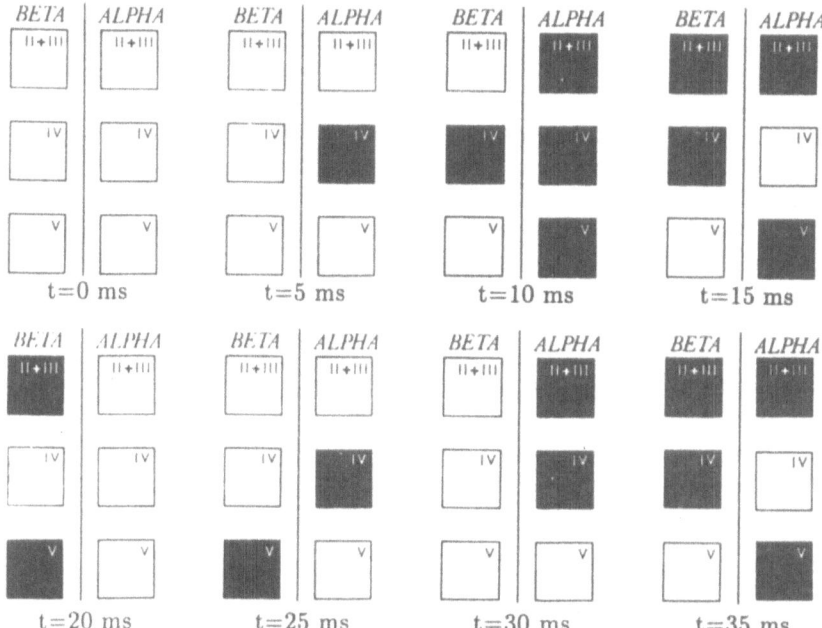

Fig. 2. Temporal evolution of the activity pattern (white: inactive; black: activity at the plateau level, at 5 ms intervals, for the relevant assemblies in interacting minicolumns in two cortical areas; activity was injected into layer IV of area ALPHA, at time zero, and the excitatory flow was thereafter passed on, in turn, to ALPHA II + III, BETA IV, BETA II + III, BETA V, back to ALPHA IV, and so on, the round-trip being 21 ms.

Each minicolumn in area ALPHA sends forward projections to only some of the minicolumns in area BETA, and it receives reverse projections from only a fraction of the minicolumns in area BETA. Moreover, there is no anatomical constraint which would cause this pattern of forward and reverse projections to be reciprocal. The closed inter-area loop suggested by Fig. 1 is thus only a minor contributor to the overall arrangement of connections between two areas such as ALPHA and BETA. Such closed inter-area loops can therefore only be minor contributors to the overall activity pattern, and the oscillations will primarily arise only when separated elements of the instantaneous pattern in a given area are in a high degree of synchrony. Indeed, looking at the arrangement of the connections within a given minicolumn, one can see that there is going to be an approximately 10 ms "window", this being imposed by the inhibitory influence of layer V on layer II + III. This requirement on synchrony will apply at each instant of the cyclic behaviour, and it will naturally also apply to the original input. Such a mechanism of discriminating coherent features in the input is similar to that which was proposed by Singer [3], but he envisaged the oscillations as arising within a single cortical area, as did Kammen et al. [8] and Eckhorn et al. [2]. We will have more to say about the differences between our model and that of these other authors later in this article.

Because (voltage-dependent) NMDA-type glutamate receptors are dense in the superficial layers and sparse in the deep layers [9], whereas the opposite is true of the kainate-type glutamate receptors and the quisqualate-type glutamate receptors, the conditional Hebbian mechanism discussed by Singer [3] might involve only reverse projections. We believe that this may be the case because the reverse projections involve synaptic connections made in the distal dendritic regions of layer IV neurons, these actually been known to extend right up into layer I. Our observed oscillations favour the NMDA mechanism, because the signals returned via the reverse projections impinge upon (layer IV) neurons whose membranes must have been depolarized within the previous 20 ms. This is less than the roughly 70 ms half-life decay time of the synaptic potential mediated by the NMDA-type receptors, and it fits in well with their observed rise time of 20–26 ms [10].

In order to investigate whether such unilateral synaptic modification would produce learning of patterns, we employed a model in which 64 minicolumns, arranged as an eight by eight array, were simulated in each of the two areas ALPHA and BETA. Each of the minicolumns in ALPHA sent 32 non-learning forward projections to (some of the) minicolumns in area BETA, and similarly, each of the minicolumns in area BETA sent 32 learning (Hebbian) reverse projections to (some of the) minicolumns in area ALPHA. The Hebbian time window was, because of the observed oscillatory period, roughly 25 ms. All of these synaptic links were exclusively excitatory, the overall activity level in the resulting patterns being controlled by the inhibitory interneurons. We believe that there is very good physiological evidence that this is the way control is achieved in the real cortex. As can be seen in Fig. 3, the time sequence for an injected activity level of 25 per cent does result in the re-establishment of the original pattern in area ALPHA, subject to minor errors for this particular activity level. We have investigated activity levels lying

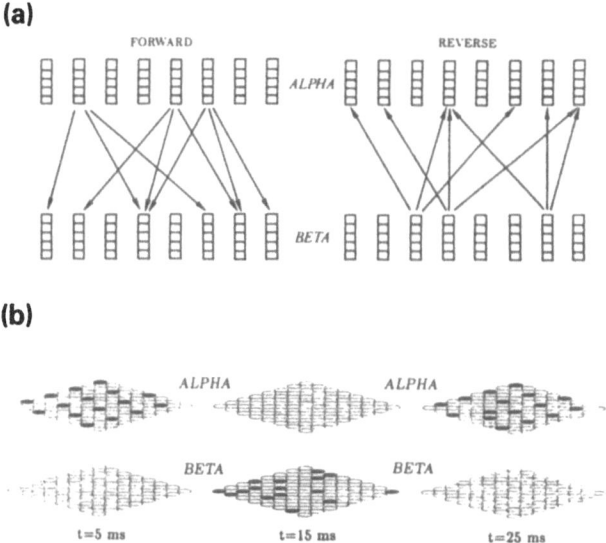

(a)

FORWARD   REVERSE

ALPHA

BETA

(b)

ALPHA   ALPHA

BETA   BETA

t=5 ms   t=15 ms   t=25 ms

Fig. 3. In Figs. 3a and 4a, the minicolumns are represented by elongated symbols, and they have been schematically drawn in one dimensional rather than two dimensional arrangements. The areas ALPHA and BETA, though actually located in different parts of the continuous cortical sheet, have been drawn in the topologically-equivalent arrangement of parallel lines, and the (exclusively excitatory) white-matter projections are indicated by the lines and arrow-heads. In Figs. 3b, 4b and 4c, the layer IV neuronal assemblies have been idealized to elipses, so that their two-dimensional arrangement can be indicated (black active, white inactive). (a) The forward projections enable certain minicolumns in BETA to detect correlated activity in ALPHA; correlations and their resultant activity pattern in BETA are detected by certain minicolumns in ALPHA, via the reverse projections, even though these are not merely reciprocals of the former projections. (b) A a time lapse sequence reveals that BETA mediates recreation of the pattern originally injected into ALPHA, with minor errors; the tensor network is able to store multiple memories in a superimposed and distributed fashion. (The illustration arbitrarily employs a symmetric input pattern, to facilitate detection of the errors.) The learning stage required 100 passes (i.e. 2s at 50Hz), for 1% learning rate.

somewhat lower and somewhat higher than this level, and no essential difference in the behaviour was observed. The activity pattern in area BETA has no geometrical significance. This area thus plays an essentially mediatory role, even though its behaviour is dictated entirely by the pattern of forward connections, as well as the pattern of activity originally injected into area ALPHA, of course. It is as if area BETA acts as a sort of "sounding board", for area ALPHA, enabling correlations in the input pattern to be captured and acted upon.

When area BETA receives forward projections for more than one area, it naturally serves to capture correlations in the patterns injected into both of those areas. To investigate this aspect, we also simulated a system in which minicolumns in two different input areas, namely ALPHA 1 and ALPHA 2, fed non-learning forward projections to a single associative area BETA, and they received learning (Hebbian) reverse projections from that area. This arrangement is shown in Fig. 4, and the resultant activity pattern in area BETA now arose from correlations provided by both sets of forward projections. The sounding-board function of area BETA was again observed, and it faithfully regenerated the two different input patterns, in their correct areas of origin. Moreover, the system was now able to function as an associator, following a suitable period of learning. Injection of only one of the input patterns belonging to a learned pair produced the other member of the pair at the appropriate input area, as can be seen in Fig. 4.

4   Discussion

Gray et al. [1] noted that oscillations in the gamma band might be mediated by neuronal interactions either within a single cortical area or between two different areas. In the simulations reported here, the oscillations could not occur in an isolated area because of the overriding inhibition return to layer II + III from layer V. It must be emphasized, however, that lateral excitatory connections within a given cortical area were not present in our model. It remains to be seen whether the inclusion of such connections would permit oscillations to occur in a single area, as Gray et al. [1] have suggested.

Our observed oscillations occur through the interactions of minicolumns in two different areas, the (globally) closed circuits being provided by the forward and reverse projections. Barlow [11] has suggested that the reason why the brain uses multiple areas is to enable it to capture correlations. Our area BETA is functioning in just such a manner, and it serves to detect coherent features in the input to area ALPHA. The recall mechanism illustrated in Fig. 4 suggests that cortical oscillations will be set up in an area that is not directly stimulated, provided that it is associatively linked with an area that is currently receiving sensory input. This possibility could serve as a test for the essential viability of the present model.

The observed latency following the injection of activity into a cellular assembly, in our model, agrees well with the duration measured by Douglas et al. [12]. Their work did not involve the non-linearities that stem from the inter-neuron interactions within a given assembly, and it naturally raises the question as to whether such interactions are strictly necessary in a simulation of the type reported here. We are currently investigating the behaviour of a model in which such interactions, (in a given minicolumn and on a given cortical layer) are simply omitted. If it transpires that the interactions are not necessary, this will be a strong indication that the primary significance of the experimentally-observed minicolumn structure is to provide such a minicolumn with alternative, but essentially equivalent, routes. In this respect, the brain could be said to exploit true parallelism. The word *true* is employed

(a)

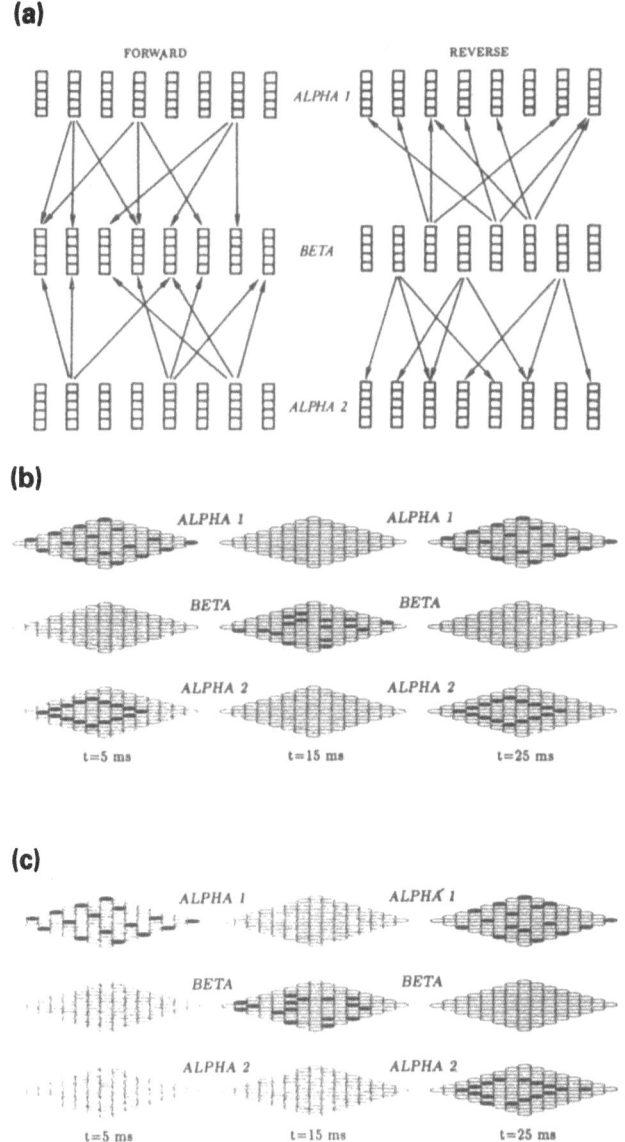

(b)

(c)

Fig. 4. (a) Area BETA is able to detect correlations in the activity patterns in two different input areas ALPHA 1 and ALPHA 2, if it receives forward projections from both of them, and (b) it is able to pass back information on those correlations if there are reverse projections to those areas. (c) When such a three-area network has been trained on pairs of patterns, injection of just one member of a pair is sufficient to provoke regeneration of the other member, with minor errors for the parameters used here.

here because the parallelism normally invoked in connection with the fan-out and fan-in arrangement often expressed by the term *parallel distributed processing* is of course not parallel at all. In the latter, the word *parallel* is being used merely to denote that processes are being carried out in different places at approximately the same time.

It is interesting to note that our observed BETA-to-ALPHA return time is about 10 ms which compares well with the approximately 6 ms measured from area 18 to area 17 by Bullier et al. [13]. But we have been reticent to identify area BETA with the anatomical area 18 because the latter also receives sensory input, whereas our area BETA does not. It might thus be better to look upon our area ALPHA as being a composite of sensory input areas. We have not, as yet, investigated a model involving actual input to two different areas, but we are currently doing just that. It remains a moot point, however, whether such an investigation should involve a model in which the two receiving areas should be connected only by the pattern of forward and reverse projections employed in the model reported on here. It may well transpire that the experimentally observed behaviour can be simulated only if further inter-area connections are incorporated.

Another point concerns the fact, which can be seen from Fig. 2, that the temporal response observed in area BETA is in approximate antiphase with that observed in area ALPHA. This fact alone indicated that it would be incorrect to identify area BETA with the anatomical area 18, because the observed oscillations in areas 17 and 18 are in phase. It remains to be seen whether further experimental investigations will produce antiphase behaviour, as is suggested by the present model. Indeed, recent magnetoencephalographic observations by Særmark et al. [14] indicate that such antiphase behaviour is observed experimentally, but that it is most prominent for oscillations in the beta band rather than the gamma band. It is possible that some of the time constants used in the present simulations are simply too short, and that lengthening them would then lead to a simulated oscillation frequency that was revised downwards towards the beta band. Were this to be the case, one would have the interesting possibility that oscillations within a given cortical area are in the gamma band, whereas those between different cortical areas lay in the beta band.

Consciousness is currently thought to be predicated on at least three different phenomena. For a start, there is very short memory, without which the senses would be deprived of their vital continuity. Such very short memory might be supplied by the reverberatry nature of the oscillations, be these in the gamma band, the beta band, or indeed by both of them. Another prerequisite for consciousness is what is known as binding, this being the mechanism whereby the responses of different modalities are kept in mutual phase when handling inputs from the same environmental stimulus. Were the brain to lack this ability, it could not establish the coherence between events that are related to the same cause. Again, the oscillations observed in the current model and experimentally would provide a manner of achieving this, through the phase locking that is an essential feature of them. Finally, there is the necessity of distinguishing coherent features in the sensory input to a given modality. This is achieved by area BETA in the present model, and it provides a distinction for coherent features in the sensory input injected into ALPHA. If it transpires that our observed oscillations are, instead, to be ascribed to the beta band, one would have to add the additional discrimination facilitated by the oscillations within a given cortical area as suggested by Kammen et al. [8], Singer [3], and Eckhorn et al. [2].

Crick and [15] Koch have mustered impressive circumstantial evidence supporting a mediatory role for gamma band oscillations in consciousness. They believe the oscillations may stem from thalamus-cortex interactions, rather than from inter-cortical interactions as observed in our model. It is possible, of course, that such gamma-band oscillations may occur in both regions. Our model did not specifically include thalamus-cortex interactions, which obviously must influence the dynamics of the overall system. The 3.4 ms average cortico-geniculate latency reported by Tsumoto et al. [16] does not preclude gamma-band thalamo-cortical oscillations. We are currently investigating the dynamical behaviour of a model in which these interactions are explicitly included.

5 Conclusions

An anatomically and biochemically realistic cortical model supports oscillations in the gamma band, as observed experimentally, and the model reveals that these are inter-area phenomena. But it is possible that some of the time constants used in the present simulations are too low, and this may necessitate a downward revision of the observed oscillation frequency, possibly bringing it into the beta band. The model predicts oscillations in areas that are not directly stimulated, provided that these are associatively linked to areas that are currently receiving sensory input. This suggests a test for the essential validity of the present model. The observed mechanism explains three components commonly associated with consciousness, namely very short memory, binding and discrimination of coherent features in the sensory input. The dynamical behaviour of a more extensive model system, which includes lateral inter-area connections as well as those between the thalamus and the cortex will be reported on at a later date.

References

[1] Gray, C. M., & Singer, W. *Soc. Neurosci. Abstr.* **404**, 3 (1987).

[2] Eckhorn, R., Bauer, R., Jordan, W., Brosch, M., Kruse, W., Munk, M. & Reitboeck, H. J. *Biol. Cybern.* **60**, 121-130 (1988).

[3] Singer, W. *Concepts in Neurosci.* 1, 1-26 (1990).

[4] von der Malsburg, C. in *The Neural and Molecular Bases of Learning* (eds Changeux, J. P. & Konishi, M.) 411-431, Wiley, Chichester, (1987).

[5] Gilbert, C. D. & Wiesel, T. N. *Vision Research* **25**, 365-374 (1985).

[6] Maunsell, J. H. R. & van Essen, D. C. *J. Neurosci.* **3**, 2563-2586 (1983).

[7] Mountcastle, V. B. in *The Neurosciences Fourth Study Programme* (eds Schmitt, F. O. & Worden, F. G.) 21-42, MIT Press, Cambridge, Mass, (1979).

[8] Kammen, D. M., Holmes, P.H. & Koch, C. In Cotterill, R.M.J. ed. *Models of Brain Function*, Cambridge Univ. Press, 273-284, (1989).

[9] Cotman, C. W., Monaghan, D. T., Ottersen, O. P. & Storm-Mathisen, J. *Trends in Neuroscience* **10**, 273-280 (1987).

[10] MacDermott, A. B. & Dale, N *Trends in Neuroscience* **10**, 280-284 (1987).

[11] Barlow, H. B. *Vision Res.* **26**, 81-90 (1986).

[12] Douglas, R,J., Martin, K.A.C. & Whitteridge, D. *Neural Computation* **1**, 480-488 (1989).

[13] Bullier, J., McCourt, M.E. & Henry, M.H. *Exp. Brain Res.* **70**, 90-98, (1988).

[14] Saermark, K., Bak, C.B. & Lebech, (to be published)

[15] Crick F. & Koch, C. *Seminars in the Neurosciences*, 2:263-275 (1990).

[16] Tsumoto, T, Creutzfeldt, O.D. & Legendy, C.R. *Exp. Brain Res.* **32**, 90-98, (1978).

Information Processing by Dynamical Interaction of Oscillatory Modes in Coupled Cortical Networks

Bill Baird

Dept Mathematics, and
Dept Molecular and Cell Biology
U.C.Berkeley, Berkeley, Ca. 94720
baird@math.berkeley.edu

Abstract

We show how hierarchical networks may be constructed of interconnected oscillatory network modules developed previously as models of olfactory cortex, or caricatures of "patches"of neocortex. The architecture is such that the larger system is itself a special case of the type of network of the submodules, and can be analysed with the same tools used to design the subnetwork modules. A particular subnetwork is formed by a set of neural populations whose interconnections also contain higher order synapses. These synapses determine attractors for that subnetwork independent of other subnetworks. Each subnetwork module assumes only minimal coupling justified by known anatomy. An N node network can be shown to function as an associative memory for up to $N/2$ oscillatory and $N/3$ chaotic memory attractors.

The modules can learn connection weights between themselves which will cause the system to evolve under a clocked "machine cycle" by a sequence of transitions of attractors within the modules, much as a digital computer evolves by transitions of its binary flip-flop states. Thus the architecture employs the principle of "computing with attractors" used by macroscopic systems for reliable computation in the presence of noise. Clocking is done by rhythmic variation of certain bifurcation parameters which hold sensory modules clamped at their attractors while motor states change, and then clamp motor states while sensory states are released to take new states based on input from external motor output and internal feedback.

Simulations show robust storage of oscillatory attractor transition sequences in a system with a sinusoidal clock and continuous oscillatory intermodule driving. The phase-locking or "binding" which occurs rapidly between coupled attractors of similar resonant frequency in different modules is important for reliable transitions. We show analytically how modular networks with more fault tolerant and biologically plausible distributed patterns can be built from "spreading activation" style networks which use single node representations.

1   Introduction

Patterns of 40 to 80 Hz oscillation have been observed in the large scale activity (local field potentials) of olfactory cortex [11] and visual neocortex [12, 13, 6, 7], and shown to predict the olfactory and visual pattern recognition responses of a trained animal. Similar observations of 40 Hz oscillation in auditory and motor cortex, and in the retina and EMG have been reported. It thus appears that cortical computation in general may occur by dynamical interaction of resonant modes, as has been thought to be the case in the olfactory system [9]. Given the sensitivity of neurons to the location and arrival times of dendritic input [17], the sucessive volleys of pulses (the "wave packet" of Freeman) that are generated by the collective oscillation of a neural net may be ideal for reliable longe range transmission of the collective activity of one cortical area to another.

The oscillation can serve a macroscopic clocking function and entrain or "bind" the relevant microscopic activity of disparate cortical regions into a well defined phase coherent collective state or "gestalt". This can overide irrelevant microscopic activity, produce coordinated motor output, and determine what goes into long term memory. Coherent ensemble activity may thus be an important medium of cortical computation. If this view is correct, then oscillatory network modules form the actual cortical substrate of the diverse sensory, motor, and cognitive operations now studied in static networks. It must ultimately be shown how those functions can be accomplished with oscillatory dynamics.

With this intent, we have constructed a parallel distributed processing architecture that is designed to model, however simplistically, the architecture of cerebral cortex. The goal is to accomplish real tasks that brains can do, using ordinary differential equations, in networks that are as faithful as possible to the known dynamics and anatomical structure of cortex. In this effort we hope to uncover novel design principles that may advance the art of computation.

The system may be viewed as a discrete-time symbol processing architecture, with analog input and oscillatory subsymbolic representations, constructed from a system of continuous nonlinear ordinary differential equations. Single network modules of the architecture have been sucessfully used for recognition of handwritten characters, and the capabilities of networks of coupled modules are being explored by application to the problem of word recognition from character sequences. Other approaches to oscillatory memory may be found in [8, 24, 16, 19].

1.1   Computing with attractors

In the design of this system, we follow an approach inspired by a particular concept of the physical structure required of macroscopic computational systems in general for reliable computation in the presence of noise. We view a computational medium as a set of structurally stable subsystems which can be coupled to form a larger system. By "structurally stable" we mean that the dynamical behavior of each subsystem is to a large extent immune to small perturbations due to noise or parameter changes. We assume that the dynamics of each subsystem is organized into attractor basins. As the overall system evolves in time (which could in principle proceed indefinitely), each subsystem passes through a sequence of attractors. *These sequences of attractors constitute the "computation" of the system.*

Present day digital computers are such systems. They are built of "flip-flops", which at the level of their transistors are continuous, structurally stable dissipative dynamical systems with two stable equilibrium states underlying the symbols we call "0" and "1". These states are attractors, i. e. returned to after small perturbations, because the flip-flops are "dissipative open systems" - each with its own source of power, and each continually dissipating energy to maintain its own equilibrium state.

We argue that the neuron itself is not the required structurally stable subsystem - it is not functionally a bistable element (flip-flop) whose activity is buffered against the effects of noise, even though it is commonly modeled as such an element in many neural networks. The output of most active neurons is a Poisson distribution of pulse intervals which suggests a firing threshold buried in noise. There are no such things as two-state neurons which go into hard saturation on either side of a threshold and stay there. An action potential is a brief pulse, not a step change of state. If repetitive firing is considered the "on" state, then the observed variation of mean firing rate with different levels of suprathreshold stimulation is unaccounted for.

We consider an intermediate "network" level of organization between the neuron and the whole brain - the "cortical area" to be the necessary structurally stable subsystem of the computational system that is the brain. We take a local population of neurons, possibly as large as a minicolumn, to be a node of the network. Its activation level is its average cell voltage or pulse output density. A network module then spans a "patch" of cortex which might be as small as a hypercoulmn in primary visual cortex, or as large as a cortical area, such as inferotemporal or prepyriform cortex. The patch then functions as a multiflop with many oscillatory attractors.

The computations of the brain that occur on the timescale of seconds are hypothesized to consist of transitions of attractors in these cortical area subnetworks that occur by interactions of the areas through learned (programmed) connections, as in cellular automata or Von Neuman machines. The tenth of a second time period required between successive voluntary eyeball movements or alterations of a motor action implies an internal clock interval at which new sensory data is sampled and motor output given. This interval allows for sucessive relaxations of internal subnetwork modules to their attractors, as is required for digital circuits.

In a digital computer, the binary flip-flop elements are made to bifurcate, say from the 1 equilibrium state being stable to the 0 state being stable, by changes in the signal or clock inputs. We hypothesize that the associative networks of the neocortex are clocked to change oscillatory attractors by the alpha rhythm at a 10 Hz "framing rate" under thalamic attention control — much as the olfactory system appears to be clocked to change attractors between 40 Hz "bursts" by the 3 - 8 Hz respiratory rhythm[2].

There is a demonstrable role for analog signal processing and motor control in the brain, but "computation with attractors" is also a necessity. Somewhere in the loop from sensation to action, an animal filters out many details of a perception to make a response choice that is invariant to those details. The hungry cat, seeing a mouse, engages in stalking behavior that is unaffected by most details of the mouse's appearance. Without the categories that can be established by basins of attraction, the world never repeats. The ability of humans and primates to manipulate internal visual and auditory symbols, as a subset of their capabilities, may be considered evidence that neural attractors are employed in some domains.

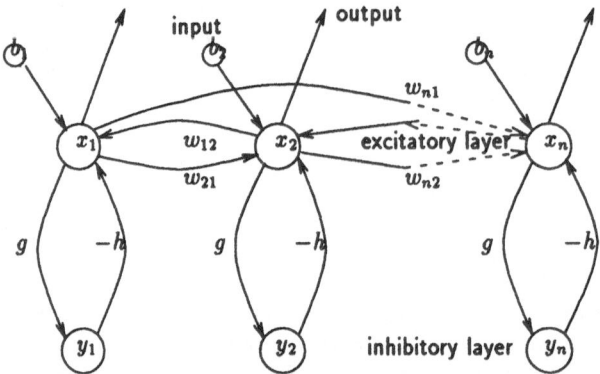

Figure 1: Biological subnetwork of excitatory cell populations x_i, inhibitory cell populations y_i, inputs b_i, adaptive excitatory to excitatory connections W_{ij}, and constant local inhibitory feedback connections g and $-h$.

2   Biological Subnetwork Module

We have determined a biologically "minimal" model that is intended to assume the least anatomically justified coupling sufficient to allow function as an oscillatory associative memory. The network is meant only as a cartoon of the real biology, which is designed to reveal the general mathematical principles and mechanisms by which the actual system might function.

Long range excitatory to excitatory connections are well known as "associational" connections in olfactory cortex[15] and cortico-cortico connections in neocortex. Since our units are neural populations, we can expect that some density of full cross-coupling exists in the system[15], and our weights are taken to be the average synaptic strengths of these connections. Local inhibitory "interneurons" are a ubiquitous feature of the anatomy of cortex [13, 7]. It is unlikely that they make long range connections (> 1 mm) by themselves. These connections, and even the debated interconnections between them, are therefore left out of a minimal coupling model. The resulting network is a fair cartoon of the well studied circuitry of olfactory (pyriform) cortex. Since almost all of cortex has this type of structure in the brains of amphibia and reptiles, our super-network of these submodules has the potential to become a reasonable caricature of the full cortical architecture in these animals. Although the neocortex of mammals is more complicated, we expect the model to provide useful suggestions about the principles of oscillatory computation there as well.

For an N dimensional system, this minimal coupling structure is described mathematically by the matrix T.

$$T = \begin{bmatrix} W & -hI \\ gI & 0 \end{bmatrix} \tag{1}$$

W is the $N/2 \times N/2$ matrix of excitatory interconnections, and gI and hI are $N/2 \times N/2$ identity matrices multiplied by the positive scalars g, and h. These give the strength of coupling around local inhibitory feedback loops. A state vector is composed of local average cell voltages for $N/2$ excitatory neuron populations $\vec{x}$ and $N/2$ inhibitory neuron populations $\vec{y}$. Intuitively, since the inhibitory units receive no direct input and give no direct output, they act as hidden units that create oscillation for the amplitude patterns stored in the excitatory cross-connections W. This may perhaps be viewed as a generalization of the analog "Hopfield" network architecture to store periodic instead of static attractors. Here the symmetric sigmoid functions are Taylor expanded up to cubic terms with third order weights (quadratic terms are killed by the symmetry). Network equations with this coupling plus these higher order excitatory synapses are shown below, in component form.

$$\dot{x}_i \;=\; -\tau x_i - h y_i + \sum_{j=1}^{N/2} W_{ij} x_j - \sum_{jkl=1}^{N/2} W_{ijkl} x_j x_k x_l + b_i, \qquad (2)$$

$$\dot{y}_i \;=\; -\tau y_i + g x_i, \qquad (3)$$

The competitive (negative) cubic terms of constitute a directly programmable non-linearity that is independent of the linear terms. Normal form theory shows that these cubics are the essential nonlinear terms required to store oscillations, because of the (odd) phase shift symmetry required in the vector field. They serve to create multiple periodic attractors by causing the oscillatory modes of the linear term to compete, much as the sigmoidal nonlinearity does for static modes in a Hopfield network [1, 3]. Intuitively, these terms may be thought of as sculpting the maxima of a "saturation" (energy) landscape, into which the modes with positive eigenvalues expand, and positioning them to lie in the directions specified by the eigenvectors to make them stable. A Liapunov function for this landscape may be explicitly constructed in a special polar coordinate system [1, 3]. We use this network directly as our biological model. From a physiological point of view, (2) may be considered a model of a biological network which is operating in the linear region of the known *axonal* sigmoid nonlinearities, and contains instead these higher order *synaptic* nonlinearities.

Adding the higher order weights corresponds, in connectionist language, to increasing the complexity of the neural population nodes to become "higher order" or "sigma-pi" units. Clusters of synapses within a population unit can *locally* compute products of the activities on incomming primary connections W_{ij}, during higher order Hebbian learning, to establish a weight W_{ijkl} (see figure 3.1). These secondary higher order synapses are then used in addition to the synapses W_{ij}, during operation of the overall network, to weight the effect of triple products of inputs in the output summation of the population.

Using only the long range excitatory em connections W_{ij} available, some number of the higher order synaptic weights W_{ijkl} could be realized locally within a neural population in the axo-dendritic interconnection plexus known as "neuropil" [2]. Only $(N/2)^2$ of these $(N/2)^4$ possible higher order weights are required in principle to approximate the performance of the projection algorithm [4]. The size of our cortical patches is limited by this number, and is itself motivation for modularity.

3 Learning by the Projection Algorithm

A key feature of a net constructed by this algorithm is that the underlying dynamics is explicitly isomorphic to any of a class of standard, well understood nonlinear dynamical systems - a "normal form" [14]. This system can be chosen in advance, independent of both the patterns to be stored and the learning algorithm to be used. This control over the dynamics permits the design of important aspects of the network dynamics independent of the particular patterns to be stored. Stability, basin geometry, and rates of convergence to attractors can be programmed in the standard dynamical system.

Here we use the normal form for the Hopf bifurcation [14] as a simple recurrent competitive k-winner-take-all network with a cubic nonlinearity shown here in Cartesian coordinate form.

$$\dot{v}_i = \sum_{j=1}^{N} J_{ij}v_j - v_i \sum_{j=1}^{N} A_{ij}v_j^2 \tag{4}$$

This network lies in what might considered diagonalized, or "mode," or "overlap," or "memory coordinates" (one memory per k nodes). For temporal patterns, these nodes come in complex conjugate pairs (with eigenvalues specified in J) which supply Fourier components for trajectories to be learned. Chaotic dynamics may be created by specific programming of the interaction of two pairs of these nodes.

The rule for learning desired spatial or spatio-temporal patterns can be shown to be equivalent to the operation of "projecting" sets of these nodes into "network" coordinates (the standard basis) using the desired vectors as corresponding columns of a transformation matrix P. The differential equations of the recurrent network itself may be viewed as linearly transformed or projected, leading to new recurrent network equations with general coupling T_{ij}, and general higher order weights T_{ijkl} corresponding to the cubic terms of the recurrent network [1]. The learning rule is,

$$T = PJP^{-1} , \quad and \quad T_{ijkl} = \sum_{mn=1}^{n} P_{im}\tilde{A}_{mn}P_{mj}^{-1}P_{nk}^{-1}P_{nl}^{-1}. \tag{5}$$

In the general case, the normal form (4) is projected to become:

$$\dot{x}_i = -\tau x_i + \sum_{j=1}^{N} T_{ij}x_j - \sum_{jkl}^{N} T_{ijkl}x_j x_k x_l. \tag{6}$$

The minimal network coupling (1) for T results from the learning rule (5) when a specific biological form is chosen, in the columns s of P, for the patterns to be stored. Only the higher order weights W_{ijkl} between excitatory populations shown in the biological module (2) are required for approximate pattern storage [4]. This special complex form for P^s and the corresponding asymptotic solutions $X^s(t)$ established are,

$$P^s = \begin{bmatrix} |\vec{x}^s|e^{i\theta_x^s} \\ \sqrt{\frac{g}{h}}|\vec{x}^s|e^{i\theta_y^s} \end{bmatrix} \Rightarrow X^s(t) = \begin{bmatrix} |\vec{x}^s|e^{i\theta_x^s + i\omega^s t} \\ \sqrt{\frac{g}{h}}|\vec{x}^s|e^{i\theta_y^s + i\omega^s t} \end{bmatrix}. \tag{7}$$

The phase θ_x, θ_y is constant over the components of each kind of neural population x and y, and differs only between them. This is basically what is observed in the olfactory bulb (primary olfactory cortex) and prepyriform cortex[2]. The phase of inhibitory components θ_y in the bulb lags the phase of the excitatory components θ_x by approximately 90 degrees.

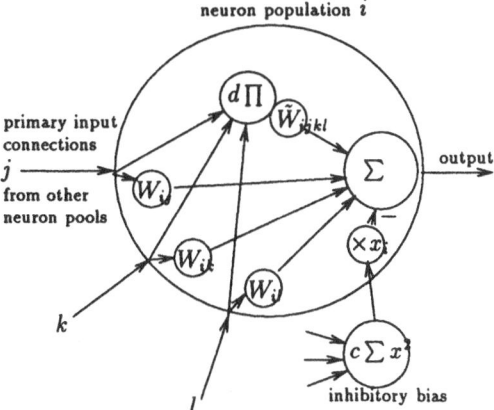

Figure 2: Neural population subnetwork acting as a sigma-pi unit. It uses secondary higher order synaptic weights $\tilde{W}_{ijkl}$ on products of the activities of incoming primary connections W_{ij}, and receives a global inhibitory bias.

3.1 Hebbian Learning

A Hebbian learning rule may be derived from the projection learning rule which allows a network to learn its attractor categories by local self organization of synapses and synaptic clusters according to pre and post synaptic activities experienced during external input driving. For orthonormal static patterns $\vec{x}^s$, $P^{-1} = P^T$, and the projection rule for the W matrix reduces to an outer product, or "Hebb" rule, and the projection for the higher order weights becomes a *multiple* outer product rule:

$$W_{ij} = \sum_{s}^{N/2} \alpha^s x_i^s x_j^s \ , \quad W_{ijkl} = c\delta_{ij}\delta_{kl} - d\sum_{s=1}^{N/2} x_i^s x_j^s x_k^s x_l^s \ . \tag{8}$$

When the Hebbian learning rule (8) is used, the higher order weights W_{ijkl} of the network model (2) can be decomposed so that (2) becomes,

$$\dot{x}_i \ = \ -\tau x_i - hy_i + \sum_{j=1}^{N/2} W_{ij}x_j + d\sum_{jkl=1}^{N/2} \tilde{W}_{ijkl}x_j x_k x_l - cx_i \sum_{j=1}^{N/2} x_j^2 + b_i \tag{9}$$

where $\tilde{W}_{ijkl}$ comes from the multiple outer product in (8), and $-cx_i \sum_{j=1}^{N/2} x_j^2$ comes from the $c\delta_{ij}\delta_{jk}$ term in (8). This single weight negative term corresponds to a shunting inhibitory bias which depends on the global excitatory activity of the network. "Shunting" here means multiplied by the current average cell voltage x_i of population i. This is an input which is identical for all excitatory neural populations and could be calculated by a single node of the network which receives input from all excitatory populations, as shown in figure 3.1. Such a node might correspond to one of the nuclei which lie below the prepyriform cortex. These send and receive the diffuse projections required to and from prepyriform cortex. The constants c and d of eq. (9) give the magnitude of the inhibitory bias c and the average higher order weight d. These constants come from the normal form matrix A, and, as we will discuss below, $c > d$ guarantees stability of all stored patterns. The greater the bias c relative to d, the greater the "competition" between stored patterns, the more robust is the stability of the present attractor, and vice versa. This is the mechanism employed later in the biological sensory-motor architecture for central control of attractor transitions within modules.

3.2   Programming the Normal Form Network

The key to the power of the projection algorithm to program these systems lies in the freedom to chose a well understood normal form for the dynamics, independent of the patterns to be learned. The Hopf normal form used here is especially easy to work with for programming periodic attractors, but handles fixed points as well. J is a matrix with real eigenvalues for determining static attractors, or complex conjugate eignevalue pairs in blocks along the diagonal for periodic attractors. The real parts are positive, and cause initial states to move away from the origin, until the competitive (negative) cubic terms dominate at some distance, and cause the flow to be inward from all points beyond. The off-diagonal cubic terms cause competition between directions of flow within a spherical middle region and thus create multiple attractors and basins. The larger the eigenvalues in J and off-diagonal weights in A, the faster the convergence to attractors in this region.

It is easy to choose blocks of coupling along the diagonal of the A matrix to produce different kinds of attractors, static, periodic, or chaotic, in different coordinate subspaces of the network. The sizes of the subspaces can be programmed by the sizes of the blocks. The basin of attraction of an attractor determined within a subspace is guaranteed to contain the subspace [3]. Thus basins can be programmed, and "spurious" attractors can be ruled out when all subspaces have been included in a programmed block [1, 3].

This can be accomplished simply by choosing the A matrix entries outside the blocks on the diagonal (which determine coupling of variables within a subspace) to be greater (more negative) than those within the blocks. The principle is that this makes the subspaces defined by the blocks compete exhaustively, since intersubspace competition is greater than subspace self-damping. Within the middle region, the flow is forced to converge laterally to enter the subspaces programmed by the blocks.

An simple example is a matrix of the form,

$$
A = \begin{bmatrix}
d & & & & & \\
& d & & & (g) & \\
& & \begin{bmatrix} d & c \\ c & d \end{bmatrix} & & & \\
& & & \begin{bmatrix} d & d & c & c \\ d & d & c & c \\ c & c & d & d \\ c & c & d & d \end{bmatrix} & \\
& (g) & & & & \ddots
\end{bmatrix},
$$

where $0 < c < d < g$. There is a static attractor on each axis (in each one dimensional subspace) corresponding to the first two entries on the diagonal, by the agrument above. In the first two dimensional subspace block there is a single fixed point in the interior of the subspace on the main diagonal, because the off-diagonal entries within the block are symmetric and less negative than those on the diagonal. The components do not compete, but rather combine. Nevertheless, the flow from outside is into the subspace, because the entries outside the subspace are more negative than those within it.

The last subspace contains entries appropriate to guarantee the stability of a periodic attractor with two frequencies (Fourier components) chosen in the J matrix. The doubling of the entries is because these components come in complex conjugate pairs (in the J matrix blocks) which get identical A matrix coupling. Again, these pairs are combined by the lesser off-diagonal coupling within the block to form a single limit cycle attractor. A large subspace can store a complicated continuous periodic spatio-temporal sequence with many component frequencies [3].

The discrete Fourier transform of a set of samples of such a sequence in space and time can be input directly to the P matrix as a set of complex columns corresponding to the frequencies in J and the subspace programmed in A. $N/2$ total DFT samples of N dimensional time varying spatial vectors may be placed in the P matrix, and parsed by the A matrix into $M < N/2$ separate sequences as desired, with separate basins of attraction guaranteed [3]. For a symmetric A matrix, there is a Liapunov function, in the amplitude equations of a polar coordinate version of the normal form, which governs the approach of initial states to stored trajectories.

3.3   Chaotic Attractors

Chaotic attractors may be created in this normal form, with sigmoid nonlinearities added to the right hand side, $v_i \rightarrow tanh(v_i)$. The sigmoids yield a spectrum of higher order terms that break the phase shift symmetry of the system. Two oscillatory pairs of nodes like those programmed in the block above can then be programmed to interact chaotically. In our simulations, for example, if we set the upper block of d entries to -1, and the lower to 1, and replace the upper c entries with 4.0, and the lower with -0.4, we get a chaotic attractor of dimension less than four, but greater than three [5].

This is "weak" or "phase coherent" chaos that is still nearly periodic. It is created by the broken symmetry, when a homoclinic tangle occurs to break up an invariant 3-torus in the flow [14]. This is the Ruelle-Takens route to chaos and has been observed in Taylor-Couette flow when both cylnders are rotated. Experiments of Freeman have suggested that chaotic attractors of the above dimension occur in the olfactory system [10]. These might most naturally occur by the interaction of oscillatory modes. We have demonstrated in simulations as well that a network with multiple Lorenz attractors can be created simply by adding off-diagonal normal form competitive terms to couple sets of the three Lorenz equations [5].

In normal form, or in a biological network, these chaotic attractors have a basin of attraction in the N dimensional state space that constitues a category, just like any other attractor in this system. They are, however, "fuzzy" attractors, and there may be computational advantages to the basins of attraction (categories) produced by chaotic attractors, or to the effects their outputs have as fuzzy inputs to other network modules. The particular N dimensional spatio-temporal patterns learned for the four components of these chaotically paired modes may be considered a coordinate specific "encoding" of the strange attractor, which may constitute a recognizable input to another network, if it falls within some learned basin of attraction. While the details of the trajectory of a strange attractor in any real physical continuous dynamical system are lost in the noise, there is still a particular statistical structure to the attractor which is a recognizable "signature".

4 Architecture of Subnetwork Modules

Because we have developed this class of mathematically well-understood associative memory networks, we can take a constructive approach to building a cortical architecture, using these networks as modules, in the same way that digital computers may be designed from well behaved flip-flop circuits. The operation of the architecture can be precisely specified, even though the outcome of a particular computation set up by the programmed connections may be unknown.

Each module is described in normal form or "mode" coordinates as the k-winner-take-all network discussed above, where the winning set of units may have static, periodic or chaotic dynamics. By choosing modules to have only two attractors, networks can be built which are similar to networks using binary units. There can be fully recurrent connections between modules. The entire super-network of connected modules, however, is itself a polynomial network that can be projected into standard network coordinates like those for the biological model. The attractors within the modules may then be distributed patterns like those described for the biological model (7), and observed experimentally in the olfactory system [11]. The system is still equivalent to the architecture of modules in normal form, however, and may easily be designed, simulated, and theoretically evaluated in these coordinates.

We show here how normal form subnetworks maybe coupled with connections learned by a sequence learning algorithm, and this larger network itself may be projected without destroying the identity of the subnetworks. The A matrix for a network module like that described above may itself become a block on the diagonal in the matrix A^* of a larger "super-network". The overall network matrix A^* is then like a large normal form A matrix with zero elements in the off-diagonal region outside the diagonal A blocks that define multiple attractors for the modules. The modules neither compete nor combine states, in the absence of A^* matrix coupling between them, but take states independently based on their inputs to each other through the weights in a matrix J^*. What is new here is that J^* is allowed to have nonzero off-diagonal elements that provide coupling between the blocks J along the diagonal that define the modules. There can be fully recurrent connections J_{ij}^* between module J blocks, but not within, so that the modules themselves remain in normal form - with J matrices having real or complex conjugate eigenvalues on the diagonal.

For simplicity, we first consider the case of modules with static attractors. For a three subnetwork system, of three N dimensional modules, for example, the matrix P^* for the supernet contains diagonal N dimensional block matrices B, C, and D with distributed attractor patterns in their columns to be assigned to the corresponding three subnetworks. Input might be wired into the units of the first subnetwork B, and output taken from the the third module D, leaving C as a "hidden" subnetwork which takes, after learning, the attractor states required to produce desired output sequences for given input sequences. Here, for simplicity, we choose identical postive real eigenvalues $\alpha = 1$ in the J matrix blocks which determine static attractors for the modules. Thus the matrix J^* of the supernet appears with the identity I (actually αI) in the diagonal blocks, but has further weights in the matrices F, G, H, K, L, and M in the off-diagonal grid of blocks that define interconnections between the subnetwork blocks,

$$P^* = \begin{bmatrix} B & & \\ & C & \\ & & D \end{bmatrix}, \quad J^* = \begin{bmatrix} I & F & G \\ H & I & K \\ L & M & I \end{bmatrix}, \quad P^{*-1} = \begin{bmatrix} B^{-1} & & \\ & C^{-1} & \\ & & D^{-1} \end{bmatrix}.$$

Now J^* can be decomposed,

$$J^* = I + J^{*'}, \ where \ J^{*'} = \begin{bmatrix} 0 & F & G \\ H & 0 & K \\ L & M & 0 \end{bmatrix}, \ so \ P^* J^* P^{*-1} = P^* I P^{*-1} + P^* J^{*'} P^{*-1},$$

$$hence \quad T^* = I + P^* J^{*'} P^{*-1} = \begin{bmatrix} I & BFC^{-1} & BGD^{-1} \\ CHB^{-1} & I & CKD^{-1} \\ DLB^{-1} & DMC^{-1} & I \end{bmatrix}.$$

Thus the diagonal and the off-diagonal blocks can be transformed independently - they do not affect each other's transform. The *higher order terms* for each subnet transform independently as well, and no terms cross-connecting subnets are generated. For all terms T^*_{ijkl} which have any index i, j, k, or l outside of a subnet block, the corresponding term of P^* or P^{*-1} is zero, and zeros all terms of the summation over m and n to guarantee that T^*_{ijkl} must be zero.

The identity of the individual subnetwork patches is preserved by the transformation (projection) from normal form to network coordinates. The connections *within* patches in network coordinates determine the particular distributed patterns that correspond to nodes in the normal form coordinates. The between-patch connections in network coordinates are transformed from those learned to effect transitions between winning nodes in normal form coordinates; they now effect transitions between the corresponding distributed patterns in the patches.

For an architecture with biological network modules, the J^* and P^* matrices contain blocks with complex conjugate eigenvalues and eigenvectors respectively. When each sub block of P^* has the form (7) shown previously for oscillatory attractors, then the connections within each diagonal block of T^* have the form (1) shown for the biological module. There are then nonzero entries in the upper left quadrants of the grid of blocks in the off-diagonal region which contain weights for the connections between excitatory elements of the subnetworks.

The higher order terms for each subnet are independent, as before, and take the same form as they would without being embedded in a super-network. Pairs of the complex conjugate coordinate axes for oscillators in normal form coordinates can be set up by the coupling for a module within an A^* matrix block to produce chaotic attractors as described above. For these systems with oscillatory or chaotic attractors, the weights between subnetworks implicitly encode frequency and vector valued amplitude and phase pattern information in order to effect transitions to the proper dynamic attractors.

A network can thus be designed or analysed in normal form coordinates as a "spreading activation" style network (only one node within a subnet is "activated" over others) where "concepts" correspond to single nodes, but can be transformed to operate with any of these more fault tolerant and biologically plausible attractors, where concepts (symbols) are distributed (possibly dynamic) patterns. For example, a super-network with can be constructed with modules in normal form coordinates that correspond to the "cortical patches" with competitive winner take all dynamics used in an architecture due to Schmidhuber [22]. The intermodule connections can then be trained in these coordinates by his "neural bucket brigade algorithm", for which simulation results demonstrating sequence learning are available. Basically, we can substitue our modules for his, use his connections, and his results apply to our system. This is true even when we use oscillatory attractors and project to get distributed activity patterns, because our network is still functionally isomorphic to his. Many other network models, such as the McClelland-Rummelhart letter recognition model[20], employ this basic structure of cooperatively connected subsets of competitive elements, and can be translated into our system to explore the effects of more complex dynamics on its operation.

4.1   Sensory-Motor Clocking

The neural bucket brigade algorithm and discrete time temporal learning algorithms like the temporal Hebbian rule, $w_{ij}(t) = w_{ij}(t-1) + \alpha x_i(t) x_j(t-1)$, require that at least the previous time step activations at each node be saved in order to calculate the weight update after the transition to the next state. Since our transition intervals are tenths of a second, it is hard to point to a specific biological process within a local neural population that might retain memory of such an activation, and feed it into the weight changing process, without interfering with the on going dynamical relaxation to the new state (although biochemistry may conceivably do it).

Without claiming positive biological evidence, but to get started and explore one network level solution to this problem, we introduce a "machine cycle" for our system. This is implemented by reciprocally varying the d "competition" (bifurcation) parameters of the sensory and motor patches, to alternately clamp one set of attractors, while the other is allowed to make attractor transitions prescribed by the present sensory states acting through the intermodule connections with weights specified by the J^* matrix [2]. Motor states feed back to sensory states to cause transitions, so that internal activity can be self-sustaining, as in any recurrent network; but this internal activity can also be guided by a sequence of sensory inputs to produce a learned sequence of motor outputs. When the inputs from one module to the next are given as impulses that establish initial conditions, the relaxation dynamics of a module is exactly predicted by the projection theorem[1]. Discrete time clocking is then done essentially by pulsing the states of the sensory modules into the motor modules and vice versa.

This alternation of sensory and motor states is inspired to some degree by the structure of cerebral cortex, with its segregation and pairing of functionally related sensory and motor areas accross the central sulcus, and because it accomplishes the task of distinguishing temporal order by "action - reaction". This allows the implementation of weight changes between time steps without requiring that neurons "store" their last activation states. Temporal transitions are always between sensory and motor areas, and the activations preceeding any motor state are always available in the present sensory state, and vice-versa. A hierarchy of temporal "chunks" can be created in the system, by allowing transitions of higher level modules only after many transitions of lower level modules. Such high level modules may thus encode "plans" that activate long sequences of low level behaviors - a notion which is also being explored by other researchers [21]. Even the attractors of the motor modules which produce final output in our system might be thought of as supplying "plan vectors" in premotor cortex to lower motor control networks, like those of Jordan [18], which generate smoothed and coordinated analog muscle activations.

5   Simulations

Preliminary simulations of this architecture show robust storage of oscillatory attractor transition sequences in a system with a sinusoidal clock and continuous oscillatory intermodule driving. Coupled attractors of similar resonant frequency in different modules rapidly become phase locked. This is similar to the apparent "binding" of sensory features by phase-locking that has been observed in visual cortex [13, 7], and used in other oscillatory memory models [23, 24, 16]. In this system, it appears that oscillating modules within the sensory set must phase-lock to the modules of the motor set in order to reliably drive them drive through the transitions of attractors that have been programmed by the intermodule connections. This perhaps models a further function of binding at a temporal level of processing.

A set of four modules, each with three oscillatory attractors, was divided into two sensory and two motor modules. Each module consisted of six differential equations of the form (4), with identical complex conjugate eigenvalues in the corresponding diagonal blocks of the J^* matrix, and a six by six dimensional A^* matrix coupling block, of the form discussed earlier that guarantees three single frequency oscillatory attractors. The super-network of coupled modules thus consisted of 24 differential equations.

Two further equations of the same form were added with a two dimensional A^* matrix block on the diagonal that formed a single stable oscillator. This was used as an autonomous clock to vary the bifurcation parameter d that allowed sensory-motor transitions. The value of one of its variables was subtracted from the off-diagonal A^* matrix coupling d of the sensory modules and added to the value of that for the motor modules. The amplitude of the oscillation was chosen to be such that, at maximum excursion, the off-diagonal A matrix coupling d equalled the diagonal coupling c in one set of modules, and was much greater in the other. At zero difference, as discussed above, there is no internal "competition" between learned attractors within a module, and a new input vector can relocate the state of a module to a new attractor basin. This causes the desired alternation of attractor transitions within the sensory and motor modules as the the oscillator variable reaches positive and negative peaks.

The period of the clock in our simulations was chosen to be five times that of the modules, to simulate the 8Hz rate of respiration in olfaction (or the cortical alpha rythum) relative to the 40Hz cortical oscillation. The convergence rate of the modules was adjusted, by setting the maximum difference of the off diagonal A^* matrix coupling (competition), to a value sufficient for modules to relax to their attractors within a clock cycle (sniff).

Particular sequences were programmed into the system by adding to the J^* matrix specific off-diagonal coupling between modules. A cyclic sequence through all attractor combinations (states of the supernet) was programmed by hand. In another experiment, the J^* matrix weights determining several non-overlapping cyclic sequences of lengths from three to seven were "learned" by a heteroassociative Hebb rule between pre-chosen states. Input (starting states) were given to the network as handwritten digits, using sensory modules previously trained to recognize digits [5]. A distributed ampitude pattern was assigned to each attractor, and placed in a P^* matrix block so that the system could be transformed into network coordinates. A menu switch allowed the activity of the system to be viewed either in mode coordinates or in terms of the activity patterns distributed over three excitatory and three inhibitory neural populations (90 degrees out of phase) that would be observed in the biological model.

The supra-system relaxed from unprogrammed states to the preprogrammed cycles, which were unpreturbed by additive Gaussian noise of a variance of up to 15% of the amplitudes of the oscillations of the attractor states. Spurious transitions were made, however, when the resonant frequencies of the attractors were randomly distributed from each other by greater than about 5%, and phase locking was lost. This indicates the importance of phase locking for reliable transitions in sinusoidally driven modules. When the system was clocked instead by pulsing the states of the sensory modules into the motor modules and vice versa to establish initial conditions for subsequent relaxation, this sensitivity was naturally gone. However, convergence times were then slower, and transitions were more sensitive to the additive Gaussian noise. Spurious transitions were observed at a variances of only 8%. This indicates that noise tolerance is confered on the system by oscillatory forcing.

5.1 Resonant Attractor Transitions

The observation here that phase locking between the driving and the driven modules is necessary to effect reliable transitions in the presence of noise, suggests an important computational role in *this* system, at least, for the kind of selective phase locking observed in visual cortex. We have some understanding of the mechanism of these transitions, in the case of phase-locked forcing, because it is similar to the process of attractor transition which we can observe in detail in two dimensional phase portraits for two static attractors with clamped inputs.

We must first view the process of the machine cycle in more detail. The larger the difference of off-diagonal A^* matrix coupling within a module created by the clock, the greater the competition between attractors and the faster the convergence to a chosen attractor. At high values of competition the module is "clamped" at its current attractor, and the effect of the changing input it receives by feedback from the modules undergoing transition is negligable. The feedback between sensory and motor modules is therefore effectively cut. The super-system can thus be viewed as operating in discrete time by transitions between a finite set of states. This kind of clocking and "buffering" of some states while other states relax is essential to the reliable operation of digital architectures. In our simulations, if we clock all modules to transition at once, the programmed sequences lose stability, and we get transitions to unprogrammed fixed points and simple limit cycles for the whole system. This is a primary justification for the use of the "machine cycle".

By this reasoning, when one set of modules is clamped at their periodic attractors, the other modules are externally "forced" by these inputs, and theoretical analysis of the transition process becomes possible. When a module is driven at the same frequency as the intrinsic resonant frequency of all its attractors, and has phase locked to the input, then we can look at its dynamics in terms of a strobed series of snapshots at a particular point of the cycle. This lets us freeze the periodic motion and construct a vector field for the competition between amplitudes of the periodic attractors independent of their phase. This is the phase portrait on a Poincare section of the system and looks like a vector field for static attractors, since equilibria in this system now describe the asymptotic states of the underlying oscillations. In the absence of input, this is exactly the vector field of the amplitudes of the polar coordinate version of the normal form equations [1, 3]. The amplitudes of the driving inputs appear in this picture as clamped static inputs, and the series of phase portraits we have calculated for static attractor transitions applies to describe the transitions between oscillatory attractors [4].

At zero difference between diagonal and off-diagonal A matrix coupling, in these studies of static attractor transitions, there is no internal "competition" between attractors within a module. The learned internal dynamics is effectively turned off, and the state vector is determined entirely by a clamped input vector. There is only a single attractor within a module then that is a scalar multiple of whatever input vector is applied. The previous attracting state of a module is completely erased at this point. As the competition increases again, this attractor is forced to a new position in state space determined by the nearest learned attractor. The other learned attractors reappear by saddle-node bifurcations at a distance from this attractor and create other basins of attraction.

A simulation similar to that described above was carried out using modules with Lorenz attractors. There is always some probability of a spurious transition in this system, since trajectories of this attractor pass arbitraily close to zero, and other attractors may take over dominance when they are released from supression by this spontaneous self-destruction. Many variations of the basic system configuration, and operation, and various training algorithms, such as reinforcement learning with adaptive critics, are being explored. The ability to operate as an finite automaton with oscillatory states is an important benchmark for this architecture, but only a subset of its capabilities. At low competition, as we have pointed out, the supra-system reverts to a continuous dynamical system. We expect that this kind of variation of the operational regime, including perhaps chaotic dynamics, though unreliable for habitual behaviors, may nontheless be important in other areas such as the the search process of reinforcement learning.

5.2 Acknowledgments

Supported by AFOSR-87-0317, and a grant from LLNL. It is a pleasure to acknowledge the invaluable assistance of Morris Hirsch, Walter Freeman, and Frank Eeckman.

References

[1] B. Baird. A bifurcation theory approach to vector field programming for periodic attractors. In *Proc. Int. Joint Conf. on Neural Networks, Wash. D.C.*, pages 1:381–388, June 1989.

[2] B. Baird. Bifurcation and learning in network models of oscillating cortex. In S. Forest, editor, *Emergent Computation*, pages 365–384. North Holland, 1990. also in Physica D, 42.

[3] B. Baird. A learning rule for cam storage of continuous periodic sequences. In *Proc. Int. Joint Conf. on Neural Networks, San Diego*, pages 3: 493–498, June 1990.

[4] B. Baird. *Bifurcation Theory Approach to the Analysis and Synthesis of Neural Networks for Engineering and Biological Modeling*. Research Notes in Neural Computing. Springer, 1992. to appear.

[5] B. Baird, W. Freeman, F. Eeckman, and Y. Yao. Applications of chaotic neurodynamics in pattern recognition. In *SPIE Proceedings Vol. 1469*, 1991. in press.

[6] R. Eckhorn, R. Bauer, W. Jordan, M. Brosch, W. Kruse, M. Munk, and H. Reitboeck. Coherent oscillations: A mechanism of feature linking in the visual cortex? *Biological Cybernetics*, 60:121, 1988.

[7] A. K. Engel, P. Konig, C. Gray, and W. Singer. Synchronization of oscillatory responses: A mechanism for stimulus-dependent assembly formation in cat visual cortex. In R. Eckmiller, editor, *Parallel Processing in Neural Systems and Computers*, pages 105–108. Elsevier, 1990.

[8] J. Freeman, W., Y. Yao, and B. Burke. Central pattern generating and recognizing in olfactory bulb: A correllation learning rule. *Neural Networks*, 1(4):277, 1988.

[9] W. Freeman. *Mass Action in the Nervous System*. Academic Press, New York, 1975.

[10] W. Freeman. Simulation of chaotic eeg patterns with a dynamic model of the olfactory system. *Biological Cybernetics*, 56:139, 1987.

[11] W. Freeman and B. Baird. Relation of olfactory eeg to behavior: Spatial analysis. *Behavioral Neuroscience*, 101:393–408, 1987.

[12] W. J. Freeman and B. W. van Dijk. Spatial patterns of visual cortical eeg during conditioned reflex in a rhesus monkey. *Brain Research*, 422:267, 1987.

[13] C. Gray, P. Konig, A. Engel, and W. Singer. Oscillatory responses in cat visual cortex exhibit intercolumnar synchronization which reflects global stimulus properties. *Nature(London)*, 338:334–337, 1989.

[14] J. Guckenheimer and D. Holmes. *Nonlinear Oscillations, Dynamical Systems, and Bifurcations of Vector Fields*. Springer, New York, 1983.

[15] L. B. Haberly and J. M. Bower. Olfactory cortex: model circuit for study of associative memory? *Trends in Neuroscience*, 12(7):258, 1989.

[16] D. Horn and M. Usher. Parallel activation of memories in an oscillatory neural network. *Neural Computation*, 3(1):31–43, 1991.

[17] J. Jack, D. Noble, and R. Tsien. *Electric Current Flow in Excitable Cells*. Clarendon Press, Oxford, 1983.

[18] M. Jordan. Motor learning and the degrees of freedom problem. In M. Jeanerod, editor, *Attention and Performance, XIII*, Hillsdale, NJ, 1990. Laurence Erlbaum.

[19] Z. Li and J. Hopfield. Modeling the olfactory bulb and its neural oscillatory processings. *Biological Cybernetics*, 61:379, 1989.

[20] J. McClelland and D. Rummelhart. An interactive activation model of context effects in letter perception. part i: an account of basic findings. *Psychological Review*, 5:375–407, 1981.

[21] M. Mozer. Connectionist music composition based on melodic, stylistic, and psychophysical constraints. *Tech Report CU-CS-495-90, Univ. of Colorado at Boulder*, 1991.

[22] J. H. Schmidhuber. A local learning algorithm for dynamic feedforward and reccurent networks. *Connection Science*, 1:719–722, 1990.

[23] C. von der Malsburg. How are nervous structures organized? In E. Basar, H. Flo, H. Hken, and A. nd Mandell, editors, *Synergetics of the Brain*, pages 238–249. Springer, 1983.

[24] D. Wang, J. Buhmann, and C. von der Malsburg. Pattern segmentation in associative memory. *Neural Computation*, 2(1):94–106, 1990.

Analysis of Oscillatory Regimes of a Coupled Neural Oscillator System With Application to Visual Cortex Modeling

Galina N. Borisyuk[1]

Roman M. Borisyuk[1]

Alexander I. Khibnik[1,2]

[1]Research Computing Center of the USSR Academy of Sciences
Pushchino, Moscow region, 142292, USSR

[2]Dept. of Computer Science, Katolieke Universiteit
Leuven B 3001, Belgium

Abstract

A system of coupled neural oscillators is considered. A neural oscillator by Wilson-Cowan consists of a system of two nonlinear differential equations that describe the interactions between excitatory and inhibitiry populations of neurons. Oscillatory regimes of two coupled oscillators is analyzed for different connections between oscillators with particular attention to phase-locking. Bifurcation diagrams of limit cycles are computed and this allow us to describe the stability and the transformations of the oscillatory regimes. In the case of connections between excitatory populations for the small connection strengths the phase-lock mode is unstable and the anti phase oscillations are stable. Increasing connection strengths gives rise to the appearance of the stable modulated oscillations. A synchronous behavior in a chain of neural oscillators is used for simulation of experimental phenomena of stimulus-dependent assembly formation in visual cortex. The role of modulated oscillations for information processing by brain structures and binding problem are discussed.

1 Introduction

Recent experimental observations on registration oscillatory and chaotic activity in primary areas of olfactory and visual cortex [1-6] cause a great number of neural networks models showing an oscillatory dynamics close to the experimentally observed one. The main functional element of the models was not a single neuron, as a rule, but a neuronal oscillator. The models can be roughly divided into three groups, according to the type of oscillator under consideration:

1. Oscillator is composed of many elements representing a sufficiently developed model of physiological neuron [7,8].

2. Oscillator consists of several neuronal populations, for example, excitatory and inhibitory ones [6]. As a rule, dynamics of each population averaged activity is considered in this group and a model of neural network is a system of differential equations. Presence of two populations is sufficient to simulate oscillatory activity in a separate oscillator. To get chaotic oscillations a system of no less than three equations is required.

3. Oscillator is described by a single variable which is a phase of oscillation (i.e. a phase of a current point along the limit cycle in the oscillator phase space) [9].

The advantage of the first group models is that they make it possible to render experimental details, for example, to allow for NMDA-receptors at a synaptio transmission or to simulate spike activity of single neurons and compare it with the experiment. The disadvantage is a great number of unknown parameters and requiring much computer power. The third group models are mathematically simple providing analytical results. The disadvantage is that the oscillation amplitudes are disregarded and the interaction between oscillators is described by a simplified scheme excluding excitatory and inhibitory neuronal populations.

In the present paper a neuronal oscillator by Wilson-Cowan is considered, which consists of excitatory and inhibitory neuronal populations. The activity dynamics of such an oscillator is described by a system of two ordinary differential equations. The detailed analysis of dynamics regimes in such system is made in the paper [10]. In section 2 we consider a neural network consisting of two identical neuronal oscillators. The oscillators may be coupled by using of various connection types, that results in different dynamics regimes. For example, in the papers [11,12] the connections between excitatory populations are called desynchronizing since they lead to nonsynchronous oscillations. At the same time the connections from excitatory population to inhibitory one are called synchronizing since they result in synchronization of oscillations.

We have carried out a bifurcation analysis of limit cycles in the system of two identical oscillators. The following four cases were analyzed:

Case 1. Connections between excitatory populations of neurons.

Case 2. Connections from neurons of excitatory population of one oscillator to neurons of inhibitory population of the other oscillator.

Case 3. Connections from neurons of inhibitory population of one oscillator to neurons of excitatory population of the other oscillator.

Case 4. Connections between inhibitory populations.

It turned out, that specific type of dynamics behavior characterizes each of these cases.For example, in case 3 complicated chaotic oscillations arise.

In section 3 we discuss the role of connection delay. Each of the oscillators is supposed to consist of neurons closely located and connection delays inside the oscillator may be neglected. However, in case of two oscillators their disposition depends on the specific simulated situation. For example, oscillators may simulate the activity of visual cortex macro columns with identical orientation preference. In this case they can be a considerable distance apart and here a connection delay between oscillators becomes essential. The numerical experiments show that typically the short delays have no influence on the system behavior, but as delay increases the dynamics may change considerably.

In section 4 we consider a one-dimensional chain of neuronal oscillators. As follows from the numerical experiments the main results obtained for the two oscillators are valid also for the chain of many oscillators. We also deal with a model of conflicting stimuli in visual cortex [13]. Our observations show that one of possible dynamic regimes in the neural network is a regime of modulated oscillations. This regime is realized in a considerable domain in the parametric space and in some cases appears to be the only stable regime in the system. In section 5 we discuss a hypothesis of the role of modulated oscillations in information processing.

The computations of bifurcation curves have been carried out using the software developed at the Pushchino Research Computing Center of the USSR Academy of Sciences: the TRAX program to compute and plot the trajectories of dynamics systems and the CYCLE program that analyzes bifurcations of limit cycles in dynamics systems [14].

2 Bifurcation analysis of oscillatory regimes in a system of two neuronal oscillators

Let us consider a neuronal oscillator by Wilson-Cowan consisting of excitatory and inhibitory subpopulations (Fig.1).

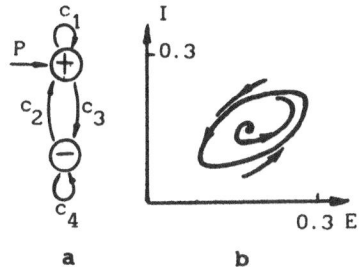

Fig. 1. A connections scheme of excitatory and inhibitory populations (1a) and phase plane (1b) of a single neural oscillator. $c_1=16$; $c_2=12$; $c_3=15$; $c_4=3$; $P=1.5$; $Q=0$; $\theta_e=4$; $b_e=1.3$; $\theta_i=3.7$; $b_i=2$.

It can be determined by the following system of equations:

$$\frac{dE(t)}{dt} = -E + (k_e - E)\, S_e(c_1 E - c_2 I + P)$$

$$\frac{dI(t)}{dt} = -I + (k_i - I)\, S_i(c_3 E - c_4 I + Q)$$

where $E(t)$ and $I(t)$ are the averaged activity of the excitatory and inhibitory subpopulations at a moment t; c_1, c_2, c_3, c_4 are the average strengths of connections between subpopulations; P and Q are external inputs to the excitatory and inhibitory subpopulations;

$S_e(x)=1/(1+\exp(-b_e(x-\theta_e)))-1/(1+\exp(b_e\theta_e))$ and
$S_i(x)=1/(1+\exp(-b_i(x-\theta_i)))-1/(1+\exp(b_i\theta_i))$ are sigmoid functions;
$k_e = S_e(+\infty)$; $k_i=S_i(+\infty)$.

Let choose the oscillator parameters to have a single stable oscillatory regime (Fig 1b). We will analyze two identical oscillators taking corresponding oscillator parameters of both oscillators as equal and choosing symmetric connections between oscillators in according to one of the four cases mentioned in the Introduction. Let α be the strength of connection between oscillators. The equations are given only for the case 1. In other cases they can be derived analogously:

$$\frac{dE_1}{dt} = -E_1 + (k_e - E_1)\, S_e(c_1 E_1 - c_2 I_1 + \alpha E_2 + P)$$

$$\frac{dI_1}{dt} = -I_1 + (k_i - I_1)\, S_i(c_3 E_1 - c_4 I_1 + Q)$$

$$\frac{dE_2}{dt} = -E_2 + (k_e - E_2)\, S_e(c_1 E_2 - c_2 I_2 + \alpha E_1 + P)$$

$$\frac{dI_2}{dt} = -I_2 + (k_i - I_2)\, S_i(c_3 E_2 - c_4 I_2 + Q)$$

At $\alpha=0$ we have two independent oscillators. If at the initial moment $t=0$ we deal with equal initial values on limit cycles: $E_1(0) = E_2(0)$, $I_1(0) = I_2(0)$, then obviously the same remains valid also for $t>0$, that is the system will exhibit synchronous oscillations. Analogously, considering initial values at various points on the limit cycle of each of the oscillators, we can observe any shift in oscillatory phases. It is clear, that a set of such trajectories forms a two-dimensional torus in a four-dimensional phase-space. Which of these oscillatory regimes will hold stability when $\alpha>0$? For small values of $\alpha>0$ either the regime of synchronous oscillations is stable or the regime of antiphase oscillations: $E_1(t) = E_2(t + T/2)$, $I_1(t + T/2)$, where T is an oscillatory period. From theoretical point of view, the stability of oscillations with other phase relations is also possible, but in our calculations we do not come across this situation.

Besides this there exist two more symmetric invariant trajectories at $\alpha=0$. They are: the product of the first oscillator stationary point by the limit cycle of the second oscillator and vice versa. These trajectories in principle can be stable for $\alpha>0$. So, for $\alpha=0$ we select four invariant trajectories:

- Symmetric limit cycle (Slc)

- Antisymmetric (antiphase) limit cycle (ASlc)

- Two nonsymmetric limit cycles (NSlc).

The problem is to study the evolution and the stability of each cycle for $\alpha>0$. Naturally, with increasing connection strength α, the above mentioned four cycles can disappear and new limit cycles can appear instead of them or together with them. We shall compute the bifurcation diagrams of limit cycles beginning from one of the four cycles. They show the stability and bifurcations of limit cycles for $\alpha \in [0;5]$.

Case 1. Connections between excitatory populations. There is a scheme of oscillators coupling in Fig. 2a and Fig. 2b shows a bifurcation diagram for limit cycles corresponding to variation of the connection strength α. Note, that for small α only ASlc is stable, so the system exhibits only antiphase oscillations. At point $b(\alpha=0.50)$ ASlc exists no longer (it disappears in a backward Hopf bifurcation). Slc becomes stable when $\alpha>1.73$ and causing branching off two more unstable and nonsymmetric limit cycles. For $1.73<\alpha<1.76$ the system exhibits three stable limit cycles and the type of oscillations depends on the choice of initial conditions. It is interesting to note that in the wide range of α changing $(0.25<\alpha<1.02)$ there are no stable limit cycles. What are the attractors for such parameters? Since two nonsymmetric limit cycles lose stability at point $c(\alpha=1.02)$ due to torus

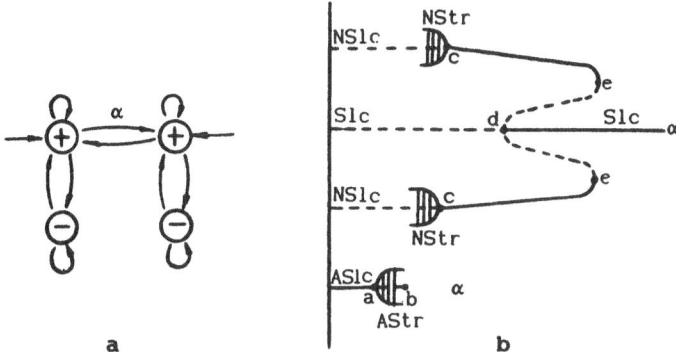

a   b

Fig. 2. A scheme of excitatory connections of two neural oscillators (2a) and a bifurcation diagram (2b) of symmetric (Slc), antisymmetric (ASlc) and nonsymmetric limit cycles. Solid line shows stable limit cycles, dashed line - unstable ones.

a(α=0.25) - torus bifurcation for antisymmetric limit cycle; stable antisymmetric torus appears for α>0.25.

b(α=0.50) - Hopf bifurcation for equilibrium point; antisymmetric unstable limit cycle arises for α<0.50.

c(α=1.02) - torus bifurcation for nonsymmetric limit cycles; two stable nonsymmetric tori arise for α<1.02.

d(α=1.73) - symmetry breaking bifurcation for symmetric limit cycle; two arising nonsymmetric limit cycles are unstable for α>1.73.

e(α=1.76) - fold bifurcation for nonsymmetric limit cycle; two of four limit cycles appearing for α<1.76 are stable.

bifurcation it is clear that stable nonsymmetric tori exist for α<1.02 (Fig.3). The numerical experiments show that attractors in the form of tori exist throughout the range of α changing (0.25<α<1.02). Two-frequency oscillations are typical for excitatory connections and are very important in our opinion for brain information processing. The hypothesis of integration of separate features to bind the whole image using multi-frequency oscillations is discussed bellow.

Case 2. Connections from excitatory population of one oscillator to inhibitory population of the other oscillator. Fig.4a shows a scheme of oscillators coupling, and fig.4b shows the results of bifurcation analysis of limit cycles. In this case there is the only stable regime of synchronous

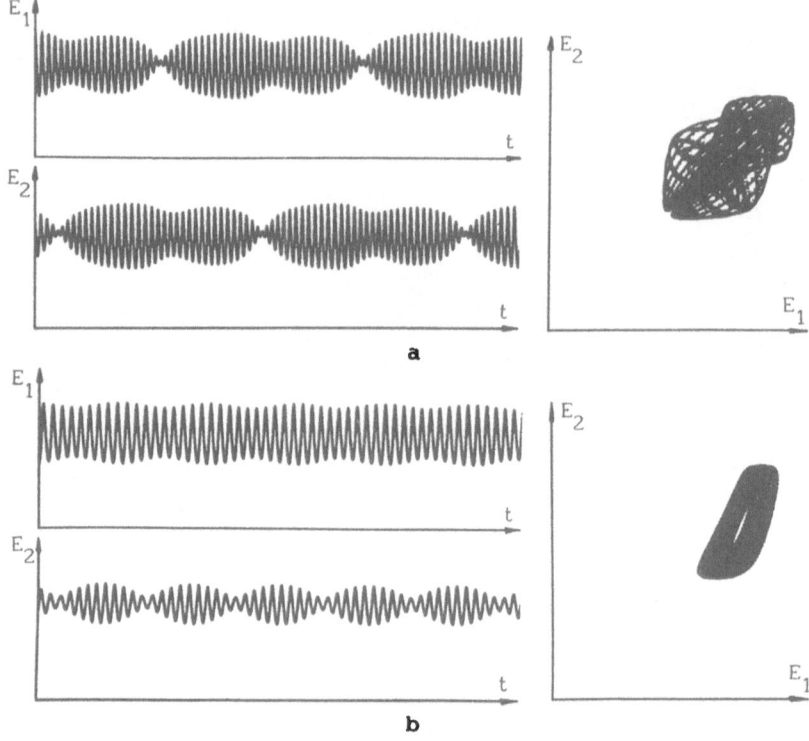

Fig. 3. Examples of modulated oscillations in case of excitatory to excitatory connections of two oscillators. Antisymmetric torus (3a) for $\alpha=0.80$ and one of the two coexisting nonsymmetric tori (3b) for $\alpha=1.00$.

oscillations of for small α and all the other limit cycles are unstable. The same picture remains with the α increasing. At point b($\alpha=1.67$) ASlc becomes stable and in the range $1.67<\alpha<2.49$ the two stable limit cycles – Slc and ASlc – coexist. As the α further increases, the system exhibits a multiple Hopf bifurcation at point c($\alpha=2.49$), when two limit cycles coincide and disappear. As α increases further more (for example, $\alpha=3.00$) the system exhibits only the steady-state behavior. At point a($\alpha=1.59$) one can see a torus bifurcation for the nonsymmetric limit cycles. Two stable antisymmetric tori and stable symmetric limit cycle coexist for $\alpha<1.57$.

Case 3. Connections from inhibitory population of one oscillator to the excitatory population of the other oscillator. Fig.5a shows a scheme of oscillators coupling and figure 5b shows the results of bifurcation analysis. Analogously to the previous case the single stable limit cycle Slc exists for

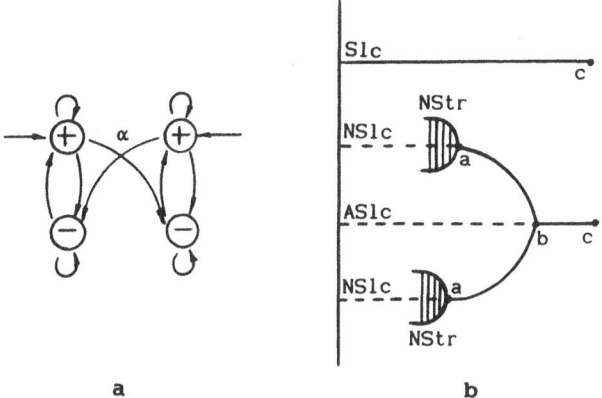

Fig. 4. A scheme of oscillators coupling (4a) for connections from excitatory population to inhibitory one and a bifurcation diagram of limit cycles (4b). Solid line shows stable limit cycles, dashed line - unstable ones.

a(α=1.59) - torus bifurcation for a nonsymmetric limit cycle; two stable tori appear for α<1.59 as limit cycles lose their stability.

b(α=1.67) - symmetry breaking bifurcation for antisymmetric limit cycle; two nonsymmetric limit cycles appear for α<1.67.

c(α=2.49) - multiple Hopf bifurcation of a symmetric equilibrium point; two stable cycles arise simultaneously for α<2.49, one is symmetric limit cycle and the other is antisymmetric limit cycle.

small α and the two oscillators oscillate synchronously. The picture becomes much more complicated as the α increases . At the point a(α=1.16), the Slc loses its stability due to period doubling bifurcation and nonsimmetric stable limit cycle appears. Then it also loses stability under symmetry-breaking bifurcation at point b(α=1.90), after which two stable nonsymmetric limit cycles arise. After that a cascade of period doubling bifurcations follows with critical parameter values accumulating near α=2.00. A strange attractor exists in the system for 2.00<α<3.30 and oscillations become chaotic.

The numerical experiments show changes of the type of chaos as α increases. Near α=3.30 the trajectory moves near one of NSlc (unstable) cycles for some time and then jumps toward the other NSlc and moves near it, then comes back etc., with the time which trajectory spends in the neighborhood of each of the cycles being random. Fig.6 gives us the examples of stochastic behavior of the trajectories.

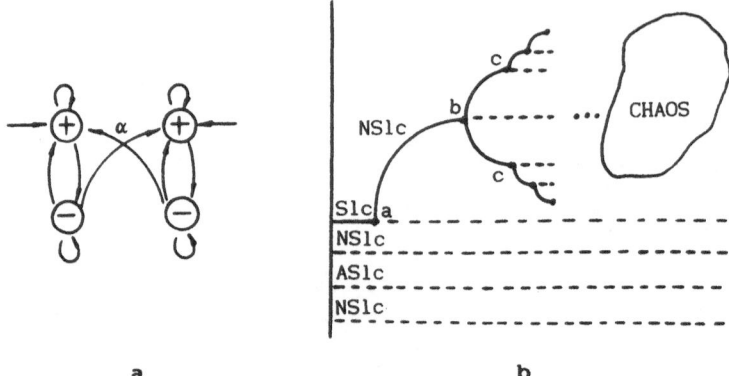

a   b

Fig. 5. A scheme of oscillators coupling (5a) for connections from inhibitory population to excitatory and a bifurcation diagram of limit cycles (5b). Solid line shows stable limit cycles, dashed line – unstable ones.

$a(\alpha=1.16)$ – period doubling bifurcation for symmetric limit cycle; nonsymmetric stable limit cycle appears for $\alpha>1.16$.

$b(\alpha=1.90)$ – symmetry breaking bifurcation for nonsymmetric limit cycle; two nonsymmetric limit cycles appear for $\alpha>1.90$.

$c(\alpha=1.94)$ – period doubling bifurcation for nonsymmetric limit cycles. A strange attractor exists in the system for $2.00<\alpha<3.3$.

Case 4. Connections between inhibitory populations. Fig.7a shows a scheme of oscillators coupling and Fig.7b – the result of analysis of limit cycles bifurcations. The only stable regime in the system for all values of α is ASlc that is the regime when the activity of neuronal oscillators changes in antiphase.

3 Influence of connections delay on the activity dynamics

As it was mentioned in the Introduction we only consider a delay in connections between oscillators supposing the two oscillators to be a considerable distance apart, so that the time for signal passing becomes essential. Delays in connections inside oscillators are disregarded since the connections are local.

As it was done above, we shall consider four cases of connections between oscillators with delay τ. The equations are given only for the case 1. In other cases they can be derived analogously.

$$\frac{dE_1}{dt} = - E_1 + (k_e - E_1) \, S_e (c_1 E_1 - c_2 I_1 + \alpha \, E_2(t-\tau) + P)$$

$$\frac{dI_1}{dt} = - I_1 + (k_i - I_1) \, S_i (c_3 E_1 - c_4 I_1 + Q)$$

$$\frac{dE_2}{dt} = - E_2 + (k_e - E_2) \, S_e (c_1 E_2 - c_2 I_2 + \alpha \, E_1(t-\tau) + P)$$

$$\frac{dI_2}{dt} = - I_2 + (k_i - I_2) \, S_i (c_3 E_2 - c_4 I_2 + Q)$$

Note that in all the cases introduction of a short delay τ does not change a picture when $\tau=0$. A dynamics regime of the system without delay remains almost the same after small delays are introduced. Thus, for example,

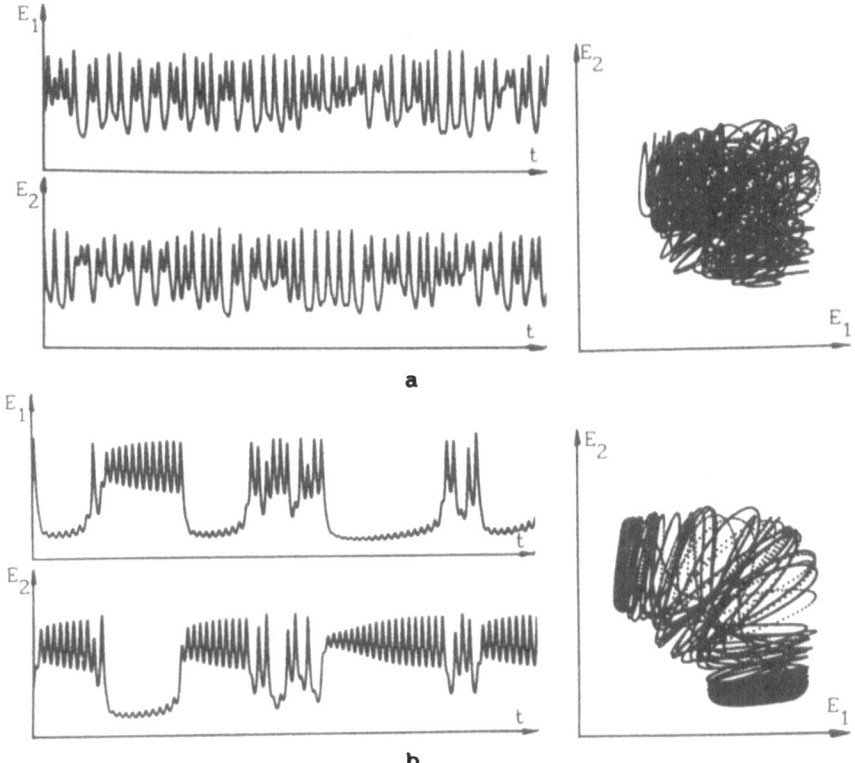

Fig. 6. Examples of a chaotic behavior in case of connections from inhibitory to excitatory populations. 6a : $\alpha=2.5$; 6b : $\alpha=3.4$.

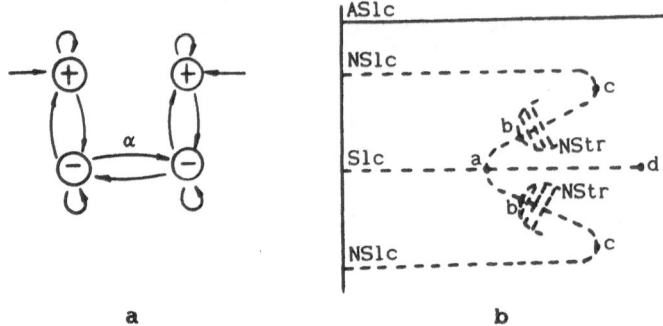

| a | b |

Fig. 7. A scheme of inhibitory to inhibitory connections of two oscillators (7a) and a bifurcation diagram (7b) of limit cycles. Solid line shows stable limit cycles, dashed line – unstable ones.

a(α=0.49) – symmetry breaking bifurcation for a symmetric limit cycle.; two nonsymmetric limit cycles appear for α>0.49; all bifurcating cycles are unstable.

b(α=0.54) – torus bifurcation; for α>0.54 two unstable tori appear.

c(α=0.55) – fold bifurcation for a nonsymmetric limit cycle.

d(α=0.61) – Hopf bifurcation for a symmetric equilibrium point; arising for α<0.61 symmetric limit cycle is unstable.

in the case 1 a delay τ~T/3 (where T is a period of oscillations and usually T~3) ensures a stable regime of ASlc for 0<α<2 and a delay more then T/3 gives a regime of Slc.

In the case 2 for α>2.49 and τ=0 there are no oscillations in the system and a delay τ=0.3 being introduced excites them. In this case for 1<α<2 a delay τ (0.5<τ<2.5) allows to obtain modulated oscillations (Fig.8), but in the absence of delay the system exhibits a stable Slc.

In the case 3 a delay plays a role of chaos destroying tool. For short delays (τ~0.1) the system exhibits chaotic oscillations (2<α<3), but the delay 0.5<τ<1 ensures the only stable regime which is the regime of synchronous oscillations (Slc).

Analogously, in the case 4 introduction of a delay can also lead to synchronization of oscillations. For example, at α=1 and 0<τ<0.5 one can observe antiphase oscillations in the system. But at delays τ~1 (i.e. τ~T/3) the system exhibits synchronous oscillations of activities of two oscillators.

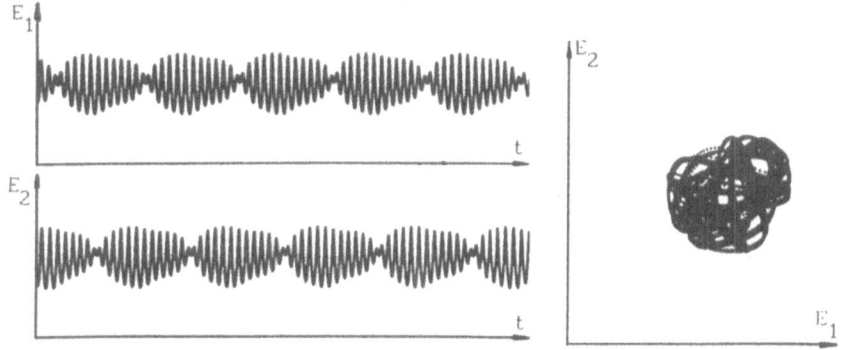

Fig. 8. An example of modulated oscillations in a case of connections delay from excitatory to inhibitory populations ($\alpha=1.0$, $\tau=0.5$).

4 A dynamics of a locally-connected chain of neuronal oscillators. An application to visual processing

Let us consider a chain, consisting of N identical locally-connected oscillators. The connections are chosen in accordance with cases 1 - 4 (see Introduction). Here we give the equations for the case 1, in other cases they can be derived analogously.

$$-\frac{dE_1}{dt} = -E_1 + (k_e - E_1)\, S_e(c_1 E_1 - c_2 I_1 + \alpha\, E_2(t-\tau) + P)$$

$$\frac{dI_1}{dt} = -I_1 + (k_i - I_1)\, S_i(c_3 E_1 - c_4 I_1 + Q)$$

$$\frac{dE_n}{dt} = -E_n + (k_e - E_n)\, S_e(c_1 E_n - c_2 I_n + \alpha\, E_{n-1}(t-\tau) + E_{n+1}(t-\tau) + P)$$

$$\frac{dI_n}{dt} = -I_n + (k_i - I_n)\, S_i(c_3 E_n - c_4 I_n + Q)$$

$$\frac{dE_N}{dt} = -E_N + (k_e - E_N)\, S_e(c_1 E_N - c_2 I_N + \alpha\, E_{N-1}(t-\tau) + P)$$

$$\frac{dI_N}{dt} = -I_N + (k_i - I_N)\, S_i(c_3 E_N - c_4 I_N + Q)$$

where n=2,3,...,N-1.

The numerical experiments show that a chain of N oscillators has the same dynamics regimes as chain of two oscillators for small values of connection

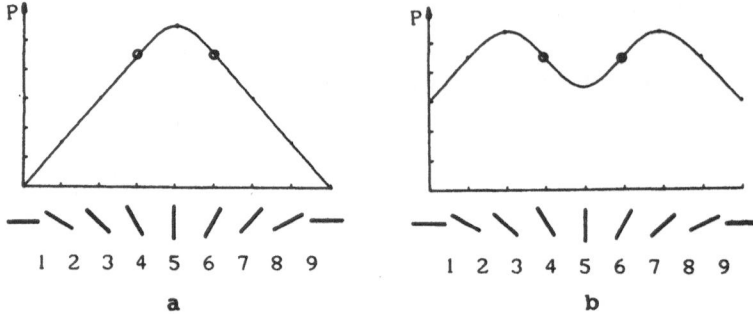

Fig. 9. The optimal orientation preferences of oscillators and a distribution of input values for the example "a" of one vertical bar stimulus (9a) and for an example "b" of two stimuli (9b).

strength α. The α values are of the other scale, of course. Thus, for example, when connections between oscillators are chosen according to the case 1 for small α values the neighboring units oscillate with half-period phase shift.

We suppose to dwell on the bifurcation regimes of the chain of oscillators in a separate paper. Here we consider a model of coupled columns of a visual cortex and show stimulus-dependent assembly formation.

4.1 A chain of oscillators: segregation by conflicting stimuli

Suppose, a chain of neuronal oscillators simulates visual cortex columns with entire receptive field and with different preferred orientations. This means that the presented stimulus (short oriented bar) causes reaction in all the oscillators-columns, but the reaction extent depends on the orientation of stimulus. Fig. 9 shows differently inclined lines, which being used as stimuli, ensure optimal response of corresponding column. In existing models of oscillators the effect of various stimuli is determined by the distribution of input values P_i. Following experimental observations we consider two examples.

Example "a": if one moves a vertical bar stimulus corresponding to preference orientation of the column N5 located in the center of the chain then the input to this column will be the largest (Fig. 9a). The inputs to other oscillators will be the less the farther the preference orientation of the oscillator from the presented one.

Example "b": Fig. 9b shows distribution of input values for two stimuli moving incoherently but presented simultaneously in a receptive field

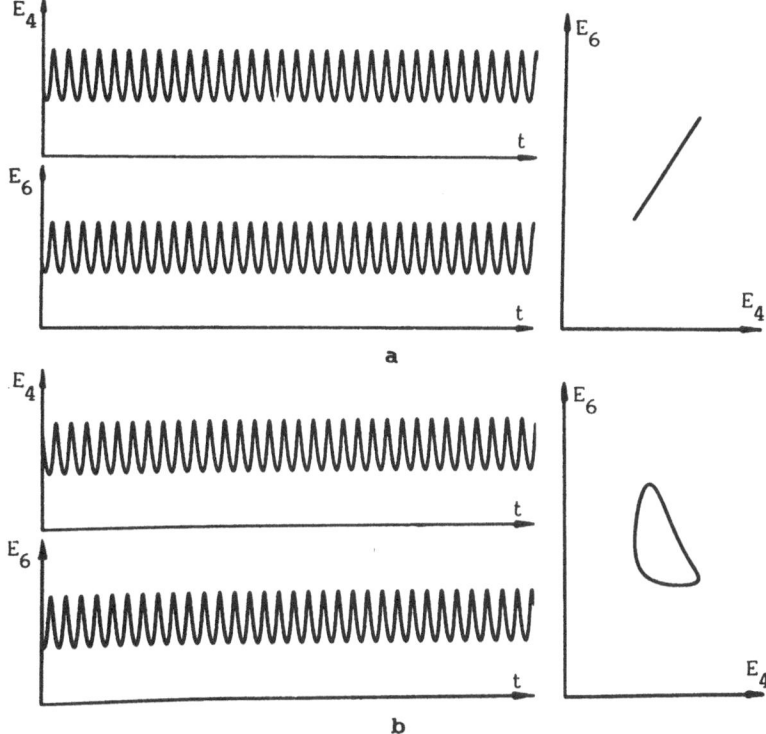

Fig. 10. The computation results for example "a" (10a) and for example "b" (10b). $\alpha=0.4$, $\tau=0.1$.

("conflicting" stimuli). This is the case of the optimal stimulus for the column N3 and the optimal stimulus for the column N7.

Let consider what happens to the oscillators N4 and N6 in the examples "a" and "b". Note, that in both cases the level of input to oscillators N4 and N6 remains unchanged: $P_4^{"a"}=P_4^{"b"}=P_6^{"a"}=P_6^{"b"}$. The results of calculations are given in Fig.10.

Example "a": Vertically oriented stimulus activates oscillations in oscillator N5 and also involves neighboring oscillators in oscillatory regime. A cluster of synchronous oscillations is formed. In particular, oscillators N4 and N6 demonstrate synchronous oscillations (Fig. 10a).

Example "b": Optimally oriented bars for the oscillators N3 and N7 make them oscillate. The oscillator N3 "engages" the neighboring ones (N2 and N3) and oscillator N7 "engages" N6 and N8 ones. As a result two clusters of synchronous oscillations are formed. But if we consider different cluster oscillators, for example, N4 and N6 we find them not to be synchronized (Fig. 10b).

Note that oscillator N5 in the case "b" is not in oscillatory mode but in stationary state. Introducing the connections delay $\tau=1$ we can obtain analogous results for examples "a" and "b", but in the latter case oscillator N5 oscillates with a period longer than oscillators N4 and N6.

Thus, the results obtained for the model are in good agreement with experimental evidence [13] that incoherent stimuli can activate coherently oscillating assemblies of cells which are not synchronized among each other.

5 A role of modulated oscillations in the information processing. Binding features of the object into integral image.

It is still unknown how information from the different cortical maps is integrated into the coherent percepts. Recent experimental observations [1-6], justified by model calculations [5-9, 11-12], make it possible to put forward a hypothesis that integration of features in the primary area of visual cortex is realized due to synchronization of oscillations. What particular areas are involved in synchronous oscillations depends not only on the stimulus local characteristics, but also on the "context". For example, stimulation by two parallel bars activates oscillations of about 40 Hz in corresponding locations of the cortex. Whether the oscillations are synchronous or not depend on the way of stimuli moving. Stimuli moving in the same direction produce a single cluster of synchronous activity. Stimuli moving in different directions form two independent clusters [4].

Many researchers suggest that synchronization plays a role of universal mechanism for binding different features of the object into the integral image. The concrete mechanism of synchronization is unknown so far. A.Damasio in paper [15] puts forward a hypothesis that there exist convergent zones of several levels where there are both feedforward and feedback connections to transform information. "The synchronization is passed by simultaneous firing from convergence zones along feedback projections towards the sites in which feedforward originated" [15].

In our opinion the idea to use feedback signal seems to be fruitful. Though, as distinct from Damasio, we would like to use this signal not for entire synchronization of high frequency activity, but to obtain synchronous modulations at a lower frequency. Upon stimulation by a simple homogeneous stimulus integration of features (synchronization of high frequency oscillations) may be realized directly on the primary areas level due to direct connections between corresponding stimulated sites [8]. When the complex nonhomogeneous stimuli are used the system does not obligatory exhibits entire synchronization of responses in all reacting subregions, for example, in a case of "conflicting" stimuli or in a case of two "scattering" bars. But from more abstract point of view, the two "scattering" bars may be the elements of one and the same object, for example, the sides of a contour, approaching an observer. Consequently after an appropriate analysis some synchronization may arise. Information converges along feedforward projections and a synchronization may appear inside some convergent zone due to local connections. The area of synchronous activity plays a role of a "common source" for information spreading along feedback projections. The "common source" is able, generally speaking, to synchronize high frequency oscillations. But in the case with stimulation by "scattering" bars this would mean that on the level of primary visual cortex the high frequency oscillations are synchronized to contradict to the experimental data [4].

We suppose that modulated oscillations of lower frequency in the cortex primary area (or in convergent zones) are caused by the influence of feedback connections. Due to low frequency modulation an assembly of neuronal populations coherently oscillating at low frequencies and thereby an integrated image is created. The high frequency oscillations of these assemblies are not obligatory synchronous on the level of primary cortex if on this level the formation of integral image did not take place.

Consideration of modulated oscillations makes it possible to introduce one more component of a signal and thereby to expand possibilities of its processing. Of course, the presented scheme of integrating features may be generalized to the case of several convergent zones or several frequencies of modulation. Thus, for example, on the level of the first convergent zone the synchronization activity may not arise. In this case the information passes to the second convergent zone, and a cluster of coherently oscillating assemblies may be formed there, etc.

The suggested hypothesis on the role of modulated oscillations in the process of integrating features makes it possible to consider in terms of this hypothesis the problems of associated memory, attention, conditioning. It allows to look upon brain as transformer of multifrequency oscillations for the analysis of entering sensory signals and their synthesis.

Acknowledgements. R.M.Borisyuk acknowledges Prof. Wolf Singer for useful discussions and support from Max-Planck Institute for Brain Research Frankfurt a.M.   A.I.Khibnik acknowledges support from Katholieke Universiteit Leuven.

References

[1]   Gray C.M., Singer W. *Stimulus-specific neuronal oscillations in the cat visual cortex: A cortical functional unit.* Soc. Neurosci. Abstr., 13 (404.3), 1987

[2]   Eckhorn R., Bauer R., Jordan W. et al. *Coherent oscillations : a mechanism of feature linking in the visual cortex.* Biological Cybernetics, v.60., pp.121-130, 1988

[3]   Gray C.M., Singer W. *Stimulus-specific neuronal oscillations in orientation columns of cat visual cortex.* Proc. Natn. Acad. Sci. USA, v.86, pp.1698-1702, 1989

[4]   Gray C.M., König P., Engel A.K., Singer W. *Oscillatory responses in cat visual cortex exhibit inter-columnar synchronization which reflect global stimulus properties.* Nature, v. 338, pp.334-337, 1989

[5]   Singer W. *Search for coherence: a basic principle of cortical self-organization.* Concepts in neuroscience, v.1, No.1,   pp.1-26, 1990

[6]   Wilson M.A., Bower J.M. *The simulation of large-scale neuronal networks.* In: Methods in Neuronal Modelling, C.Koch, I.Segev (eds), MIT Press, Cambridge, MA, pp.291-334,   1989

[7]   Freeman W.J., Yao Y., Burke B. *Central pattern generating and recording in olfactory bulb: a correlation learning rule.* Neural Networks, v.1, n.4, 1988

[8]   Borisyuk G.N., Borisyuk R.M., Kirillov A.B., Kryukov V.I., Singer W. *Modeling of oscillatory activity of neuron assemblies of the visual cortex.* In: Proc. IJCNN-1990, San Diego, v.2, pp. 431-434, 1990

[9]   Kammen D.M., Holmes P.J., Koch C. *Cortical arhitecture and oscillations in neuronal networks: feedback versus local coupling.* In: Models of brain function, R.M.J. Cotterill   (ed.),   Cambridge   University   Press, Cambridge, pp. 273-284,   1989

[10] Borisyuk R.M., Kirillov A.B. *Bifurcation analysis of neural network model.* Biological Cybernetic, 1991 (in press)

[11] König P., Schillen T.B. *Stimulus-dependent assembly formation of oscillatory responses: I. Synchronization.* Neural Computation, v.3, pp.155-166, 1991

[12] Schillen T.B., König P. *Stimulus-dependent assembly formation of oscillatory responses: II. Desynchronization.* Neural Computation, v.3, pp.167-177, 1991

[13] Engel A.K., König P., Gray C.M., Singer W. *Synchronization of oscillatory responses: A mechanism for stimulus-dependent assembly formation in cat visual cortex.* In: Parallel Processing in Neural Systems and Computers, R.Eckmiller et al. (eds), Elsevier, pp.105-108, 1990

[14] Khibnik A.I., Kuznetsov Yu.A., Levitin V.V., Nikolaev E.V. *Continuation techniques and interactive software for bifurcation analysis of ODEs and iterative Maps.* Physica D, 1991 (in press)

[15] Damassio A.R. *The brain binds entities and events by multiregional activation from convergence zones.* Neural Computation, v.1, pp.123-132, 1989

Systems of Relaxation Oscillators with Time-Delayed Coupling

Ernst Niebur
Computation and Neural Systems Program
California Institute of Technology
Pasadena CA 91125, USA.

Heinz G. Schuster
Institut für Theoretische Physik
Universität Kiel
D-2300 Kiel 1, Germany.

Daniel M. Kammen
Department of Physics
Harvard University
Cambridge, MA 02138, USA.

October 18, 1991

Abstract

We study systems of relaxation oscillators in the presence of nearest-neighbor coupling. It is shown that introduction of delay in the coupling leads to a depression of the frequency of individual oscillators as well as of the average frequency of the system. In certain parameter ranges, we also observe the existence of metastable states. Both phenomena can be understood in a simple mean-field like theory.

The recent exciting observations of stimulus evoked synchronized oscillations in the visual cortex of the cat [4, 6, 10] has ellicited a number of theories that identify the oscillations as a functional mechanism linking neuronal and perceptual events [2, 5]. While at present no direct evidence of this relationship exists, the hypothesis is supported by psychophysical studies [19]. On more general grounds, emerging techniques of recording neuronal activity in large populations of neurons [1, 11], and computational advances[20] in providing realistic models of these systems – each of which surely include complex dynamics of interacting but time-delayed units – suggests that a general theoretical analysis may prove fruitful.

Omitting the details of excitable cells, we begin with two observed facts: stimulus specific oscillations are present, and, under suitable circumstances, the oscillations are synchronized over large distances and numbers of intervening neurons, even across the cerebral hemispheres [7].

We therefore consider a system consisting of elements with only two properties: (a) they show periodic behavior

(b) their interaction favors synchrony.

An isolated element is then simply described by the equation:

$$\frac{d\phi_i(t)}{dt} = \omega_i \tag{1}$$

where ϕ_i is the state variable of oscillator i and ω_i is the intrinsic frequency of this oscillator. Adding a simple interaction term which favors synchrony, we obtain

$$\frac{d\phi_i(t)}{dt} = \omega_i + K \sum_j \sin(\phi_j(t) - \phi_i(t)) \tag{2}$$

where the sum runs over the subset of the N oscillators which are coupled to oscillator i. We have also introduced the coupling constant $K > 0$.

This and similar systems have been studied extensively over the last years [13, 9, 14, 8, 3, 15, 16, 18]. In this report, we will introduce a seemingly small change in eq. 2: Instead of assuming instantaneous interaction between coupled oscillators, we assume that it takes some time τ until the changed state of oscillator j can affect oscillator i:

$$\frac{d\phi_i(t)}{dt} = \omega_i + K \sum_j \sin(\phi_j(t - \tau) - \phi_i(t)) \tag{3}$$

$$\tau \geq 0$$

It is obvious that this is a more realistic model for interactions in a nervous system than eq. 2: interaction between neurons is always subject to a delay due to the finite conduction velocity of neural signals along the nerve fibers ($\sim 1\ mm/msec$). In the case of a chemical synapse, the delay is even larger due to synaptic delay.

In fact, equation 3 is a more realistic model than eq. 2 for *all* physical systems, because of the finite propagation velocity inherent in causal signals. In the following, we will therefore make no use of specific properties of neural systems and, instead, study eq. 3 as a general model of a variety of systems.

In this report we confine our investigation to the case of nearest-neighbor interactions, i.e., the sum runs over all nearest neighbors of oscillator i. We also assumed $\omega_i = \omega_0$ for all i, although most of our results do not depend on this assumption (see below). In order to achieve larger generality, we added a Gaussian noise-term (or temperature T) in the usual way:

$$\frac{d\phi_i(t)}{dt} = \omega_0 + K \sum_j \sin(\phi_j(t - \tau) - \phi_i(t)) + \eta_i(t) \tag{4}$$

$$< \eta_i(t) > = 0$$
$$< \eta_i(t)\eta_j(t') > = 2T\delta(i,j)\delta(t - t')$$

where $\delta(t)$ is the Dirac delta "function", defined by:

$$\delta(t) = 0 \text{ for all } t \neq 0$$
$$\int_{-\infty}^{\infty} \delta(t)dt = 1 \tag{5}$$

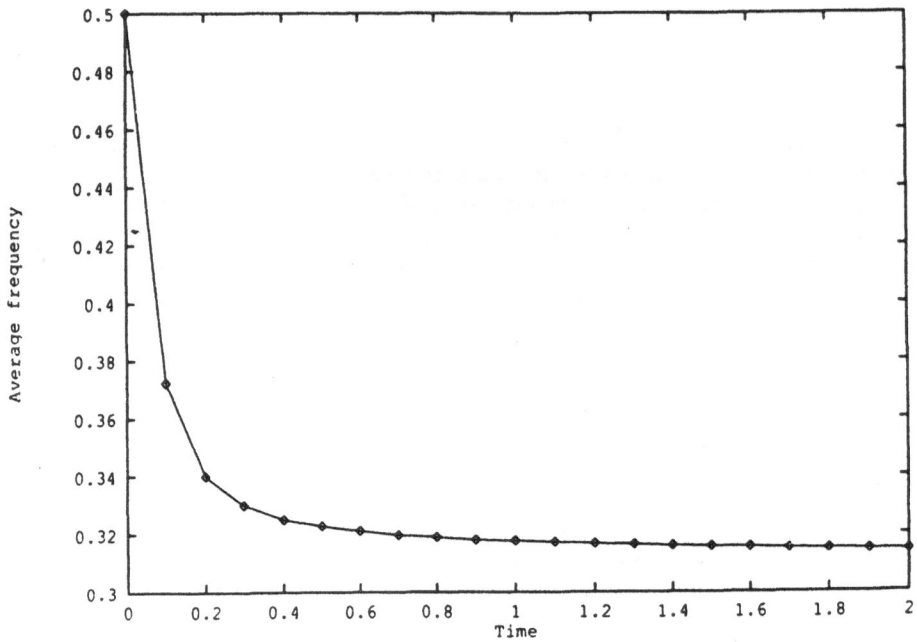

Figure 1:
Depression of the average frequency Ω of the system of 128×128 oscillators, described by eq. 5. At $t = 0$, the average frequency (see eq. 6) is $\Omega = \omega_0 = 0.5$. The frequency drops to the value computed in eq. 9. Parameters: $T = 0, K = 2.5, \tau = 0.01$.

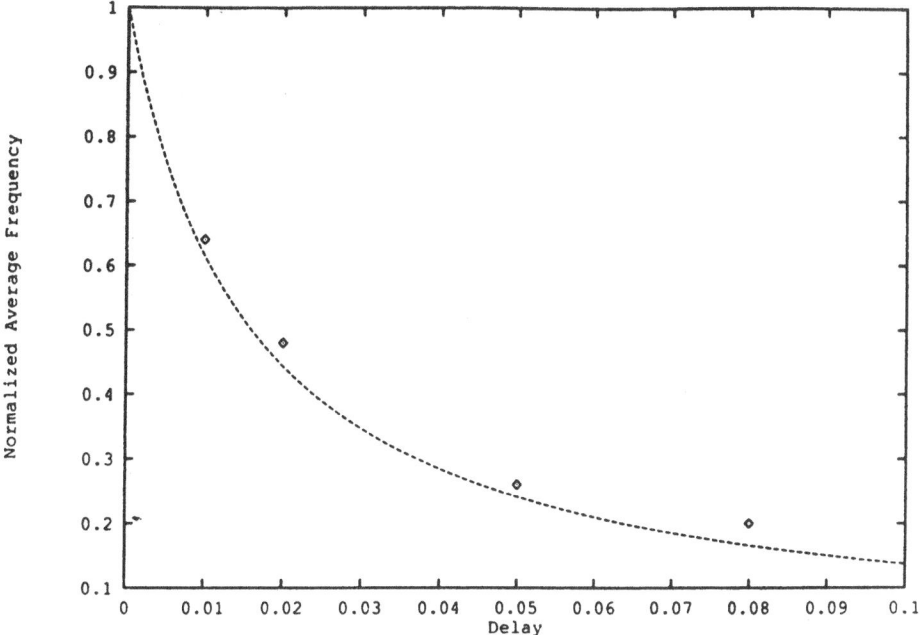

Figure 2:
Frequency suppression as a function of time delay τ (in units of $2\omega_0^{-1}$) for a two-dimensional array of 16,384 oscillators (diamonds) and prediction from eq. 8 (line). The average frequency Ω is plotted as a fraction of the intrinsic frequency, ω_0. Temperature, $T = 10^{-4}K$.

We simulated this system for $N = 16,384$ (128×128) oscillators and for $\omega_i = \omega_0$ for all i on the CM-2 Connection Machine, using a two-dimensional square lattice with periodic boundary conditions. Figure 1 shows the system exhibits a strong "frequency suppression:" Very rapidly, the average frequency

$$\Omega = \frac{1}{N}\sum_i <\dot{\phi}_i>$$ (6)

(the brackets denote the average over the random noise $\eta_i(t)$ and the dot the derivative with respect to time) of the system drops from the mean intrinsic frequency to a smaller value. This value depends on the coupling constant and the delay. With increasing coupling and delay, the mean frequency is depressed more and more, as can be seen in Figure 2 (as a function of τ). We obtain a similar frequency depression if instead of a single frequency ω_0 the oscillators have different intrinsic frequencies with a distribution that has a mean ω_0 and a width comparable to ω_0 (data not shown).

This effect can be understood in a mean-field like theory. Consider a situation where all angles change with the same frequency Ω:

$$\phi_i = \Omega t + \alpha \text{ for all } i \tag{7}$$

For $T = 0$, Ω is then determined by the self-consistency relation

$$\Omega = \omega_0 - Kn\sin(\Omega\tau) \tag{8}$$

where n is the number of neighbors (4 in the case of a square lattice with nearest-neighbor interaction). Depending on the values of its parameters, this equation has one or more than one solutions. In Fig. 1 we plot the lowest stable frequency

$$\Omega_{min} \approx \omega_0/(1 + Kn\tau) \tag{9}$$

and obtain good agreement with our simulations.

How about the other solutions? We have shown numerically [17] that, by a careful choice of the initial conditions, the system can be prepared in a way that it will enter a state with $\Omega > \Omega_{min}$. The system can be driven out of this state by thermal fluctuations. We have also presented an analytically solvable model of two delay-coupled oscillators which elucidates this behavior [17]. In this report we present a related model which also shows the observed metastable states and which involves only one oscillator.

In order to derive this model, consider eq. 4 for one oscillator, i.e. $N = 1$. We drop the subscript and obtain for $T = 0$:

$$\frac{d\phi(t)}{dt} = \omega_0 + K\sin(\phi(t-\tau) - \phi(t)) \tag{10}$$

Using eq. 5, this can be rewritten as

$$\frac{d\phi(t)}{dt} = \omega_0 + K\int_{-\infty}^{\infty} \delta(\tau - \tau')\ \sin(\phi(t-\tau') - \phi(t))\ d\tau' \tag{11}$$

Replacing $\delta(\tau' - \tau)$ by a decaying exponential with the characteristic time τ, it is then easy to see that eq. 11 is equivalent to the following system of equations:

$$\frac{d\phi(t)}{dt} = \Omega - K\sin(\phi(t) - \psi(t)/\tau) \tag{12}$$

$$\frac{d\psi(t)}{dt} = \phi(t) - \psi(t)/\tau \tag{13}$$

We have chosen the initial conditions as $\psi(0) = 0$. Taking the difference of these equations and defining

$$x = \phi - \psi/\tau \tag{14}$$

we find that x is determined by a potential function V:

$$\frac{dx}{dt} = -\frac{dV}{dx} \tag{15}$$

$$V(x) = -\Omega\,x + \frac{1}{2\tau}x^2 - K\cos x \tag{16}$$

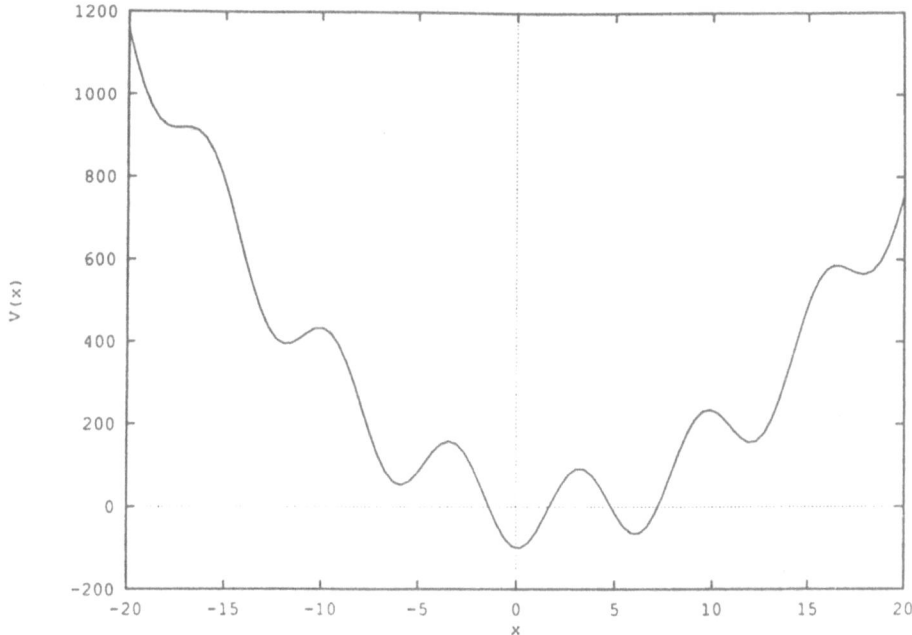

Figure 3:
Metastable states in the potential function $V(x)$ (see eq. 16). The absolute minimum occurs for the value of x which is given by eq. 9. All other minima are metastable. Parameters: $\Omega = 10, K = 100, \tau = .2$.

The minima $\{x_0\}$ of $V(x)$ are the stationary solutions of eqs. 15. They are proportional to the synchronization frequencies of eqs. 12-13 as can be seen from the following argument. For $x = x_0$, we have from eq. 14 $\phi - \psi/\tau = x_0$ and this yields from eq. 13 $\frac{d\psi}{dt} = x_0$, i.e. $\psi(t) = x_0 t$ or $\phi(t) = x_0 + x_0/\tau\ t$ which means that x_0/τ is a synchronization frequency. Figure 3 shows that there can be many metastable frequencies but only the solution to eq. 9 is absolutely stable.

The drastic decrease of the synchronization frequency (which occurs even for small delays if the coupling strength is large) should be observed in a wide range of dynamic systems and may be useful in the analysis of physical processes ranging from the behavior of liquid crystals to atmospheric convection. The existence and the functional form of the potential $V(x)$ depend on the details of the coupling between the oscillators [12], but the existence of the frequency depression does not. We believe that the investigation of the nature of metastable states in dynamic systems with internal delay times which are abundant in nature is a promising direction of further research.

Acknowledgement

We are grateful to D. Ruderman for writing part of the Connection Machine code. We would like to thank B. Ermentrout and H. Sompolinsky for stimulating conversations and C. Koch for his continuing support and encouragement. Part of the computations have been performed on the Caltech/Argonne Connection Machine. E. N. is supported by the Swiss National Science Foundation through Grant No. 8220-25941. H. G. S. is supported by the Volkswagen Foundation, and D. M. K. by the Division of Biology and grants from the Air Force Office of Scientific Research and the James S. McDonnell Foundation (both to C. Koch).

References

[1] G.G. Blasdel and G. Salama. Voltage-sensitive dyes reveal a modular organization in monkey striate cortex. *Nature*, 321:579–585, 1986.

[2] F. Crick and C. Koch. Towards a neurobiological theory of consciousness. *Seminars in the Neurosciences*, pages 1–36, 1990.

[3] H. Daido. *Phys. Rev. Lett.*, 61:231, 1988.

[4] R. Eckhorn, R. Bauer, W. Jordan, M Brosch, W Kruse, M. Munk, and H.J. Reitboeck. Coherent oscillations: a mechanism of feature linking in the visual cortex? *Biological Cybernetics*, 60:121–130, 1988.

[5] R. Eckhorn, H.J. Reitboeck, M. Arndt, and P. Dicke. A neural network for feature linking via synchronous activity: Results from cat visual cortex and from simulations. In Cotterill; R.M.J., editor, *Models of brain function*, pages 255–272. Cambridge Univ. Press, 1989.

[6] A.K. Engel, P. Koenig, C.M. Gray, and W. Singer. Stimulus-dependent neuronal oscillations in cat visual cortex: inter-columnar interaction as determined by cross-correlation analysis. *Europ. J. Neurosci.*, 2:588–606, 1990.

[7] A.K. Engel, P. Koenig, A.K. Kreiter, and W. Singer. Interhemispheric synchronization of oscillatory neuronal responses in cat visual cortex. *Science*, 252:1177–1179, 1991.

[8] G. B. Ermentrout and N. Kopell. *SIAM J. Appl. Math.*, 50:125, 1990.

[9] W. Freeman. *Scientific American*, 264(2):78, 1991.

[10] C.M. Gray, P. Koenig, A.K. Engel, and W. Singer. Oscillatory responses in cat visual cortx exhibit inter-columnar synchronization which reflects global stimulus properties. *Nature*, 338:334–337, 1989.

[11] A. Grinvald, E. Lieke, R.D. Frostig, C.D. Gilbert, and T.N. Wiesel. Functional architecture of cortex revealed by optical imaging of intrinsic signals. *Nature*, 324:361–364, 1986.

[12] N. Kopell and G. B. Ermentrout. Symmetry and phaselocking in chains of weakly coupled oscillators. *Comm. Pure Appl. Math.*, 39:623–660, 1986.

[13] C. M. Marcus and R. H. Westervelt. *Phys Rev. A*, 39:347, 1990.

[14] P. C. Matthews and S. H. Strogatz. *Phys. Rev. Lett.*, 65:1701, 1990.

[15] E. Niebur, D.M. Kammen, and C. Koch. Phase locking in 1-d and 2-d networks of oscillating neurons. In W. Singer and H. G Schuster, editors, *Nonlinear Dynamics and Neuronal Networks*, pages 173–204. VCH Verlag, Weinheim, FRG, 1991.

[16] E. Niebur, D.M. Kammen, C. Koch, D. Ruderman, and H. G Schuster. Phase coupling in two-dimensional networks of interacting oscillators. In D. Touretzky and R. Lippman, editors, *Advances in Neural Informations Processing Systems 3*, pages 123–129. Morgan-Kaufmann, San Mateo, CAA, 1991.

[17] E. Niebur, H. G Schuster, and D.M. Kammen. Collective frequencies and metastability in networks of limit cycle oscillator with time delay. *Physical Review Letters*, 1991.

[18] E. Niebur, H. G Schuster, D.M. Kammen, and C. Koch. Oscillator phase coupling for different two-dimensional network connectivities. *Physical Review A*, 1991.

[19] E. Poeppel and N. Logothetis. Neuronal oscillation in the human brain. *Naturwissenschaften*, 73:267–268, 1986.

[20] M.A. Wilson, U.S. Bhalla, J.D. Uhley, and J.M. Bower. Genesis: a system for simulating neural networks. In D. Touretzky, editor, *Advances in Neural Network Information Processing Systems*. Morgan Kaufmann Publ., San Mateo, California, 1989.

Cortical Coherent Activity
Induced by Thalamic Oscillations

A. Destexhe[1] and A. Babloyantz

Université Libre de Bruxelles, CP 231 - Campus de la Plaine,

Boulevard du Triomphe, B-1050 Bruxelles, Belgium

Collective behavior in a simple model of the thalamo–cortical interaction is compared to the various rhythms seen in the electroencephalogram (EEG). Field potentials provide a global view of the network activity and may be characterized by dimensions and Lyapunov exponents. We show that the slow rhythms are those corresponding to the highest level of synchronization and coherence.

The thalamic reticular nulcleus is a key structure in the generation of brain rhythms. A model of this network is built from recently published voltage clamp data of thalamic neurons. In this model, various rhythms of different degree of spatiotemporal coherence may be observed as a function of the value of a single conductance. Here again, the slower rhythms are the most synchronized.

1 Introduction

The electroencephalogram (EEG) reflects the global electrical activity of millions of cortical neurons. Therefore, it is clear that EEG ocillations are the sign of synchronized rhythmic behavior in large pools of neurons. Such oscillations are seen for various behavioral states, such as the slow waves of the deep sleep and the alpha rhythm in higher mammals (awake, eyes closed).

A closer scrutiny shows that these EEG rhythms are not periodic but undergo irregular oscillations with various degree of coherence from one EEG epoch to the next. Moreover, an increasing amount of experimental data [4, 5, 15, 37, 53] suggest that this coherent activity could be described by deterministic chaos. In other words, the irregular oscillations in some stages of the EEG seem to be under the control of a dynamical law which may involve only a few independent variables.

In the context of studying chaotic dynamics in brain activity, two alternative approaches are possible. First, one could consider that chaotic dynamics has a determinant role in higher brain function thus its cognitive power must be elucidated.

---

[1] E-mail: adestex@bbrbfu60.bitnet

Such an approach is presently considered by our group in Brussels. Second, one could use chaotic dynamics, as demonstrated from time series analysis, for the purpose of modeling cerebral rhythmical activity. In this case, chaotic dynamics appears as a constraint that must satisfy any model of brain activity. This latter approach is the one used through this paper.

Numerous evidence of chaotic dynamics have been found in models of formal neural networks [1, 6, 7, 13, 14, 26, 38, 40, 42, 49]. These models are obviously too simple for being considered as relevant for describing EEG activity. However, chaotic dynamics may also be seen in physiologically more realistic models of the cortex [20, 48]. Such an approach is more close to the one followed in this paper.

Modeling complex rhythmical activity of the EEG requires a good knowledge of the underlying physiological events which trigger oscillatory activity at the cortical level. It appears now clearly that the thalamic reticular (RE) nucleus constitutes the pacemaker responsible for spindle type of rhythmic activity [45, 46, 47]. For the other types of synchronized EEG oscillations, at least two properties suggest an important role for the thalamus. First, the alpha rhythm and sleep spindles occur synchronously over large cortical areas, which are connected to the thalamus. In this case, the different specific relay nuclei show synchronized oscillations. The best candidate for pacemaker activity is the RE nucleus which projects to all specific relay nuclei, and could potentially synchronize distant cortical areas [43]. Second, oscillations of frequency similar to the EEG have been reported in the thalamus. Thalamic bursts of 1-4 Hz are observed *in vivo* [27, 44] as well as *in vitro* [28, 29, 32]. Bursts of 7-14 Hz are seen during sleep spindles [43] and of 8-10 Hz during alpha rhythm [2, 30].

Recently, we have introduced a simple model of cerebral cortex subject to various type of thalamic oscillations [16, 17]. The neurons were modeled by classical neuronal membrane equations based on the electrical analogue of the neuron. The thalamus was modeled as a simple external oscillator which displays various types of oscillations. We found that this model was characterized by different types of coherent oscillations of various degree of synchrony.

The comparison between the model and EEG data was provided by the average membrane potential. If this average activity is considered as a time series, we showed that the nonlinear properties such as dimensions and Lyapunov exponents are very close to those evaluated from experimental recordings [17].

In this paper, we briefly review (Section 2) the essential features of this model. In order to provide a more realistic description of the global activity of the network, we reconstruct the field potentials using an approach outlined by Nunez [34]. This approach provides another type of global activity of the network which is closer to the EEG.

In spite of the relatively good consistency of the qualitative results of the model with experimental EEG data, the architecture of this model remains obviously simple compared to the actual thalamo–cortical system. In order to provide a more realistic model of the thalamus instead of a simple oscillator, we introduce here a network model of the thalamic RE nucleus, based on voltage-clamp experiments (Section 3). The latter model is part of a more refined model of the thalamo–cortical interaction which will be presented in a forthcoming paper.

2 A simple model of thalamo–cortical rhythms

We describe here a model of the thalamo–cortical system introduced recently [16, 17]. The field potentials generated by such a system of neurons are computed and monitored for different types of rhythmical activities in the model. Various methods from nonlinear time series analysis are used to compare these simulations with EEG activity.

2.1 Description of the model

In this model, the cerebral cortex is represented by a set of leaky integrator neurons divided into two populations of excitatory and inhibitory cells. The thalamus is represented by a simple two-variable oscillator introduced by Rose and Hindmarsh [39].

The basis of the model is the electrical analogue of the membrane introduced by Hodgkin and Huxley [23]. According to this description, the dynamics of a network of N excitatory and M inhibitory neurons of membrane potential X_i and Y_i respectively, is given by [16]:

$$
\begin{aligned}
\frac{dX_i}{dt} &= -\gamma(X_i - V_0) - (X_i - E_1)\left[\sum_k \omega_{ki}^{(1)} F(X_k(t - \tau_{ki})) + T_i\, g(x)\right] \\
&\quad -(X_i - E_2)\sum_l \omega_{li}^{(2)} F(Y_l(t - \tau_{li})) \\
\frac{dY_j}{dt} &= -\gamma(Y_j - V_0) - (Y_j - E_1)\sum_k \omega_{kj}^{(3)} F(X_k(t - \tau_{kj})) \\
&\quad -(Y_j - E_2)\sum_l \omega_{lj}^{(4)} F(Y_l(t - \tau_{lj}))
\end{aligned}
\tag{1}
$$

$$
i, k = 1...N \quad , \quad j, l = 1...M
$$

Here, X_i and Y_j are the postsynaptic potentials of the N excitatory and M inhibitory neurons, $\gamma = 0.25\ ms^{-1}$ is the inverse of the time constant of the membrane and $V_0 = -60\ mV$ is the resting potential. $E_1 = 50\ mV$ and $E_2 = -80\ mV$ are the excitatory and inhibitory transmitter equilibrium potentials. $\omega_{ji}^{(1)}, \omega_{ji}^{(2)}, \omega_{ji}^{(3)}, \omega_{ji}^{(4)}$ are respectively the excitatory-to-excitatory, inhibitory-to-excitatory, excitatory-to-inhibitory and inhibitory-to-inhibitory synaptic weights. $F(x) = 1/[1 + \exp(-0.2(x + 25))]$ describes the nonlinear properties of neurons such as the firing threshold and the saturation of the firing rate. τ_{ji} is the propagation delay between sites i and j of the network.

The connectivity of the model is a simplified version of the two-dimensional cortical tissue connectivity. The two types of neurons are arranged on a regular lattice and τ_{ki} is 2 ms per lattice length. A given neuron connects to all neurons lying within a fixed neighborhood. First and second neighbor interactions as well as random connectivity have been considered. The boundary neurons have the same connectivity, except that a "mirror" image of the network is repeated outside the boundaries.

For each type of interaction, the synaptic weights of all neurons are identical and the total sum of the inputs is constant. Therefore, $\sum_k \omega_{ki}^{(1)} = \Omega_1$, $\sum_l \omega_{li}^{(2)} = \Omega_2$, $\sum_k \omega_{kj}^{(3)} = \Omega_3$ and $\sum_l \omega_{lj}^{(4)} = \Omega_4$. The dynamical properties of the model are very similar for a wide range of these parameters.

A small fraction of cortical excitatory neurons are submitted to an oscillatory input which mimicks thalamic activity. A phenomenological model of the thalamic oscillations was introduced by Rose and Hindmarsh [39]. The two variable version of this model reads:

$$\frac{1}{c}\frac{dx}{dt} = f_1(x) - z + I$$

$$\frac{1}{c}\frac{dz}{dt} = r(h_2(x) - z) \tag{2}$$

where x is the membrane potential and z is an adaptation current. The details of the model can be found in ref. [39] (see Fig.5 of this paper for the parameters used).

This model accounts qualitatively for some of the electrophysiological properties of thalamic neurons such as the coexistence between resting and oscillating activities. I is the control parameter allowing the transition from steady states to oscillatory states. c is a parameter which rescales the time axis.

The thalamic oscillator is connected to 2 % of randomly chosen excitatory neurons via the function $g(x) = 1/[1 + \exp(-10(x - 0.9))]$ with a strength of $T_i = 15$. This input is identical for all receiving cortical neurons.

The set of eqs. (1) and (2) are integrated numerically using a Runge-Kutta algorithm [35] modified for integration of delay differential equations. The values of the steady states and bifurcation points of eqs. (1) found by linear stability analysis (Destexhe & Babloyantz, unpublished) have been confronted with success to the values obtained by numerical integration.

2.2   Generation of field potentials

Although the exact origin of the EEG remains unknown, experimental evidence [9, 10, 11] points to the fact that its main origin is the postsynaptic potentials of excitatory pyramidal neurons in the cortex, while the contribution due to action potentials seems negligible. Such a model of the EEG was discussed by Nunez [34] and provide an expression of the field potential at a given point r_j in the extracellular space in function of a set of different current sources:

$$V(\mathbf{r}_j, t) = \frac{\rho}{4\pi} \sum_i \frac{I_m(\mathbf{r}_i, t)}{|\mathbf{r}_i - \mathbf{r}_j|} \tag{3}$$

Here $\mathbf{r}_i$ are the location of the current sources I_m, $\rho = 230 \ \Omega \ cm$ is the conductivity of the extracellular medium [36], and $|\mathbf{r}_i - \mathbf{r}_j|$ is the distance between $\mathbf{r}_i$ and $\mathbf{r}_j$.

In our model, the current sources are the postsynaptic currents given by the relation:

$$I_m(\mathbf{r}_i, t) = C_m \left\{ -(X_i - E_1) \left[\sum_k \omega_{ki}^{(1)} F(X_k(t - \tau_{ki})) + T_i \ g(x) \right] \right.$$

$$\left. -(X_i - E_2) \sum_l \omega_{li}^{(2)} F(Y_l(t - \tau_{li})) \right\} \tag{4}$$

$$i, k = 1...N , \ l = 1...M$$

where $C_m = 0.08 \ pF$ is the membrane capacitance of the neuron [31]. The intercellular distance (lattice length) of the two dimensional lattice of neurons is of 50 μm. The position of the recording site $\mathbf{r}_j$ is chosen at 500 μm perpendicularly above the plane of the network.

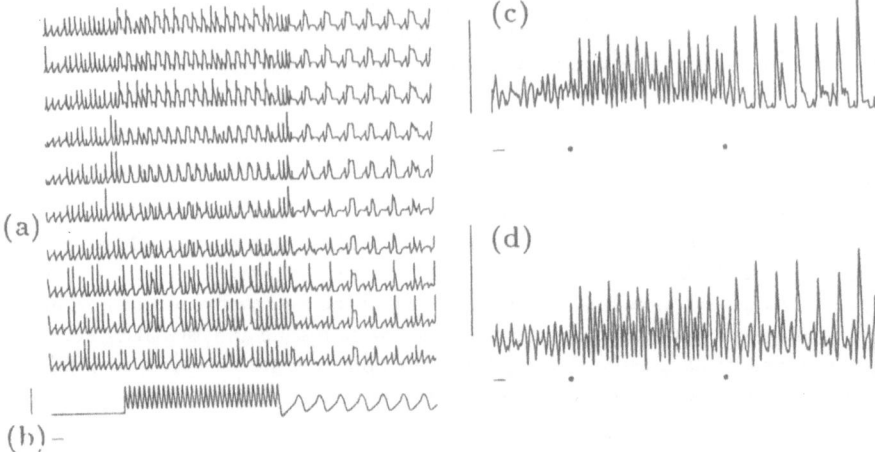

Figure 1: Transition between different patterns of rhythmic activity in the model.
(a) From top to bottom: activity of the 10 first cells in the network ($N = 400$, calibration bars:
100 mV and 100 ms). (b) Pacemaker. (c) Field potentials produced by the network (calibration
bars: 100 μV and 100 ms, intercellular distance: 50 μm, recording electrode at 500 μm perpendicular to the network). (d) Averaged membrane potential of the excitatory cells given for comparison
(calibration bars: 100 mV and 100 ms). The system is submitted successively to 600 ms without
pacemaker (flat trace in b), 1200 ms of fast rhythm ($I = 2.6$, $c = 0.125$) and 1200 ms of slow
rhythm ($I = 0.6$, $c = 0.06$). In (c)-(d), the dots indicate a change in pacemaker oscillation. The
synchronization induced by the fast rhythm of the pacemaker appears as oscillations of larger amplitude in the field potentials. A further increase of amplitude is seen following the onset of the
slow rhythm. $N = 400$, $M = 100$, $\Omega_1 = 15$, $\Omega_2 = \Omega_3 = 12.5$, $\Omega_4 = 0$ and up to second neighbor
connections were used.

2.3   Field potential oscillations

The working hypothesis in this section is that synchronization of the cortical system
occurs following periodic inputs from the thalamus. We induce here transitions
in the dynamics of the cortical network due to input change from the thalamic
pacemaker. The rhythms produced in the field potentials will be analyzed with the
same methods as those used for EEG data (see ref. [17] for a more detailed overview).

Let us first consider the dynamics of the cortical network in the absence of
thalamic input ($T_i = 0$).

The activity of the cortical tissue as described by eqs. (1) is a function of the
total synaptic weights $\{\Omega_1, \Omega_2, \Omega_3, \Omega_4\}$. For weak values of these parameters, all cells
of the network relax to the unique value of the -60 mV resting potential. However,
as the synaptic weights increase, spontaneous sustained activity may appear.

For $\Omega_2 = \Omega_3 = 12.5$ and $\Omega_4 = 0$, which are representative of the typical behavior
of the system, and for moderate values of Ω_1, the neurons oscillate periodically in
unison and one sees a bulk oscillation. As Ω_1 is increased further, a critical point
may be reached and spatiotemporal turbulence may appear [16, 17]. In the range of
parameters considered, the spatiotemporal turbulence is not seen in small networks.
However, for reasonably large number of neurons ($N \sim 400$), the turbulence is
always present.

Let us now consider the dynamics of the network in the presence of oscillatory
input. Although a small minority of cells receive the input, the vast majority of the

neurons may be entrained into a coherent behavior.

The dynamics of the system is investigated for two values of the input I and parameter c, $\{I = 0.6, c = 0.06\}$ and $\{I = 2.6, c = 0.125\}$ which correspond to two oscillating states of high and low frequency of different amplitude and wave form (see Fig. 1).

In Fig. 1, a system of 500 cortical neurons is submitted successively to a short period without pacemaker, a short period of fast rhythm and a short period of slow rhythm. In the absence of pacemaker ($T_i = 0$), the network shows desynchronized oscillations as described above. As the pacemaker sets in, the neurons switch into a partially synchronized dynamics where the membrane potential oscillations become more phase-locked. Although these oscillations are not strictly regular, the mean frequency of the network is of the same order as that of the pacemaker. A transition in the value of the amplitude is visible in the average potential as well as in the field potentials.

The first transition in Fig. 1 from the desynchronized state to a more synchronized state shows similarities with the transition from beta to alpha rhythm. Fig. 2 describes such a transition for a larger system of 8000 neurons. The synchronization of neurons at the onset of the pacemaker is manifested as a striking increase of amplitude of the field potentials.

Fig. 1 also show that the onset of the slower rhythm corresponds to a different type of collective behavior. In this second transition, the parameter I is decreased and the pacemaker switches to a slower oscillating regime. Again the network responds by a synchronization of neural activity. The system is characterized by a higher degree of coherence, as shown by the increase of amplitude in the field potentials when the pacemaker switches to the slow oscillation.

The level of synchronization between neurons can also be quantified by evaluating the spatial autocorrelation function. For the turbulent state, we have shown [16] that this function vanishes after several lattice lengths, indicating a loss of spatial coherence and the absence of long range spatial correlations. However, as the fast oscillatory input is switched on, the dynamics of the network synchronizes and the autocorrelation function shows a slower spatial decay. During this state, long range spatial correlations appear as a consequence of the more coherent synchronized dynamics. Spatial correlations increase further for the slow periodic input.

In a previous study [17], we could show that the dominant parameter which controls the level of synchronization and coherence is the *frequency* of the pacemaker rather than its waveform.

2.4 Nonlinear dynamics of the network

The system is integrated for each type of oscillatory input separately such that between 200 and 300 cycles of the field potential oscillations are covered. The correlation dimension is estimated from the Grassberger-Procaccia algorithm [22]. Time series from the field potentials and averaged membrane potentials both give rise to nearly identical values of the correlation dimension.

In the absence of pacemaker, the algorithm does not converge to a dimension lower than 10 [16]. As the method does not give reliable results for such high dimensions, this indicates only that the system is high dimensional. This behavior is

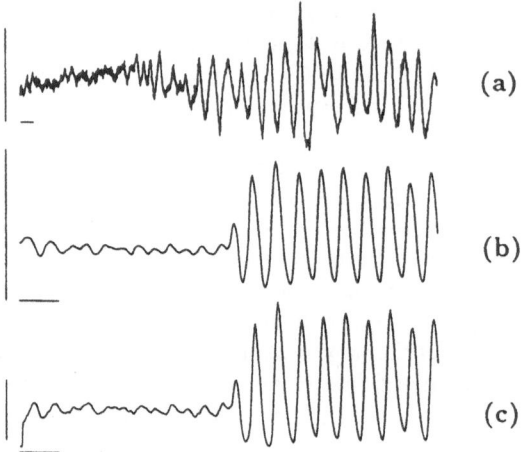

Figure 2: The onset of alpha rhythm as compared to synchronization in the model.

(a) Typical onset of alpha rhythm of a normal human subject when the eyes are closing (calibration bars: 100 μV and 100 ms.; P3-O1). (b) Field potentials of the network (calibration bars: 100 μV and 100 ms., intercellular distance: 50 μm, recording electrode at 2000 μm above the network). (c) Averaged membrane potential of excitatory neurons of the simulated network (calibration bars: 100 mV and 100 ms). The simulation was made with $N = 6400$ excitatory neurons and $M = 1600$ inhibitory neurons. 160 randomly chosen excitatory cells were subject to a 19 Hz pacemaker activity ($I = 0.6$, $c = 0.185$). The remaining parameters are the same as in Fig. 1.

very similar to the desynchronized states of the EEG which also show no convergence [5, 4].

As the pacemaker sets in, the more coherent type of behavior is indeed characterized by low dimensional chaotic behavior [16, 17]. Moreover, the correlation dimension appears as a linear function of the pacemaker frequency [16]. This behavior is remarkably similar to the results obtained from the analysis of EEG activity: the slower rhythms of the EEG also correspond to the lower dimensions.

The spectrum of Lyapunov exponents has been evaluated [17] from the algorithm of Eckmann et al. [19]. A very good convergence has been obtained for both rhythms described in Fig. 1. The data length and other parameters for reconstruction of phase portraits were the same as those used for the evaluation of the correlation dimension. The rhythm corresponding to the lowest dimension (the "slow" rhythm of Fig. 1 with $I = 0.6$, $c = 0.06$) was found to possess two positive Lyapunov exponents [17], whereas the dynamics corresponding to the fast rhythm ($I = 2.6, c = 0.125$) possesses three positive Lyapunov exponents [17]. The presence of positive Lyapunov exponents constitutes a further indication of chaotic dynamics for these rhythms.

The use of the Kaplan-Yorke conjecture [25] for estimating the dimension from the spectrum of Lyapunov exponents leads to values close to 10 - 15% to the values obtained from the Grassberger-Procaccia algorithm [17]. Therefore, the results from the two algorithms show a good consistency as it has been shown for EEG data by Gallez and Babloyantz [21].

The nonlinear properties of such a simple model of the thalamo–cortical interaction are remarkably consistent with EEG data. However, a more realistic model of EEG oscillations must consider the actual architecture and properties of cortical neurons, as well as the complex rhythmical properties of the thalamic networks. This latter point is the focus of the next section.

3   A model of the reticular thalamus

In the previous section, the thalamus was modeled as a two variable oscillator presenting the main features of thalamic neurons, namely the coexistence between oscilltory and resting states. The purpose of the present section is to show how these features may be accounted by a more realistic modeling approach.

The spontaneous oscillations observed in the disconnected RE nucleus suggest that these neurons should be characterized by a set of conductances allowing the production of rhythmic oscillations. Experimental data suggest that the occurence of these oscillations depends on intrinsic membrane properties as well as on collective parameters such as the connectivity [47].

The model described in this section attempts to make use of both of these properties. In a first step, thalamic neurons are modeled in term of several voltage-dependent ionic conductances. The various oscillatory and resting states found are described for single neurons. In a second step, we use this model as the basis of a network mimicking the connectivity of the RE nucleus. We give a brief overview of the spatiotemporal properties of this network.

3.1   Modelling single thalamic neurons

The electrophysiological study of RE neurons as well as thalamo–cortical relay (TCR) neurons reveals the presence of a low-threshold Ca^{2+} current, termed I_T, responsible for the generation of low-threshold spikes (LTS) following hyperpolarization [24]. The voltage-clamp study of this current [8, 12] shows that the kinetics of I_T may be descibed by a Hodgkin-Huxley-type formalism with the m^3n format, similarly to the kinetics of the Na^+ current underlying fast action potentials [23]. Taking the activation functions $m_\infty(V)$ and $n_\infty(V)$ provided by the experiments [8], and chosing voltage dependent time constants $\tau_m(V)$ and $\tau_n(V)$ as close as possible to experimental data [8], one obtains the following set of equations:

$$
\begin{aligned}
C_m \frac{dV}{dt} &= -g_L \left(V - V_L\right) - \bar{g}_{Ca}\, m^3 n \left(V - V_{Ca}\right) \\
\frac{dm}{dt} &= -\frac{1}{\tau_m(V)} \left(m - m_\infty(V)\right) \\
\frac{dn}{dt} &= -\frac{1}{\tau_n(V)} \left(n - n_\infty(V)\right)
\end{aligned}
\tag{5}
$$

where $C_m = 1\mu F/cm^2$ is the membrane capacitance, $g_L = 0.05\ mS/cm^2$, $V_L = -85\ mV$ are the leakage parameters and $V_{Ca} = 120\ mV$ is the calcium equilibrium potential. This kinetic scheme is a simplified version of an existing model proposed recently [51]. The various parameters were adjusted to the *in vivo* conditions (temperature of 36°C, extracellular calcium concentration of 2 mM; for more details, see refs. [18, 51]).

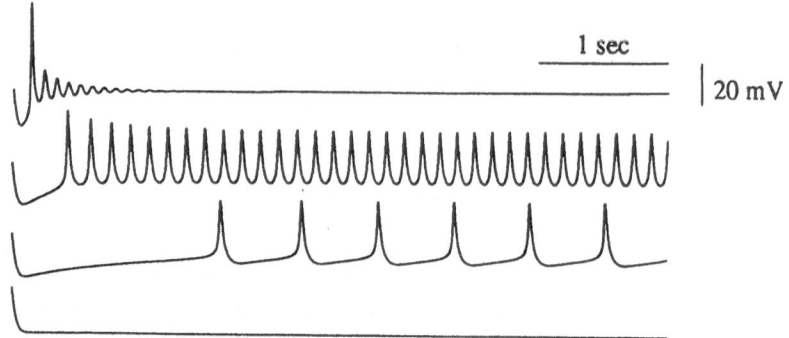

Figure 3: Oscillations in the model of a single thalamic neuron.
The resting and oscillatory states are shown for different values of $\bar{g}_h$. From bottom to top: $\bar{g}_h = 0$ (hyperpolarized resting state), $\bar{g}_h = 0.013 \ mS/cm^2$ (slow oscillation of about 1.6 Hz), $\bar{g}_h = 0.03 \ mS/cm^2$ (fast oscillation of about 7.5 Hz) and $\bar{g}_h = 0.15 \ mS/cm^2$ (depolarized resting state). $\bar{g}_{Ca} = 1 \ mS/cm^2$.

In addition to this current, several other currents were characterized in TCR and RE neurons [24, 46, 47]. In particular, a Na^+ and K^+ inward current I_h, often called anomalous rectifier, has been shown to play an important role in the generation of spontaneous pacemaker-like membrane oscillations [32, 41]. The spontaneous membrane oscillations observed in TCR neurons are reversibly abolished by blockage of I_h [32, 41]. The voltage-clamp studies also show that, similarly to the low-threshold Ca^{2+} current, I_h is activated by hyperpolarization below threshold [32].

Let us assume that this current is also present in RE neurones and introduce a simple kinetic scheme for I_h. As suggested by the apparent single exponential form of I_h following activation or de-activation [32], I_h seems to be associated with a single activation variable. The kinetics of this non-inactivating current is then given by:

$$C_m \frac{dV}{dt} = -g_L (V - V_L) - \bar{g}_{Ca} \, m^3 n \, (V - V_{Ca}) - \bar{g}_h \, h \, (V - V_h)$$

$$\frac{dh}{dt} = -\frac{1}{\tau_h(V)} (h - h_\infty(V)) \tag{6}$$

where $\bar{g}_h$ is the maximum conductance of the h-current and $V_h = -43 \ mV$ is the equilibrium potential. The functions $h_\infty(V)$ and $\tau_h(V)$ are chosen as close as possible to experimental data (from ref. [32]).

As shown in Figure 3, the combination of the two currents I_T and I_h, described by the above equations, leads to various types of oscillating behavior in a single cell. For weak values of $\bar{g}_h$, the membrane does not oscillate and the neuron is in a hyperpolarized resting state near -84 mV. If $\bar{g}_h$ is increased above some threshold value, the membrane displays slow oscillations of about 1.6 Hz. If $\bar{g}_h$ is increased further, the frequency of the oscillations also increases. Finally, for high values of $\bar{g}_h$, the membrane is in a depolarized resting state, near -62 mV, closer to the firing threshold.

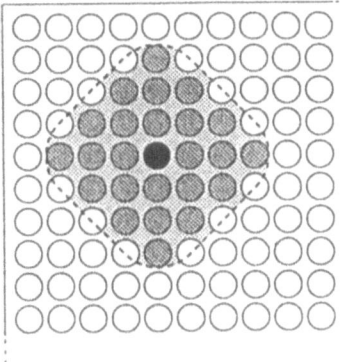

Figure 4: Local connectivity in the model of reticular nucleus.
Each circle represent one of the 400 RE neurons. The extent of the connectivity of a given neuron (black circle) is shown by indicating its neighbors by grey circles. The same rules of connectivity and the same number of neighbors hold for every neuron ($n_v = 24$ here).

3.2   Network of reticular neurons

Physiological data indicate that the RE nucleus is made of a homogeneous population of a single type of neurons [46]. It is also known that RE neurons are connected via dendro-dendritic inhibitory synapses [46]. Therefore, we consider a two dimensional network of the same neurons as described above. Each unit of the network is described by eqs. (5-6) and the neurons are connected via the variable V. The dynamics of such a network is given by:

$$C_m \frac{dV_i}{dt} = C(V_i) - (V_i - V_K) \, K_r \, \sum_j F(V_j)$$

$$C(V_i) = -g_L \, (V_i - V_L) - \bar{g}_{Ca} \, m_i^3 n_i \, (V_i - V_{Ca}) - \bar{g}_h \, h_i \, (V_i - V_h) \qquad (7)$$

$$i = 1...N$$

The equations describing the evolution of the variables m_i, n_i and h_i are identical to eqs. (5-6). The sigmoidal function $F(x) = 1/\left[1 + \exp\left(-0.4 \, (x + 35)\right)\right]$ describes the nonlinear properties of dendro-dendritic synapses. The connectivity is defined locally: each neuron connects to its n_v first neighbors with the same synaptic strength K_r, as illustrated in Fig. 4.

Assessing the conditions of occurence of coherent oscillatory activity in the RE nucleus is of primary importance for understanding cortical rhythmicity. Thalamic RE neurons send their axons into the various relay nuclei of the thalamus. As these nuclei are reciprocally connected to the cortex, an homogeneous oscillation inside the RE nucleus may trigger synchronized oscillations over large cortical territories. We will give a brief description of the type of coherent oscillation in this model of the RE nucleus.

We describe here the type of oscillating behavior found for a network of 400 neurons, with $n_v = 24$ connections per neuron. In the range of parameters considered, this configuration is representative of the typical behavior of the network.

244

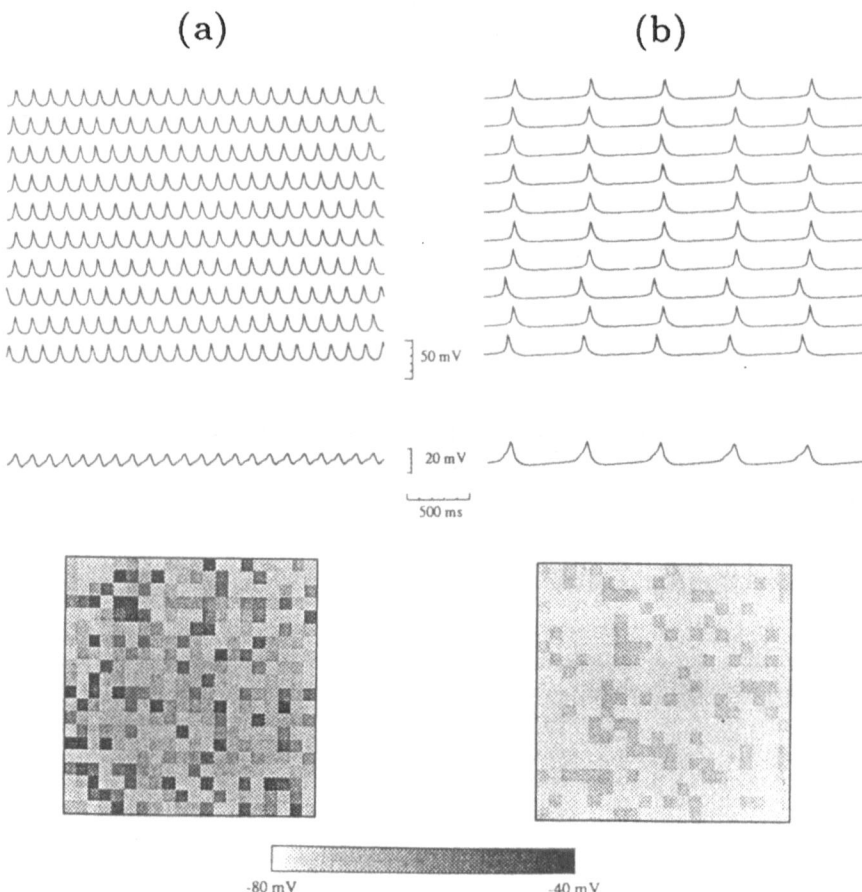

Figure 5: Spatiotemporal activity of the reticular network.
The top figures show the activity of 10 cells chosen along the diagonal of the network. The middle trace depicts the average membrane potential and the bottom figure is a snapshot of the instantaneous activity of the system (cfr. scale for calibration of grays). (a) fast oscillation with $\bar{g}_h = 0.03 \ mS/cm^2$, (b) slow oscillation with $\bar{g}_h = 0.013 \ mS/cm^2$. Same parameters as in Fig. 3, $N = 400$, $K_r = 0.06$.

As for single neurons, the network also exhibits a hyperpolarized and a depolarized resting state. These resting states will be seen for the highest and smallest values of $\bar{g}_h$, as it has been shown for single cells in Fig. 3. As both of these steady states are below threshold, there is no synaptic interaction and the network behaves as a set of independent units. Therefore one sees a uniform steady state.

However, for intermediate values of $\bar{g}_h$, in the range of values for which a single cell oscillates, the network also oscillates with different degrees of spatiotemporal coherence. Figure 5 shows the behavior of several cells in the network as well as the corresponding snapshots of activity and average potential.

It can be seen that for both examples, the frequency of the network oscillation is of the same order as the frequency of the single cell. This property is unexpected since reciprocal inhibitory connections tend to produce out of phase oscillations [52]. However, for first neigbor connections, we found that neighboring neurons oscillates out of phase and the network frequency is about twice the single cell frequency (not shown here).

For both examples of Fig. 5, individual neurons show a seemingly periodic oscillation while the corresponding snapshots of the network show that there is no perfect phase locking. However, the collective behavior may be thought of as being synchronized, as seen by the relatively high amplitude oscillations in the average potential. If one monitors the time evolution of the snapshots, one sees clearly a pulsation of activity (not shown here).

When comparing the two rhythmic behavior in Fig. 5, it also appears that the slower rhythm (Fig. 5b) manifests the higher degree of spatiotemporal coherence. This is shown by the higher amplitude in the average value and the relatively homogeneous snapshots. The fast rhythm (Fig. 5a) displays a relatively complex spatial activity comparing to its seemingly periodic temporal activity.

This behavior is generally seen for different set of values of the parameters such as conductances, size and connectivity. Provided the connectivity extends to relatively distant neighbors (as shown in Fig. 4), the slow rhythm shows the highest synchronization and spatiotemporal coherence.

4 Discussion

In this paper we have presented a simple model of cortical tissue, submitted to thalamic input. The field potentials calculated from this model exhibit transitions of amplitude and frequency which show some similarity with EEG rhythms. In particular, we showed [16] that the slow synchronized rhythms are of higher spatial and temporal coherence whereas the faster rhythms show a lower degree of synchronization.

An elementary model of the cortical tissue subject to an two-variable thalamic oscillator is therefore sufficient to account for the occurence of high and low dimensional chaos in the human electroencephalogram. The methods of nonlinear time series analysis have been used here to compare the output of the model with experimental data. In this respect, both for the model and for the real cerebral cortex, the gobal activity of neural masses turns out to show deterministic chaos.

In order to construct a more realistic model of the thalamus instead of a simple oscillator, a network of biologically more relevant neurons was considered. It seemed that for single neurons, the combination of the low-threshold calcium current and the anomalous rectifier is sufficient to reproduce the main features of the oscillating and resting behavior of a single thalamic cell.

Moreover, the construction of a homogeneous network of such oscillators show coherent collective behavior. The network exhibits spatiotemporal activity with mean frequency of the same order as the frequency of the single cell oscillations. Moreover, as seen in the model of the cortex, the slow rhythms also appear as being the most synchronized.

Experimentally, it has been shown from simultaneous microelectrode recordings [50] that thalamic oscillations seem to be non homogeneous. Circulating waves of activity were seen throughout the thalamus. As we never observed homogeneous oscillations (bulk oscillation), our model of the RE nucleus tends to corroborate these data.

Our results also show that, even at the level of the reticular thalamic nucleus, there are various type of rhythms with various degree of spatiotemporal coherence. Following Steriade and col. [43, 45, 47], we note that the RE nucleus projects to the entire thalamic relay structures, which in turn project to the cortex. Therefore we may expect that finding different degree of spatiotemporally coherent behavior in this nucleus give the potential ability of the thalamus to entrain the entire cerebral cortex into various type of synchronized behavior.

Moreover, we showed that the various types of oscillatory behavior in the RE nucleus may be entirely determined by a single conductance, namely the anomalous rectifier I_h. As this conductance has been shown to be under the control of brain stem afferents to the thalamus [33, 46], our simulations show that the brain stem is potentially able to control directly the transition between resting behavior, coherent slow oscillations and less coherent fast oscillations in the thalamus.

In order to study the various type of sychronized behavior at the level of the cerebral cortex, we must consider a more realistic cortical network, including bidirectional interactions with thalamic and brain stem networks (in preparation). A more detailed account of the oscillatory behavior of the single cell is also in preparation [3, 18].

References

[1] Aihara, K., Takabe, T and Toyoda, M. Chaotic neural networks. *Phys. Lett. A* **144** 333-339, 1990.

[2] Andersen, P. and Andersson, S.A. Thalamic origin of cortical rhythmic activity. in: *Handbook of EEG and Clinical Neurophysiology*. Edited by Remond, A. Amsterdam: Elsevier, 1974, pp. 91-118.

[3] Babloyantz, A. and Destexhe, A., in preparation, 1991.

[4] Babloyantz, A. and Destexhe, A., Strange attractors in the cerebral cortex. in: *Temporal Disorder in Human Oscillatory Systems*. Edited by Rensing, L., an der Heiden, U. and Mackey, M.C., *Springer Series in Synergetics*, **36**. Berlin: Springer, 1987, pp. 48-56.

[5] Babloyantz, A., Nicolis, C. and Salazar, M., Evidence for chaotic dynamics of brain activity during the sleep cycle. *Phys. Lett. A* **111**: 152-156 , 1985.

[6] Bauer, M. and Martiensen, W. Quasi-periodicity route to chaos in neural networks. *Europhys. Lett.* **10**: 427-431, 1989.

[7] Choi, M.M. and Huberman, B.A. Dynamic behavior of nonlinear networks. *Phys. Rev. A* **38**: 3116-3124, 1983.

[8] Coulter, D.A., Huguenard, J.R. and Prince, D.A. Calcium currents in rat thalamocortical relay neurones: kinetic properties of the transient, low-threshold current. *J. Physiol.* **414**: 587-604, 1989.

[9] Creutzfeldt, O. Neuronal Basis of EEG waves. in: *Handbook of EEG and Clinical Neurophysiology.* Edited by Remond, A. Amsterdam: Elsevier, 1974, pp. 6-55.

[10] Creutzfeldt, O., Watanabe, S. and Lux, H.D. Relation between EEG phenomena and potentials of single cortical cells. I. Evoked responses after thalamic and epicortical stimulation. *EEG Clin. Neurophysiol.* **20**: 1-18, 1966.

[11] Creutzfeldt, O., Watanabe, S. and Lux, H.D. Relation between EEG phenomena and potentials of single cortical cells. II. Spontaneous and convulsoid activity. *EEG Clin. Neurophysiol.* **20**: 19-37, 1966.

[12] Crunelli, V., Lightowler, S. and Pollard, C.E. A T-type Ca^{2+} current underlies low-threshold Ca^{2+} potentials in cells of the cat and rat lateral geniculate nucleus. *J. Physiol.* **413**: 543-561, 1989.

[13] Degn, H., Holden, A.V. and Olsen, L.F. (eds.) *Chaos in biological systems,* NATO ASI series, life sciences, vol.138, New York: Plenum Press, 1987.

[14] Derrida, B. and Meir, R. Chaotic behavior of nonlinear networks. *Phys. Rev. A* **38**: 3116-3124, 1988.

[15] Destexhe, A., Sepulchre, J.A. and Babloyantz, A. A comparative study of the experimental quantification of deterministic Chaos. *Phys. Lett. A* **132**: 101-106, 1988.

[16] Destexhe, A. and Babloyantz, A. Pacemaker-induced coherence in cortical networks. *Neural Computation* **3**: 145-154, 1991.

[17] Destexhe, A. and Babloyantz, A. Deterministic chaos in a model of the thalamo-cortical system. in: *Self-Organization, Emerging Properties and Learning,* Edited by A. Babloyantz, ARW Series, Plenum Press, New York, 1991, pp. 127-150.

[18] Destexhe, A. and Babloyantz, A. The interplay between ionic conductances and the various types of oscillations in thalamic neurons, to be submitted to *J. Neurophysiol.*, 1991.

[19] Eckmann, J.P., Kamphorst, S.O., Ruelle, D. and Ciliberto, S. Lyapunov exponents from time series. *Phys. Rev. A.* **34**: 4971-4979, 1986.

[20] Freeman, W.J., Simulation of chaotic EEG patterns with a dynamical model of the olfactory system. *Biol. Cybernetics* **56**: 139-150, 1987.

[21] Gallez, D. and Babloyantz, A. Predictability of human EEG: a dynamical approach. *Biol. Cybernetics* **64**: 381-391, 1991

[22] Grassberger, P. and Procaccia, I. Characterization of strange attractors. *Phys. Rev. Lett.* **50**: 346-349, 1983.

[23] Hodgkin, A.L. and Huxley, A.F. A quantitative description of membrane current and its application to conduction and excitation in nerve. *J. Physiol.* **117**: 500-544, 1952.

[24] Jahnsen, H. and Llinas, R.R. Ionic basis for the electroresponsiveness and oscillatory properties of guinea-pig thalamic neurons *in vitro*. *J. Physiol.* **349**: 227-247, 1984.

[25] Kaplan, J. and Yorke, J. Chaotic behavior of multi-dimensional difference equations. in: *Functional Differential Equations and Approximations of Fixed Points*, Eds. Peitgen, H.O. & Walther, H.O. (Springer, Berlin), *Lectures Notes in Mathematics* Vol. **330**, 1979, pp. 228-236.

[26] Kürten, K.E. and Klarck, J.W. Chaos in neural systems. *Phys. Lett. A* **114**: 413-418, 1986.

[27] Lamarre, Y., Filion, M. and Cordeau, J.P. Neuronal discharge of the ventro-lateral nucleus of the thalamus during sleep and wakefulness in the cat - I. Spontaneous activity. *Exp. Brain Res.* **362**: 122-131, 1971.

[28] Leresche, N., Jassik-Gerschenfeld, D., Haby M., Soltesz, I. and Crunelli, V. Pacemaker-like and other types of spontaneous membrane potential oscillations in thalamocortical cells. *Neurosci. Lett.* **113**: 72-77, 1990.

[29] Leresche, N., Lightowler, S., Soltesz, I., Jassik-Gerschenfeld, D. and Crunelli, V. Low frequency oscillatory activities intrinsic to rat and cat thalamocortical cells. *J. Physiol.* **441**: 155-174, 1991.

[30] Lopes da Silva, F.H., Van Lierop, T.H.M.T., Schrijer, C.F.M. and Storm van Leeuwen, W. Organization of thalamic and cortical alpha rhythm: spectra and coherences. *EEG Clin. Neurophysiol.* **35**: 627-639, 1973.

[31] Lux, H.D. and Pollen, D.A. Electrical constants of neurons in the motor cortex of the cat. *J. Physiol.* **29**: 207-220, 1966.

[32] McCormick, D.A. and Pape, H.C. Properties of a hyperpolarization-activated cation current and its role in rhythmic oscillations in thalamic relay neurones. *J. Physiol.* **431**: 291-318, 1990.

[33] McCormick, D.A. and Pape, H.C. Noradrenergic modulation of a hyperpolarization-activated cation current in thalamic relay neurones. *J. Physiol.* **431**: 319-342, 1990.

[34] Nunez, P.L. *Electric Fields of the Brain. The Neurophysics of EEG.* New York: Oxford University Press, 1981.

[35] Press, W.H., Flannery, B.P., Teukolsky, S.A. and Vetterling, W.T. *Numerical Recipes. The Art of Scientific Computing.* Cambridge: Cambridge University Press, 1986.

[36] Ranck, J.B. Specific impedance of rabbit cerebral cortex. *Exp. Neurol.* **7**: 144-152, 1963.

[37] Rapp, P.E., Bashore, T.R., Martinerie, J.M., Albano, A.M., Zimmerman, I.D. and Mees, A.I. Dynamics of brain electrical activity *Brain Topography* **2**: 99-118, 1989.

[38] Riedel, U., Kühn, R. and van Hemmen, J.L. Temporal sequences and chaos in neural nets. *Phys. Rev. A* **38**: 1105-1108, 1988.

[39] Rose, R.M. and Hindmarsh, J.L. A model of a thalamic neuron. *Proc. Roy. Soc. Lond. Ser. B.* **225**: 161-193, 1985.

[40] Sandler, Y.M. Models of neural networks with selective memorization and chaotic behavior. *Phys. Lett. A* **144**: 462-466, 1990.

[41] Soltesz, I., Lightowler, S., Leresche, N., Jassik-Gerschenfeld, D., Pollard, C.E. and Crunelli, V. Two inward currents and the transformation of low frequency oscillations of rat and cat thalamocortical cells. *J. Physiol.* **441**: 175-197, 1991.

[42] Sompolinsky, H. Crisanti, A. and Sommers, H.J. Chaos in random neural networks. *Phys. Rev. Lett.* **61**: 259-262, 1988.

[43] Steriade, M. and Deschênes, M. The thalamus as a neuronal oscillator. *Brain Res. Rev.* **8**: 1-63, 1984.

[44] Steriade, M., Deschênes, M., Domich, L. and Mulle, C. Abolition of spindle oscillations in thalamic neurons disconnected from nucleus reticularis thalami. *J. Neurophysiol.* **54**: 1473-1497, 1985.

[45] Steriade, M., Gloor, P., Llinas, R.R., Lopes da Silva, F.H. and Mesulam, M.M. Basic mechanisms of cerebral rhythmic activities. *EEG Clin. Neurophysiol.* **76**: 481-508, 1990.

[46] Steriade, M., Jones, E.G. and Llinas, R.R. *Thalamic Oscillations and Signalling*, John Wiley & Sons, New York, 1990.

[47] Steriade, M. and Llinas, R.R. The functional states of the rhalamus and the associated neuronal interplay. *Physiol. Rev.* **68**: 649-742, 1988.

[48] Traub, R.D. and Miles, R. *Neuronal Networks of the Hippocampus.* Cambridge Univ. Press, Cambridge, 1991.

[49] Tsuda, I., Koerner, E. and Shimizu, H. Memory dynamics in asynchronous neural networks. *Prog. Theor. Phys.* **78**: 51-71, 1987.

[50] Verzeano, M. and Negishi, K. Neuronal activity in cortical and thalamic networks. A study with multiple microelectrodes. *J. Gen. Physiol.* **43**: 177-195, 1960.

[51] Wang, X.J., Rinzel, J. and Rogawski, M.A. A model of the T-type calcium current ald the low-threshold spike in thalamic neurons. *J. Neurophysiol.* **66**: 839-849, 1991.

[52] Wang, X.J., Rinzel, J. and Rogawski, M.A. Low-threshold spikes and rhythmic oscillations in thalamic neurons. in: *Analysis and Modeling of Neural Systems*, University of Berkeley, July 1990.

[53] West, B.J. *Fractals and Chaos in Medicine.* Berlin: Springer, 1989.

A 'microscopic' model
of collective oscillations in the cortex

J.Leo van Hemmen, Wulfram Gerstner, and Raphael Ritz
Physik-Department der TU München
D-8046 Garching bei München

Abstract

The discovery of coherent oscillations in the primary visual cortex of the cat has aroused considerable theoretical interest. Most model networks that try to simulate these collective oscillations use some kind of oscillatory element as the basic unit of the network. It is, however, not clear how these oscillations should be described on a more microscopic level. Here we present a network that is based on a couple of measurable neurobiological quantities: (i) A distribution of axonal delay times for the transmission of spikes. (ii) A postsynaptic response described by realistic excitatory or inhibitory postsynaptic potentials (EPSP or IPSP). (iii) A threshold dynamics for the model neurons that includes refractoriness and noise. For a realistic set of parameters, the network shows collective oscillations only while an external signal is applied. If the parameters are changed significantly, other scenarios result with a behaviour which is qualitatively different in that it shows prolonged oscillations or no oscillations at all.

1 Introduction

Neurons communicate via the exchange of spikes, action potentials that are strongly localized in space *and* time. If, then, a spatio-temporal configuration of spikes has to code the information presented to the network, one may wonder how several aspects of the same object are either discerned (pattern segmentation) or considered as belonging together (feature linking). A possible solution could be, for instance [1], that feature linking is realized through a *coherent* spiking of different regions of the cortex. The discovery of 50 Hz oscillations in the primary visual cortex of the cat during presentation of a stimulus provided the first experimental evidence [1, 2] that this kind of feature linking might indeed be possible. Its modeling has attracted quite a bit of theoretical interest – just scan this book.

Most models networks are based on some kind of nonlinear oscillator [3]-[7] or phase equation [8, 9] which are not derived but just postulated phenomenologically. These equations are assumed to describe either the internal dynamics of a single neuron

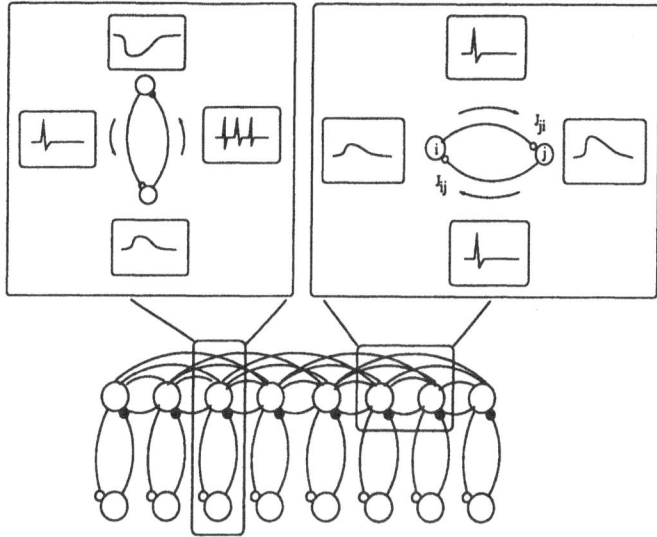

Figure 1: *Network structure.* The network consists of a fully connected layer of neurons with Hebbian synapses and a layer of inhibitory neurons that are *locally* connected to the 'Hebbian' layer. The neurons communicate with each other via the exchange of spikes that are transmitted along the axons and evoke an EPSP or IPSP in the postsynaptic neuron.

or else the average activity of local ensembles of excitatory or inhibitory neurons. In any case, the equations describe an intrinsic oscillatory behavior of the elements of the network. Collective oscillations of the network as a whole are understood as 'locking' of these oscillatory elements.

Assuming intrinsic oscillators as the basic units of the network, however, seems questionable. We may ask how these oscillations are produced on the level of single neurons communicating with each other via the exchange of spikes. We try to answer this question by going back to some measurable neurobiological quantities. In particular, we consider the axonal transmission delays that are distributed in some realistic range, the excitatory and inhibitory postsynaptic potentials (EPSP and IPSP) that are produced at the soma of the postsynaptic neuron after receival of a spike, and the threshold voltage that must be reached in order that a neuron fires. While the model stays close to neurobiology, the network structure is simple enough to allow for mathematical analysis as well as for straightforward simulations.

2   The model network

The model network consists of two different populations of neurons that we consider as organized in two layers (Fig.1). The top layer is a fully connected net of N neurons ($i = 1 \ldots N$) and their axonal connections that end in Hebbian synapses [10]. Each neuron of this Hebbian layer is *locally* connected to one of the inhibitory neurons that form the bottom or inhibitory layer. The inhibitory neuron controls the activity of its 'local partner-neuron' which has *long-ranged* connections all over the Hebbian net.

The Hebbian network has to learn q patterns by adjusting the efficacy J_{ij} of the synaptic connection from neuron j to neuron i according to a Hebbian rule. A pattern μ is a set of random variables ξ_i^μ $(i = 1, \ldots N)$ that are distributed stochastically with mean activity a, i.e., $\xi_i^\mu = \pm 1$ with probability $(1 \pm a)/2$. Learning these patterns yields an asymmetric efficacy matrix [11]

$$J_{ij} = \frac{1}{N(1 - a^2)} \sum_{\mu=1}^{q} \xi_i^\mu (\xi_j^\mu - a). \tag{1}$$

Thus, each pair of neurons has axonal connections in both directions but, in contrast to most other Hebbian models, the synaptic efficacy J_{ij} for a transmission from neuron j to neuron i may be, and in general is, different from the transmission efficacy in the other direction.

The neurons in the network communicate with each other via the exchange of spikes which we describe by an Ising variable $S_i = \pm 1$. If a neuron j in the Hebbian layer fires, the signal of the spike is transmitted along the axon and over the synaptic cleft to the neurons of the Hebbian layer as well as to the partner neuron in the inhibitory layer. Let us consider the effect on a neuron i in the Hebbian layer first (Fig. 1, inset top right).

If neuron j fires at time $t = t_n$, the spike variable is set to $S_j(t_n) = +1$. A postsynaptic neuron i that is connected to neuron j through a synapse of efficacy J_{ij} will receive the signal of this spiking event only after some transmission delay Δ_i that we assume to depend on the postsynaptic neuron only. After this delay an excitatory (or inhibitory) potential is evoked at the soma of the postsynaptic neuron. Its time-course will be described by a response function $\epsilon(\tau)$ (see Fig.2, top curves for the typical shape of an EPSP), its amplitude is determined by the synaptic efficacy J_{ij}. If we add the contributions of all neurons, we find the total postsynaptic potential at the soma of neuron i

$$h_i(t_n) = \sum_{j=1}^{N} J_{ij} \sum_{\tau=0}^{\infty} \epsilon(\tau)[S_j(t_n - \tau - \Delta_i) + 1] + h_i^I(t_n) + h_i^S(t_n), \tag{2}$$

where $h_i^I(t_n)$ is the contribution of the inhibitory partner neuron of neuron i and $h_i^S(t_n)$ is the input by an external signal. Note that the axonal transmission delay is not identical for each neuron but may be a stochastically distributed variable.

The inhibitory contribution can be obtained as follows (Fig.1, inset top left). If neuron i has fired at some earlier time t_m, a spike has been transmitted to the inhibitory partner neuron where it evokes an EPSP. This effect is assumed to be strong enough to excite spiking of the inhibitory neuron. Its spikes produce a series of inhibitory postsynaptic potentials (IPSP) at the soma of neuron i. Summing then yields an effective inhibitory contribution $\eta_i(\tau)$, the time course of which is drawn schematically in the lower part of Fig. 2. Its exact duration depends on the specific pair of excitatory and inhibitory neurons, as indicated by the subscript i. Putting things together, the firing of neuron i results in an inhibitory feedback to its own potential at some later time t_n,

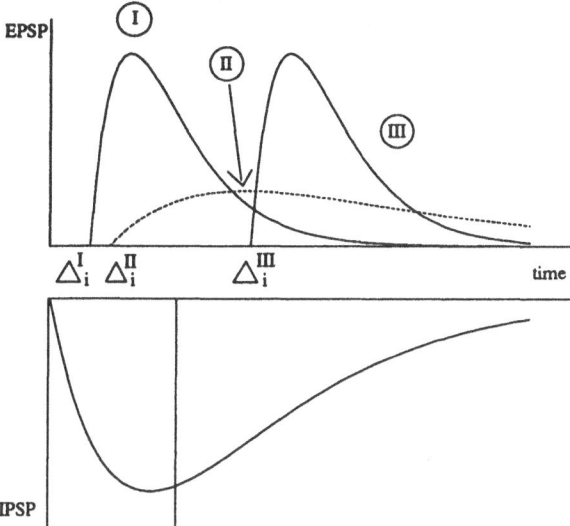

Figure 2: *The three scenarios.* Top – excitatory postsynaptic potential (EPSP); bottom – inhibitory postsynaptic potential (IPSP); both plotted as a function of time after emission of a presynaptic spike. Scenario I: sharply peaked EPSP (short rise time of 2 *ms*) and short axonal delays (distributed between 1 and 4 *ms*); Scenario II: broad EPSP (rise time of 6 *ms*) and short axonal delays (2 – 5 *ms*); Scenario III: sharply peaked EPSP (rise time of 2 *ms*) but long axonal delays (12 – 15 *ms*). The vertical line in the bottom part of the figure indicates the duration of the absolute refractory period of the neurons.

$$h_i^I(t_n) = \sum_{\tau=0}^{\infty} \eta_i(\tau) \frac{1}{2}[S_i(t_n - \tau) + 1]. \tag{3}$$

Due to the inhibition, the neuron is turned off after firing and kept quiet for some time thereafter. If the inhibitory potential decays, threshold can be reached again. Instead of a strict threshold θ, we assume that firing occurs stochastically with probability

$$\text{Prob}[S_i(t_{n+1}) = +1] = \frac{1}{2}\{1 + \tanh[\beta(h_i(t_n) - \Theta)]\}, \tag{4}$$

where the parameter β measures the amount of noise in the system. For $\beta \to \infty$ we regain the noiseless case with a sharp threshold condition. In the following we always assume that updating of the system is done for all neurons in parallel.

3 Macroscopic states of the network

It is convenient to analyze the macroscopic states of the network in terms of the *overlap* with the patterns the system has been trained on. The overlap $m^\mu(t_n)$

measures the correlation between a network state $S_j(t_n)$ and pattern μ and is defined by

$$m^\mu(t_n) = \frac{1}{N(1-a^2)} \sum_{j=1}^{N} (\xi_j^\mu - a)[S_j(t_n) + 1]. \tag{5}$$

If the network state is identical with pattern μ, then $m^\mu = 1$, otherwise $m^\mu < 1$. If we use (5) in (2), then we find

$$h_i(t_n) = \sum_{\mu=1}^{q} \xi_i^\mu \sum_{\tau=0}^{\infty} \epsilon(\tau) m^\mu(t_n - \tau - \Delta_i) + h_i^I(t_n) + h_i^S(t_n). \tag{6}$$

In our simulations for a network of $N = 4000$ neurons trained on 5 patterns we have assumed a small threshold $\theta = 0.05$ and a limited amount of noise $\beta^{-1} = 0.015$. The transmission delays and postsynaptic potentials are chosen according to three different scenarios as explained in Fig. 2. From equations (4) and (6) it is clear that independent of the choice of scenario the trivial state $m^\mu = 0$ for all μ is a stable state of the system as long as no external signal is applied. This is seen in figure 3 during the first 200 time steps. If an external signal $h_i^S(t_n) = \gamma(\xi_i^\mu + 1)$ is presented that supports pattern μ with a strength $\gamma = 0.05$, a finite overlap with this pattern evolves. The overlap can be either stationary (Fig. 3, middle) or oscillatory (Fig. 3, top and bottom) indicating synchronized spiking of the neurons. If the external signal is removed, the oscillations persist in scenario III, whereas in scenario I and II the network returns to the resting state. Thus, depending on the shape of the EPSP and the duration of the transmission delays we find three qualitatively different and mutually exclusive scenarios. It can be shown analytically [12] that it is the EPSP slope $\frac{\partial \epsilon(\tau)}{\partial \tau}|_T$ where T is the oscillation period that determines whether an oscillation is stable or not.

4 Discussion

Experimental axonal delays are of the order of $1 - 2$ ms, measured postsynaptic responses have a rise time of about 5 ms and inhibitory effects last for approximately $15 - 20$ ms. Thus scenario I seems to be a realistic description of the elementary neurobiological processes. The simulations revealed a number of attractive features of this scenario. First, oscillations persist only while an external signal is applied, a result that compares well to measurements in the cortex. The oscillation period of about 50 Hz is consistent with the experiments. Second, coherent oscillations are possible even though there is a wide distribution of delay times. Due to noise and different durations of the IPSP, any single neuron shows a certain degree of randomness in its spiking (see the spike raster in Fig. 4), but the overall synchronicity of the spiking is nevertheless preserved. In addition to the results shown here we have found that two hemisheres connected by delay lines in the range of 3 to 7 ms do oscillate coherently. Finally, the capability of the network for separation of up to 4 simultaneously presented patterns (see Fig. 4 for two patterns) supports the idea that collective oscillations in the cortex might also be useful in the context of pattern segmentation [1] – as alluded to in the introduction.

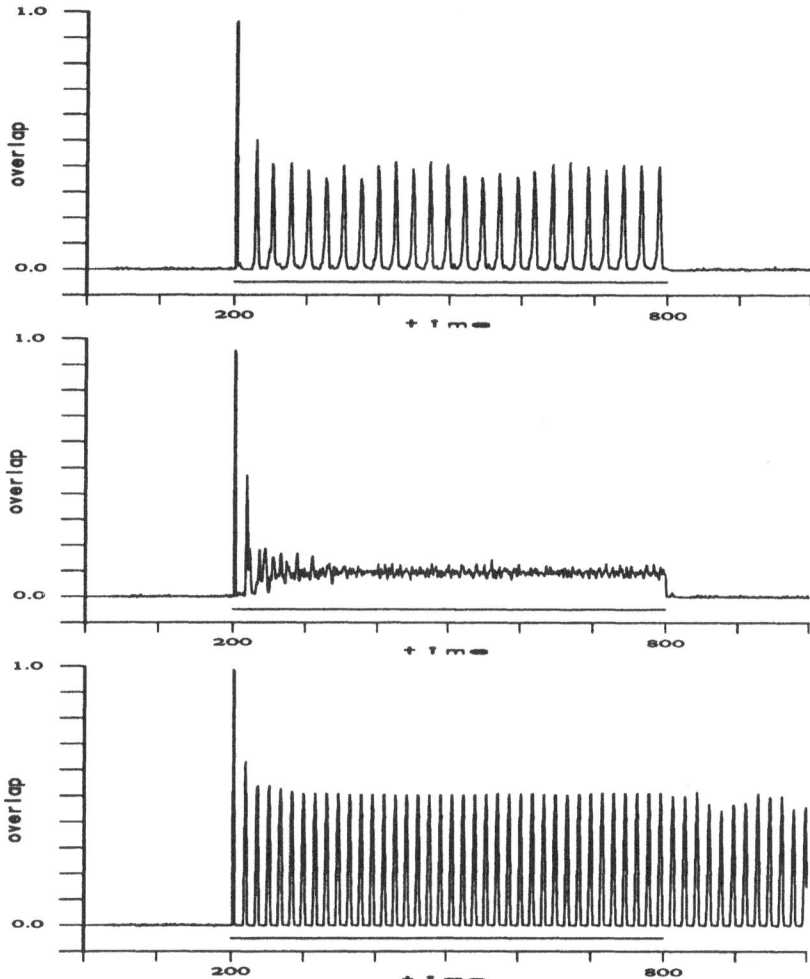

Figure 3: *Simulation results.* Overlap with a specific pattern as function of time for the three different scenarios. This pattern is supported by a weak external signal for a time between 200 and 800 time steps as indicated by the horizontal bar.
Top – scenario I, oscillations occur only while the external signal is applied.
Middle – scenario II, transient behavior to a stationary retrieval state.
Bottom – scenario III, oscillations remain even after the signal has been turned off.

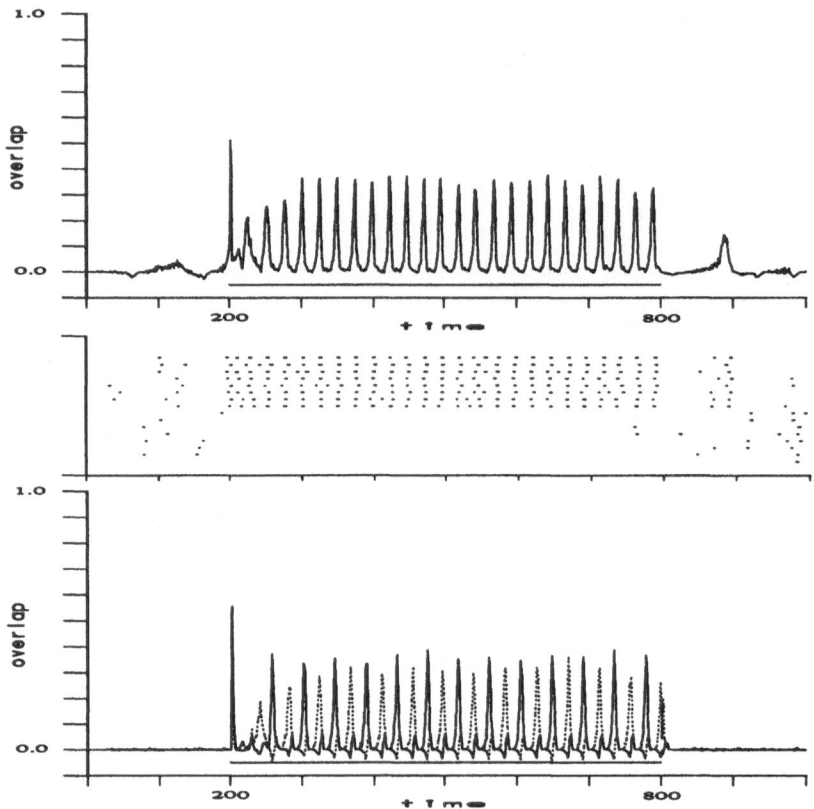

Figure 4: *Simulation results with scenario I.* Top: Overlap with pattern 1 which is supported by an external signal (horizontal bar); all parameters are as in Fig. 3 except the noise ($\beta^{-1} = 0.02$). Even if no signal is present ($t < 200$ or $t > 800$), noise can induce spontaneous activity bursts of the network. This is seen more clearly in the next plot (middle) showing a *spike raster* of 16 neurons observed in this run. For each neuron, the spikes are indicated by dots and plotted in a string parallel to the time axis. Eight of these neurons are active during retrieval of the pattern and show collective oscillations (vertical columns) while the signal is applied (upper 8 traces). Neurons that are inactive should be suppressed during retrieval but show spontaneous activity if no signal is present (lower 8 traces). Bottom: The signal now supports two different patterns with equal strength, i.e., $h_i^S \propto (\xi_i^1 + 1) + (\xi_i^2 + 1)$. Note that the overlap with pattern 1 (solid line) oscillates phase – shifted to the overlap with pattern 2 (dotted line). Pattern segmentation also works with 3 and 4 patterns as input (data not shown).

Acknowledgments

We thank Reinhard Eckhorn for stimulating discussions and Andreas K. Engel as well as Peter König for helpful comments.

References

[1] Eckhorn, R., Bauer, R., Jordan, W., Brosch, M., Kruse, W., Munk, M. and Reitboeck, H.J. 1988. Coherent oscillations: A mechanism of feature linking in the visual cortex? *Biol. Cybern.* **60**, 121-130

[2] Gray, C.M., König, P., Engel, A.K. and Singer, W. 1989. Oscillatory responses in cat visual cortex exhibit inter-columnar synchronization which reflects global stimulus properties. *Nature* **338**, 334-337

[3] Baird, B. 1990. Learning with synaptic nonlinearities in a coupled oscillator model of Olfactory Cortex. *preprint*

[4] Kurrer, C., Nieswand, B., and Schulten, K. 1990. A model for synchronous activity in the visual cortex. In: *Self-Organization, emerging properties and learning* A. Babloyantz, Ed., Plenum Press

[5] Schuster, H.G. and Wagner, P. 1990. A model for neuronal oscillations in the visual cortex. *Biol. Cybern.* **64**, 77-82

[6] Wang, D., Buhmann, J. and von der Malsburg, C. 1990. Pattern segmentation in associative memory. *Neural Computation* **2**, 94-106

[7] König, P. and Schillen, T.B. 1991. Stimulus – dependent assembly formation of oscillatory responses: I. Synchronization. *Neural Computation* **3**, 155-166

[8] Sompolinsky, H., Golomb, D., and Kleinfeld, D. 1990. Global processing of visual stimuli in a neural network of coupled oscillators. *Proc. Natl. Acad. Sci. USA* **87**, 7200-7204

[9] Niebur, E., Kammen, D.M., Koch, C., Ruderman, D., and Schuster, H.G. 1991. Phase-coupling in two-dimensional networks of interacting oscillators. In: *Advances in Neural Information Processing Systems 3*, 123-129 Morgan Kaufmann

[10] Buhmann, J. 1989. Oscillations and low firing rates in associative memory neural networks. *Phys. Rev. A* **40**, 4145-4148

[11] van Hemmen, J.L., Gerstner, W., Herz, A.V.M., Kühn, R., Sulzer, B. und Vaas, M. [1990] *Encoding and decoding of patterns with are correlated in space and time.* In: G. Dorffner, Ed., Konnektionismus in Artificial Intelligence und Kognitionsforschung, Springer–Verlag Berlin Heidelberg, (1990)

[12] Gerstner, W., Ritz, R., and van Hemmen, J.L. [1991] *Collective oscillations in the cortex: the importance of axonal transmission delays and postsynaptic response* preprint

Temporal Processing in Brain Activity

J G Taylor
Centre for Neural Networks
Department of Mathematics, King's College London
London, UK

Abstract

A framework is presented in terms of which models of temporal sequence storage, attention, consciousness and self-consciousness are given. The framework incorporates various features of neurons - stochasticity, short, and long-term temporal processes - together with simple forms of net architecture.

The sequence storage uses topographic or coupled feedback networks and local learning rules, and leads to context sensitivity. The attention and consciousness modelling is at systems level, and uses various known cortical and sub-cortical structures involved in the subject as well as new results from magnetoencephalography. The models are related to a relational automata approach to consciousness and to plant modelling in control theory.

1   Introduction

Time is fundamental in all physical and hence in all physiological, processes. Yet it enters in the latter at what appears to be a bewildering array of scales and in a variety of guises. Thus in human responses there is the twenty to thirty millisecond temporal order threshold for auditory, visual or sensory events [1], [2] and for pursuit latency periodicities [2]. At slightly longer scales, there is the one to two hundred milliseconds of human reaction time, the ten Hertz oscillations of the Parkinson tremor, and the two to three hundred millisecond lapse between visual saccades. Longer still is the roughly three second duration of behavioural episodes as observed in a variety of interpersonal interactions and human cultures [3]. At even longer scales are the approximately hourly sleep/wake cycles, the daily sleep cycle and the monthly female menstrual cycle. We will not consider the longer time scales here, but limit the time duration under discussion to at most the two to three second duration of behavioural episodes. That is not to say that the longer temporal scales are not of interest or importance in understanding human activity. However the physiological structures necessary to analyse in modelling the longer temporal durations are outside the scope of our own personal knowledge and extend beyond the cortex and certain mid-brain structures (especially thalamus and hippocampus) on which we wish to concentrate.

The purpose of this article is to attempt to construct a neuronal modelling framework in which these various temporal processes can be hoped to be explained, and to give tentative explanations for the processes themselves. These latter will be taken specifically to be

(a)   memory itself, considered as temporal sequence storage (TSS),

(b)   attention, regarded as a temporal process involving a sequence of at least three disparate activities (disengage, move and re-engage [4]) and at two different levels (exogenous and endogenous),

(c)   consciousness and self-consciousness, the latter seen as an iterative process of modelling the modeller, etc.

The models of the above psychological processes are discussed in subsequent sections, following a description of the neuronal modelling framework in the next section. This gives an analysis of the basic tools in terms of which the models are couched. The structure and function dilemmas facing all such modelling attempts is first outlined and the enormous armory of single neuronal and network models at our disposal is described. The basic philosophy behind our approach is then presented, so allowing the modelling framework to be finally specified. The paper itself can be seen to lie in the gap between the two disciplines of computational neuroscience and artificial neural networks, a gap which is increasingly being bridged in order to give rise to more fruitful interchanges between the two fields. It is hoped that the paper will help strengthen the bridge.

2   The neuronal modelling framework

2.1   The structure and functional dilemmas

The two main dilemmas which have to be faced by any serious attempt to model the psychological processes mentioned in the previous section are

(1)   the structural dilemma: what level of complexity must be included (of single neurons, of their connection in an area network, and of the connections between areas)?

(2)   the functional dilemma: what are the functions being performed by the various components, either in each neuron, by each neuron or each area, in

contributing to the process under consideration?

Some details of these two dilemmas have been discussed elsewhere [5], and we will only outline the main features which need to be addressed. A list of single neuron or architectural features and the responses they confer are outlined in table I.

We begin with the structural dilemma. The subtlety, especially in the temporal domain, of the responsiveness of single neurons is slowly being unravelled. One aspect of this is the plethora of ionic channels and their detailed time courses [6], which give a decidedly non-trivial temporal feature to the response of such neurons. Moreover, there appear to be different ionic currents in neurons in different brain areas, so helping confer considerably different response patterns to thalamic nuclei [7], for example, compared to cortical areas. The effects of having delayed ionic currents will, in general, be to emphasise response to signals time delayed by a corresponding amount. Non-trivial effects of the interaction between various potential-dependent ionic currents may, in special circumstances, produce bi- or even multi-phasic responses of neurons [6]. Thus a depolarization from the resting membrane potential leads to a graded response of a certain class of cells, whilst depolarization from a suitably hyperpolarised cell produces a burst of spikes. Such bi-phasic responses can be modelled directly in terms of a set of differential equations for a set of suitable coupled variables [8], so is considered as a separate feature in table 1 to that of ionic channels (item 2), although it should properly come under that heading. Another subtlety of neurons is the presence of capacitative neuronal membrane. This leads to the leaky integrator model, which allied with the non-trivial neuronal geometry of pyramidical cells in, say, cortex or hippocampus, can again give subtle temporal response powers to inputs with a variety of time courses. In general temporal summation effects arise from leaky integrator neurons.

There is also the nature of short- or long-term modification of synaptic weights under a range of experiences [9], which will in general cause one type of temporal filter being carried out by a neuron (or neural net) to be transformed into another. Synaptic noise is also relevant in the temporal content, especially since it can build up over time in a leaky integrator neuron [10]. Such noise will modify the response properties of a neuron considerably, changing, for example, its powers of generalisation [11]. One of the basic questions on neuronal signalling presently under active discussion is the level of precision occurring in the temporal domain. The earlier result of Singer and his co-workers on synchronised oscillations between a pair of nerve cells in visual cortex, with similar receptive field or orientation sensitivity, (in the gamma frequency range (20-80Hz) [12], [13] have been brought into question by other workers. They claim that it is synchronisation of neuronal activity which is important in cortical information processing [14], and not the existence of well-defined oscillations. In order for such synchronisation to be achieved over suitable ensembles of neurons in a module it may be necessary to include temporal effects in a very precise manner. Even the shape of the nerve impulse may be important here to allow for precision of each neurons response to within a millisecond; to take account of this, active membrane must be incorporated in the axon hillock, as described under entry 7 in table 1.

Another feature of timing relevant to the above question of cortical oscillations v cortical synchronisation is that of the possible presence of intrinsically oscillatory inhibitory interneurons in cortex [15] (and in sub-cortical structures [16]). It is possible to use these to build the ICON model of the author [17], which gives an underpinning of the Singer results, and may also be used for the related synchronisation results of [14]; these appear as entry 8 in table 1.

Other temporal features of neurons that may or may not be included in modelling are refractory period, dendritic spikes, second messengers, nerve impulse feedback over the neuron after firing (the 'reset' wave) and time delays, among others. At the same time the nature of the non-linearity of the response, in its dependence on the inputs, may be modified by non-standard synapses, as dendro-dendritic, serial, glomerular, reciprocal, axo-axonal, etc. Modifying a standard synapse into one or other of these types will change the resulting temporal responses of neurons. These various features are summarised in table 1. Some of the temporal response properties which a given feature imbues in a neuron possessing it are given in the adjacent column of the table; these will be discussed further in the following sub-section. A useful discussion is given in [18] of the static properties conferred on neurons by various of the above features.

Beside the problem of complexity of single neurons is that of neuronal types and their connections. Beside the variety of excitatory neurons, with long-range as well as short-range connections are the preponderantly local interneurons. These have already been noted when imbued with intrinsic oscillatory properties, as giving certain interesting temporal features to a net, for the ICON model, as noted above. More generally interneurons can function in a feedforward or feedback manner. In the former mode they can perform temporal differentiation of inputs by means of the well-known time-delayed inhibitory post-synaptic responses (IPSPs) in thalamic and hippocampal excitatory neurons. Feedback inhibition can be used to keep activity local, such as in the formation of topographic maps, or to preserve stability, or to perform differencing of output from later input to lead to temporal difference learning, as in the hippocampal model of [19]. There are also numerous further features of gross architecture, which we will discuss under functional properties.

The functional dilemma is one which has faced neuroscience ever since localisation of function in the dog cortex in 1865 was discovered by Fritsch and Hitzig, and which has been added to with increasing detail since then. Use of anatomical, physiological and psychological methods have indicated the division of cortex into many areas with different functions, as well as giving increasing detail for sub-cortical structures involved in information processing. Yet due to the high level of inter-connectivity between the various cortical areas, and between them and sub-cortical structures, it has proved difficult to say with precision what function each structure is performing in the total scheme. For example it is clear that the various early visual areas V1,V2,V3, V4,V5, etc are engaged in analysis of orientation, colour, texture, motion of visual inputs, etc [20], [21]. However the detailed manner in which these features are computed is unknown; for example the importance of feedback from 'higher' areas, or of processing between cortical layers 3,4 and 5, or of lateral inhibition, is still relatively unclear. Similarly the role of the heavy cortico-thalamic feedback to the lateral geniculate nucleus is yet to be explained convincingly, in spite of interesting attempts [22]. Even greater uncertainty exists over the function of areas in associative or prefrontal cortex as it similarly does with hippocampus and with thalamic nuclei. That the hippocampus is crucial to memory is by now well-documented, but there have been at least a dozen suggested rules for it, including the recent one that it is well adapted to store temporal sequences by its tri-synaptic feedback structure [19].

The functional dilemma arises then, not only from the possible complexity of the processing performed by each cortical area but also the added inter-area interaction. This latter makes it seem as if the information processing problem can only be solved at the global level. All areas (or nearly all) must be accounted for simultaneously in the information-handling scheme of things before the modus operandi of the brain can be understood. The moral of this is "All or none".

It would appear that we meet here the nub of the combined structural/functional dilemma. The multitude of features (and their parameters) of single neurons, sketched briefly under the structural dilemma heading earlier in this sub-section lead to a combinatorial explosion of possibilities when being tried out as models for neurons in each of the areas of the brain. In the absence of microscopic variables describing activity in an area, it would seem difficult to test each of the possible neuronal models when the many areas are put together to give the total response. The structural/functional dilemma now faces us in a related guise: how are local and global processing related? We must try to bridge the gap between specified local structure and the hoped-for global response. How, then, can we proceed to bridge this gap?

One important feature, which has so far been omitted, is the possibility of experimental clues as to global brain processing as based on local or semi-local activity but measured simultaneously over the whole brain. These clues are already becoming available in terms of measurements of the global magnetic field arising from brain activity during information processing. The use of high-sensitivity many-channel (SQUID) detectors allows for the activity of ensembles of nerve cells to be detected at both cortical and sub-cortical level [23],[24]. Coupled with already available EEG measurements it should be possible to develop models of area and coupled area activity which incorporate and/or explain these experimental findings. This has already begun with the ICON model [17] and will be discussed in more detail later in this paper. A further window on the brain exists by the use of voltage-sensitive dyes to measure movement of neural activity over millimetres of cortical surface [25].

These new windows on the brain are clearly of great importance in our programme - they begin to fill in the temporal nature of the on-going global activity in terms of that in localised cortical and sub-cortical areas monitored by each of the various magnetic or electric electrodes. However it does not quite resolve the structural/functional dilemma of the previous but one paragraph, since the structural dilemma, and its concomitant combinatorial explosion, is still with us. We still have to answer the question 'which neuron is to be used?' before we can begin to analyse the function.

We might start at the most complicated extreme, putting in all of the features of table 1 (and many more still left out) in the model neuron. This has already been attempted in numbers of studies. Although these are of great value in understanding the experimentally observed properties of single cortical, hippocampal or thalamic neurons, they have not led to any guiding principles allowing the solution of the global information processing problem. In a sense the old tag "one cannot see the wood for the trees" is appropriate here. Moreover, recent studies, such as [26], indicate that certain gross features of global network activity (such as activity spreading across the net) can arise from simplified neuron models based on mean firing frequency and time delays only.

The other extreme is to start with the simplest possible neuron and add on the different features of table 1 to see which are crucial to obtain suitable information processing capabilities. These latter are to be taken from the whole range of experimental data of neurophysiology and neuropsychology. Allied to this would be the use of the developing theory of artificial neural nets based on statistical mechanical and information theoretic ideas. In the former case, there have been recent results on capacity [27] and generalisation [28] for leaky integrator neurons which are of value. In the latter there are presently only results for binary decision neurons (BDNs) without temporal summation [29]. The program of sequentially complexifying the BDN neuron has been followed by the author over the last few years (and started in 1971 [30]). We will consider the general features of the programme in a little more detail in the next sub-section.

2.2 Models of neurons

In order to prevent the above-mentioned combinatorial explosion arising from the plethora of features of single neuron activity, it is necessary to place these features roughly in order of their expected importance in resulting information processing properties. Three important parallel strands can be recognised in the properties of table 1, and these are indicated in figure 1. They are:

(a)   the addition of synaptic noise (#3 of table 1)

(b)   the addition of leaky membrane characteristics (#1 of table 1)

(c)   the addition of spike generation (# 7 of table 1).

Each of these leads to interesting and useful applications, even at hardware level in the case of pRAMs [31] and of the silicon retina arising using a lateral inhibitory net of leaky integrator neurons [32], [33].

The above three strands emphasise the three distinct properties of (1) stochasticity, (2) relatively slow and smooth time course processes (longer than 5-100 msec) (3) relatively fast and singular time course processes (less than 5 msec) in neuronal response to inputs. The smooth characteristics of (2) arise from first order time differential equation whilst the singular characteristics of (3) stem from sharp dependence of neuronal response on membrane potential.

It is now possible to loosely group the various features of table 1 under these three headings:

(1)   stochasticity: features 6 of table 1

(2)   smooth time course processes: features 1, 2, 4, 5, 8, 11, 12, 14, 15.

(3)   singular time course processes: features 3, 7, 9, 10, 13.

The above division is certainly not absolute, but can be regarded as a rough and ready guide to the manner in which the neuronal response depends on its inputs and slow variations of its parameters.

Our problem is thus reduced to that of exploring in parallel the expected information processing powers obtained by the addition of single neuron features under the stochastic (1), smooth time course (2), or singular time course (3), headings above. There are an increasing number of results being obtained from exploring various of these features in the artificial neural network framework. That associated with branch (1) may be seen in its most general context in pRAMs, and is described in [34], [35], [36]. That associated with smooth time course processes will be discussed in the next section, under models of temporal sequence processing. The singular time course aspects will be considered briefly in section 4 under models of attention.

The set of mathematical equations embodying the details of the various features of table 1 have been presented by the author elsewhere [37], [38], as well as having been discussed in many other places. They will not be discussed in such detail here, but can be summarised as follows. Let $\underline{X}$ (t) denote the state of a net, composed of neurons possessing certain features, at any time t. This state will in general denote the levels of membrane potential in the various compartments of each neuron, the levels of opening or closing of ionic channels, the probability distribution at each synapse for release of quanta of chemical transmitter, and other variables. The general equation of motion for the net is assumed to be first order in time, and is of causal, but in general time-delayed form

$$d\underline{X}/dt = \underline{F}\left(\{\underline{X}\,(t^1 \text{ earlier than t})\}, t, \underline{I}\,(t)\right) \tag{1}$$

where $\underline{I}$ (t) denotes the set of inputs to the net, $\{\underline{X}(t^1$ earlier than t)$\}$ indicates that the dynamics involves states of the net at earlier times, and the non-linear function $\underline{F}$ contains both the dynamics of on-going neural activity and that of synaptic modifications. As such it incorporates both the smooth processes, such as augmentation of membrane potential and its flow over the neuronal geometry, and the change of the synaptic parameters with experience, and also the singular processes, in particular the production of the nerve impulse and its flow along axon collaterals.

The dynamical systems approach to (1) has been followed increasingly (see, for example [37]). We have to explore both the asymptotic behaviour of (1) - the attractor states (fixed points, cycles, quasi-periodic orbits and strange attractors) and their basins of attraction, and the transients. In the former case it is usual to neglect variations of the inputs I (t) in (1) once a trajectory has started. It is also common to make the adiabatic assumption that (1) can be separated into the on-going part describing neural activity and that corresponding to learning - the process of structural modification. The former is assumed to be taking place at a faster time scale than the latter. The former dynamics can then be divided into either relaxational (to attractors) or transient. We will consider this division, and other aspects of the dynamics in due course where it is appropriate.

3   Models of temporal sequence storage

There have been numerous models of temporal sequence storage by neural networks. Thus time-delayed neural nets (TDNNs) have been analysed, and used in the process of speech recognition [39]. This transient approach, and the related one of using time delays in a relaxational network [40], have not used the smooth temporal processes of neurons discussed under heading (2) of the previous section, nor do they satisfy a number ofria of biological reality. These latter have been given in [19] as:

(1)   a relatively fast unsupervised learning algorithm (at most ten or so training cycles needed)

(2)   no restriction on sequence length, modulo that given by the storage capacity of the net,

(3)   time-invariant storage (so sequence regeneration can start from any point in a sequence),

(4)   is biologically realistic,

(5)   achieves disambiguation (can store, for example, the sequence ABCBD ...),

(6)   gives recall with almost identical time course to the pattern sequence being stored.

TDNNs [39] are excluded by criterion (2), since they require a fixed set of (T+1) input lines to input the time-delayed sequence I(t), I(t-1), ..., I(t-T). Relaxational nets with internal time delays [40] seem to be excluded by (1) and (6) (there is no natural learning rule, and the transition between patterns does not seem to be flexible). The recent developments of temporal back-error propagation (TBEP) [41] look powerful, especially in application to time-series prediction, but fail criterion (4). The approach of [19], however, appears to pass the above criteria. Since it has led to a new model of the hippocampus, it would seem appropriate to expand on it a little here.

The general architecture of the system is shown in figure 2. It involves two nets L and M. The input 'IN' feeds directly onto the net L, which is composed of leaky integrator neurons with a range of time constants. The threshold output of these neurons is fed onto the single-layer perceptron net M. The weights of the neurons in this net are modified according to the delta-learning rule, which may be made biologically realistic in terms of Hebbian-type synaptic modification. In the testing mode the initial (or later) pattern of a learnt sequence, when fed into the L net, will generate from the M net the next pattern of the sequence, (after some time delay t_d) and so cause M to generate the full sequence. The various detailed features of error levels, capacity, etc are analysed by simulation in [19]; the capacity is analysed theoretically in [27], and generalisation in [28].

The approach may also be used [19] to model the hippocampus, schematically shown in fig 3, with the identification EHC = IN, DG = L, CA3 = M, the modifiable synapse being denoted 3 in that figure. There are numerous predictions of a biological nature which flow from this model which may be tested in the near future.

One of the important questions to be answered by the model is the relative importance that various temporal features of neurons may play in the storage described above. For example, in what manner is the capacitative membrane crucial, or is it just the time delay t_d related to more general biological features of the net? One aspect, noted in [19], was the need for threshold leaky integrators in order to achieve disambiguation. A 'crumbling history' of earlier patterns occurs on the net L of leaky integrators, and leads to disambiguation by means of the context dependence of this history extending over several earlier patterns. Thus in the sequence ABCBD, the second B has a different earlier history on L, ABC, than does the first B; this is coded by membrane activities of neurons of the L net. A further feature, noted also quite forcefully in [19], was the need for channel variables, describing the time course of the PSP. This is usually regarded as an 'alpha-function,' according to [42], and corresponds to the opening and closing of channel gates by first order dynamics. Without the channel variables/alpha functions, a fixed time-delay t_d (considerably beyond the 0.5 msec synaptic delay) seemed necessary in order to achieve suitable temporal sequence storage. Work is presently under way [43] in learning the alpha-variable, which is often regarded as a crucial variable in LTP. Further features involved with slow processes are presently under investigation.

Another approach to analysing the temporal powers of leaky integrator neurons (LINs) has been to incorporate the LIN as an integral part of Kohonen's topographic map [44]. The resulting temporal topographic map [45] has useful powers which indicate its sensitivity to context. For example, consider the 16 sequences of length two on two binary inputs (with the inputs (0,0), (0,1), (1,0), (1,1) denoted 0, 1, 2, 3 respectively). A 4 x 4 net of LINs trained by the temporal topographic map perfectly partitions these 16 sequences as in figure 4, where the label (a, b) denotes the winning node for the sequence a then b. It is seen from the figure that the last input b of the sequence [a,b] gives a partition of the net into four quarters, further subdivision of each of these quarters then occurring according to the earlier (content) input a. The corresponding partitioning by non-LINs (BDNs) is given in figure 5; it shows no recognition of content. This has been extended to earlier contexts by following the winner trajectory through the net as the input occurs; we refer the reader to [45].

We conclude that slow processes, such as LINs, channel variables and the like, and biologically realistic learning rules, are important in storage and recognition of context in temporal patterns. The time scales for such storage are expected to be in the range of 10-200 msec or so. Longer time scale ionic currents could be included (and may be needed to explain some features) to lengthen the time scale although it is more natural to consider inter-area interactions at the longer time course end. Shorter time scales will require consideration of the short time course processes (3) of the preceding section.

4   Modelling attention

There is now a wealth of data [4], [46] on a wide range of psychological and physiological features of attention. To this are to be added the multi-unit recordings of [12], [13] and [14] from visual cortex, and the related suggestions on consciousness and attention [47], [48] and on information processing by synchronisation [49], [50] or oscillation (for review see [51]). In addition there are results beginning to come in from the new window of magneto-encephalography (MEG) on global temporal brain activity obtained by using multi-channel SQUID detectors. In order to begin to make sense of this enormous amount of material let us summarise some of the crucial findings.

The conclusions of [4] and [46] are that alteration of attention involves three stages: disengage (mediated by the posterior parietal lobe), move (in which the superior colliculus and frontal eye fields are involved) and re-engage (controlled by thalamic and nucleis reticularis structures). These latter localisation results have been obtained from studies of attentional deficits in humans with correspondingly placed lesions; the disengage, move and re-engage sequence most naturally fits the reaction time deficits in such patients observed under suitable stimulus conditions. Moreover, it is generally accepted that there are two forms of attentional processing, one involving control by peripheral stimuli (exogenous) and the other by top-down mechanisms (endogenous). The latter involves an alerting system in right prefrontal cortex, and also involving the norepinephrine system arising in locus coeruleus and feeding to frontal lobe, posterior lobe, pulvinar and superior colliculus. To this body of results is to be added the 'spotlight' aspects involved in the serial attentional processing of objects containing specific conjunctions of two or more features in an array of objects (with a range of values of these features such as orientation, colour, etc), in contrast to the 'pop-out' aspect when only one feature in an object is being searched for. For example the time taken to detect a blue T amongst blue T's and red P's increases linearly with the number of distracting P's, whilst a blue T can be detected in a time independent of the number of red T distracters. Finally the correlated activity of visual cortical cells across centimetres of cortex (even between two hemispheres) [12], [13], [14], [52] is considered by many to be of great relevance in attentional processing, although details of the effect of attention on such activity is relatively scarce (most experiments are on anaesthetised animals).

Finally there are the MEG results on human global brain activity [23], [24]. These are obtained during awake, attentional processing, and appear to indicate that there is an important component of activity at about 40 Hz in auditory processing (as already known from EEG studies [53]) and more surprisingly that there appears to be a sweep of such cortical activity from frontal lobe backwards to occipital lobe in about 6 msec, preceded by 3 milliseconds by a similarly forward to backward directed sweep in the thalamus and nucleus reticularis.

The ICON model was introduced in [17] to begin to correlate these results. ICON (denoting intrinsic coupled oscillatory neuron) uses the recently discovered intrinsic inhibitory neurons of cortex [15] and thalamus [16] as clocks to give local synchronisation of cortical and thalamic cell activities. Partial support for this model of oscillations in both thalamus and cortex where both occur, (as seen from the data of [24]), is that there may be fewer appropriate feedback circuits in thalamus to achieve oscillation by feedback inhibition in a similar manner to that proposed in feedback inhibition models based on accepted cortical circuitry. Moreover there is a need for precise timing of synchronised activity (even to a milli-second or so) which, on the face of it, seems more natural in the ICON model, by the precision given by the inhibitory neurons' intrinsic oscillatory response than that of simple feedback inhibition. Thus the inhibitory interneurons of the ICON model can be turned on by an input to thalamus (lateral or medial geniculate), and from the results of [15] these neurons will continue oscillating to control responsiveness of a group of nearby relay neurons. Control of layer 4 cortical input could then occur similarly, with the expected 3 msec time delay. The control by inhibition makes for more sensitivity here, since oscillation will cease immediately on cessation of an input, in spite of the continued periodic oscillation of the inhibitory neurons's membrane potential.

It was suggested [23] that the forward-backward global sweep of activity is controlled by the thalamic nucleus reticularis (NR). This is a sheet of inhibitory neurons which receives axon collaterals locally from both thalamo-cortical and cortico-thalamic axons crossing it, but locally only feeds back to thalamic regions sending to it.

The structure of the NR is of interest to test this hypothesis, and even develop it to a stronger one [55]:

The Template Hypothesis.

The NR acts as a (set of) templates or masks which only allows certain correlated activities through it from thalamus to cortex and back again.

The idea here is that in a region of NR associated with a particular cortical area or set of cortical areas [56] there is strong inhibitory coupling between the inhibitory neurons of the NR (possibly by dendro-dendritic and/or electrical synapses). The NR sheet, with long dendritic processes, can be modelled along the lines of the horizontal cells of the outer plexiform layer of the retina [33]. With inhibition, and the extra condition that the input is inhibited when NR is positive (assuming zero threshold for NR cells), there results a restriction on allowed inputs that are able to persist under the NR feedback inhibition. It is in this way that the NR can act as a mask on input and cortical activity. The spatial extent of the mask depends on that of the NR correctivity which may be enough to cover the whole thalamus, not only the lateral and medial geniculate nuclei. Furthermore the existence of a structured wave of activity - a 'moving mask' on the NR, generated by primary input - may also be similarly explicable.

The backward-going direction of the NR activity wave may be explained, neurophysiologically, by the presence in anterior NR of spontaneous active neurons [57]. It is also natural to have such a forward-to-backward sweeping mask on the basis of the corollary discharge theory of Luria [58] and Teuber [59]. Earlier input activity will have set up in frontal lobe an expectancy response from hippocampal and nearby temporal structures by the way of the 'what' visual circuit from primary visual input. This response sweeps back, governed by the moving NR mask, to be compared with actual activity entering into parietal lobe from primary cortex by the 'how' circuit from primary visual cortex [60]. If there is too great a discrepancy between the top-down expectancy wave from frontal lobe and the bottom-up input, then it seems reasonable that attention to the new inputs be alerted; otherwise the system will continue its current actions, with attention focussed on other than current input. This is a general model of endogenous attention, outlined in (2), but needing a great deal of detail to be inserted of the relevant structures and time courses involved.

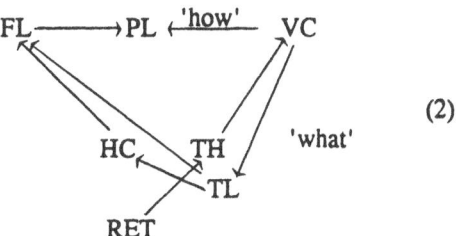

$$(2)$$

Involvement of NR and different thalamic nuclei still has to be included in (2), where TL = temporal lobe, TH = thalamus, RET = retina, VC = visual cortex, PL = parietal lobe, FL = frontal lobe, and HC = hippocampus. The arrow-heads denote the main direction of flow of information from retina. We see that there is a global circulation of cortical activity associated with a particular visual input in this model; this gives a clear prediction of the time course to be detected by MEG when, say, a subject opens his/her eyes to view a particular visual pattern. Use of an oscillating pattern would make the flow easier to detect by spectral analysis.

The process of exogenous attention, and in particular the disengage, move, re-engage sequence mentioned earlier can also be modelled at a systems level using results being gathered on responses in superior colliculus (SC) and inferior parietal cortex [60], [61]. The move process is already specified by the general model in [60] of a moving locus across deep SC to the anterior (fixation) pole. The disengage process may arise from the modification of responses of the two classes of light-sensitive (LS) [62] and fixation (F) [63] cells in monkey 7a in inferior parietal cortex. The first of these fires when a new peripheral light stimulus occurs, the second when fixation of attention to a certain position is taking place.

A systems-theoretic modelling approach to this will be in terms of the sequential process:

$$LS \xrightarrow{\text{inhibit}} F \xrightarrow{\text{excitation}} SC \text{ (controlled gaze shift)} \quad (3)$$

where F is assumed to be spontaneously active. Thus when no peripheral stimulus is present the F cells in area 7a prevent saccade generation in the deep SC layers by direct and continued encitation of the anterior pole of the SC [60], and so preserve fixation. A new peripheral visual stimulus activates a set of LS cells which inhibit (by lateral inhibition of the F cells) the SC fixation, and so a saccade may then be made. The determination of the position of the next fixation point of attention has, of course, to be specified. Indeed the tripartite model of disengage   move   re-engage has a lacuna in that 'movement of attention' cannot be efficiently initiated until and unless the new position is already known to which attention is to be directed. Thus the model should be a quadripartate one: disengage   compute next fixation position   move   re-engage.

There are cells in lateral intra-parietal cortex (LIP) which appear to hold a memory of the new position to which attention should be directed [64]; these cells can fire for up to a second while a trained monkey may delay a saccade response, and appear to code the error signal of (new minus old) fixation position. These LIP neurons are fed visual inputs from area 7a, so may be regarded as coding 'where to move'. This is assumed to be fed on to SC from the LIP neurons to bring about the desired movement, as described in [60]. The net result of this is to modify the model of (2) to be

$$IN \xrightarrow{+} LS \xrightarrow{-} F \xrightarrow{+} SC$$
$$\text{LIP} \quad \text{FL(?)} \quad (4)$$

A top-down inhibitory input is shown in (4) from frontal lobe (FL) so that the memory stored in LIP does not cause attentional movement until the desired time (when the inhibition is released). The systems model (4) is only one of a variety of models which may be developed to describe attentional movement. The model (4) is deficient in that it does not describe in detail the wiring diagram involved, and in particular does not incorporate the pulvinar nucleus of the thalamus. This latter acts as a way station for outputs of parietal cortex to SC and vice versa.

We have already introduced the template hypothesis concerning a possible functioning of the NR. The connectivity of that structure allows us to make the hypothesis more precise, as follows: for an area of cortex, the NR computes the winning input signal of a set of topographically localised ones. It does this by lateral disinhibition, and feedback inhibition from NR to thalamus. This possibility fits with known local connectivity between NR and thalamus. The idea of NR being the final arbiter of inputs to cortex may be extended to non-primary cortex by using the cortico-thalamic and thalamo-cortical feedback loops. It is known from detailed studies that a given region of cortex feeds back to the same region of thalamus which feeds it. Such a feedback-loop system is being gated by NR. The extended template hypothesis, applied to non-primary cortex, leads to the resulting conjecture:

NR Competetive Hypothesis

The nucleus reticularis NR acts as the arbiter of competition in associative cortex between different local regions in an area of active cortex.

This hypothesis implies that NR and its thalamic neighbour (especially pulvinar) should be focal point for the re-engage activity of attention, being the site of competition. This agrees with the re-engage deficits experienced by patients with lesions in thalamus and NR [69].

How does the global front-to-back sweep of activity fit in with this model? That must arise by involvement of the 'what' circuit of (2), through temporal lobe, hippocampus and frontal lobe, and so back to parietal lobe. Thus the FL output in (2) could now be used as in a similar manner to the unknown FL input in the flow diagram (4).

A given input from retina will arrive by the 'how' circuit from primary visual cortex to PL so as to meet the activation by the 'what' circuit from primary visual cortex to PL so as to meet the activation by the 'what' circuit from VC through TL to HC, FL and back to PL which has arisen from earlier inputs. This timing is important in a closed loop comparison circuit, and corresponds to the structure of fig 2 in testing mode.

A possible way in which the FL feedback from PL combines with the LIP signal for movement has already been suggested elsewhere [17] by means of a phase comparison process using coupled oscillators [17]. Alternatively it may involve a straightforward but longer-lasting inhibition on the LIP cells so as to cancel an identical excitatory feedback. Again the ICON model will help in prolonging such an inhibitory effect. Competition will also be expected to occur in NR, as described above.

The temporal aspects of attention (and subsequent motor acts) naturally depend on the circuits being used, the particular features of the neurons, and the functional methods (relaxation v direct transformation) used in the information processing. To summarise this section, then, we have proposed various circuits for attention of both endogenous (by (2)) and exogenous form (by (4)). The neurons are assumed to have smooth temporal features of type (2) of section 2 so as to enable nearby context to be kept, but mainly with direct transformation properties. A hint of need for fine timing (synchronisation) was noted, but careful simulation is required in order to determine the necessity for the sharp time features of type (3) of section 2. That is presently proceeding [66], and it is hoped to compare results with available EEG and the new MEG data as soon as possible.

5   Models of consciousness

We will follow the arguments of [67] that attention and consciousness are distinct. The latter confers the ability of having an intention to attend, which is itself conscious.   As remarked in [67], "That means, phenomonologically, that consciousness and attention are not the same thing: the former uses the latter to attain strategical control over lower order cognitive processes". Thus it is necessary to determine what brain areas are relevant for consciousness, beyond the attentional areas mentioned in the last section, and attempt to model their temporal activity.

It is clear that inputs to the consciousness system must be effective in order for awareness to occur. The case of the patient DF of [66] is a case in point, in which there was a striking dissociation between her ability to perceive object orientation (at which she was very poor) and to direct accurate reaching movements towards objects in different orientations (at which she was normal). Magnetic resonance imaging showed that DF had lost most of primary visual areas 18 and 19, though not 17. Input to the ventral 'what' system seems lacking in DF, whilst that to the dorsal 'how' system proposed in [66], granting DF manipulative, non-conscious skills, was available. Even more startling are the cases of blindsight investigated by Weiskrantz and colleagues [68].

In the modelling of attention in the previous section, exogenous attention was apparently well understood as being somewhat circumscribed to posterior parietal lobe, thalamus and nucleus reticularis, and superior colliculus; possible specific involvement of the first of these areas was outlined in the flow chart (4). On the other hand endogenous attention was noted as also involving the anterior cortex, as shown in (2), with feedback control on the exogenous attention centres in PL shown clearly there.

There are two particular anterior regions associated with the control of attention, which have been described in [4]. These are the right prefrontal cortex (RPFC) and the anterior cingulate gyrus (ACG). The ACG appears to be involved in target detection, with its activity reduced when target detection - in the alert state - occurs, when that in the RPFC concomitantly increases. There are strong reciprocal connections between RPFC and ACG [69], and the RPFC is also involved in neural activity during delayed response tasks in monkeys.

Can we therefore put the consciousness command module in RPFC and ACG, which can delegate activity (endogenous attention) or lose control (exogenous attention) to the posterior attention circuits of (4), thalamus, NR, and SC? The consciousness levels of lobotomised patients indicate that such an identification must be done with care since they are still conscious, although such cases would appear to lose RPFC as an alerting control system but not the ACG. This may explain the loss of forward planning ability after lobotomy. Support for the importance of ACG is given in [70], in which patients who had undergone complete commissurotomy were noted as suffering an important change: " ... characterised by gaps or holes lasting fifteen sec or longer during which patients utterly failed to respond." Consciousness was described by these patients as full of gaps, "but like an old stocking, the fabric was mostly preserved, but there were many holes." Interestingly such a degradation did not occur if only partial commissurotomy had been performed. This may be explained in terms of the need for access of the right PFC and/or ACG to the left attentional and linguistic centres; partial commissurotomy was not affective of consciousness. However it appeared that the posterior part of the corpus callosum was most important, so emphasising the posterior cortex's role in attention and consciousness.

Let us now return to the global sweep of activity discovered in [23], and consider how that may be involved in consciousness, as modelled above. In so doing the role of the structures mentioned above may be clarified. We note first the proposed origin for this sweep, which we suggested in the previous section to arise from spontaneous activity in the anterior (dorsal) pole of the nucleus reticularis. Secondly we may now understand how this becomes sculptured into the 'competitive mask' described earlier by noting the strong reciprocal connectivity between the posterior cingulate gyrus and the medial pulvinar of the thalamus [69], which will have collaterals to the NR. Thus cortical inputs from the 'what' circuit can activate the anterior-posterior sweep. Thirdly by inhibition of posterior NR and disinhibition of anterior NR at about the same time, these cortical inputs interact with the limbic system by the classical circuit. This latter activity can then be used by frontal lobe in future planning (resulting in control of attention in RPFC). There will also be slightly later involvement of posterior cortex and the interconnected medial pulvinar [69]. In all of this thalamo-cortical interaction the NR will play a role as moving mask acting as an arbiter of local cortical competition.

It may be conjectured that the purposes of NR beyond that of local competition are two-fold:

(a)   to act as a moving mask, so as to correlate cortical and thalamic activity in different regions in a spatial manner,

(b)   to act so as to co-ordinate this latter activity in a temporal manner. This may occur either in the oscillatory manner reported in [23], or by synchronisation and time windowing. In either manner NR acts as a type of clock acting in either a regular beating mode or stop-watch or timing mode.

We may label our model the stroboscopic one since in all of this activity there will naturally arise a forward-backward sweep controlled by NR in re-engagement of attention, along the lines described earlier.

In summary, then, we regard consciousness as arising from the conjoint activity of several neural centres - RPFC, ACG, NR, TH, SC, PL, VC plus a suitable level of excitability of these centres as determined, say, by activation of the brain stem reticular system. Some of these centres are necessary but not sufficient for consciousness (we suspect ACG, NR, TH, PL, VC), the remaining ones making the system more effective by extra features. We suggest that NR and ACG are necessary for preserving the continuity and unity of consciousness. The masking/competitive nature (in space and time) of NR appears particularly crucial, although strong cortico-cortical links will also play their role in preserving the integrity of the system.

The model of consciousness presented here can be partially subsumed under the approach of the author presented earlier in [71]. This latter considered consciousness as determined by a relational structure set up by present input to past, stored, activities. The details of the relational structure were not delineated in [71]. We see here that the suggested comparator nature of the PL attentional system (comparing FL activity determined by memories and motives in HC and near CG against VC input) fits in perfectly with this scheme. However there has been an attempt in our present suggestions to consider the additional temporal features related to the presumed forward-backward sweep of cortical and thalamic activity of [23]. This has brought in the NR as a candidate for explaining the unified nature of consciousness. The unitary nature of consciousness is to be expected in terms of competition between inputs for a limited response channel. In the neural network models proposed above there is assumed to be only one focal point to which attention is directed at any one time, as evinced by the unique error signal on SC describing the next position to attend to. Only by commissurotomy would it seem possible to use the two SCs to have two separate foci of attention in the 'same' brain.

There could, conceivably, have been more than one focus of attention without suffering commissurotomy to produce two brains. The survival value of such a situation would not seem to be high since a situation corresponding to deadlock in parallel processing or multi-task computing could occur: two or more processes competing for access to a shared response (in this context this could be control of motor circuits, for example). To prevent this, it would be necessary to have a competition between the various processes to choose a winner. The winning process would thus be the candidate for the 'unified' stream of consciousness at a higher level.

It would seem, therefore, that only a unified stream of consciousness is expected and that to have arisen by genetic programming of the connectivity and activity of the associated neural networks. The nature of the connectivity and output functions needed for such unitary response patterns is clearly of great interest to investigate further.

We suspect that this is achieved by a further global competition gated by NR, as hinted at earlier. We present our final hypothesis:
NR Unification of Consciousness.

The nucleus reticularis of thalamus is the unifier of consciousness by its long range inhibitory interconnectivity and its consequent control of cortical activity.

It is perhaps of relevance to note that the NR is solely composed of inhibitory cells, which are not usually regarded as having temporality. This leads to the suggested division of neural activity between NR as the fast mask/competitor arbiter, with memory relatively slowly changing in cortex. It may be therefore that NR gives the unity of consciousness, cortex its 'unified stream' character. The difference of temporal scales suggested here may be determined by careful simulations, using the short and long term processes for neurons mentioned in section 2; these are presently being performed [74].

A prediction resulting from our model is that animals which have a brain structure similar to the TH-NR-Cortex triumvirate are expected to display the characteristics of conscious beings. It would appear of interest to investigate the comparative anatomy of brain structures to determine if there is a correlation of this sort. On the other hand the existence of such a structure may be used to characterise the behaviour of animals as controlled by consciousness or otherwise.

Finally we should note that self-consciousness may be modelled in a control theoretic manner [73], as a process of building and manipulating a model of the activities, abilities, and emotional needs and responses of the self in a similar manner to plant modelling. The initial consciousness process can be regarded as storing in memory these various features of the self. That is the 'plant model'. The next level up is that of storing the responses when these features occur in reaction to various situations, so as to build a 'model of the plant modelling'; in other words to attend to the particular responses being chosen out of the total repertoire that could have been chosen and store that. The next step is to attend to and store the process of attending to and storing at the previous level, and so it goes to higher levels. The storage at each stage is to be done, in an as yet unidentified manner, through hippocampus, and later laid down in nearby cortex; the manner in which attention and memory storage interact is also yet to be understood.

6 Discussion

We have presented, as promised in the introduction, a broad framework of neural networks in which we have shown how temporal sequence storage may be achieved, and in terms of which sketched models of attention, consciousness and self-consciousness. The framework itself, explored in section 2, identified the three strands of short-term processes, long term processes, and intrinsic (synaptic) stochasticity for neuron features. Each strand had increasing levels of complexity and hence processing power. The general properties which each feature conferred on the neuron were summarised (especially in table 1), as were those related to some special architectures.

More detailed architectures, involving coupled nets, were explored in section

3 for temporal sequence storage. This was extended to numerous nets in the discussion on attention in section 4 and consciousness in section 5, although specific features of these nets were not presented in detail, but only a systems analysis was given. In particular a possible model of the backward sweep of global activity (suggested by MEG measurements) was given in section 4, with the guidance of the sweep, in space and time, being determined by the nucleus reticularis of the thalamus. The manner in which that might occur was noted by analogy to the horizontal cell layer of the retina. This model lead to the further proposal that NR is the arbiter of competition between cortical activity in local areas. Detailed modes of action of the other nets involved in attention and consciousness were not discussed, except for suggesting cortex as the unifier of consciousness and NR as making it unique. More specific features of the models will have to be determined when the systems models are being attempted to be simulated [73].

The material presented in the previous two sections is to be regarded as the outline of a program. At this early stage of the work, what can we claim for the expected success of the program? Firstly we have made a little progress in setting out the flow charts of the various features associated with attention and consciousness, delineating in what manner various cortical and sub-cortical structures may enter in the phenomena. There seems no reason to suspect that simulation of such structures, using the framework of section 2 and 3, will not be effective in explaining further details. Some specific features, such as the pop-out effect, have not been explained. In fact our purpose was not to attempt to model at such detail yet, and even at the systems level our modelling is incomplete and possibly premature. There still are, in particular, crucial features of the global MEG activity of [23] and [24] which are unknown. The activity during visual processing is not yet known, although experiments are being performed on this [74].

The lack of such details should not deter us from attempting to model such high level activity. For, as noted earlier, the 'all or none' aspect of brain activity indicates the need to understand the highest levels of brain function in order to help clarify the lower ones. Such models could help guide us to new experiments at various levels. The suggestion on the division of labour between cortex and diencephalon made in the last section, and in particular the differences of time courses required in the two brain regions, already indicates the crucial need for inclusion of detailed temporal features of neurons and architectures as outlined in section 2.

References

[1]   I J Hirsch and C Scherrick, J. Exp. Psychol. 26, 423 (1961)

[2]   E Poppel and N Legothetis, "Neuronal Oscillations in the Human Brain", Naturwiss, 73, 267-8, 1986.

[3]   M Scheidt, I Eibl-Eibesfeldt and E Poppel, "Segmentation of Human Short-Term Behaviour", Naturwiss 74, 289-290, 1987

[4]   M I Posner and S E Petersen, "The Attention System of the Human Brain," Ann.Rev Neurosci 13, 25-42, 1990.

[5]   J G Taylor, The Promise of Neural Networks, Springer-Verlag, 1992

[6]   R Llinas, "The intrinsic electrophysiological properties of mammalian neurons", Science 242, 1654-1664, 1988.

[7]   V Crunelli and N Leresche, "A role for $GABA_B$ receptors in excitation and inhibition of thalamocortical cells", Trends in Neurosciences 14, 16-21, 1991.

[8]   R M Rose and J Hindmarsh, "A model of thalamic neuron", Proc.R.Soc.Lond. B225, 161-193, 1985.

[9]   M Baudry and J Davis (eds), Long-Term Potentiation, Bradford Book, MIT Press, Cam. Mass, 1991.

[10]   P C Bressloff and J G Taylor, "Temporal Sequence Storage Capacity of Time-Summating Neural Networks," J.Phys.A.(in press), 1992.

[11]   T G Clarkson, Y Guan, D Gorse and J G Taylor, "Generalisation by pRAMs in the presence of training noise", KCL preprint 1992.

[12]   C Gray and W Singer, IBRO. Abstr. Neurosci. lett.suppl. 22, 1301, 1987.

[13]   R Eckhorn, R Bauer, W Jordan, M Brosch, W Kruse, M Munk and H J Reitbock, "Coherent Oscillations: A Mechanism of Feature linking in the Visual Cortex?", Biol.Cyb. 60, 121-130, 1988.

[14]   J I Nelson, P A Salin, M.H-J Munk, M Arzi and J Bullier, "Spatial and temporal coherence in cortico-cortical connections", Visual Neuroscience (in press) (1992).

[15]   R R Llinas, A A Grace and Y Yarom "In vitro neurons in mammalian cortical layer 4 exhibit intrinsic oscillatory activity in the 10 to 50 Hz frequency range," Proc. Natl. Acad. Sci USA 88, 897-901, 1991.

[16]   R Llinas and Y Yarom, "Oscillatory properties of guinea-pig inferior olivary neurons and their pharmacological modulation in and in vitro study", J Physiol. 376, 163-182, 1986.

[17]   CLT Mannion and J G Taylor, "Information Processing by Oscillating

Neurons", in Coupled Oscillating Neurons, J Taylor and C L Mannion (eds), Springer-Verlag (in press); J G Taylor, "Neural Networks: From Spin Glasses to Consciousness", in Proc 2nd Wigner Symposium, Goslar, World Sci.Publ, 1992.

[18]   C Koch, T Poggio and V Torre, "Nonlinear Interactions in a dendritic tree: localisation, timing and role in information processing", Proc.Nathl.Acad.Sci.USA 80, 2799-2802, 1983.

[19]   M Reiss and J G Taylor, "Storing Temporal Sequences", Neural Networks 4 773 -788, 1991; M Reiss and J G Taylor, "On Temporal Sequence Storage," pp129-133, Proc 2nd IEE Int Conf. Art. Neural Networks, Bournemouth, IEE Conf.Publ.No 349, 1991.

[20]   J H R Maunsell and W T Newsome "Visual Processing in monkey extrastrate cortex", Ann. Rev Neurosci 10, 363-401, 1987.

[21]   S zeke and S Shipp, "The Functional logic of cortical connections", Nature 335, 311-317, 1988.

[22]   S M Sherman and C Koch, "The control of retinoginiculate transmission in the mammalian lateral geniculate nucleus." Exp. Brain Res 63, 1-20, 1986.

[23]   R Llinas and U Ribary "Rostocaudal Scan in Human Brain: A Global Characteristic of the 40 Hz Response During Sensory Input" in Induced Rythms in the Brain, E Basar and T Bullock eds, Birkhauser (in press) 1992.

[24]   N Ribary, A A Ioannides, K D Singh, R Hasson, R P R Bolton, F Lado, A Mogilner and R Llinas "Magnetic field tomography of coherent thalamocortical 40-Hz oscillations in humans", Proc.Natl. Acad. Sci (in press), 1991.

[25]   A Grimwald (private communication).

[26]   H Liljenstrom, "Modelling the dynamics of olfactory cortex using simplified network units and realistic architectures," Int.J. Neurosci (in press), 1991

[27]   J G Taylor "Neural Network Capacity for Temporal Sequence Storage", Int J Neural Systems 2, 47-54, 1991.

[28]   P C Bressloff and J G Taylor, "On the Capacity and Generalisation Ability of More Realistic Neurons" pp II-157-II-161 in Proc.Int.Joint.Conf Art.Neural Nets, Seattle, 1992.

[29]   S-I Amari and N Murata, "Statistical Theory of learning Curves under Entropic loss Criterion", Fac of Engineer, Univ of Tokyo preprint METR 91-12, Nov 1991.

[30]   J G Taylor, "Spontaneous behaviour in neural networks", J.Thor.Biol. 36, 513-528, 1972.

[31]   D Gorse and J G Taylor, "On the identity and properties of noisy neural and

probabilistic RAM net", Phys.letts. A131, 326-332, 1988; ibid, "An analysis of noisy RAM and neural nets", Physica D34, 90-114, 1989.

[32]   C A Mead and M A Mahowald, "A silicon model of early visual processing", Neural Networks 1, 91-97, 1988.

[33]   J G Taylor "A Silicon Model of Vertebrate Retinal Processing", Neural Networks 3, 171-178, 1990.

[34]   D Gorse and J G Taylor, "A General model of stochastic neural processing", Biol.Cyb. 63, 299-306, 1990.

[35]   D Gorse and J G Taylor, "A continuous Input RAM-Based Stochastic Neural Model", Neural Networks 4, 193-202, 1991.

[36]   T G Clarkson, D Gorse and J G Taylor, "Biologically Plausible learning in hardware Realisable Nets", pp 195-199 in Artificial Neural Networks, ed T Kohonen et al, Elsevier 1991.

[37]   J G Taylor "Dynamical Systems and Artificial Neural Networks" pp31-76 in Theory and Applications of Neural Networks, J G Taylor and C L T Mannion (eds) Springer-Verlag (1991).

[38]   J G Taylor "Living Neural Nets", pp31-52 in New Developments in Neural Computing, J G Taylor and CL T Mannion (eds), Adam Hilger (1989).

[39]   A Waibel, "Modular Construction of Time-Delay Neural Networks for Speech Recognition", Neural Comp 1, 39-46, 1989.

[40]   A C Coolen and C C Gielen, "Delays in Neural Networks", Europhys.lett. 7, 281-285, 1988.

[41]   B A Pearlmutter, "Learning State Space Trajectories in Recurrent Neural Networks", pp II-365-II372 in Proc.Int.Joint Conf.Neural Networks, IEE TAB Neural Networks Committee, 1989.

[42]   J Jack, D Noble and Tsien, Electric Current Flow in Excitable Cells, Clarendon Press Oxford, 1975.

[43]   D Gorse and J G Taylor, work in progress.

[44]   T Kohonen, "Self-Organisation and Associative Memory", Springer-Verlag, 1984.

[45]   G J Chappell and J G Taylor, "Temporal Topographic Maps", KCL preprint, 1991.

[46]   G W Humphreys and V Bruce, Chap 5., Visual Cognition, Lawrence Erlbaum Assoc, 1989.

[47]   F H Crick, "Function of the thalamic reticular complex: The searchlight hypothesis", Proc.Natl.Acad.Sci, USA, 81, 4586-4590, 1984.

[48]   F H Crick and C Koch, "Towards a Neurobiological Theory of Consciousness," Seminars in the Neurosciences, (in press).

[49]   C von der Malsburg and W Schneider, "A neural cocktail-party processor," Biol.Cyb. 54, 29, 1986.

[50]   M Abeles, Local Cortical Circuits, Springer-Verlag, 1982.

[51]   C L T Mannion and J G Taylor, "Coupled Excitable Cells", pp285-305 in Theory and Applications of Neural Networks, ed J G Taylor and C L T Mannion, Springer-Verlag, 1991.

[52]   A R Engel, P Konig, A K Kreiter and W Singer, "Interhemispheric Synchronisation of Oscillatory Neuronal Responses in Cat Visual Cortex", Science 252, 1177-1179, 1991.

[53]   R Galambos, S Makeig and P J Talmachoff, "A 40 Hz auditory potential recorded from the human scalp", Proc.Nath.Acad Sci USA, 78, 2643-2647, 1981.

[54]   M E Scheibel and A E Scheibel, "Specialised Organisational Patterns within the Nucleus Reticularis Thalami of the Cat", Exp.Neurol.34, 316-322, 1972.

[55]   J G Taylor, in preparation

[56]   A M Graybiel and D M Berson, "Families of related cortical areas in the extrastriate visual system: summary of an hypothesis", in C N Woolsey (ed.) Multiple Cortical Sensory Areas, The Humana Press, NJ, 1982.

[57]   M Steriade, L Domich, G Oakson and M Deschenes, "The Deafferented Reticular Thalamic Nucleus Generates Spindle Rythmicity", J.Neurophysiol. 57, 260-273, 1987.

[58]   A R Luria The Working brain, trans.B.Haigh, Basic Books, New York, 1973.

[59]   H L Teuber, "The frontal lobes and their function", Int.J.Neurol 5, 282-300, 1966.

[60]   M A Goodale and A D Milner, Trends in Neurosci 15, 20 (1992).

[61]   D P Munoz, D Pelisson and D Guitton, "Movement of Neural Activity on the Superior Colliculus Motor Driving Gaze Shifts", Science 251, 1358-1360, 1991.

[62]   R Anderson, Ann.Rev.Neurosci, 12, 377-403 (1989).

[63]   B C Motter and V B Mountcastle, "The functional properties of the light-sensitive neurons of the posterior parietal cortex studied in waking monkeys", J.Neurosci. 1,3-26, 1981.

[64]   V B Mountcastle, B C Motter, M A Steinmetz and C J Duffy, "Looking and seeing: The usual functions on the parietal lobe", pp159-193 in Dynamic Aspects of

Neocortical Function, ed G M Edelman, W E Gall and W M Cowan, Wiley 1984.

[65]   J W Gradt and R A Andersen, "Memory related motor planning activity in posterior parietal cortex of macaque" Exp.Brain Res 70, 216-220, 1988.

[66]   M A Goodale, A D Milner, L S Jakobson and D P Carey, Nature 349, 154 (1991)

[67]   C Umilta "The control operations of consciousness", 334-355 in Consciousness in Contemporary Science, ed A J Marcel and E Bisiach, Clarendon Press, Oxford (1988)

[68]   L Wishrantz, Blindsight, Clarendon Press, Oxford, 1986.

[69]   P S Goldman-Rakic "Topography of Cognition", Ann.Rev. Neurosci. 11, 137-156, 1988.

[70]   S J Dimond, "Brain Circuits for Consciousness", Brain Behav.Evol. 13, 376-395, 1990.

[71]   J G Taylor, Neural Network World 1, 4-12, 1991.

[72]   W T Miller, R S Sutton and P J Werbos (eds), Neural Networks for Control, Bradford Book, MIT Press, 1989.

[73]   F Alavi and J G Taylor, ongoing work.

[74]   A Ioannides, private communication.

Table 1 Structural Properties of Neurons

Feature	Response Property
1. Capacitative membrane	Leaky integrator (temporal integration)
2. Slow ionic channels	Emphasises earlier (by the corresponding time-delay inputs to the time course of the ionic channels
3. Multi-phasic firing patterns	Change of temporal filter properties.
4. Neuronal geometry (with capacitative membrane)	Emphasises time-courses of inputs according to positioning of synapes in the geometry.
5. Short/long term synaptic modification	Changes temporal filter properties.
6. Synaptic noise	Gives generalisation powers; increases in a leaky integrator-neuron.
7. Active membrane for nerve impulse	Sensitivity to high frequency (greater than 500Hz) aspects of neuronal outputs are allowed.
8. Intrinsically oscillatory interneurons	Allows global 'clocking' for synchronised oscillatory activity.
9. Refractory period	High frequency cut-off; changes spread of wave activity in a net.
10. Dendritic spikes	Emphasises otherwise weak slightly earlier inputs; affects non-linear response of neuron.
11. Second messengers	Affects time-course of post-synaptic membrane response.
12. Reset wave	Determines how long temporally summed activity persists, especially on the cell body.
13. Time-delays at synapses and in or between neurons	Emphasises time course of inputs to different neurons to obtain maximal response (context sensitivity)
14. Feedforward inhibition	Temporal difference on inputs
15. Feedback inhibition	Self-teaching difference learning for localisation of activity; stability; temporal sequence storage

EXAMPLES OF REVERSE ENGINEERING:

	NEURONS	
+ Noise	+ Leaky Membrane	Spike Gen
STOCH LIN.NEURONS	TEMPORAL SEQ.STORAGE	COUPLE D OSCILLATORS
+ Non-linear		
pRAMS (STOCH. I-II)	MODEL OF HIPPOCAMPUS	VISION MACHINE
		ATTENTIONAL MACHINES
STOCH REINF. LEARNING	TIME SERIES ANALYSIS	
	KBES	PREPROCESSING
ROBOT CONTROLLERS		
	LEARNING GRAMMARS	

Figure 1

Various examples of reverse engineering, based on the binary decision neuron.

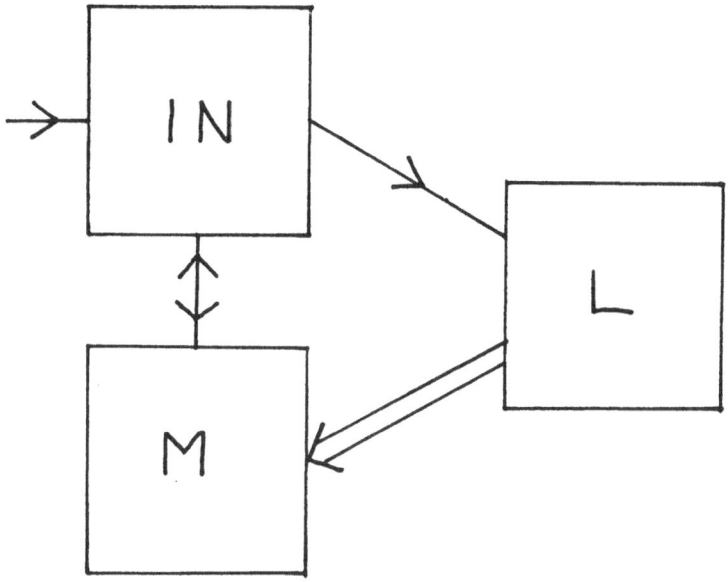

Figure 2

The coupled net system for temporal sequence storage. Net L, composed of leaky integrators with a range of time constants, receives inputs IN a 1:1 manner. The outputs of the neurons in L are sent to M, where the modifiable synapses are trained in an adaptive manner by means of teacher-forcing, the teacher being the next input to IN. In the teaching mode the training signal is built using the input at IN fed directly to M; in the testing mode the output from M is fed back to IN and used to generate the next pattern of the stored sequence.

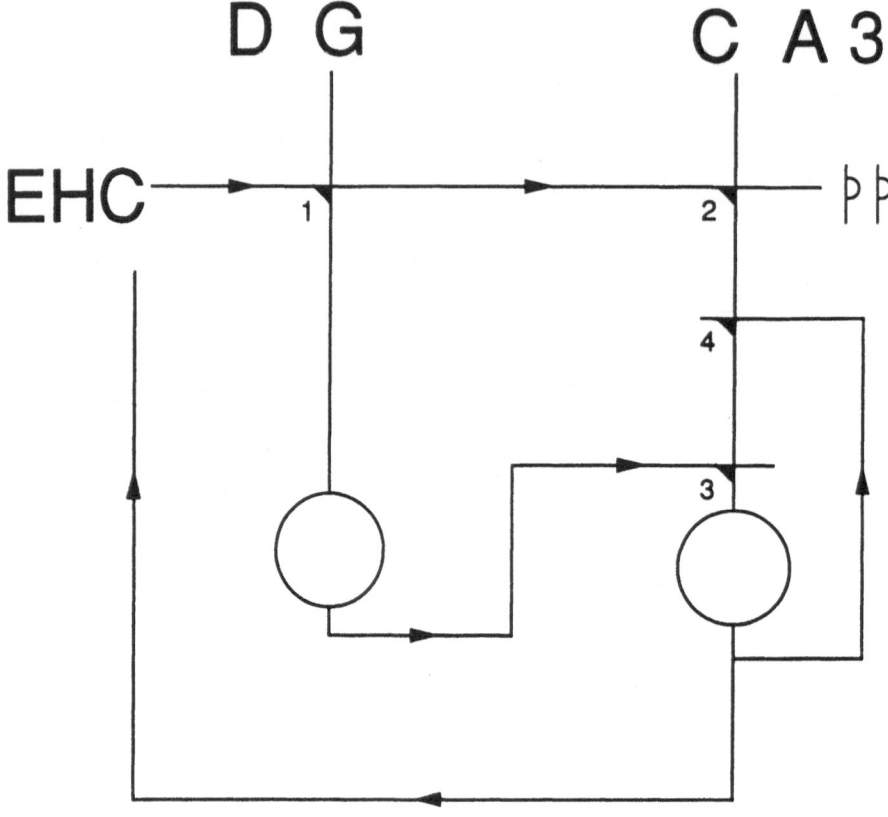

Figure 3

An application of the temporal sequence storage model of figure 2 to storage in hippocampus. The net L of leaky integrators is identified with the dentate gyrus (DG), and the sequence generating net M as the CA3 field. The perforant path pp acts so as to give the IN to M net teaching input; the sequence regeneration phase occurs on flow of activity through the entorhinal cortex (EC) from CA3 back to DG. The cell field CA1 has been neglected.

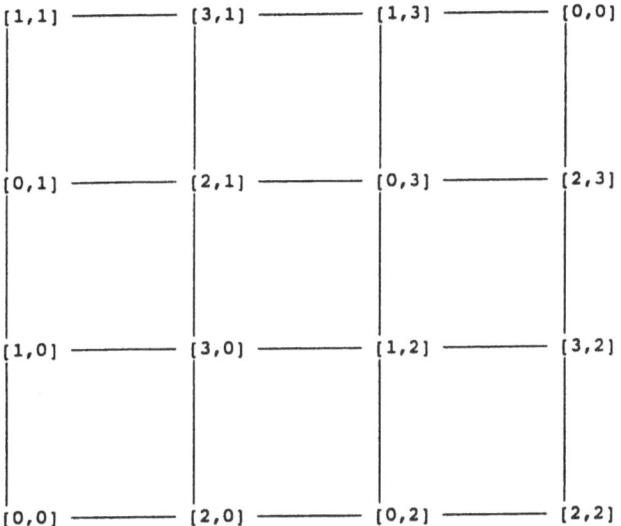

Figure 4

Results of the temporal topographic map applied to the 16 sequences of length 2 built from the 4 binary inputs to a 4 x 4 net; the inputs (0 0), (0 1), (1 0), (1 1) are denoted by 0, 1, 2, 3 respectively, and the symbol [a,b] attached to a node indicates it is the winner for the sequence whose first input was a, second b (a , b = 0, 1, 2 or 3). The map resulted after 750 training epochs, with decay constant 0, 3.

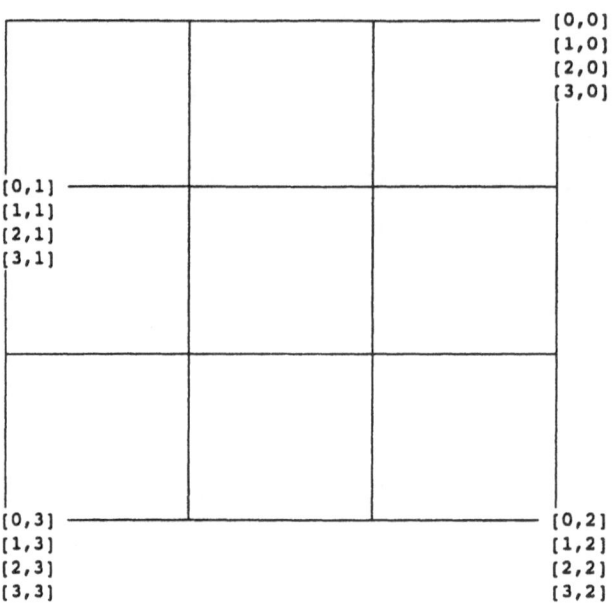

Figure 5

The same map as figure 3, but now with no time decay (decay constant = 0).

SCIENTIFIC
APPLICATIONS
OF NEURAL
NETWORKS

STRUCTURAL PROPERTIES OF PROTEINS PREDICTED BY NEURAL NETWORKS.

H. Bohr

Noyes Laboratory, University of Illinois at Urbana-Champaign, IL 61801 USA.

Abstract

Structural properties of proteins are being analysed with the help of feed forward neural networks of the perceptron type with hidden layers of neurons. After being trained on known structures the networks can predict local properties of new proteins on the basis of their sequence. Of the structural properties that the networks could predict with reasonable success were the surface structure, H-bond occurrence and secondary structure content. Prediction of the local surface properties means that the networks assign a number to each residue in the sequence signifying whether that residue is deeply buried in the protein or positioned on the surface of the protein. The networks were up to 70 % correct in predicting surface structures of proteins novel to the trained network. A similar score was obtained for the prediction of H-bond occurrence, e.g. if a certain residue participated in forming an H-bond, and for the prediction of secondary structures, i.e. if a certain residue was part of a particular secondary structure. A theoretical model for protein dynamics from an informational processing viewpoint will also be presented.

1. Introduction

Within the class of knowledge based techniques to predict protein structures from sequence information neural network methods have in the last years shown great promises due to their robustness and relatively simple ussage. Up to now most efforts in the biotechnological applications of neural networks have been concentrated on the limited task of predicting secondary structures of proteins (ref. 1) from sequence data since the result of that task can be a crucial step in modelling the more complex tertiary structure of proteins.

In this presentation we shall discuss different applications of neural networks to predict protein structures but within the same framework as that of secondary structure prediction and exclusively with the use of the same type of networks, the feed forward, multi-layer perceptrons. Recently, however, other types of networks such as recurrent ones have also shown great potentials for prediction of protein structure and functionality but discussions of that will be beyond the scope of this presentation. This study is based on investigations carried out with Drs R. Goldstein and P. G. Wolynes reported in ref. 5

and with additional results on Hydrogen bond predictions.

Since this study is utilizing the same neural network methodology as that of secondary structure predictions we shall begin with a discussion of the significance of secondary structure determination in the overall scheme of formation of 3-dimensional protein structures. Some experiments suggest (e.g. ref. 2) that more than half of all secondary structures (up to 70 %) in folded proteins are formed before the initial collapse in the beginning stages of folding. This would suggest that there is a local code, given by the sequence of amino acids, for the formation of secondary structures, possibly related to the fact that feed forward neural networks can predict up to 70 % of the secondary structures in the native proteins correctly from sequence data when trained on a large set of native proteins.
Even 70 % (or even more) correctly predicted secondary structures, however, does not provide enough information for determining the tertiary structure of proteins. We shall try to see if other properties of the protein structure, such as hydrogen bonding patterns and the surface structures, can be determined from local codes and be predicted with the use of neural networks, when trained on data sets of native structures and whether such information can help in the determination of tertiary structure.

Many of the hydrogen bonds are closely connected to the formation of secondary structures since the former provide their stability and possibly also a signal for their endpoints. It turns out that a feed forward, multi-layered, neural network (ref. 3) can determine with resonable accuracy when hydrogen bonds are present or not at a given residue along the sequence when trained on the Kabsch and Sander classification (see ref. 4).

Similarly a very sought-after property is the surface structure of a protein, or to be more precise, the information of what residues are exposed to the surface and what residues are buried in the core of the protein (ref. 5). The importance of that information is obvious in anti-genic investigations of proteins and in the design of drugs. Actually the surface exposed area of proteins is quite hard to calculate even from crystalographic structures. We shall here propose an easy algorithm for the calculation of local (i.e. per residue) surface exposed area in terms of contact densities, and then establish a data set of surface exposed areas per residue, "superficiality" of known proteins for the neural network to be trained on. Such technique and concept was developed by Bohr, Goldstein and Wolynes and described in their article of reference 5. It is reasonable to believe that the superficiality is determined to some degree by local codes, since the hydrophobicity of the side-chains influence whether a residue is on the inside or outside of a protein. While knowledge of a residue's hydrophobicity allows some prediction of superficiality, it turns out that feed forward neural networks, even on the basis of a small reading frame (window) of input sequence data, can predict superficiality with significantly greater accuracy than mere knowledge of hydrophobicity allows. It is on the average 20 % better. To be precise this means in this context that for a neural network judging whether a residue is positioned on the surface of a protein or not, the score in percentage of correctly determined residues over the whole sample is on the average 20 percent higher than a score based on the distribution of hydrophobic sidechains (see fig 4) where most are considered to be inside the protein. The neural network is superior when having to determine more precisely what exact grade of contact density or superficiality a given residue has (i.e. more precise location inside the protein) based only on information of sequence data.

Neural network predictions of the surface structure of proteins can also be used as initial information for larger schemes of molecular dynamics and associative memory techniques (ref. 6) in protein folding analysis.

2. Contact density for proteins

We define first a contact quantity for residues in a given protein. Consider the protein as being a long folded chain of amino acids or residues (see figure 1). Two residues are in contact with each other if they are within the distance of ρ from each other. In that case their corresponding contact quantity σ_{ij}^ρ is equal to 1; otherwise it is 0. The full set of σ_{ij}^ρ is often denoted as the binary distance matrix for the given protein. The contact density or superficiality σ_i^ρ for a particular residue i is then defined as:

$$\sigma_i^\rho = \sum_j \sigma_{ij}^\rho \tag{1}$$

where the index j runs over all the residues. It is clear that a large value for the contact density σ_i^ρ means that the particular residue i has many close neighbours and hence is buried in the interior of the protein, while a small value of σ_i^ρ could mean that the residue is on the surface of the protein.

FIG 1

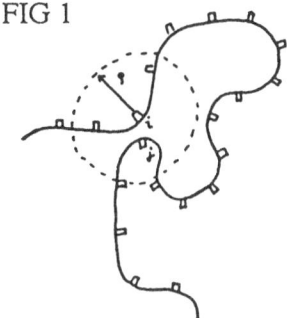

Figure 1 shows graphically a contact between residue i and j.

We could also define a vector quantity which indicates in which direction the sidechain is pointing. Thus we will have to specify two positions for each side-chain (residue). The most obvious points is the C_α coordinates where the side-chain is attached to the backbone, and then the coordinates for the side-chain center of mass. We shall as an approximation to the latter rather use the C_β coordinates. The difference between the two positions should roughly measure the direction in which the side-chain points. Accordingly we define the vector contact density, or vector superficiality $\sigma_{i(\beta-\alpha)}^\rho$ as

$$\sigma_{i(\beta-\alpha)}^\rho = \sum_j (\sigma_{ij(\beta)}^\rho - \sigma_{ij(\alpha)}^\rho) \tag{2}$$

This sum is over all j but one of the σ-values are mostly only different from 0 in the range where j runs between $i - N$ and $i + N$ and where N is typically of the order of 10 when ρ is taken to be $8\mathring{A}$. Then a negative value means that the side-chain for the given residue points outwards and a positive value that the side-chain points towards the interior center of the protein. In ref. 5a we have depicted the relation between the surface exposed area of residues calculated by the algorithm of F. M. Richards, reference 7, using the MIDAS program, reference 8, and the corresponding calculated vector superficiality for a set of crystallographic protein structures. The relation is linear but with a lot of noise.

2a. Protein folding as evolution of neural networks

In the framework of contacts and contact densities it is possible to develop a theory of contact dynamics for the protein folding processes, ref. 9, where it turns out that the initial stages of fast "down-hill" energy minimization of the protein folding processes are well described by equation of motions that are similar to the evolution equations for feed forward and Hopfield neural networks. This serves to remind us that neural networks have a natural application in various stages of protein folding. Before continuing with the next chapters of more practical neural network applications let us just briefly formulate in mathematics, ref. 9, the statement above. In terms of the fundamental contact variables σ_{ij}, the free energy for forming contacts on a protein chain can be written as:

$$
\begin{aligned}
\mathcal{F} &= \sum_{ij} kT[(1 - \sigma_{ij}log(1 - \sigma_{ij}) + \sigma_{ij}log\sigma_{ij}] \\
&- \sum_{ij} W_{ij}^o \sigma_{ij} - \sum_{ij} \sum_{kl} W_{ijkl}\sigma_{ij}\sigma_{kl} - \sum_{ij\alpha} \gamma_{ij}^\alpha \sigma_{ij}^\alpha \sigma_{ij}
\end{aligned}
\tag{3}
$$

where the first two terms are entropy terms, the third term measures the energy gain for creating the contact (i, j), the fourth term measures the energy gain for forming the contact (i, j) in the presence of the contact (k, l) and the last term is an interaction term with some side-chain charges $\gamma_{ij}^\alpha(q_i, q_j, q_i^\alpha, q_j^\alpha)$ and instructed from real patterns $\{\alpha\}$. The coefficients W_{ij}, W_{ijkl} in the third and fourth terms can be derived from polymer theory. The next step is to derive the equations of motion for fast "down-hill" energy processes, which we envisage occur in the early stages of protein folding. The fast "down-hill" equation is a kind of Langevin equation without the noise term and thus describing a steepest descent process:

$$
\frac{d\sigma_{ij}}{dt} = -\frac{\partial \mathcal{F}}{\partial \sigma_{ij}}
\tag{4}
$$

From the time-independent mean field equation: $\frac{\partial \mathcal{F}}{\partial \sigma_{ij}} = 0$, and with a redefinition of the variable $\sigma_{ij} \rightarrow (\sigma_{ij} + 1)/2$ and by writing the interaction term as $W_{ijkl}^I \sigma_{kl}^\alpha \sigma_{ij} = q_i q_j \sum_\alpha q_k^\alpha q_l^\alpha \sigma_{kl}^\alpha \sigma_{ij} = q_i q_j \omega \sigma_{ij}$ (q_i represent side-chain properties), we obtain by differentiation:

$$
\sigma_{ij} = tanh[W_{ij}^o + q_i q_j \omega + \frac{1}{2} \sum_{kl\rho'} W_{ijkl}\sigma_{kl}^{\rho'}]
\tag{5}
$$

which is the evolution equation for a feed forward neural network that predicts contacts (distances between residues in a protein) on the basis of sequence data $\{q_i\}$. Such a network is similar to the feed forward neural network employed in ref. 10.

From the time-dependent equation: $\frac{d\sigma_{ij}}{dt} = -\frac{\partial \mathcal{F}}{\partial \sigma_{ij}}$ we instead obtain, in the low temperature limit, the following equation:

$$\sigma_{ij}(t+1) = sgn[\sum_{ijkl} W_{ijkl}\sigma_{kl}(t) + W_{ij}^o + W_{ij}^I] \tag{6}$$

which is the evolution equation for a feed back neural network, a Boolean net. Actually a more appropriate description of the fast protein dynamics processes is given by the full evolution equation valid in all temperature regimes:

$$\sigma_{ij}(t+1) = tanh[(k_BT)^{-1}(\sum_{ijkl} W_{ijkl}\sigma_{kl}(t) + W_{ij}^o + W_{ij}^I)] \tag{7}$$

Both these networks are "trained" by the adjustment of their thresholds, while their synaptic weights mostly are given by the dynamics of polymer chains. To be more precise the synaptic connections W_{ijkl} are calculated from second order effects in contact dynamics as the effect of forming a contact or loop (i,j) in the presence of the contact or loop (k,l). It is interesting that there are only three topologically distinct ways of connecting two loops depending on whether $i < k < j < l$, $i < k < l < j$ or $i < j < k < l$ and these topological classes correspond to the three distinct types of secondary structures being respectively helices, anti-parallel beta-sheets and random coil. Therefore finding fixed point solutions to the evolution equation above forces one into considering the well-known classes of secondary structures. Thus in the language of contacts, neural networks play an unavoidable role in the description of the first stages of protein folding, where most of the the the secondary structures are supposed to be formed.

The networks can be analysed with the help of an equation for the overlap m_{ij} between a contact (i,j) and the correct pattern. The evolution equation for m_{ij} can be written with the help of the error function and which, in the case of dilute nets, becomes:

$$m_{ij}(t+1) = \int_{-\infty}^{\infty} \frac{dz}{\sqrt{2\pi}} exp(-z^2/2)tanh[\beta(\sum_{kl} W_{ijkl}m_{kl}(t) + W_{ij}^o + \sqrt{\alpha}z)] \tag{8}$$

where α is a noise term arrising from the "non-condensed" memories.

The size of the basins of attraction (i.e. the efficiency in recalling a certain desirable protein contact pattern) are determined from the slope of the error function near the fixed points.

Our questions in the introduction concerning protein folding were about the existence of a local code for the first collapse of a random chain to a molten globule state and the fact that around 70 % of all secondary structures are formed in the beginning. Those questions can partly be understood by the appearance of these natural neural nets, especially since feed forward neural nets for protein secondary structure prediction take local sequence data and quickly transform them into secondary structure data. Since the networks we use for secondary structure prediction are trained on structure data from native folded proteins we will expect such neural nets to be up to 70 % correct in their prediction compared to the native structures, which they also turn out to be!

It is interesting if the dynamical nature of these network equations, eqs. 7 and 8, can give some hints to why neural networks for predicting secondary structures actually reach the upper limit of the 70% performance. To answer that one could try to solve the equations numerically with a trial protein containing primitive contact patterns of the 3 types of secondary structures, helical, sheets and coil, as studied in ref. 11. Thus the question is rephrased as how well a given type af contact can be recalled by the network obeying the evolution equation or overlap equation written above. Naively one could argue that since such networks can be shown to recall specific contacts with an accuracy of at least 90% in the pressence of just another type (of secondary structures) and away from the critical storage capacity limit, and assuming that contacts different from zero are evenly distributed on the three types of secondary structures, it seems that at least the upper limit of around 70 % correctness in the predictions can be met. Actually the assumption that all three types of contacts occur evenly is not correct since helical contacts occut more often than sheet contacts which also explains why helices are better predicted.

3. Neural network methodology

The neural network we employed was a multi-layered feed forward network of the perceptron type. Different configurations of networks were tried out but typically the input layer contained around 50 neurons, the hidden layer around 20 and the output layer around 5. The input information generally included sequence information about the residue of interest with two on either side (for a window of 5), although other window sizes were used. Generally 4 input neurons were used for each residue encoding that residue's charge, hydrophobicity, polarity and size. In the case of 4 classes of sequence data and with a window size of 5 the total number of input neurons is 20. We also tried including information about predicted secondary structures in the input layer. Ordinarily we used 11 output neurons to classify the contact density values, ranging from -10 to 10.

In order to optimize the architecture of the network (i.e. the number of hidden layers, neurons and adjustable synapses) we started out with our chosen input layer, 1 hidden neuron, and 1 output neuron, and then slowly added more hidden neurons and increased the number of layers. This expansion was done during the training procedure such that whenever new synapses were included their weights were chosen by a random number generator. The most optimal configuration, depending on the training set, turned out to be several hidden layers each with a few neurons.

The training of the neural network was performed with the back-propagating error algorithm. The training set consisted of around 6000 values of input-output combinations and the test set of 2000 values. These values originated from 50 very different proteins with a well-determined 3-dimensional (X-ray crystalographic) structure. The network could be trained to up to 95 % correctness (i.e. the number of contact density values correctly predicted within a certain tolerance of the correct real value and taken over the whole sample of values) and with a test of around 60 % correct (defined again as above). The results depended only marginally on the input window size and with an improved performance when secondary structure information was included. This information was obtained from another neural network (ref. 1) that predicted secondary structures of proteins from their sequence data. The output of such network was then fed into our contact density predicting network together with sequence data. The total network arrangement could then be considered as two sequentially connected feed forward neural networks, (figure 2). The training and test curve for the contact density prediction from a particular neural network configuration is shown in figure 3.

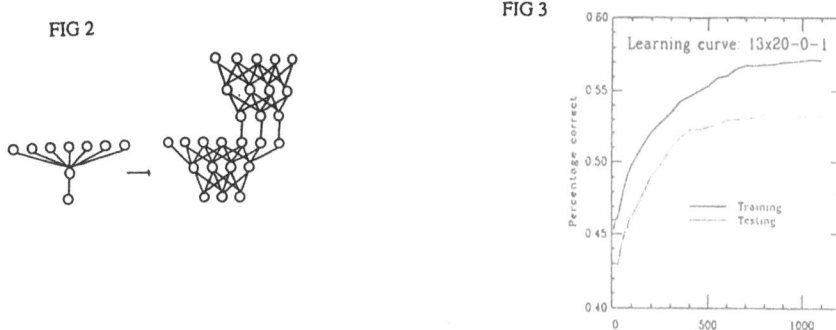

FIG 2

FIG 3

Figure 2 shows the configuration of two sequential feed forward neural networks employed for this study where one NN predicts secondary structures from sequence data input that together with the secondary structure output is used as input for the next NN that predicts contact density.

Figure 3 shows the learning and test curve for a neural network with the configuration 260 input neurons, no hidden layer and 1 output neuron. The percentage of correctly predicted values compared to the whole set are plotted against the number of learning cycles.

4. Results on protein structure prediction

In the next subsections we shall present some results on the prediction of various structural properties of proteins exclusively with the use of feed forward neural networks of the perceptron type. Previously mostly the use of neural networks to secondary structure prediction have been reported in the literature, e.g. ref. 1, so we shall here describe some other applications for protein structure determination.

4a. Results from surface prediction

One of the main goals of this study has been to see if neural network methods could be used to predict what amino acids in a given protein are positioned at the surface of the protein and what amino acids are buried in the interior of the protein. It is wellknown that the hydrophobicity of the amino acids to a certain extend can determine whether

that the hydrophobicity of the amino acids to a certain extend can determine whether they are on the surface or not. This is because hydrophilic side-chains tend to be at the surface where most water molecules are found and hydrophobic side-chains are attracted to the interior of the protein in order to avoid water. Therefore we also observe, when doing a statistical analysis of all side-chains in the training set in relation to their contact density values, that the distribution of hydrophobic side-chains has the biggest weight on positive values of the vector contact density $\sigma^\rho_{i(\beta-\alpha)}$ while the distribution of hydrophilic side-chains is peaked at negative values of vector contact densities. These distributions are showed in figure 4 prediction made on the basis of such distributions and simply assigning positive values of contact density σ to hydrophobic side-chains and negative values to hydrophilic ones can, in the notion of our input correlation window, be considered as a 1-unit window method where each side-chain is independent of the others. In judging our neural network method it is important to see whether it is better than just the primitive 1-unit window hydrophobicity prediction of the local surface property and whether a multi-unit window neural network is better than a single-unit net.

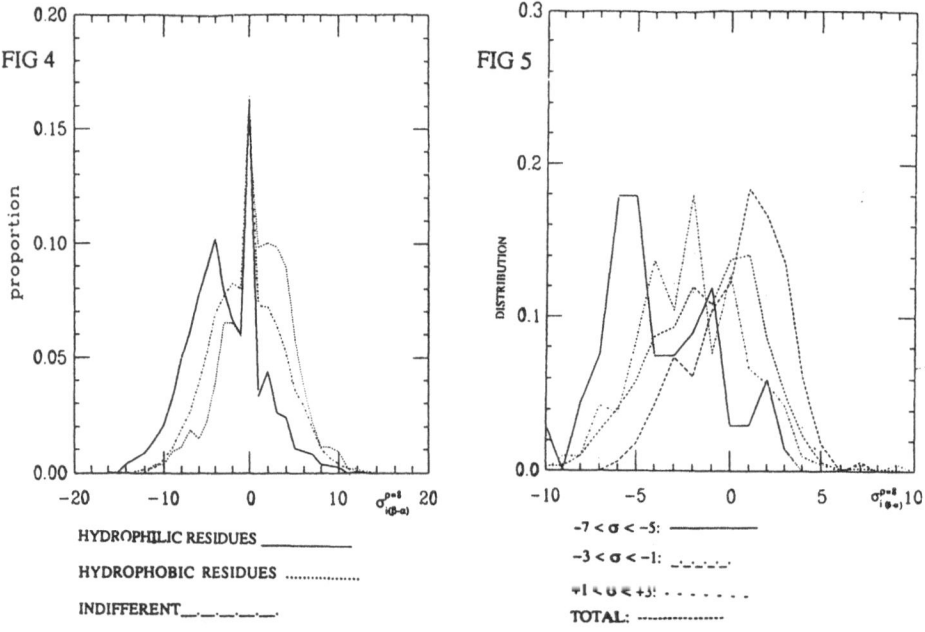

HYDROPHILIC RESIDUES _____

HYDROPHOBIC RESIDUES ....

INDIFFERENT ._._._._.

$-7 < \sigma < -5$: _____

$-3 < \sigma < -1$: _._._._.

$+1 < \sigma < +3$: . . . . . .

TOTAL: ....

Figure 4 shows the distribution of hydrophobic and hydrophilic side-chains as a function of their contact densities (superficiality). The full line corresponds to hydrophilic side-chains, the dashed line to hydrophobic side-chains and the semi-dashed (dashes-points) line to indifferent ones.

Figure 5 shows the distribution of the NN predicted values of contact density when real values of contact density lie in the middel of a narrow interval that indicates tolerance for correctness.

In figure 5 we have depictured the predicted σ-distributions of test cases within a nar-

distribution for the NN predicted values of σ for residues that have a real (correct) value of σ in the middle of the interval $-7 < \sigma < -5$. The network used for these predictions had a window size of 5 and had altogether 20 input neurons, 90 hidden neurons in two hidden layers and 11 output neurons. The network was trained on 6000 values during 200 learning cycles and up to 70 % correct (i.e. training score which measures how well the network can recall learned patterns. The network performed on a new set of data with a test score of 55 % correctness which measures the ability of generalization. The figure clearly shows that this type of neural network is superior to just a 1-window predictor based on the hydrophobicity of the residues, and the predictions seem quite correct although the hydrophilic residues are predicted better than the hydrophobic ones.

In Table I we have presented a more detailed comparison between performances of different types of neural network architectures with different size of windows and with correlation to extra information about secondary structures. The table indicates that the network performes slightly better with larger sizes of windows and much superior to a 1-window predictor. Including predicted secondary structure in the input makes an improvement of the networks performance. The last network in the table is just predicting if residues are on the surface or not (yes/no).

TABLE I

NN architecture (w=windowsize) input+hid.+output (w)	sec.struc. extra input	training cycles	train score percent	test score percent
12 + 20 + 11 (w-3)	no	1000	62	51
20+30+30+11 (w-5)	no	600	76	53
36+80+11(w-9)	no	200	70	51
20+90+90+11 (w-5)	no	100	65	55
104+40+5+11 (w-13)	yes	500	84	57
35+20+5+11 (w-5)	yes	100	76	65
91+20+1(yes/no)(w-13)	yes	1100	98	68

4b. Results on H-bond prediction

We shall finally briefly discuss the results from a network that was trained to predict the occurrence of H-bond structures in a protein purely on the basis of its sequence of amino acids. The training set for the prediction of the H-bond structure was formed from the Kabsch and Sander data base and using their classification (ref. 4). One can basically group the H-bond structures at the residues in the following way: A residue can participate in a H-bond pair in a helix structure where it can either be paired with a residue outside or inside the helix and in the end, in the middle or the beginning of the structure. A residue can also paticipate in an H-bond pair in a sheet structure (either parallel or anti-parallel beta-sheet), and a residue can of course have no participation in any H-bond pair. Therefore these classes, all together 7, were used as output categories for the network, while the sequence of amino acids, as usual, was the input to the network represented in a number cooding. The network employed for this task was very similar to the ones used for the surface prediction. It had a hidden layer of around 50 neurons and mostly with a window size of 13 units for reading the sequence. The training set consisted of around 14 proteins and the test was performed on 3 proteins novel to the network. The network performed very well in predicting whether a given residue participating in a H-bond pair of any kind or not. It could predict that up to 90 % correct but on average with a score of 70 % correct and where random score is 50 %. Thus the neural network was reasonably successfull in predicting such H-bond presence or deficiency, see table II. This fact indicates that there is a local code in the information of amino acid sequences for determining the presence or deficency of hydrogen bonds

TABLE II

NN architecture (w=windowsize) input+hid.+output (w)	out-put categories	training cycles	train score percent	test score percent
180 + 20 + 7 (w-9)	7	2200	87	40
260 + 40 + 3 (w-13)	3	400	96	65
260 + 20 + 2 (w-13)	2	600	93	69

The network was less successfull in predicting whether a residue formed an H-bond in the beginning or the end of a helical structure (which then could be understood as an identification of a helix start or a helix break). The network was around 65 % correct in such predictions (random is 33 %) and the network was 40 % correct (random is 14 %) in predicting what specific class of H-bond structur, out of 7 possible classes, a given residue participated in. The network for identifying residues as helix starters or helix breakers can be used in combination with a network for secondary structure prediction in order to improve the latter.

5. Conclusion

We presented a novel application of multi-layered feed forward neural networks. The applications were mainly the prediction of local surface structures of proteins based on the knowledge of their primary structure of amino acids. The networks performed this task superior to any known methods based on single amino acid properties such as hydrophobicity and the network improved when correlating the input sequence data with information about secondary structures of the given protein. Such information was also obtained from a neural network with only sequence data as input. The network configuration with the highest score was for obvious reasons the one which just descided whether an amino acid was at the surface or not. A similar network was quite successfull in predicting H-bond presence or deficiency just on the basis of the primary structure, but less correct in predicting specific H-bond structures.

Acknowledgement

L. Walsh and A. Crofts are acknowledged for a stimulating lecture and poster pointing out the significance of predicting surface properties of proteins, and Peter Wolynes and Richard Goldstein are acknowledged for participation in this study. Calculations were performed at the National Center for Supercomputer Applications in Urbana-Champaign. This work was supported by NIH grant PHS GM 44557-01.

References

1. N. Qian and T. J. Sejnowski J. Mol. Biol. V. 202, 865, (1988),
H. Bohr, J. Bohr, S. Brunak, R. M. J. Cotterill, B. Lautrup, L. Nørskov, O. Olsen and S. Petersen, FEBS Lett, V.241, 223, (1988) and
L. H. Holley and M. Karplus, Proc. Nat. Acad. Sci. USA, V.86, 152, (1989).

2. O. B. Ptitsyn et al., FEBS Lett, V.263, 54, (1990).

3. H. Bohr, "Determination of internal bondings and surface structures of complex protein molecules by neural networks. Abstract for the workshop on "Complex dynamics in neural networks", June 1991, IIASS, Vietri, Salerno, Italy.

4. W. Kabsch and C. Sander, Biopolymers, V.22, 2577 (1983).

5. H. G. Bohr, R. A. Goldstein and P. G. Wolynes, AMSE Periodicals, Modelling, Measurement and Control, C, Vol. 31, No 2, 55 (1992) and
A. Shrake and J. A. Rupley, J. Mol. Biol., V.79, 351 (1973) and
B. Lee and F. M. Richards, J. Mol. Biol., V.55, 379, (1971).

6. M. S. Friedrichs and P. G. Wolynes, Science, V.246, 371, (1989) and
M. S. Friedrichs, R. A. Goldstein and P. G. Wolynes, Generalized protein tertiary structure recognition using associative memory Hamiltonians, U. of I. preprint (1991), subm. to J. Mol. Biol.

7. F. M. Richards, Ann. Rev. Biophys. Bioeng. (1977).

8. UCSF MidasPlus Users Manual, Computer Graphics Lab. Univ. Of California, San Francisco (Nov. 1989).

9. H. Bohr and P. G. Wolynes: "Protein Folding: A Physical View of Neural Network Approaches". Contribution to the proceedings of the workshop on "Neural Networks: From Biology to High Energy Physics", Marciano Marina, Elba, Italy, June (1991).

10. H. Bohr, J. Bohr, S. Brunak, R. M. J. Cotterill, H. Fredholm, B. Lautrup and S. B. Petersen, FEBS Lett, V. 261, 43 (1990).

11. H. Bohr and P. G. Wolynes, The early stages of protein folding from an information processing viewpoint. (Submitted to J. Chem. Phys.) (May 1992).

Nuclear Phenomenology with Neural Nets

John W. Clark and Srinivas Gazula

McDonnell Center for the Space Sciences
and Department of Physics
Washington University, St. Louis, MO 63130 USA

Henrik Bohr

School of Chemical Sciences
University of Illinois, Urbana, IL 61801 USA

Abstract

We propose a new method of phenomenological analysis of physical systems based on adaptive neural networks. When trained with the backpropagation algorithm, multilayered networks are capable of learning the associations between dependent and independent variables implicit in large data sets and may show reliable predictive power when tested on examples absent from the training set. The approach is illustrated through applications to several problems relating to the stability of atomic nuclei.

1 Introduction

Artificial neural networks are systems of neuron-like units that store information in the connections between the units [1-4]. Since there are many pathways by which signals can travel from input to output through an intricate mesh of connections, processing in a neural network is said to be massively parallel.

This feature of parallel processing of information is reminiscent of the manner in which visual images are processed in the human brain. It should then be no surprise that, with a suitable choice of wiring diagram or network architecture and a suitable learning algorithm for determining the algebraic weights of connections, neural nets can become very adept at pattern recognition and at classifying input patterns into two or more categories. In other words, they may be able to learn a set of associations between input patterns and appropriate patterns of output response. All but the simplest classification tasks require neural networks to form internal representations of their environments, i.e., of the mapping that underlies the ensemble of associations. If the classification is to be performed reliably with limited numbers of neuronal units and interconnections, a network must discover economical rules for describing the correlations between input and output patterns. In part, the creation of such rules may involve the development, under training, of neuronal receptive fields attuned to essential regularities in the input patterns. Thus certain neurons become feature detectors that exercise a critical influence on the output categorization decision. Suppose a network has indeed developed working rules that gives a reasonably faithful representation of a set of experienced associations (the training set), in the sense that the response of the network to the input patterns of the training set is nearly always correct. The broader applicability of these rules, or the generalization ability of the net, may then be tested by exposing the network to novel patterns (the test set) and observing its response. A high percentage of correct responses to unfamiliar stimuli indicates that the system is not merely using its free parameters to make a lookup table, but is actually capturing the most important rules governing the composition of the world of input stimuli.

Now, re-read the last paragraph, with these substitutions: *data* for *patterns*; *independent physical variable* for *input pattern*; *dependent physical variable* for *output pattern*; *model* or *theory* for *rules*; and *prediction* for *response to unfamiliar stimuli*. It may then be recognized that, in essence, what the neural net is doing in the above scenario is just what a scientist does when doing science!

It is possible that this analogy between the functioning of an adaptive artificial neural net and the activities of a human scientist may be exploited to create new and fruitful theoretical structures. The idea is to train a neural network on a body of scientific data — especially on complex data generated by complicated many-particle systems — and let it formulate its own laws about the regularities implicit in these data. The experimental data on a given class of physical systems consists of a set of associations between measured variables. Coded versions of these variables provide the input and output patterns for the implementation of a supervised learning procedure in a multilayered neural network. Under favorable circumstances, the internal model built by the network during the learning process may possess useful predictive power, yielding correct values of the dependent physical quantities (or categories) corresponding to unfamiliar values of the independent variables.

Thus, we envision an unorthodox adaptive phenomenology subserving collective computation of properties of complex physical systems. This approach will have obvious practical merit if it produces reliable results in interesting physical contexts. The approach is most likely to be successful in cases where a large data base exists, furnishing some thousands of training patterns for the creation of an accurate representation of the relevant associations. Since feedforward nets are much better at interpolation than extrapolation, their predictive faculty is most likely to be useful for filling gaps in the data base, rather than projection far beyond the range of current data. With these qualifications, it is conceivable that neural network algorithms may become competitive with conventional methods for data analysis.

Beyond such utilitarian considerations, more intriguing possibilities and issues may arise, especially as more advanced architectures and learning rules are developed. In building a workable internal model, the scientific neural network may arrive at laws (or merely rules) we already know, or it may represent the data in ways alien to us. There is the tantalizing prospect that the net may uncover aspects of nature that might otherwise elude us. Of course, the "theory" postulated by a neural network is buried in the connections and their weights — and in practice it may be difficult or impossible to derive a set of clearly expressed rules from the array of "learned" neuron-neuron interactions. One is confronted with a new and challenging class of ill-posed inverse problems whose analysis has scarcely begun.

We shall not take on these deeper issues here, but rather set ourselves the limited task of showing that neural networks are able to grasp well-known regularities in a well-characterized data base gathered for large class of physical systems, regularities that underlie accepted models of these systems.

2   Neural nets for modeling nuclear physics

Scientific applications of neural networks are still in a formative stage and are viewed by many as mere curiosities. However, a scheme resembling that employed for text-to-phoneme conversion [5] ("NETtalk") has already achieved notable successes in protein chemistry, furnishing a valuable new approach to the prediction of secondary and tertiary structure of protein molecules from the amino-acid sequence specifying their primary structure (see, for example, Bohr et al. [6,7] and the article by Bohr in this volume [8]). Currently, we are witnessing a rapid proliferation of other promising implementations of neural-network techniques across a broad range of scientific disciplines. To name just a few instances, neural nets are being used in the identification of ^{1}H-NMR spectra of complex oligosaccharides [9] in carbohydrate chemistry; for star/galaxy discrimination [10] and the recovery of atmospheric phase distortion from stellar images [11,12] in astronomy; and to perform triggering, event classification, track reconstruction, and other data management tasks in experimental high-energy physics [13,14,15,16].

The field of nuclear physics provides rich territory for testing the power of neural network phenomenology. Among the possible choices of physical systems, nuclei are especially appealing, since their structure and dynamical behavior reflect both the basic laws of quantum mechanics and the behavior of strong, weak, and electromagnetic forces over the fermi scale of distances. In the low-energy domain of traditional nuclear physics, the properties of an isolated nucleus, or nuclide, are dictated entirely by its proton and neutron numbers, respectively denoted by Z and N. The Brookhaven National Nuclear Data Center offers on-line access to an extensive collection of experimental results for such properties as (i) the mass (or binding energy), spin, parity, magnetic and electric moments, radius, and other observables of the ground state of a nuclide; (ii) decay modes, branching ratios, lifetimes, and decay chains of unstable nuclei; (iii) level schemes and data on excited states; and so on. In principle, one should be able to calculate all these properties from fundamental theory as embodied in the Standard Model of the strong and electro-weak interactions, or, less ambitiously, from the currently popular effective-interaction models based on nucleonic or hadronic degrees of freedom. The former option faces the intractability of quantum chromodynamics in the nonperturbative regime pertinent to nuclear physics (where the coupling constant is of order unity). While effective-interaction theories have generally been very useful for the formulation of tangible physical mechanisms, they are of limited accuracy and scope. Thus, the current status of nuclear theory leaves room for novel phenomenological approaches to nuclear physics.

We have performed a wide range of computer experiments that demonstrate the efficacy of multilayered, feedforward neural networks in capturing salient regularities of the nuclear world. In most of the experiments discussed here, the input pattern imposed on the neurons of the input layer represents the integers Z and N that characterize a particular nuclide. The corresponding pattern of activity of the output neurons represents the value computed by the network for the desired property of that nuclide. For example, the output may code for the ground-state mass of the input nucleus, or its spin-parity assignment, or both.

We have considered a variety of coding schemes for representing the input and output data. The networks contain one or more hidden layers, with full feedforward connectivity between adjacent layers. The notation $^c(I+H_1+H_2+...+H_L+O)_{c'}[P]$ is employed to identify specific choices of architecture and coding. In this expression, I and O are the numbers of input and output neurons and H_l is the number of neurons in the lth hidden (or intermediate) layer; c and c' denote the input and output coding schemes, respectively; and P is the number of adaptive weights and thresholds. The thresholds of the input neurons do not contribute to P, since these units act simply as data registers. For input, hidden, and output neurons, we adopt the standard labels k, j, and i, respectively. Generic neurons are labeled m, m'. Given an input pattern, the system computes an output according to the following rules: (i) All units within a layer update their states in parallel. (ii) Successive layers are updated sequentially, starting at the input layer and proceeding forward until the output layer is reached.

The system is taught by example, in a supervised learning scheme known as backpropagation [1,4]. The input patterns of the training set are presented to the system in random order, errors in the responses of the output neurons are observed, and the weights and thresholds that parametrize the state of knowledge of the network are adjusted in accordance with the standard backpropagation algorithm supplemented by a momentum term. The input to generic neuron m is a linear superposition $\sum_{m'} V_{mm'} a_{m'}$ of the activation levels $a_{m'}$ of the neurons that extend connections to m, the coefficients $V_{mm'}$ being the connection weights. The squashing function $g(x)$ that transforms this weighted sum of input signals into the analog response $a_m \in [0,1]$ of neuron m is taken to be of the usual logistic form, $g(x) = [1 + \exp(-x)]^{-1}$. Also as usual, the threshold V_{mo} of neuron m is incorporated as a weight through the introduction of a "true unit" [1] that is always maximally active and extends a connection to m having weight $-V_{mo}$. The backpropagation algorithm minimizes the cost function $C = \sum_{\mu,i}[t_i^{(\mu)} - a_i^{(\mu)}]^2/2$, where $a_i^{(\mu)}$ is the actual activity level of output neuron i that results when the system is exposed to input pattern μ and $t_i^{(\mu)}$ is the corresponding target value.

Typically, some hundreds of passes through the training set are required before the cost function is effectively reduced to its asymptotic value. Since the initial values of the weights and thresholds are chosen by random sampling from a uniform distribution, and since the order of presentation of the training patterns is random, different instances of the learning routine will yield different trained networks. We have performed a sufficient number of independent training sequences to ascertain that the behaviors described below are representative.

In the following sections, we examine specific applications focusing on various aspects of nuclear stability: (a) the construction of networks that distinguish stable from unstable nuclides, (b) learning and prediction of atomic masses, and (c) analysis of neutron separation energies, including an attempt to extrapolate established trends to the proposed magic island of superheavy nuclei.

3 Nets that detect stable nuclei

At the most basic level, nuclei can be classified as stable or unstable. Admittedly, there is some problem in defining stability. On the one hand it is only possible to give lower limits on the lifetimes of putatively stable nuclei, and on the other it seems natural to include very long lived unstable nuclides in the stable category. A reasonable condition for inclusion in the "stable" class would be a lifetime exceeding, say, 5×10^8 years.

Feedforward neural networks with architecture $16 + H + 1$ have been developed that approximately solve this categorization problem (see Fig. 1). A binary coding of input patterns is adopted, to emphasize the integral character of Z and N: the first 8 of the 16 input units are clamped "on" ($a_k = 1$) or "off" ($a_k = 0$) to represent Z as a binary number; the remaining 8 encode N in a similar manner. The response $a_i \in [0,1]$ of the single analog output neuron i measures the confidence with which the net classifies the input nuclide (Z, N) as stable. (In our general notation for network types, we would put $c = b$ and $c' = a$ to designate binary input coding and analog output coding.)

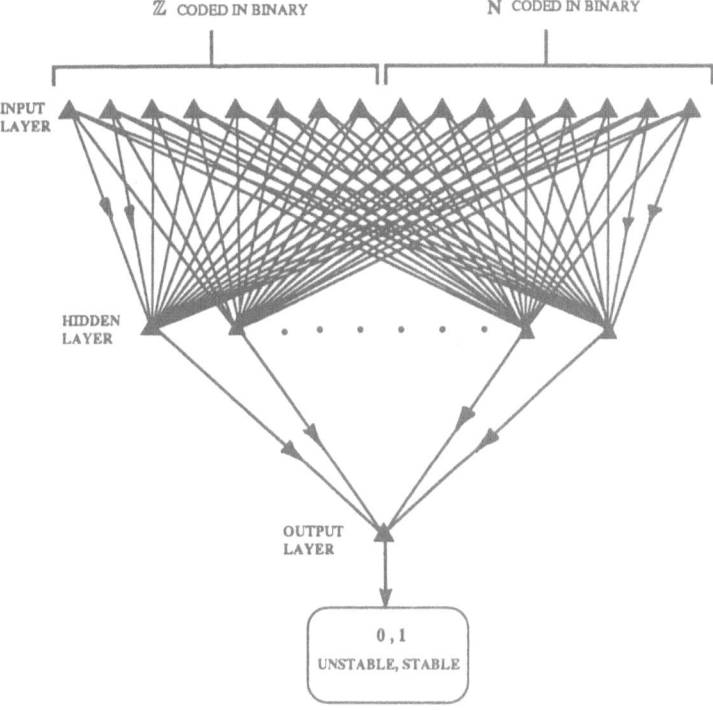

Fig. 1. Architecture for neural net that learns to distinguish between stable and unstable nuclei. Window at bottom shows target activities.

The full data base chosen for the stability study consists of the 2226 entries in the General Electric Chart of the Nuclides [17]. Nuclides with grey patches on their squares are counted as stable. The stable nuclides so identified are outnumbered by the unstables by a factor of about 9 to 1. To equalize exposure of a net to the two categories during the learning phase, each stable example was presented 9 times and each unstable example once, in each pass through the training set. An "epoch" is defined as one such pass through the training data. The learning rate is generally taken as $\eta = 0.5$ (rather than 0.05 as reported previously [18,19]) and the momentum parameter as $\alpha = 0.9$, while initial weights and thresholds are restricted to $[-0.5, 0.5]$.

There are two primary aspects of network performance: *learning* and *prediction*. For satisfactory learning, one requires accurate response to the patterns on which the network has been taught; in prediction, the network is required to use its generalization ability to assign unfamiliar patterns to the correct category. In measuring performance, either for taught or unfamiliar patterns, we consider the response of the network to a nuclide (Z, N) as "correct" if $a_i \geq 0.5$ $[a_i < 0.5]$ when that nuclide is stable [unstable]. On this basis, typical learning accuracy is at the 94% level overall and 75% and 96% for the stable and unstable nuclei respectively, for a network with $H = 19$ trained on the full data base. Performance in the learning task appears to saturate around $H = 20$ (hence around $P = 350$), with little gain for larger numbers of hidden units. Prediction was tested by deleting randomly selected subsets of approximately 15% of the stable examples and a like fraction of the unstables, training on the remaining cases, and asking for responses to the unfamiliar patterns. The process was repeated for reductions by approximately 25% from the original stable and unstable training sets. In representative runs with $H = 19$, the percentages of correct responses for stable nuclides among the smaller and larger test samples were 69% and 63%, respectively, the corresponding measures being 94% and 93% for unstable test nuclides. Similar performance figures are recorded when an alternative training procedure, conjugate-gradient minimization of the cost function [20], is employed instead of backpropagation [21].

Due to pairing and shell effects [22], nuclei divide naturally into even-Z-even-N, even-Z-odd-N, odd-Z-even-N, odd-Z-odd-N, magic-Z, and magic-N classes. The learning curves for these six classes, i.e., the corresponding percentages of correct responses to the training patterns plotted against number of training epochs, reveal a significant feature of the neural network model being explored. The nets with hidden units are quick to grasp the importance of both pairing and shell phenomena for stability. In particular, they learn, on a relatively short time scale, that even-even nuclides as well as nuclei with *magic numbers* of neutrons or protons (Z or $N = 2, 8$, 20, 28, 50, 82, and $N = 126$) carry an enhanced likelihood of stability. Furthermore, examination of the receptive fields of the hidden-layer units of trained networks shows that (a) hidden neurons which function (in part) as feature detectors of odd Z or odd N are not uncommon and may act to incorporate the pairing effect; that (b) certain units tend to vote for stability when the network is stimulated with one or more specific magic values of Z or N; and that (c) some units assume the task of mapping out unstable boundary regions of the (Z, N) plane and inhibit activation of the output neuron for inputs in such regions. However, the receptive fields that are developed by the hidden and output neurons of competent networks are generally quite complex and difficult to decipher – very complicated processing is taking place even at the single-unit level. (A more detailed discussion of similar results from earlier stability experiments may be found in [18].)

It is to be stressed that our networks based on binary coding of Z and N do not merely compile lookup tables as they are trained. Rather, they expend their limited parametric reserves to develop rules which approximately characterize the data base and especially its chief regularities, capturing fundamental aspects of nuclear structure. While these nets do not learn perfectly, they do show respectable predictive ability.

This behavior is in strong contrast with the findings of another set of experiments in which the nuclidic input patterns are encoded *locally* by 126 neurons for Z and 184 neurons for N. Each possible value of Z (or N) has its own "grandmother" neuron, which turns fully "on" when that Z (or N) value is presented as input, all the other neurons in the input bank being clamped "off". In this case, no preference was given to stables over unstables in the frequency of presentation of training examples. For $H = 5$, learning is almost perfect. In a specific example, the overall accuracy is 98.7% (94.0% for the stables, with the best performance for even-even and magic-N nuclides; and 99.2% for the unstables). On the other hand, prediction is unreliable. In one run, stability was correctly predicted for only 9 out of 62 stable test nuclides. It appears that the network is exploiting its substantial parametric resources ($P = 1561$ adjustable connection weights and thresholds) to "memorize" the training data, although it does recognize the simple fact that most nuclides are unstable. Predictive performance on the stables actually improves somewhat as the number of hidden neurons is reduced to 2 or 1, although at $H = 1$ (thus $P = 313$) the accuracy of learning has declined to 90.9% overall.

4   Nets that learn and predict nuclear masses

It is unrealistic to expect a complete solution of the the stability/instability classification problem by neural networks of the type we have constructed, since the networks do not receive any information about the *degrees* of stability or instability of nuclei. Indeed, we consider it unlikely that significantly better performance on the combined learning-prediction task can be achieved with further refinements and parameter searches within the $^b(16 + H + 1)_a$ class of nets. This position is supported by the similarity of the available results obtained with backpropagation and conjugate-gradient optimization algorithms.

The requisite graded information on stability comes into play when networks are trained on nuclear binding energies or masses. Accordingly, we have carried out an extensive set of experiments in which layered feedforward nets were assigned the tasks of accurate representation of the nuclidic (or atomic) mass surface $M(Z, N)$ and reliable prediction of masses for novel nuclides.

Most tabulations characterize the mass of a particular nuclide (Z, N) in terms of the *mass excess* $\delta(Z, N) = M - A$, where $M(Z, N)$ is the mass of the corresponding neutral atom and $A = Z + N$ is the mass number. In turn, M is measured in atomic mass units, defined such that $M(6, 6) = 12$, i.e., such that the mass excess of the ^{12}C atom is zero. Values of $\delta(Z, N)$ are commonly quoted in MeV.

The Brookhaven data bank supplies target values of $\delta M(Z, N)$ for 2291 nuclides, from which training sets of various sizes may be selected. We have studied the performance of nets of several different architectures, with two kinds of coding for the input variables Z and N. The learned or predicted value of $\delta M(Z, N)$ is read from the sigmoidal analog response $a_i \in [0, 1]$ of a single output neuron by multiplication with a scaling factor equal to the range of experimentally determined (or expected) mass excesses.

The quality of the results obtained in a number of runs for different network types is indicated in Table 1, in terms of the rms deviation and mean deviation of learned or predicted responses from the experimental or database masses. In this table (as opposed to Fig. 2), we follow [25] and define "deviation" as: calculated mass − experimental mass. For learning, the rms deviation is directly proportional to the square root of the cost function minimized by the backpropagation algorithm. The mean deviation measures systematic overbinding or underbinding.

Table 1

Characterization of errors in learning and prediction of atomic masses by neural networks of various types, for representative runs. Conventions for rms and mean deviations, cited in MeV, are as in [25]. The last line gives the error measures for one of the most accurate global mass fits by traditional methods, based on an homogeneous partial difference equation [26] and involving 471 adjustable parameters and 1504 database nuclei.

Net type	Learning error		Prediction error	
$^c(I + H_1 + \cdots + H_L + O)_{c'}[P]$	rms	mean	rms	mean
$^a(2 + 20 + 1)_a[81]$	3.384	0.313	3.389	0.625
$^a(2 + 60 + 1)_a[241]$	3.848	0.362	–	–
$^a(2 + 10 + 10 + 1)_a[151]$	1.807	-0.053	–	–
$^b(16 + 20 + 1)_a[361]$	1.919	0.268	2.278	-0.038
$^b(16 + 10 + 10 + 1)_a[291]$	2.043	0.632	2.180	-0.278
$^b(16 + 10 + 10 + 10 + 1)_a[401]$	1.008	0.005	3.612	0.396
$^b(16 + 10 + 10 + 14 + 1)_a[449]$	0.932	-0.049	–	–
Masson-Jänecke fit [471]	0.346	0.014	–	–

In the simplest scheme, Z and N are represented by the analog activities a_k of two dedicated input neurons, after accommodation to the interval $[0, 1]$ by an appropriate scaling factor. Thus one considers $^a(2 + H + 1)_a$ networks, with $c = c' = a$ to indicate analog input and output coding. Learning ability, i.e. accuracy in the representation of given data, was evaluated for such nets after training on the full data base. The differences $\Delta(Z, N) = M_{exp} - M_{calc}$ between "experimental" or database masses and the values "calculated" or learned by a trained network exhibit some intriguing

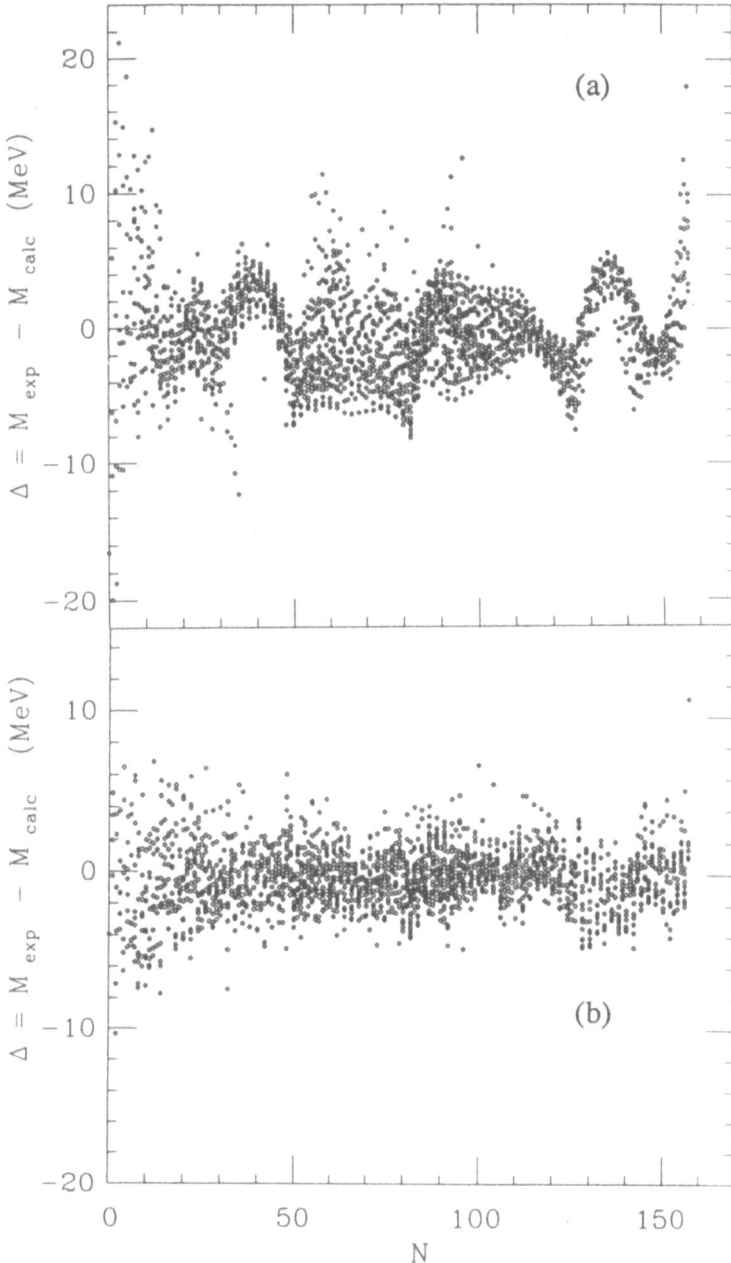

Fig. 2. Projected errors for neural nets of types (a) $^a(2+20+1)_a[81]$ (with analog input and output coding) and (b) $^b(16 + 20 + 1)_a[361]$ (with binary input and analog output coding).

features. Fig. 2(a) shows, for a typical run, the projection of individual errors onto a plane of constant Z. From the large negative errors at or near the magic numbers $N = 20, 28, 50, 82, 126$, it is obvious that, with the chosen architecture and coding, the trained network *does not* recognize shell effects. Rather, the system creates a (generally) smooth mapping from (Z, N) to ΔM, in accordance with the continuous nature assigned to the input and output variables by the analog coding prescription. In fact, the error plot of Fig. 2(a) displays a striking — even semi-quantitative — resemblance to the corresponding projection of the "experimental shell correction" determined by Myers and Swiatecki [23] (see also [24]) from the differences between the experimental masses and the predictions based on the liquid-droplet model. This model entails a semi-classical, continuum picture of nuclei which (like the analog input coding prescription) ignores the discrete character of Z and N.

The neural-network representation of the mass data is dramatically improved when we adopt the binary input coding scheme used in the stability/instability problem, while maintaining one hidden layer of 20 units, thus working with $^b(16 + 20 + 1)_a[361]$ nets (where $c = b$, for binary input coding). Binary coding of Z and N explicitly incorporates their integral nature and permits the system to make disjoint mappings for the different shell regions of the (Z, N) domain. Consequently, the large shell-edge errors and the associated shell oscillations disappear from the error projection (Fig. 2(b)) — just as they do when theoretical shell corrections are added to the liquid-droplet fits [23,24]). If the error data are instead projected on a plane perpendicular to the N axis, we find a completely analogous behavior: conspicuous shell oscillations, with minima near proton magic numbers, occur when Z and N are encoded by single analog neurons, but these errors are suppressed upon reverting to binary input coding. Since the $^b(16 + 20 + 1)_a[361]$ networks have substantially greater parametric resources than the simpler $^a(2 + 20 + 1)_a[81]$ nets, it should be no surprise that they achieve a better representation of the data base. Quantitatively, this superior performance is reflected in decreases in the rms deviation and mean deviation of the learned masses from experiment, as seen in Table 1. However, the qualitative global failure of the 2-unit analog input coding scheme persists even when the number of hidden units is increased by a factor three: in $^a(2 + 60 + 1)_a[241]$ networks the shell oscillations show no significant decrease of amplitude. It is rather surprising that the rms and mean error measures are not reduced (but instead are increased somewhat) on going from $H = 20$ to $H = 60$. This lack of improvement could merely reflect the sensitivity of behavior to the random starting point in weight space. On the other hand, it might be another symptom of the limitations of the $^a(2 + H + 1)_a$ network type in approximating the physical mapping $(Z, N) \rightarrow M$; presumably the minimum rms deviation attainable by such nets already reaches its asymptotic value for $H \sim 20$ or less. At any rate, no improvement is seen in a further run with H raised to 90 ($P = 361$). Insertion of a second hidden layer, to create a $^a(2 + 10 + 10 + 1)_a$ architecture with pure analog coding, does produce considerable improvement in the accuracy of learning and some reduction in the amplitude of the shell oscillations, but the discontinuities in the error surface at magic numbers are still quite evident in the constant-Z and constant-N projections.

Fig. 3 shows projected error data for one of the better networks listed in Table 1, plotted against N.

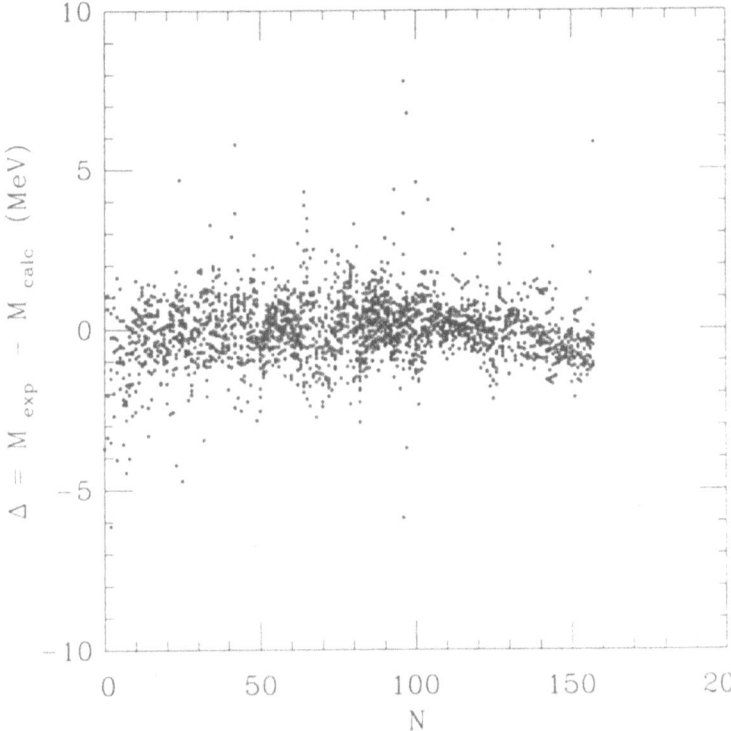

Fig. 3. Projected errors for 5-layer feedforward net $^b(16 + 10 + 10 + 10 + 1)_a[401]$, with binary input and analog output coding schemes, and 401 weight parameters.

The predictive accuracy of these networks is of critical importance, since their principal utility would lie in interpolation between existing data points (and possibly in modest extrapolation from the valley of β stability). Generalization ability was investigated by removing 572 nuclides at random from the data base (about 25% of the total), training on the remaining 1719, and testing the predictive response for the deleted nuclei. Results for four examples are entered in Table 1, in terms of rms and mean deviations of the predicted masses from the database values. As expected, prominent shell oscillations are visible in error plots for the predicted masses when 2-analog-unit input coding of Z and N is employed.

The tabulated results for three- and four-layer nets with analog and binary input coding demonstrate that the accuracy of prediction need not be seriously reduced from that for learning — again, these particular networks are not merely doing "rote memorization." On the other hand, the results for the $^b(16 + 10 + 10 + 1)_a$ net show that good generalization is hardly a universal property.

In application to the modeling of atomic masses, neural network phenomenology is not yet competitive with highly developed conventional techniques [25]. However, it may become so, since a reduction of the rms and mean error measures by another factor of one-half (without increasing the number of parameters) would ensure a quality of fit similar to that of the better mass models surveyed by Haustein (see last row of Table 1, and Table A of [25]).

The applications to neutron separation energies described in the next section give some indication that the required accuracy is attainable. Significant improvements on the network models constructed to date may be gained through (a) optimization of the representation of integer- or real-number input or output data in terms of the activities of input and output neurons [27] and (b) utilization of advanced network-construction, training, and pruning schemes such as cascade-correlation [28], skeletonization [29], and optimal brain damage [30], which promote generalization ability and parametric efficiency. In relation to (b), some fault-tolerance experiments [31] suggest that the current networks contain a lot of "fat" — that it should be possible to eliminate a substantial fraction of the hidden units and hence substantially reduce the number of adaptive parameters, with no degradation of performance.

5 Nets that calculate neutron separation energies

In this section, attention is shifted from atomic masses to another facet of nuclear stability, namely nucleon separation energies. Once again, we are concerned with the discovery and prediction of nuclear shell structure by neural networks. From the technical standpoint, the two exercises to be described serve to illustrate the dual aspects of interpolation and extrapolation.

The first study is a straightforward one involving interpolation between known values of separation energies. Thus, the input to the neural network is again simply (Z, N) and the output is the real-valued neutron separation energy defined by $S(N; Z) = B(Z, N) - B(Z, N - 1)$, where the B's are the binding energies of the neighboring nuclear species. We specialize to odd neutron numbers N and even proton numbers Z. With this choice, the even-odd periodicity in N due to the pairing effect is avoided, but clear signs of nuclear shell structure will remain. The data set consists of 460 examples that are well determined experimentally. When the data points belonging to a common value of $N - Z$ are joined by lines [22], sharp peaks or cusps, followed by sudden drops, are seen near the neutron magic numbers 20, 28, 50, and 82. The net was trained on around 90% of the examples and then required to predict the separation energies of the missing nuclides. We experimented with several network architectures, as specified below.

Analog representations were used at both input and output interfaces. However, to obviate the shortcomings of the simple analog treatment employed in the mass study, we have increased the flexibility and precision of the input and output representations by implementing a certain "real-number" coding prescription (thus $c = c' = r$ in our notation for network types). Each of the variables Z and N is now encoded by *several* analog input neurons, which are assigned nonoverlapping ranges of Z and N. A similar real-number coding scheme is used to represent the target values of the output variable in the backpropagation process, the range of $S(N; Z)$ being encoded in a disjoint manner by several analog output neurons. A detailed description of this coding scheme, including the associated procedure for readout of a computed value for the analog output variable, has been given elsewhere [19], and will not be repeated here.

Networks $^r(I+H+O)_r$ utilizing this coding strategy exhibited good performance in both learning and predictive aspects of the separation-energy problem. The larger nets give a somewhat better representation of the training data, but, as usual, the greater accuracy is won at the expense of increased parametric complexity. In this problem, it is meaningful to assess performance (in either learning or prediction) in terms of the average of $|(S_{exp} - S_{calc})/S_{exp}|$, expressed as a percentage. Selected results are reported in Table 2. In all cases, elimination (or special treatment) of a few difficult examples would decrease the error measures substantially. These results support the view that neural-network modeling of the nuclear binding problem can achieve an accuracy rivaling that of conventional theoretical approaches. (For purposes of comparison of the percentages given in Table 2 with the rms error values shown in Table 1, it may be noted that an rms deviation of 1 MeV corresponds, "typically," to about 2% accuracy in the determination of the nuclidic masses. On the other hand, the entries for the $18 + 18 + 18$ network correspond to rms deviations from the experimental separation energies amounting to 0.98 and 0.117 MeV for learning and prediction, respectively, figures that are to be compared with typical separation energies of 6 MeV.) The well-known tradeoff between accuracy of learning and reliability of prediction (generalization) is reflected in the table: the largest net learns with the highest accuracy, but its predictive marks are actually slightly worse than those for the smallest net.

Table 2

Average errors in learned and predicted values of even-Z, odd-N neutron separation energies, for three network types. The learning errors refer to the responses of the mature net for the 90% of the database used in training.

Net type	Learning	Prediction
$^r(10 + 10 + 9)_r[209]$	1.63%	1.8%
$^r(18 + 18 + 18)_r[684]$	0.89%	1.6%
$^r(18 + 38 + 18)_r[1424]$	0.69%	1.9%

A demanding test of the predictive ability of the $^r(18 + 18 + 18)_r$ network type was made in an additional experiment. A whole line of data, corresponding to $N - Z = 19$, was included in the 10% sample held for predictive trials. As seen in Fig. 4, the network is able to produce an excellent approximation to the unfamiliar line, especially in the region of the $N = 82$ shell closure cusp.

In the second study of nucleon separation energies, an attempt is made to derive information on nuclei in the vicinity of the hypothetical "magic island" of stable – or nearly stable – superheavy nuclei beyond the known "peninsula" of stable

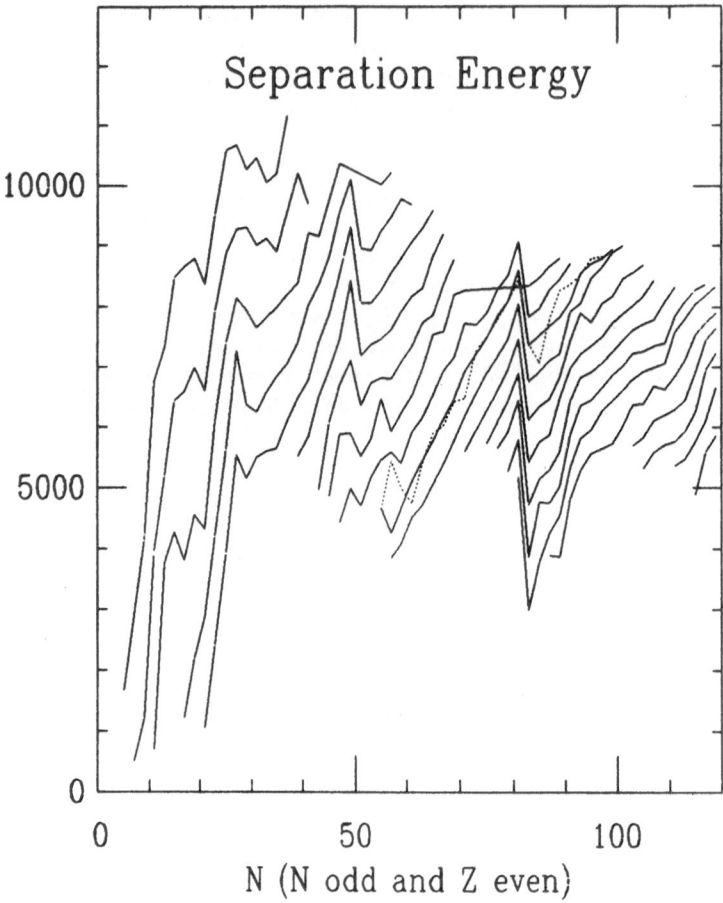

Fig. 4. Separation energies of odd-N-even-Z nuclei, in keV. Data points corresponding to the same $N - Z$ are connected by solid lines. The dotted curve is the prediction of a $^r(18 + 18 + 18)$, network for the $N - Z = 19$ line.

nuclear species. Superheavies have been the subject of much speculation, as well as serious theoretical and experimental effort, extending back to the 1960s [32,33]. In contrast to the preceding analysis of neutron separation energies, which was mainly a matter of interpolation, the neural network models are now confronted with the much more challenging task of extrapolating far from the range of the training set: very few data are available between the last stability region of proton number $80 < Z < 94$ and the postulated stability region somewhere around $106 < Z < 130$. Although neural networks are generally weak at extrapolation, this weakness can be mitigated in the current context by systematically training a network to move from one stability region to another. Applying the backpropagation algorithm, a

39+27+9 net with multi-neuron "real-number" coding of input and output variables was taught with a series of input vectors having five components: $(\delta Z, \delta N, S(r-1),$ $S(r), S(r+1))$. The first two components are the differences in proton and neutron numbers of the reference and target nuclides from those of the most stable isotopes of the pertinent major shells, while the last three components are the separation energies $S(r-1)$, $S(r)$, and $S(r+1)$ of the corresponding reference nuclei of the $N \sim 28$ $(r-1)$, $N \sim 50$ (r), and $N \sim 82$ $(r+1)$ stability regions. The 39 neurons in the input interface are allocated as follows: 3 to represent δZ, 9 for δN, and 9 each for $S(r-1)$, $S(r)$, and $S(r+1)$. The output of the network, coded also by 9 neurons, represents the separation energy $S(r+2)$ of the target nuclide of the given δZ, δN in the *next* stability region $r+2$, which corresponds to $N \sim 126$. The values of $S(r+2)$ were learned with high accuracy, the mean error being only 0.008% as a consequence of the large number of adjustable network parameters (1332) and the relatively small data set (comprised of 48 input vectors plus the corresponding outputs). The trained network was then used to predict the values $S(r+3)$ corresponding to an input vector $(\delta Z, \delta N, S(r), S(r+1),$ $S(r+2))$ – thus accomplishing an extrapolation of separation-energy systematics to the magic-island domain based on a training scheme that incorporates known semi-periodic regularities of nuclear physics. Of paramount interest are the (even) proton and neutron numbers Z_s, N_s that correspond to the values of $S(r+3)$ situated at the cusps of the separation energy in plots versus Z or N. We find $Z_s \approx 118$ and $N_s \approx 180$; i.e., the positions of the cusps are shifted somewhat from the nominally assumed shell-model values of 126 and 184, respectively, for the proton and neutron magic numbers of the superheavy stability region. While the reliability of these predictions can obviously be questioned, the conventional approaches are also subject to considerable uncertainty. It is well known that the location of the magic island cannot simply be determined from the familiar shell model with spin-orbit coupling [32,33]. In particular, the importance of level splittings due to high angular-momentum couplings makes the magic-island search a nontrivial problem within traditional nuclear theory.

6   Interpretation and outlook

We close with a few comments and caveats.

Examples have been presented to demonstrate that feedforward neural networks, equipped with suitably designed input and output interfaces and trained with the backpropagation algorithm, are suited to phenomenological analysis of complex physical systems. Specifically, we have shown that neural nets are capable of grasping the essential features of the nuclear stability problem and that they may exhibit a useful facility for generalization and prediction. It must be stressed that, at this stage, the results presented are purely empirical in nature; that is, we do not have a satisfactory theoretical understanding of why neural nets are effective in the representation of the nuclear properties examined, nor of the limitations of such representations.

Our attitude in this initial foray into neural network phenomenology has been to start with the simplest architectures, coding schemes, and learning algorithms. If the approach works at all, we know that we can always do better, perhaps much better.

We are pursuing further applications of neural network methods to the nuclear data base, considering such aspects as (i) ground-state spins and parities, (ii) nuclear shapes and deformations, (ii) decay modes, branching ratios, and lifetimes, and (iv) atomic and isotopic relative abundances in terrestrial and extraterrestrial material. Other fields of science also appear amenable to fruitful phenomenological analysis and modeling based on neural networks. For example, in materials science, this approach can be applied to the prediction of structural and thermodynamic properties of novel compounds, and in molecular physics, feedforward nets can be used in the analysis and classification of spectra.

Some final remarks on the interpretation of the "parameters" of the neural models — the connection weights — is in order. The most straightforward view of the present work, and notably the investigations of the mass table and of neutron separation energies, is that the subset of training data has been fitted with rather complicated functions involving meshed sigmoids, by adjusting a rather *large* number of parameters (the weights). In the mass analysis, the number P of weights still remains substantially smaller than the number D of data points (training examples); whereas in the studies of separation energies, P may approach or even exceed D. In another view, the sterile notion of weights as fitting parameters is suppressed. The neural network procedure is seen as automating what a model-building scientist does. It is a highly flexible, adaptive procedure for determining a model of the data environment, given only the *few* gross parameters characterizing the architecture, coding scheme, and learning rule (e.g. I, H, O, η, α) and a random initial position in weight space. This alternative view has merit to the extent that one can actually look inside the "black box" of the network, and determine what model, what rules, the system has arrived at through its experience. The deduction of this system of rules from the neuronic receptive fields is a highly nontrivial inverse problem which is beginning to receive serious attention (for example, see [34]). In the solution of this challenging problem lies the prospect of discovering radically new models of physical systems.

7 Acknowledgments

This research was supported by the U. S. National Science Foundation under Grant No. PHY-9002863. We have benefited from numerous discussions with S. Brunak, R. M. J. Cotterill, K. A. Gernoth, J. Hasenbein, and J. S. Prater.

References

[1] Rumelhart, D. E., Hinton, G. E., and Williams, R. J.: Learning internal representations by error propagation. In: Rumelhart, D. E., McClelland, J. L., *et al.* (eds.) *Parallel Distributed Processing: Explorations in the Microstructure of Cognition*, Vol. 1. MIT Press, Cambridge, MA, 1986

[2] Müller, B., and Reinhardt, J. *Neural Networks – an Introduction.* Springer, Heidelberg, 1990

[3] Hertz, J., Krogh, A., and Palmer, R. G. *Introduction to the Theory of Neural Computation.* Addison-Wesley, Redwood City, California, 1991

[4] Clark, J. W. Neural network modelling. *Physics in Medicine and Biology* 1991; in press

[5] Sejnowski, T. J., and Rosenberg, C. R. Parallel networks that learn to pronounce English text *Complex Systems* 1987; **1**: 145-168

[6] Bohr, H., Bohr, J., Brunak, S., Cotterill, R. M. J., Lautrup, B., Nøskov, L., Olsen, O. H., and Petersen, S. B. Protein secondary structure and homology by neural networks: the α-helices of rhodopsin *FEBS Letters* 1988; **B241**: 223-228

[7] Bohr, H., Bohr, J., Brunak, S., Cotterill, R. M. J., Fredholm, H., Lautrup, B., and Petersen, S. B. A novel approach to prediction of the 3-dimensional structures of protein backbones by neural networks *FEBS Letters* 1990; **261**: 43-46

[8] Bohr, H., elsewhere in this volume.

[9] Meyer, B., Hansen, T., Nute, D., Albersheim, P., Darville, A., York, W., and Sellers, J. Identification of the ^{1}H-NMR spectra of complex oligosaccharides with artificial neural networks *Science* 1991; **251**: 542-544.

[10] Odenwahn, S. C., Stockwell, E. B., Pennington, R. L., Humphreys, R. M., and Zumach, W. A. Automated star/galaxy discrimination with neural networks. *Ap. J.* (submitted).

[11] Angel, J. R. P., Wizinowich, P., Lloyd-Hart, M., and Sandler, D. Adaptive optics for array telescopes using neural network techniques. *Nature* 1990; **348**: 221-224

[12] Sandler, D., Barrett, T. K., Palmer, D. A., Fugate, R. Q., and Wild, W. J. Use of a neural network to control an adaptive optics system for an astronomical telescope *Nature* 1991; **351**: 300-302

[13] Denby, B. Neural networks and cellular automata in experimental high energy physics. *Comput. Phys. Commun.* 1988; **49**: 429-448

[14] Peterson, C. Track finding with neural networks. *Nucl. Instr. Methods* 1989; **A279**: 537-545

[15] Denby, B., and Linn, S. L. Spatial pattern recognition in a high energy particle detector using a neural network algorithm. *Comput. Phys. Commun.* 1990; **56**: 293-297

[16] Humpert, B. On the use of neural networks in high-energy physics experiments. *Comput. Phys. Commun.* 1990; **56**; 299-311

[17] Walker, F. W., Miller, D. G., and Feiner, F. *Chart of the Nuclides*, Thirteenth Edition, General Electric, San Jose, CA, 1984

[18] Clark, J. W., and Gazula, S.: Artificial neural networks that learn many-body physics. In: Fantoni, S., and Rosati, S. (eds.) *Condensed Matter Theories*, Vol. 6. Plenum, New York, 1991

[19] Clark, J. W., Gazula, S., and Bohr, H.: Teaching nuclear systematics to neural networks. In: Benhar, O., Bosio, C., Del Giudice, P., and Tabet, E. (eds.) *Neural Networks: From Biology to High-Energy Physics*, in press

[20] Luenberger, D. G. *Linear and Nonlinear Programming*, 2nd ed. Addison-Wesley, Reading MA, 1984

[21] Prater, J. S., private communication

[22] Bohr, A., and Mottelson, B. R. *Nuclear Structure*, Vol. I. W. A. Benjamin, New York, 1969

[23] Myers, W. D., and Swiatecki, W. J. Nuclear masses and deformations. *Nucl. Phys.* 1966; **81**: 160

[24] Möller, P., and Nix, J. R. Nuclear masses from a unified macroscopic-microscopic model. *Atomic Data and Nuclear Data Tables* 1988; **39**: 213-223

[25] Haustein, P. E. An overview of the 1986-1987 atomic mass predictions. *Atomic Data and Nuclear Data Tables* 1988; **39**: 185-200

[26] Masson, P. J., and Jänecke, J. Masses from an inhomogeneous partial difference equation with higher-order isospin contributions. *Atomic Data and Nuclear Data Tables* 1988; **39**: 273-280

[27] Liisbjerg, C., private communication

[28] Fahlman, S. E., and Lebiere, C.: The cascade-correlation learning architecture. In: Touretzky, D. (ed.) *Neural Information Processing Systems*, Vol. 2. Morgan Kaufmann, Denver, 1990

[29] Mozer, M. C., and Smolensky, P.: Skeletonization: a technique for trimming the fat from a network via relevance assessment. In: Touretzky, D. (ed.) *Neural Information Processing Systems*, Vol. 1. Morgan Kaufmann, Denver, 1989

[30] Le Cun, Y., Denker, J. S., and Solla, S. A.: Optimal brain damage. In: Touretzky, D. (ed.) *Neural Information Processing Systems*, Vol. 2. Morgan Kaufmann, Denver, 1990

[31] Prater, J. S., private communication

[32] Thompson, S. G. and Tsang, C. F. Superheavy elements. *Science* 1972; **178**: 1047-1055

[33] Nix, J. R. Calculation of fission barriers for heavy and superheavy nuclei. *Ann. Rev. Nucl. Part. Sci.* 1972; **22**: 65-120

[34] Sestito, S., and Dillon, T. The use of sub-symbolic methods for the automation of knowledge acquisition for expert systems. *Avignon'91, Expert Systems and their Applications, Avignon, France, June 1991*

Applying Neural Networks to Resonance Search in High Energy Physics

Jochen Rau, Berndt Müller, and Richard G. Palmer

Department of Physics
Duke University, Durham, NC 27706 USA

Abstract. It is the aim of many modern experiments in high energy physics to discover and investigate the properties of rare particles. However, often so few of these particles are produced in an experiment that it is very difficult to discover their decay signature against the background. There are various techniques to suppress the background and thus to enhance the relative strength of the signal, but none of the techniques currently used is optimal. In view of the future operation of even larger accelerators, such as the Superconducting Supercollider, where a signal may occur once in a billion events, and millions of events will have to be analyzed each second, it is desirable to optimize the techniques for resonance search. Recently it has been suggested that neural networks may be used for this task. It is still unclear, however, whether neural networks can perform an unbiased data analysis or whether they may produce artificial signals due to information acquired during the training process.

1   What is the problem?

In recent years neural networks have been successfully applied to various tasks in the data analysis of high-energy physics experiments, such as track reconstruction, calorimeter cluster finding or generic peakfinding [1, 2, 3, 4]. Here we discuss another potential application, namely to the problem of identifying particle resonances against a noisy background [5]. The problem of resonance search is of great importance in experimental high energy physics, and any fast, efficient algorithm would have important applications. At the planned Superconducting Supercollider (SSC) in Texas, for example, experiments will be designed to search for exotic particles with very low production cross sections. It will then become essential to have an efficient system, possibly on-line, for optimized resonance search.

Consider as an example the experiment shown schematically in Fig. 1. Nuclei collide and produce many pions (π^+, π^-) via hadronic interactions. However, some rare particle resonances such as kaons or rho mesons may also be produced, followed by subsequent decay into $\pi^+\pi^-$ pairs. Detectors measure the (spatial) momentum $\vec{p}$ and charge q of each outgoing pion. For every pair of pions, the position of the respective detectors and the pions' momenta can also be used to reconstruct the

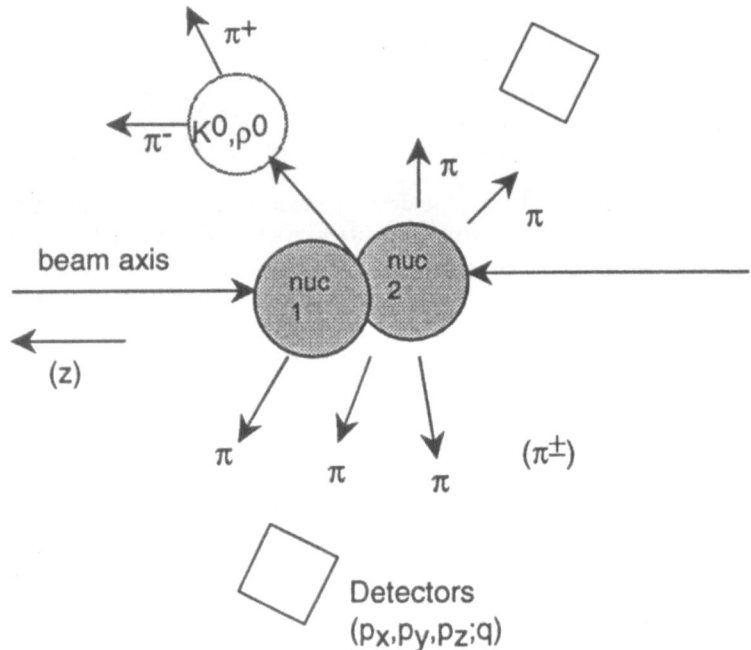

Figure 1: Example of a high-energy physics experiment.

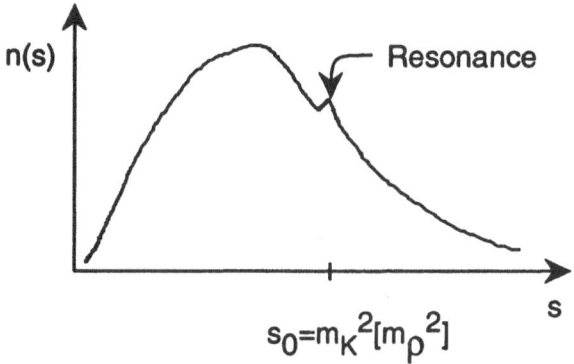

Figure 2: Typical invariant mass distribution.

(hypothetical) vertex where the pair was produced; the experimental setup allows for the determination of z, the coordinate of this vertex along the beam axis. Hence for any $\pi^+\pi^-$ pair one can measure the 7 parameters $(\vec{p}_1, \vec{p}_2, z)$. The problem we are faced with is to distinguish the pion pairs coming from a resonance (K^0, ρ^0) decay from those produced via direct hadronic interactions.

For this purpose the invariant mass $s = (p_1 + p_2)^2$, where p_i are the relativistic four-momenta, is calculated for every $\pi^+\pi^-$ pair. (The four-momentum of a pion can be calculated from its spatial momentum and mass.) The invariant mass distribution of those pion pairs coming from a resonance decay will be peaked around the mass-squared of the resonance (i.e. m_K^2 or m_ρ^2) whereas those produced directly will have a broad range of s values. It is very difficult to identify the resonance peaks against the broad and noisy background distribution. (A typical distribution is shown schematically in Fig. 2.) It is therefore desirable to have some technique to suppress the background and thus, in effect, enhance the signal in the s-distribution. By calculating and plotting only the invariant mass, we lose information contained in the seven parameters measured in the experiment; most methods to enhance the signal of the resonance are therefore based on using additional information contained in these parameters. Traditionally, one introduces cuts in the parameter space, e.g. on the transverse momentum $p_\perp$. Many of these traditional methods, however, are neither systematic nor optimal, but rather are based on the experimenter's experience and intuition.

We thus find ourselves confronted with an optimization problem. An exact mathematical treatment, of course, would be best. However, this would require full knowledge of the background distribution — which in general is not available. In particular, the two-particle correlations are not exactly known. Perhaps a neural network can provide the "second best" solution; it is this option which we explore in this paper.

Before we present the proposed neural network solution, let us briefly outline what the ansatz for an exact mathematical treatment would have to be. Apart from the invariant mass s, additional parameters can be extracted from the measured quantities $(\vec{p}_1, \vec{p}_2, z)$; we denote these additional parameters by α. As shown schematically in Fig. 3, we then have a distribution $\phi(s, \alpha)$ from which the invariant mass distri-

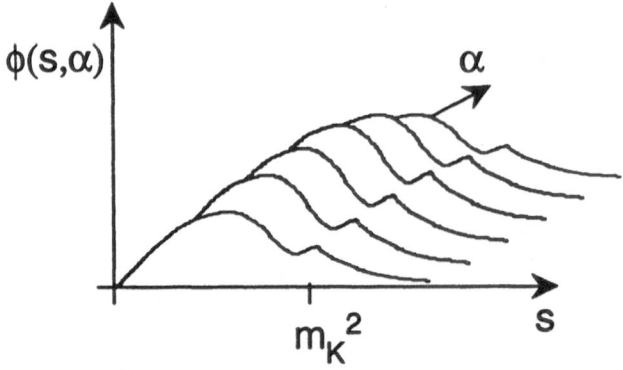

Figure 3: Distribution $\phi(s, \alpha)$.

bution can be calculated by

$$\phi(s) = \int d\mu(\alpha)\phi(s, \alpha) \quad , \tag{1}$$

where μ is a suitable measure. In order to suppress the background, we introduce a weight function $w(\alpha)$, $w(\alpha) \le 1$, to obtain the weighted invariant mass distribution

$$\varphi(s) = \int d\mu(\alpha)w(\alpha)\phi(s, \alpha) \quad . \tag{2}$$

(Note that the traditional cuts are a special case in which the weight function is a characteristic function on parameter space, i.e. it takes the value 1 in a certain region of parameter space and 0 elsewhere.) The weight function is then chosen such that the weighted invariant mass distribution $\varphi(s)$ has an "optimum" enhanced signal, where the criteria for optimality are yet to be determined. As an example, one might think of the signal-to-noise ratio or the ratio of peak height and measurement uncertainty. This leads to an optimization problem for the weight function which, as mentioned before, could be solved analytically only if the background distribution $\phi_0(s, \alpha)$ were known exactly.

2 A proposed neural network solution

Recently it has been suggested that neural networks can be applied to resonance search [5]. Here we present the basic ideas of this approach. In [5] a feed-forward network with one hidden layer and continuous-valued units was used. The network architecture is shown in Fig. 4; there are 7 input units (for the measured parameters $p_x^1, p_y^1, p_z^1, p_x^2, p_y^2, p_z^2, z$), 6 units in the hidden layer and 1 output unit which takes values between 0 and 1. The network was trained using error backpropagation [6, 7]. The output unit was trained to be 0 for background events and 1 for resonance decays. The set of training patterns consisted of experimentally measured $\pi^+\pi^+$ or $\pi^-\pi^-$ pairs, and decay events generated by Monte Carlo simulation (where detector inaccuracies were taken into account). The $\pi^+\pi^+$ and $\pi^-\pi^-$ pairs obviously

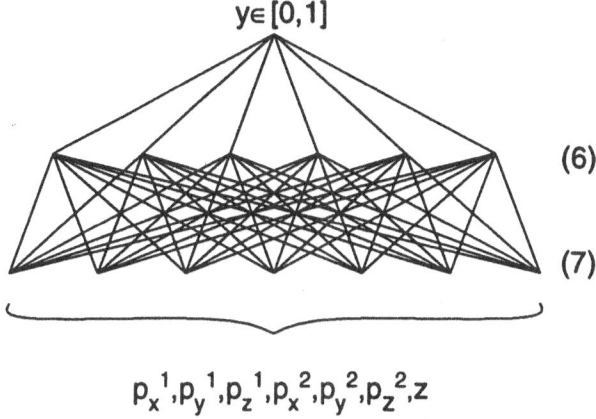

$$y \in [0,1]$$

(6)

(7)

$$p_x^1, p_y^1, p_z^1, p_x^2, p_y^2, p_z^2, z$$

Figure 4: Architecture of the feed-forward network.

do not come from resonances and were assumed to have the same distribution as background $\pi^+\pi^-$ pairs. After training, for any given input $(\vec{p}_1, \vec{p}_2, z)$ the value of the output unit should then be a qualitative measure of the probability of a decay event. Introducing an arbitrary threshold y_0, $0 < y_0 < 1$, one defines the network as having identified a resonance if and only if the value of the output unit is above the threshold.

The neural network can now serve as a filter: By selecting only those events which give a network output above the threshold y_0, we can effectively select those events with a high probability of being a resonance decay. This selection procedure again amounts to a cut in parameter space, but, in contrast to conventional methods, the neural network has learned to optimize the region in parameter space which is being cut. The procedure for identifying resonances is shown schematically in Fig. 5 and works as follows: The measured $\pi^+\pi^-$ distribution is passed through the NN-filter (with threshold y_0), yielding a modified distribution of those pairs which the network identified as coming from a resonance decay. Obviously, this new distribution is narrowly peaked around the invariant mass of the resonance. However, the distribution may still contain many background events which happen to have an invariant mass near the mass-squared of the resonance, and which the network incorrectly identified as decay events. It is therefore necessary to subtract the modified (i.e. filtered) background distribution. In order to obtain this distribution, the measured distribution of $\pi^+\pi^+$ and $\pi^-\pi^-$ pairs — which is assumed to be representative for the background $\pi^+\pi^-$ distribution — is passed through the same NN-filter, using the same threshold y_0. Clearly, the two filtered distributions should differ by a signal which is due to resonance decays. Indeed, this procedure of filtering and subsequent background subtraction allowed Alexopoulos [5] to extract a clear signal from a noisy original invariant mass distribution. It must be remarked, however, that this neural network approach only allows a qualitative, not quantitative analysis: resonances can be identified, but their strength cannot be determined.

328

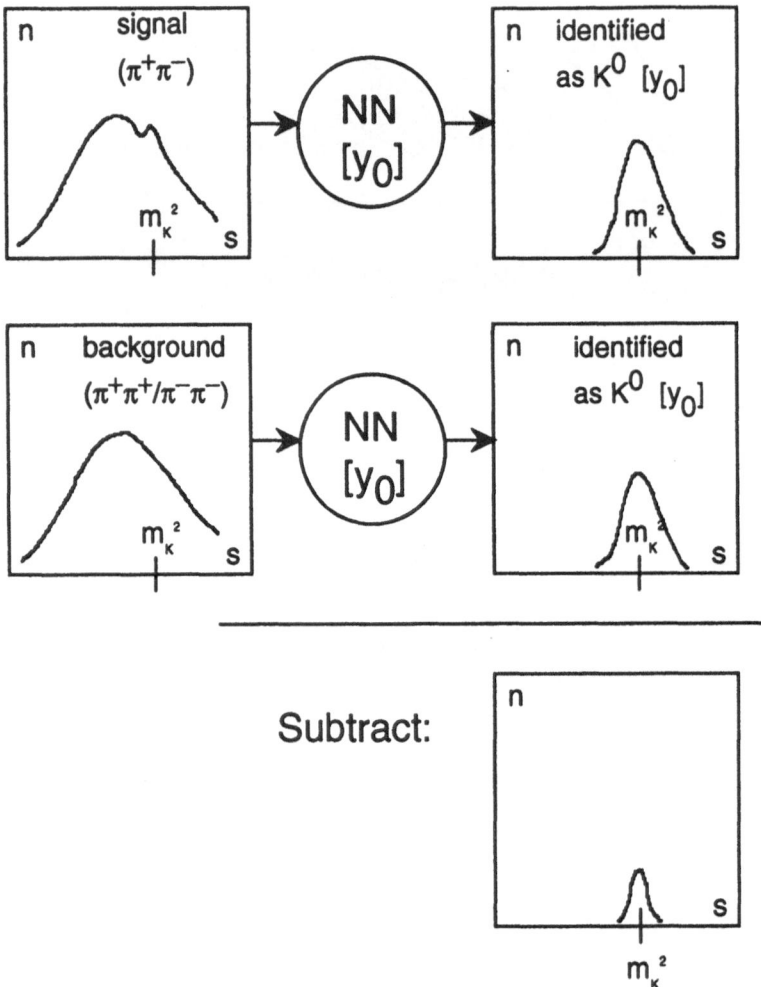

Figure 5: Procedure for identifying resonances.

3   Outlook

Several open questions, of both theoretical and practical nature, remain. First we have to address the fundamental problem of whether a neural network can perform a truly unbiased resonance search or whether there is the possibility of its producing artificial signals due to information acquired during the training phase. This question is currently under investigation; we study a simplified model in a two-dimensional parameter space where both the signal and the background distribution are exactly known and where we are thus able to test the network performance in detail. Once this theoretical problem is resolved, it will be desirable to optimize the network architecture, which will involve modifying the number of hidden layers and units. In addition, the network performance might be improved by preprocessing the experimental data (e.g. calculating the invariant mass, transverse momentum etc.) before feeding them to the neural network. Making effective use of symmetries of the experimental setup, such as azimuthal symmetry, may also reduce the required number of input units. Finally one might envision a combination of an (optimum) analytical treatment of the resonance search problem with the neural network approach.

It is important to note that the technique presented here only allows the search for resonances whose properties, especially mass, are known beforehand (since these properties are needed in the training phase). Many high energy physics experiments, however, involve the search for new particles with unknown properties, e.g. the Higgs boson. It will therefore be necessary to modify the search procedure in such a way that also new resonances, which have not been trained before, can be discovered. One possibility may be to use the network at least to mask out known, disturbing resonances. In addition, if the mass range of a new resonance is known, several nets might be trained for different (hypothetical) masses and then applied in parallel.

References

[1] Denby, B. Neural networks and cellular automata in experimental high energy physics. *Comput. Phys. Commun.* 1988; **49**: 429-448

[2] Peterson, C. Track finding with neural networks. *Nucl. Instr. Methods* 1989; **A279**: 537-545

[3] Denby, B., and Linn, S. L. Spatial pattern recognition in a high energy particle detector using a neural network algorithm. *Comput. Phys. Commun.* 1990; **56**: 293-297

[4] Humpert, B. On the use of neural networks in high-energy physics experiments. *Comput. Phys. Commun.* 1990; **56**; 299-311

[5] Alexopoulos, T. Ph.D. thesis, University of Wisconsin – Madison 1991 (unpublished)

[6] Müller, B., and Reinhardt, J. *Neural Networks – an Introduction.* Springer, Heidelberg, 1990

[7] Hertz, J., Krogh, A., and Palmer, R. G. *Introduction to the Theory of Neural Computation.* Addison-Wesley, Redwood City, California, 1991

VISUAL COMPARISON OF INFORMATION STORAGE IN VARIOUS NEURAL NETWORK MODELS

C.Aberger, R.Folk, K.E.Kürten[*] and H.Schweng

Institut für Theoretische Physik, Universität Linz, Österreich
[*]Institut für Neuroinformatik, Ruhr-Universität, Bochum, BRD

Abstract

The performance of neural networks strongly depends on the learning procedure used for the information to be embedded. We present a visual comparison of various learning rules demonstrating the specific self organization process of the neuron system. Special emphasis is given to sparsely connected networks with pattern dependent architecture and greatly increased efficiency.

Introduction

The storage of information (patterns) in a neural network is buried in the strength of the connections c_{ij} of the neurons. These strengths depend on the learning mechanism used. In principle no conclusion on the patterns stored can be drawn directly from the synaptic couplings c_{ij}. Moreover one and the same information can be differently stored by networks, whose performance in the retrieval process may be quite similar. An interesting question in this context is, in which respect the organization of the networks differs or is alike for the various learning mechanism. Especially we are interested, how the couplings are organized in networks with large storage rate in comparison to networks, with learning rules which fail to store the information. Furthermore one may ask how correlations within and between the patterns influence the neural connections.

A first global picture is obtained by considering the distribution of the strengths of the couplings. Again, for special cases this distribution can be calculated e.g. for random patterns or Hadamard patterns [1]. For structured patterns, besides the distribution, the arrangement of the couplings plays an important role. We present a visual comparison of different networks, which are supposed to store strongly correlated patterns. It is known that the Hebbian learning rule is not sufficient for the storage of such patterns, not to mention the retrieval of defect patterns. Therefore, other learning algorithm have to be taken into account. For certain learning rules the synaptic strengths are explicitly known functions of the particular pattern set to be stored; in other cases these can be found only by numerical iteration procedures. Some of the problems mentioned will be considered in networks with the following learning rules

(1)   The Hebbian learning rule [2]
(2)   The pseudo-inverse learning rule [3]
(3)   Learning by unlearning [4]
(4)   Learning by optimal pattern specific dilution (OSD) [5]

Display of the synaptic matrix by NEURONET

The visualization of the network couplings uses the software package NEURONET [6] which has been developed to demonstrate the retrieval process of an autoassoziative neural network. A pattern editor, the Hebbian and the pseudo-inverse learning rule as well as learning by unlearning are implemented in this software package. Several other plot facilities regarding the overlap, the energy and the histogram of the coupling strengths are also available. General synaptic coupling matrices c_{ij} can be loaded and displayed by a spectral pattern of the synaptic strengths.

The networks displayed here contain 100 neurons. The synaptic matrix is therefore a 100 by 100 matrix with zero diagonal. The strength c_{ij} of a connection from neuron j to neuron i corresponds to a spectral color. The spectrum from the minimal to the maximal strength is indicated on a color scale. The diagonal of the coupling matrix always containes the spectral color of the value zero, so it is easy to distinguish regions of small and strong couplings. The representation of one connection of two neurons is given by a small rectangle best seen in the diagonal of the coupling matrix. The place of such a rectangle in the matrix scheme corresponds to the numbers of the two neurons connected.

Discussion of some examples
Patterns with equal correlations

Let us start with an instructive although very special example. For the information to be stored we take the 20 patterns ξ_i^μ shown in fig. 1a), which all have equal correlations

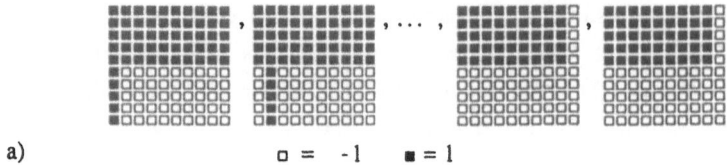

a)   □ = -1   ■ = 1

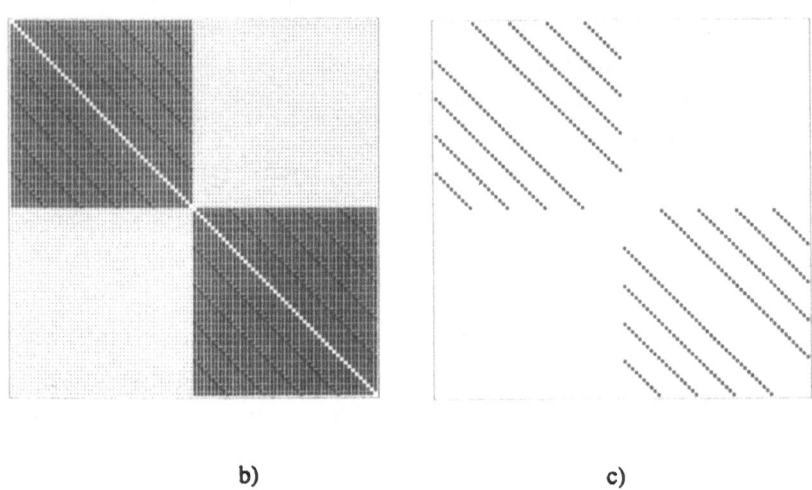

b)   c)

Fig.1: a) Patterns to be learned, b) Coupling matrix for the Hebbian learning rule (· = -0.18 ≠ = 0.18 ■ = 0.2 blank = 0), c) Coupling matrix for the pseudo-inverse learning rule and OSD procedure of [5] (■ = 0.2 blank = 0)

$$C^{\mu\nu} = (1/N) \sum_i \xi_i^\mu \xi_i^\nu \tag{1}$$

and therefore (with I the matrix with all elements equal to 1)

$$C^{\mu\nu} = (1-c) \delta^{\mu\nu} + cI^{\mu\nu} \tag{2}$$

The Hebbian learning rule

$$c_{ij} = \sum_\mu \xi_i^\mu \xi_j^\mu \quad \text{for } i \neq j \text{ and} \quad c_{ij} = 0 \quad \text{for } i = j \tag{3}$$

leads to only two attractors (the first 50 neurons exited and the other ones quiet as well as the inverse state) with half of the state space as basin under the dynamics

$$S_i(t+1) = \text{sign}(\sum_j c_{ij} S_j(t)) \tag{4}$$

This is immediately obvious from the structure of the couplings, shown in fig. 1b where in fact the nearly constant couplings, apart from the diagonal and a faint structure coming from the spikes in the patterns, lead to a quasi majority rule for each half of the pattern. For the pseudo-inverse learning rule we have

$$c_{ij} = \sum_{v,\mu} \xi_i^v (C^{-1})^{v\mu} \xi_j^\mu \quad \text{for } i \neq j \text{ and} \quad c_{ij} = 0 \quad \text{for } i = j. \tag{5}$$

For this example one can easily calculate the inverse correlation matrix

$$(C^{-1})^{v\mu} = 1/(1-c)[\delta^{\mu v} - c/(1 + (p - 1)c) I^{\mu v}] \tag{6}$$

and a quite different picture arises. Only the faint structure (the strongest positive couplings) seen in the Hebbian network remains leading to 20 decoupled networks for 5 neurons (equivalent to a small Hebbian network for one spike). This of course increases the numbers of attractors since now every combination of the spike structure is attractor (again with a majority rule for each spike). The same OSD network architecture arises in this case when one optimizes the minimal stability coefficients as explained in [5] starting from the Hebbian network. The couplings correspondingpseudo-inverse learning rule can also be determined from an iterative algorithm [7], which for linearly independent patterns converges to (1) and leads to stability coefficients

$$\gamma_i^\mu = \frac{\xi_i^\mu \sum\limits_{i}^{N} c_{ij} \xi_j^\mu}{\left(\sum\limits_{j}^{N} c_{ij}^2 \right)^{1/2}} \tag{7}$$

independent of the pattern index ($\gamma_i^\mu = \gamma_i$) because one iterates until the denominator has reached 1. The OSD procedure of [5] improves the pattern dependent stabilities of the Hebbian network for each pattern leading to non symmetric couplings and unequal stabilities of a neuron in different patterns.

For the case where less than the 20 patterns of fig.1a are to be stored the pseudo-inverse learning rule and the OSD procedure of [5] lead to different network architectures, the latter leading to an asymmetric coupling matrix c_{ij} as is generally the case for that procedure. This is demonstrated in fig. 2, where we display the networks emerging from learning only the first 10 patterns. A characteristic feature of the pseudo-inverse learning rule is again an almost completely decoupling of the network into a network for the upper part of the patterns and 10 networks for the "spikes". This is achieved by the concentration of couplings around zero, keeping only a few large positive couplings. The optimization procedure of [4] also leads to a decoupling in the network, but only of the lower part of the pattern from the upper. Nevertheless, the small couplings in the pseudo-inverse model has the effect, that other mixed states appear than in the model optimized by dilution. E.g. the pattern with the upper half inverted is unstable

334

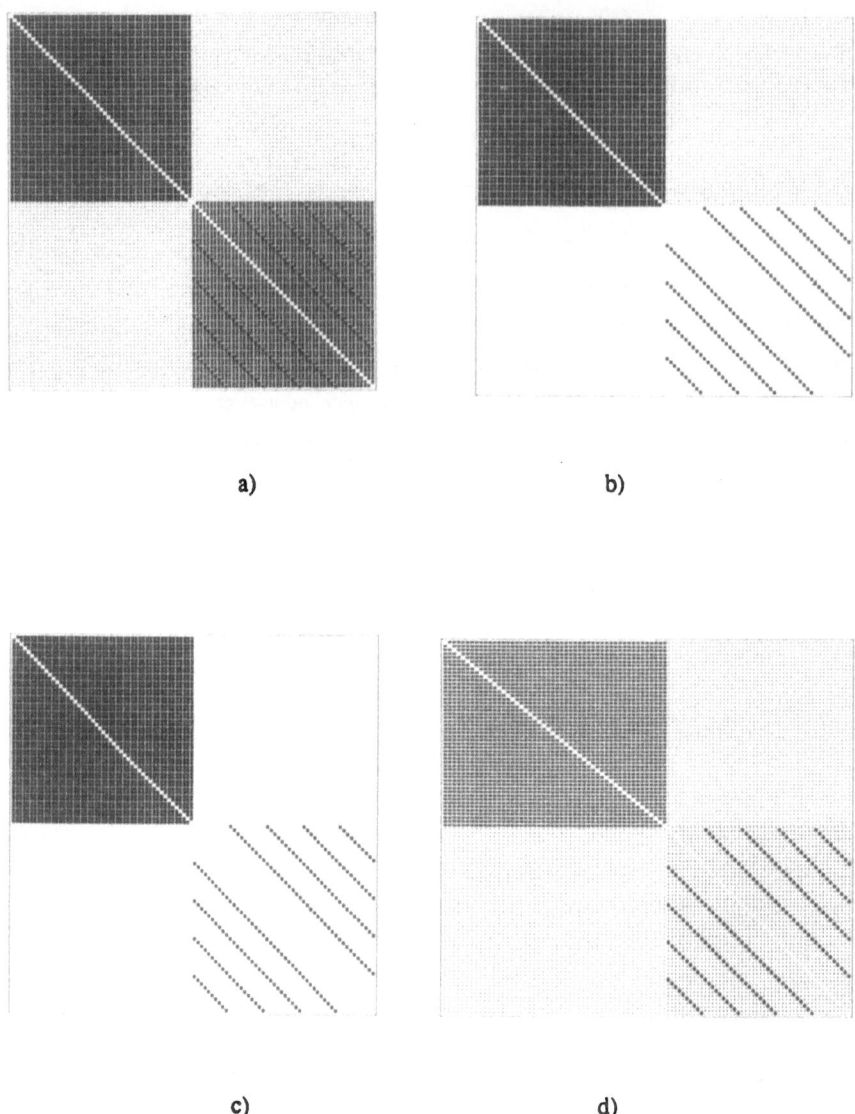

Fig.2: Coupling matrix a)for the Hebbian learning rule (· = -0.08 ≢ = 0.06 ■ = 0.1 blank = 0), b) for the OSD procedure of [5], c) after optimization and symmetrization and d) for the pseudo-inverse model (: = -0.012 · = -0.01 = = 0.012 ■ = 0.18

in the pseudo-inverse model, in the other model it is stable.

In asymmetric networks the energy function is not a Ljapunov function for the dynamics. We therefore have also developed a procedure leading to a symmetric network by the following steps. We symmetrize the optimized couplings by calculating new couplings as

$$c_{ij}^{new} = [\, (c_{ij}^{old} + c_{ji}^{old})/2 \,] \qquad (8)$$

where [x] is the largest integer smaller or equal to x. Then we reapply the optimization procedure of [5], symmetrize and so on, as long as an increase of the minimal stabilities can be observed. We note, that now couplings different from the Hebbian ones arise, with a tendency for small couplings. While the non symmetrized procedure leads to equal or larger stabilities than those for the Hebbian model, this is now not guaranteed. However in most of the cases we reached an improvement upon the Hebbian model.

The minimal stabilities for the neurons of the upper half of the patterns is reduced from 9 for the pseudo-inverse model to 7 for the symmetric diluted model and for the lower part from 2.08 to 2.0 repectively. But this relatively small reduction is compensated for by an dilution of 72%, thus increasing the efficiency of the network drastically. It is worth to note that in no case the network is able to "recognize", that each pattern has only one spike. For that feature to be implanted one would have to get rid of the unwanted mixture states.

A general example

Some of the features mentioned for this special set of patterns can also be found for the example of the 10 patterns shown in Fig.3. They have correlation of different size and are quite anisotropic. In this case we also display a network, which has been obtained by unlearning [4]. The procedure is the following. We start in the Hebbian network the dynamical process, equ. (4), from a random pattern and subtract the Hebbian couplings corresponding to the end pattern multiplied by a conveniently choosen small parameter ("dreaming phase"). This process is then repeated for the new network. The network shown here resulted from 380 "dreams" and an unlearning parameter equal to 0.02 according to [4]. The interesting result is that the overall structure of the network remains quite the same as for the Hebbian network.

Conclusion

The display of the coupling matrix by NEURONET may help to explore neural networks and offers a convenient way to extricate features, regularities and rules from the

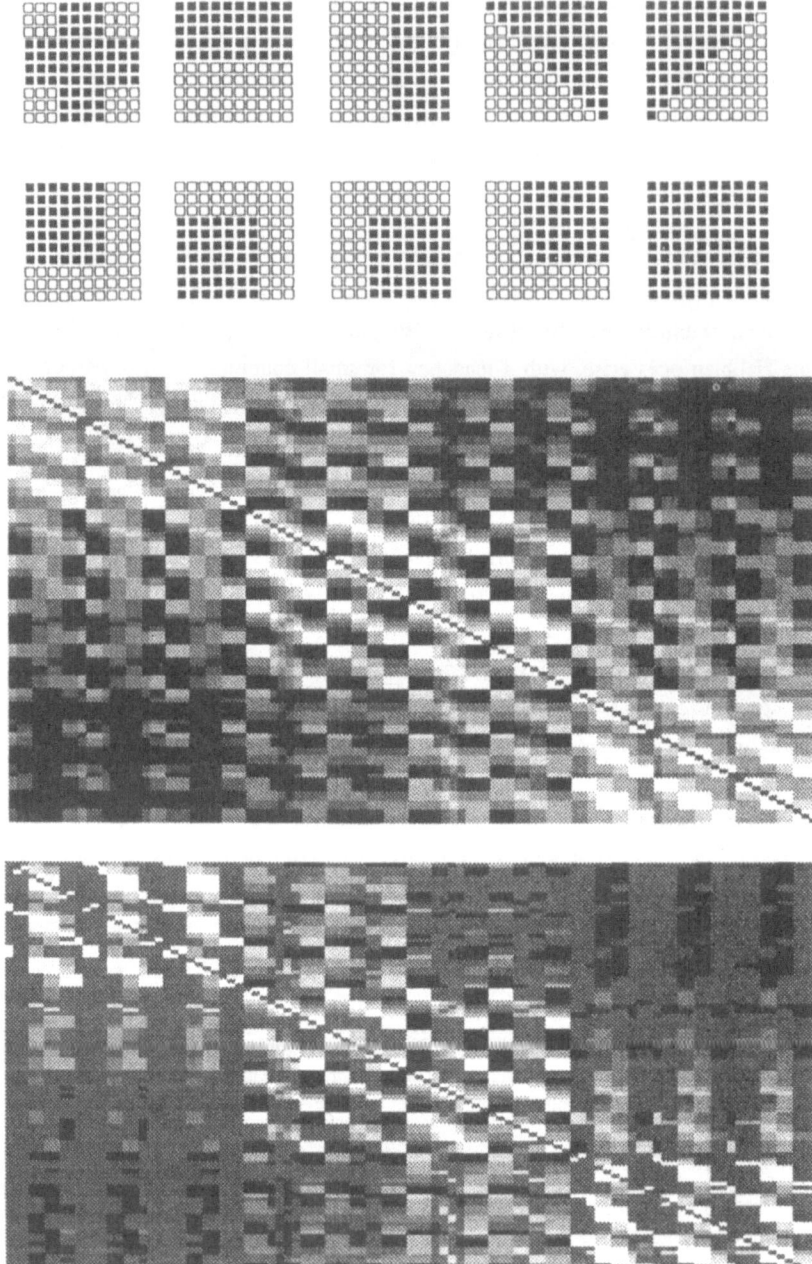

Fig.3a: Pattern set and corresponding coupling matrices for the Hebbian learning rule and after optimization. Strength from smallest values (black) to largest values (white). The diagonal is always zero.

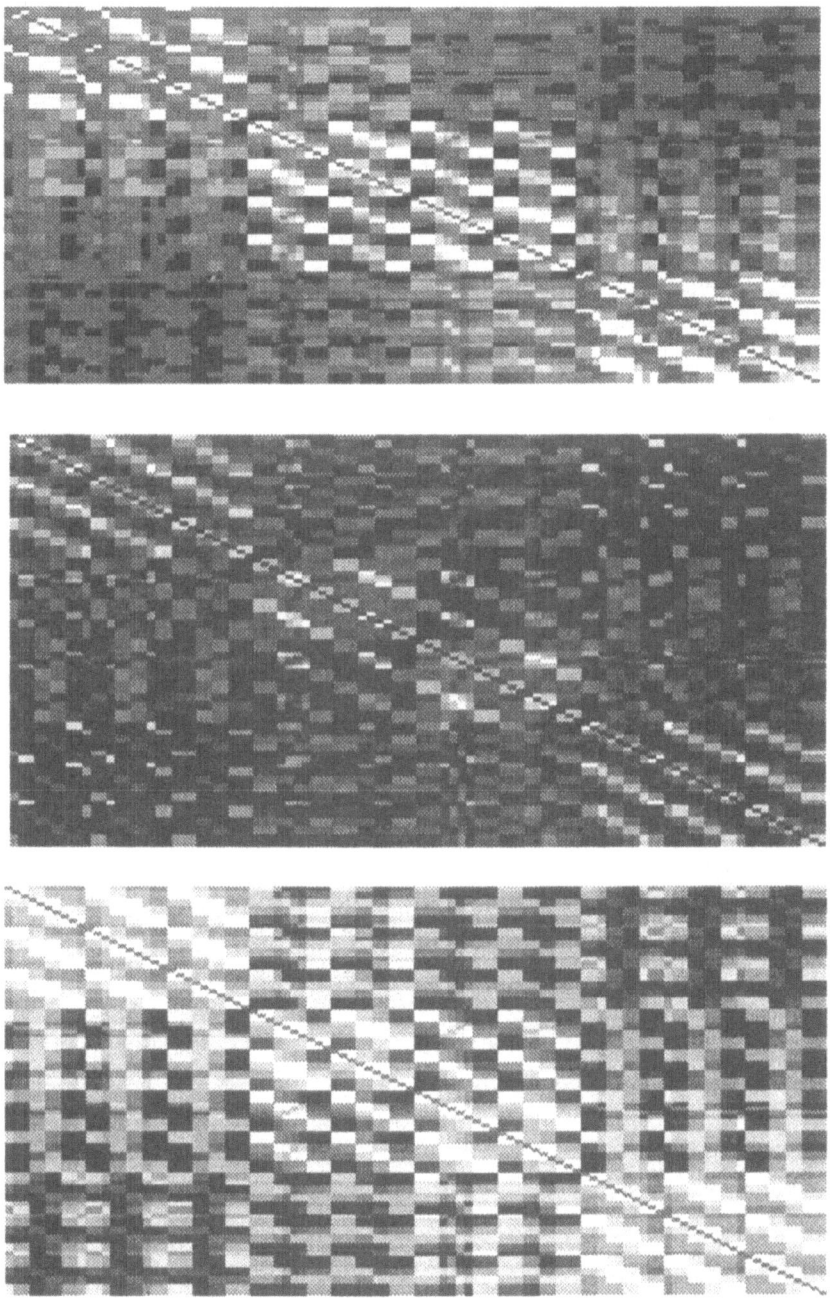

Fig.3b: Corresponding coupling matrices for optimization and symmetrisation, the pseudo inverse learning rule and for unlearning for the patternset of Fig.3a.

patterns of the learned neuron-neuron interactions [8]. In more complicated pattern sets the freedom in permuting the neurons together with e.g. the optimization procedure of [5], may help to recognize less connected "subnetworks" thus opening the possibility to reduce the size of the network constructed for a specific recognition problem.

References

[1]   O.Krisement, A Hopfield model with Hadamard prototypes, Z.Phys.B **80**, 1990, 15-421

[2]   J.J.Hopfield, Neural networks and physical systems with emergent collective computational abilities, Proc. Natl. Acad. Sci. USA **79**, 1982, 2554-2558

[3]   L.Personnaz et.al., Collective computational properties of neural networks: New learning mechanism, Phys. Rev. A **34**, 1986, 4217-4228 and I.Kanter and H.Sompolinsky, Associative recall of memory without errors, Phys. Rev. A **35**, 1986, 380-392

[4]   J.L.van Hemmen et.al., Increasing the efficiency of a neural network through unlearning, Physica A **162**, 1990, 386-392, and, Unlearning in neural networks (this conference)

[5]   K.E.Kürten, Optimal dilution of a Hopfield network, Workshop on Neurodynamics, Clausthal-Zellerfeld 1990, World Scientific Singapore (in print) and, Optimal architectures and higher order networks (this conference)

[6]   C.Aberger und R. Folk, NEURONET Hopfield - Network Simulation, presented at the WORLD TECH 1990 and 5.CIP Congress, Berlin 1991

[7]   S.Diederich and M.Opper, Learning of correlated patterns in spin-glas networks by local learning rules, Phys. Rev. Lett. **58**, 1987, 949-952

[8]   J.W.Clark, Teaching nuclear physics to neural networks (this conference)

BIOLOGICAL
APPLICATIONS
OF NEURAL
NETWORKS

Activation Dynamics of Space–Variant Continuous Networks[1]

*Hanspeter A. Mallot**
Fotios Giannakopoulos[†]

*Institut für Neuroinformatik, Ruhr–Universität–Bochum
W-4630 Bochum, FRG
[†]Mathematisches Institut der Universität zu Köln
W-5000 Köln, FRG

Abstract

Artificial neural networks are usually built on rather few elements such as activation functions, learning rules, and the network topology. When modelling the more complex properties of realistic networks such as the visual cortex, however, a number of higher level structural principles become important. In this paper, we present a theoretical framework for one of the most prominent of these higher level architectural features, i.e. neural mapping. Thereby, we entirely omit the question of map formation (e.g. by self organization). Instead we focus on phenomenological models and their interaction with spatio–temporally continuous activation functions.

1 Elements of Activation Dynamics

One important element of all neural network modells is the *activation function* describing the summation of inputs and the formation of the new output states (excitation). Table 1 summarizes a number of popular activation functions for various applications. In the first three of them, cells are labeled by an index i. While this is very useful to model arbitrary graph structures, it is not easily applied to networks where connectivity is largely determined by spatial distance. The most obvious way to introduce space is to simply identify a "neuron" with a point $\mathbf{x} = (x_1, x_2)$ in a twodimensional layer. In this case, the simple input summation is replaced by a convolution, or, more generally, by some linear integral operation as indicated in Table 1. We combine output nonlinearity and the explicit representations of space and time for n interconnected layers to obtain the system of integro–differential equations

$$\tau \frac{d}{dt} e_j(\mathbf{x}, t) = -e_j(\mathbf{x}, t) + f_j \left(\int \sum_i^n W_{ij}(\mathbf{x}, \mathbf{x}') s_i(\mathbf{x}', t - T_{ij}) d\mathbf{x}' \right). \tag{1}$$

Here, $e_i(\mathbf{x}, t)$ and $s_i(\mathbf{x}, t)$ are taken to be spatio–temporal *densities* of excitation and stimulus in layer i, respectively. In the discussion of magnification factors, it will be important to note that their dimension is $mm^{-2} sec^{-1}$.

What do the connectivity kernels W_{ij} look like? One simple case, where the influence of a stimulus at location $\mathbf{x}'$ on the excitation at location $\mathbf{x}$ depends only on

---

[1]Supported by the *Deutsche Forschungsgemeinschaft* Grant Ma 1038/3-1

Table 1: Linear activation function and specializations. Combinations of spezializations (such as nonlinear temporally continuous) are not shown.

Simple Summation	$e_j = \sum_i w_{ij} s_i$
Output Nonlinearity	$e_j = \phi\left(\sum_i w_{ij} s_i - \theta\right)$

Input Nonlinearity
      "Sigma–Pi–Unit"
 	
      "Shunting Inhibition"
	$e_j = \sum_{k=1}^{K} w_{kj} \prod_{n=1}^{N_k} s_{nk}$
	
	$e_j = \frac{1 + \sum_i w_{ij} s_i}{1 + \sum_i v_{ij} h_i} - 1$

Explicit Representation of Time	$\tau \frac{de_j}{dt}(t) = -e_j(t) + \sum_i w_{ij} s_i(t - T_{ij})$
Explicit Representation of Space	$e(\mathbf{x}) = \int W(\mathbf{x}, \mathbf{x}') s(\mathbf{x}') d\mathbf{x}'.$

e	excitation	w	transmission weight	τ	time constant
s	stimulus	W	4D weight kernel	T	time delay

the vector distance $\mathbf{x} - \mathbf{x}'$ is of course spatial convolution. Spatially continuous convolution networks have been investigated quite intensively (e.g., [1,2,3,4]). However, cortical organization includes a number of space–variances (neural mappings) that require modifications of the convolution model. In the remainder of this Section, we will summarize some types of neural mappings found in the mammalian visual cortex. Models of these maps will be given in the subsequent sections.

Let us consider a cortical area as a sheet of neurons to which the activation dynamics of Eq. 1 can be applied. Then, there are basically three types of space–variance, or mappings:

Input Map. Input into the area can be spatially distorted by some point–to–point mapping. Examples for this are topographic maps and ocular dominance stripes.

Intrinsic Map. Processing within the area can be different at different positions. This is sometimes called "functional mapping"; an example is given by the orientation columns in area 17.

Output Map. This case becomes relevant only if inter–area connections are considered. Output from different locations within one area can be of different strength or may be directed to different target areas ("segregator areas").

These space–variances can occur on different spatial scale, affecting either the entire area or local columns etc. A summary of mapping types is given in Table 2.

Table 2: Various types of space–variance or mappings in the visual cortex

Type	Global	Local	Model
Input	Topographic Map [5]	Ocular Dominance [6]	Point–to–point maps, $\mathcal{R} : \mathbf{R}^2 \mapsto \mathbf{R}^2$; Recipient cell densities $c_1(\mathbf{x}), c_2(\mathbf{x})$
Intrinsic		Orientation columns [7] 1mm	Functional Map $\mathbf{x} \mapsto$ receptive field parameters
Output	Density of retinal ganglion cells [8]	"Segregator Areas" [9]	Projection cell densities $p_i(\mathbf{x})$

2   Mapping Functions

In this Section we derive mapping functions for a particularly important case, i.e. topographic mapping.

2.1   The Constant Cellular Magnification Assumption

Retinal ganglion cell density has long been used as a starting point for the construction of mathematical coordinate transforms modelling retinotopic mapping. The basic assumption underlying this approach is that cellular magnification is constant for each retinal ganglion cell. Previous studies have used one–dimensional formulations of the problem that are restricted to rotationally symmetric distributions of ganglion cell density. Moreover, additional restrictions were made concerning the sought mapping function, most notably that of conformallity (isotropic linear magnification). Here we study mathematically the relation between areal magnification and retinotopic mapping functions in two dimensions. Analytical results will be presented for a number of biologically relevant cases, including non-isotropic distributions of areal magnification such as visual streaks. With these analytical results at hand, mapping functions can be fitted to electrophysiological data [10]. By adding the areal magnification data obtained from these fits to ganglion cell counts from the retina (e.g., [11]) a reliable independent measurement for the question of globally constant cellular magnification is obtained.

A *retinotopic mapping function* $\mathcal{R}$ is defined as a piecewise continuous and differentiable function mapping a source area $\mathbf{S} \subset \mathbf{R}^2$ onto a target area $\mathbf{T} \subset \mathbf{R}^2$.

$$\mathcal{R} : \mathbf{S} \to \mathbf{T}; \quad \mathcal{R}(x, y) = (u, v) \tag{2}$$

The same map in polar coordinates is denoted by $\mathcal{R}^*$:

$$
\begin{aligned}
\mathcal{R}^*(r, \varphi) \quad &= \quad (s, \vartheta) \\
\underbrace{(r, \varphi) \overset{\mathcal{P}}{\mapsto} (x, y)}_{\mathbf{S}} \quad &\overset{\mathcal{R}}{\mapsto} \quad \underbrace{(u, v) \overset{\mathcal{P}^{-1}}{\mapsto} (s, \vartheta)}_{\mathbf{T}},
\end{aligned}
\tag{3}
$$

where $\mathcal{P}$ denotes the polar coordinate transform.

The relation of retinal ganglion cell density, areal and cellular magnification, and retinotopic mapping is described by the Jacobian of the mapping function. For a given distribution of ganglion cells, $p(x, y)$ or $p^*(r, \varphi)$, respectively, the constraint of constant cellular magnification can than be formalized by the partial differential equation

$$|\det \mathbf{J}_\mathcal{R}(x, y)| = \left| \frac{\partial u}{\partial x} \frac{\partial v}{\partial y} - \frac{\partial u}{\partial y} \frac{\partial v}{\partial x} \right| \quad = \quad p(x, y), \tag{4}$$

or, in polar coordinates,

$$s|s_r \vartheta_\varphi - s_\varphi \vartheta_r| \quad = \quad r p(r, \varphi) \tag{5}$$

Estimates of areal magnification can be obtained from the density of retinal ganglion cells [12], visual acuity [13], etc. In order to infer possible mapping functions from these estimates, one of the above partial differential equations has to be solved. In this paper, we study solutions for different distributions of areal magnification.

Figure 1: Contour lines for a distribution of retinal ganglion cells derived from Eq. 9, illustrating area centralis, visual streak, and assymmetry of upper and lower retina.

2.2 Functions Modelling Ganglion Cell Density

We approximate distributions of retinal ganglion cell density (for both fovea and visual streaks) in two steps:

1. For a given meridian (without loss of generality, we chose the one with angle $\varphi = 0$), the decrease is described by a function f, e.g. a power law:

$$p^*(r,0) \;=\; f(r) = \left(\frac{r}{\kappa} + r_0\right)^\alpha \tag{6}$$

for some $\alpha < 0$, $\kappa > 0$.

2. For different meridians, the ganglion cell density may decrease with different "speeds" $\kappa(\varphi)$. The shape of the decrease, f, is not affected:

$$p^*(r,\varphi) \;=\; f\left(\frac{r}{\kappa(\varphi)}\right) = \left(\frac{r}{\kappa(\varphi)} + r_0\right)^\alpha \tag{7}$$

This family of functions is general enough to model most existing data of retinal ganglion cell density. Examples are given in Fig. 1. Contour lines of the function $f(r/\kappa(\varphi))$, with density p_0 are given by the curves:

$$r = f^{-1}(p_0^*)\kappa(\varphi) \tag{8}$$

By construction, contour lines for various values of p_0 are similar, i.e., they are scaled versions of each other. Fig. 1 shows contour lines derived from the function

$$\kappa(\varphi) = \left(\kappa_0 + \frac{1}{1 + \left(\frac{\varphi}{\varphi_0}\right)^2}\right) \frac{1}{1 + a\sin\varphi} \tag{9}$$

Here, κ_0 determines the area centralis, φ_0 the width of the visual streak, and a the amount of the unisotropy of upper and lower field.

2.3 Classes of Mapping Functions

Eq. 5 places only a one–dimensional constraint on the two dimensional mapping function. Therefore, solutions are generally not unique. More specifically, if $\mathcal{R}$

is a solution and $\mathcal{E}$ any equal-area mapping (i.e., $\det J_{\mathcal{E}} \equiv 1$), $\mathcal{R} \circ \mathcal{E}$ is another solution. Examples for equal-area transforms are shifts, linear transforms with unit determinant, or the "tangential compression" $\mathcal{T}$:

$$\mathcal{T}^* : (r, \varphi) \;\mapsto\; (s, \vartheta) := (\alpha r, \frac{\vartheta}{\alpha}); \quad \alpha \in \mathbf{R}\backslash\{0\}, \tag{10}$$

which has been used to refine mapping models in [14].

One way to deal with the uniqueness problem is to define an algebraic group G of maps with respect to the composition "$\circ$", within which the identity is the only equal aera map. Then, if $\mathcal{P}, \mathcal{Q} \in G$ are two solutions of Eq. 5, we have $\det J_P \equiv \det J_Q$. Since G is a group, $\mathcal{P}^{-1} \circ \mathcal{Q}$ is in G. Since $\mathcal{P}^{-1} \circ \mathcal{Q}$ is equal area, it must thus be the identity, i.e. $\mathcal{P} \equiv \mathcal{Q}$. We introduce two closely related groups of functions, generalized radial compressions and radially separable compressions.

An idea put forth by Fischer [15] is to constrain the mapping functions by the condition that radii in the retina map to radii in the map. With respect to anisotropic distributions of ganglion cell density (Fig. 1), there are two extreme ways to achieve this:

Generalized radial compressions simply shift a point along its radius. The amount of displacement depends on both, the absolut distance from the origin, r, and the direction, φ. In polar coordinates, generalized radial compressions are given by

$$\mathcal{R}^*(r, \varphi) \;=\; \left(\sigma\left(\frac{r}{\kappa(\varphi)} \right), \varphi \right). \tag{11}$$

Note that $\vartheta \equiv \varphi$ and σ is monotonically increasing with $\sigma(0) = 0$.

Radially separable compressions incorporate the anisotropy of ganglion cell density not in a compression factor $\kappa(\varphi)$ but rather into variing angular distances between the images of retinal meridians. In polar coordinates, we obtain:

$$\mathcal{R}^*(r, \varphi) \;=\; (s(r), \vartheta(\varphi)) \tag{12}$$

where $s(0) = 0$, $\vartheta(-\pi) = -\pi$, $\vartheta(\pi) = \pi$ and both σ and ϑ increase monotonically.

For isotropic distributions of ganglion cell density, both types of compression are identical. We state without proof that each type has group structure with respect to the composition operation and that the identity is the only equal area map in each group. Hence, solutions in either group are unique.

2.4 Solutions

Consider a radially separable densitity

$$p(r, \varphi) = \tilde{p}\left(\frac{r}{\kappa(\varphi)} \right) \tag{13}$$

and a mapping function $(r, \varphi) \mapsto (s, \vartheta)$.

For the generalized radial compression (eq. 11) we have $\vartheta_r \equiv 0$, $\vartheta_\varphi \equiv 1$. From eq. 5, we obtain

$$s_r(r, \varphi) s(r, \varphi) \;=\; r\tilde{p}\left(\frac{r}{\kappa(\varphi)} \right), \tag{14}$$

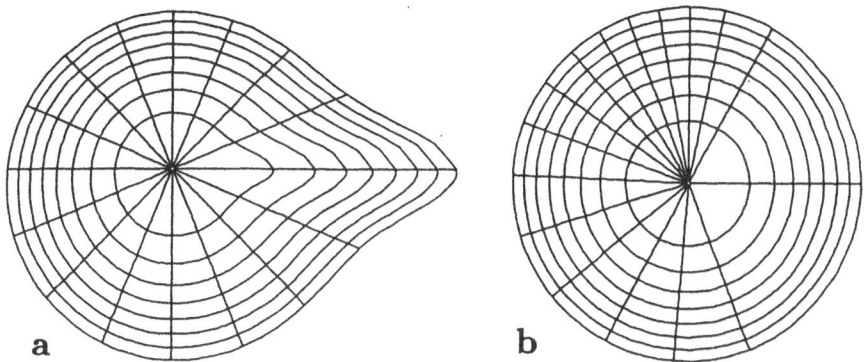

a   b

Figure 2: Solutions of eq. 5 for the anisotropic ganglion cell density from Fig. 1. a. Generalized radial compression. b. Radially separable compression.

which, using the substitution $u(r,\varphi) := \frac{1}{2}s^2(r,\varphi)$, yields the equation:

$$s^2(r,\varphi) = 2\int_0^r r'\tilde{p}\left(\frac{r'}{\kappa(\varphi)}\right)dr' = 2\kappa^2(\varphi)\int_0^{r/\kappa(\varphi)} r'\tilde{p}(r')dr'. \tag{15}$$

From here, we have the solution:

$$\begin{aligned}
s(r,\varphi) &= \kappa(\varphi)\sqrt{\sigma\left(r/\kappa(\varphi)\right)} \quad \text{where} \quad \sigma(r) := 2\int_0^r r'\tilde{p}(r')dr' \\
\vartheta(r,\varphi) &\equiv \varphi
\end{aligned} \tag{16}$$

For a radially separable function (eq. 12) we have $s_\varphi \equiv 0$ and $\vartheta_r \equiv 0$ and the basic equation (5) becomes

$$s_r(r)s(r)\vartheta_\varphi(\varphi) = r\tilde{p}\left(\frac{r}{\kappa(\varphi)}\right). \tag{17}$$

Separating the variables r and φ leads to

$$\frac{s_r(r)s(r)}{r\tilde{p}(r)} = \frac{\kappa^2(\varphi)}{\vartheta_\varphi(\varphi)} \tag{18}$$

Since eq. 18 must hold for all r, φ, we conclude that both sides are equal to a constant, c. We can now simply integrate both sides and calculate c from $\vartheta(\pm\pi) = \pm\pi$:

$$\begin{aligned}
s(r) &= \sqrt{c\sigma(r)} \quad \text{where} \quad \sigma(r) := 2\int_0^r r'\tilde{p}(r')dr' \\
\vartheta(\varphi) &= -\pi + \frac{1}{c}\int_{pi}^\varphi \kappa^2(\varphi')d\varphi' \\
c &= \int_{-\pi}^\pi \kappa^2(\varphi')d\varphi'
\end{aligned} \tag{19}$$

Clearly, for $\kappa \equiv 1$, solutions (16) and (19) coincide. Examples for the ganglion cell density of Fig. 1 are given in Fig. 2.

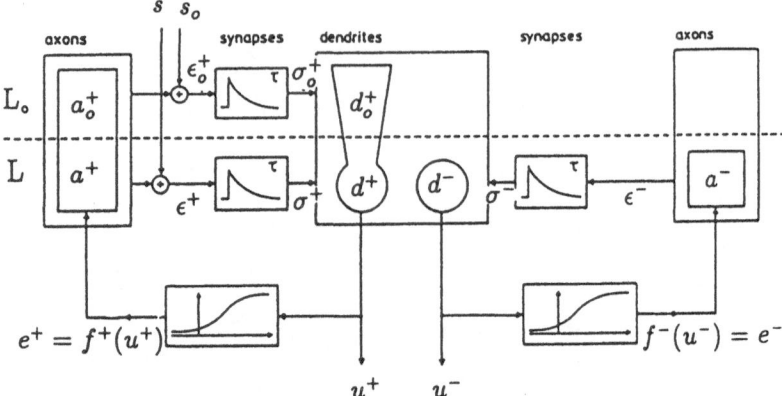

Figure 3: Scheme of the model cortex. The dendrites of the excitatory cells (d_o^+, d^+) collect the postsynaptic potentials σ_o^+, σ^+ und σ^- which sum up to the total potential u^+ at the soma. The activity e^+ generated by the total potential $(e^+ = f^+(u^+))$ is spread via the axonal arborizations (a^+, a_o^+) to layers L, L_o where it combines with the external stimuli s und s_o to form the presynaptic activities ε^+ und ε_o^+. By passing the synapse (i.e. delay and lowpass), these activities are transformed into the new inputs σ for the dendrites. An analoguous feedback loop exists for the inhibitory cell population.

3 Nonlinear Cortical Dynamics

In this Section, we present a nonlinear model of the dynamics of a cortically orga-nized network such as a cortical area. Model areas of this type can serve as basic elements of *cortical area networks* that will be discussed in the next section. First, let us introduce the model.

3.1 The Model

Consider two populations of cells (excitatory *pyramidal cells* and inhibitory *stellate cells*) distributed in a lamina L. A second lamina L_o contains axons and apical dendrites of the excitatory cells extending from layer L. We assume that both populations comprise an infinite number of units and that both L and L_o are two–dimensional continua which will be identified with the plane, R^2. Fig. 3 summarizes the structure of the model.

The spatio–temporal potentials u^+, u^- of the excitatory and the inhibitory cell type are given by the following equation (for detail see [16, p. 45 ff.]):

$$
\begin{aligned}
\tau \frac{\partial}{\partial t} u^+(x,t) \;=\; & -u^+(x,t) \\
& + d_o^+ * \; [\quad a_o^+ * f^+(u^+(x,t-T_o^{++})) + s_o(x,t-T_o^+) \,] \\
& + d^+ * \; [\quad a^+ * f^+(u^+(x,t-T^{++})) \\
& \qquad\qquad - a^- * f^-(u^-(x,t-T^{+-})) + s(x,t-T^+) \,] \qquad (20) \\[4pt]
\tau \frac{\partial}{\partial t} u^-(x,t) \;=\; & -u^-(x,t) \\
& + d^- * \; [\quad a^+ * f^+(u^+(x,t-T^{-+})) - a^- * f^-(u^-(x,t-T^{--}))
\end{aligned}
$$

$$+ s(x, t - T^-)].$$

Here, $d_o^+, d^+, d^- : \mathbf{R}^2 \longrightarrow \mathbf{R}_+$ denote dendritic and $a_o^+, a^+, a^- : \mathbf{R}^2 \longrightarrow \mathbf{R}_+$ the axonal density distributions of excitatory and inhibitory neurons in layers L_o und L, respectively. These distributions are modelled by Gaussians:

$$g(x) = \frac{A}{2\pi B^2} \exp\{-\frac{x_1^2 + x_2^2}{2B^2}\}, \quad x = (x_1, x_2) \in \mathbf{R}^2 ; \quad A, B > 0 . \quad (21)$$

$f^+, f^- : \mathbf{R} \longrightarrow \mathbf{R}$ are monotonically increasing functions describing the nonlinear transformation of the total potentials u^+, u^- of the excitatory and inhibitory neurons into the according activities. For the sake of simplicity, we choose:

$$f^+(u^+) = \frac{M_f}{1 + \exp\{-\frac{4 M_{f'}}{M_f}(u^+ - \theta)\}} \quad (22)$$

and

$$f^-(u^-) = u^- \quad (23)$$

where $M_{f'}, M_f > 0$ and $\theta \in \mathbf{R}$.

Carrying on with Eq. 20, τ is a positive time constant describing the synaptic lowpasses. $T_o^{++}, T^{++}, T^{+-}, T^{-+}, T^{--}, T_o^+, T^+, T^- \geq 0$ are delays modeling both synaptic delay and propagation times along dendrites and axons. Spatial convolution is denoted by the symbol $*$. Finally, s_o, s are the external stimuli impinging on layers L_o and L, respecively.

Except for the amplitudes A of the spatial coupling functions (Eq. 21) and the maximal slope $M_{f'}$ of the nonlinear compression function, all parameters of the model are infered from neurophysiological and neuroanatomical data (cf. [17]). A classification of the free parameters $(A, M_{f'})$ can be derived for the slightly simplified network of Eq. 24, whose properties are discussed in the next subsection.

3.2 Classification of Parameters

Consider the case $T_o^{++} = T^{++} = T^{+-} = T^{-+} = T^{--}, T_o^+, T^+, T^- = 0$ and s_o, s constant over space. In this situation, the network of Eq. 20 has space–independent solutions (cf. [16]). These solutions satisfy the equation:

$$\begin{aligned} \tau \, \dot{u}^+(t) &= -u^+(t) + q^{++} \, f^+(u^+(t)) - q^{+-} \, u^-(t) + s^+(t) \quad (24) \\ \tau \, \dot{u}^-(t) &= q^{-+} \, f^+(u^+(t)) - (1 + q^{--}) \, u^-(t) + s^-(t) . \end{aligned}$$

Here, we used the notations

$$q^{++} := q_o^{++} + q_m^{++} \quad \text{where}$$

$$q_o^{++} := \iint_{\mathbf{R}^2} d_o^+(x_1, x_2) \, dx_1 dx_2 \iint_{\mathbf{R}^2} a_o^+(x_1, x_2) \, dx_1 dx_2 ,$$

$$q_m^{++} := \iint_{\mathbf{R}^2} d^+(x_1, x_2) \, dx_1 dx_2 \iint_{\mathbf{R}^2} a^+(x_1, x_2) \, dx_1 dx_2$$

$$q^{+-} := \iint_{\mathbf{R}^2} d^+(x_1, x_2) \, dx_1 dx_2 \iint_{\mathbf{R}^2} a^-(x_1, x_2) \, dx_1 dx_2 ,$$

$$q^{-+} := \iint_{\mathbf{R}^2} d^-(x_1, x_2) \, dx_1 dx_2 \iint_{\mathbf{R}^2} a^+(x_1, x_2) \, dx_1 dx_2 ,$$

$$q^{--} := \iint_{\mathbf{R}^2} d^-(x_1, x_2) \, dx_1 dx_2 \iint_{\mathbf{R}^2} a^-(x_1, x_2) \, dx_1 dx_2 ,$$

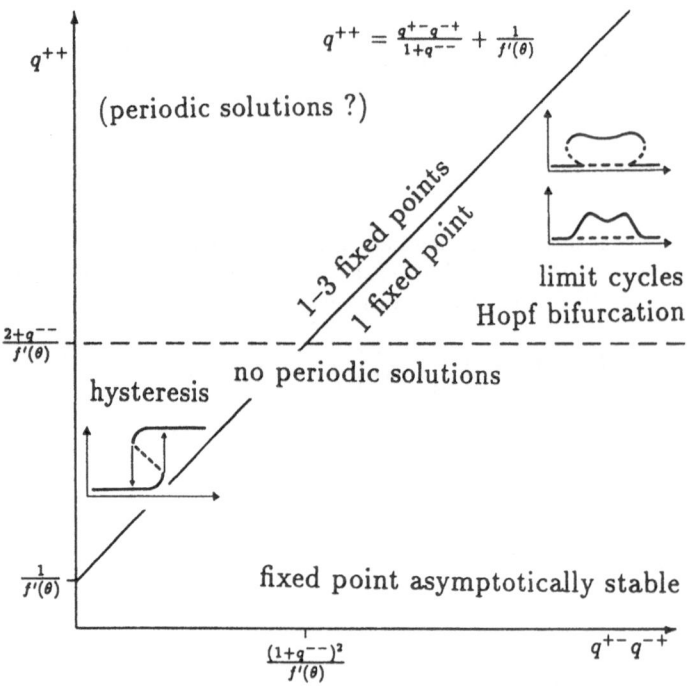

Figure 4: Classification of system (24) in terms of positive q^{++} and negative feedback $q^{+-}q^{-+}$.

$$s^+ \; := \; q_o^+ s_o + q^+ s \; , \quad s^- := q^- s \quad \text{where}$$
$$q_o^+ := \iint_{\mathbf{R}^2} d_o^+(x_1, x_2) \, dx_1 dx_2 \; ,$$
$$q^+ := \iint_{\mathbf{R}^2} d^+(x_1, x_2) \, dx_1 dx_2 \; ,$$
$$q^- := \iint_{\mathbf{R}^2} d^-(x_1, x_2) \, dx_1 dx_2 \; .$$

It has been shown analytically that the system described by Eq. 24 exhibits characteristic nonlinear behaviour such as hysteresis, Hopf bifurcation, and limit cycles [16]. This behaviour is controled by just two parameters, i.e., positive q^{++} and negative feedback $q^{+-}q^{-+}$. The most important properties are summarized in Fig. 4.

Many of these properties have been confirmed numerically for space dependent solutions of Eq. 20 (cf. [16]). An example of a spatio–temporally oscillating response is shown in Fig. 5 by a series of snapshots taken over about one cycle of the oscillation. Similar models have been used successfully to simulate neural activity in visual cortical areas (cf. [17]).

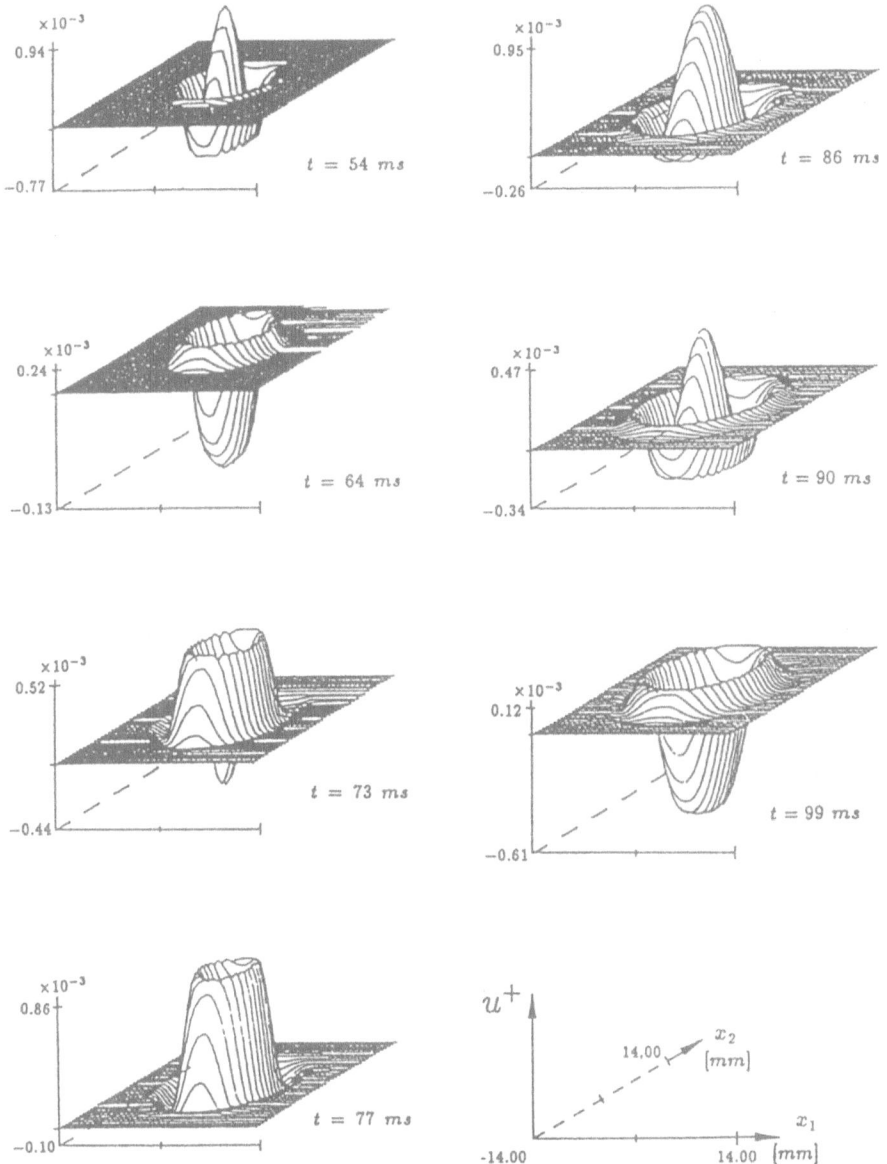

Figure 5: Numerical simulation of the spatio–temporal behaviour of the non–linear system (20). Each plot shows the spatial distribution of the excitatory potential u^+ after the specified time. Units of space and time are derived from the anatomical and physiological parameters of the model (synapse delays, fiber length etc.) At time $t = 0$, the system had been "stimulated" by a spatio–temporal Dirac δ.

352

Node (Area A_i):

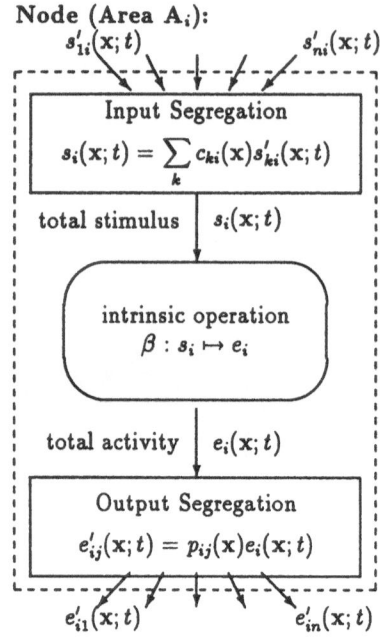

Edge $i \longrightarrow j$

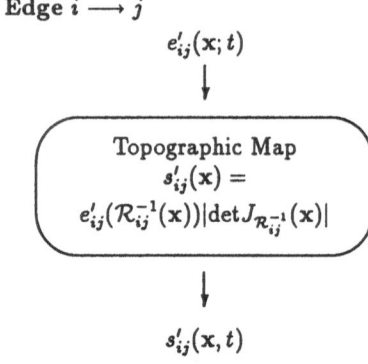

$$s'_{ij}(\mathbf{x}, t)$$

Figure 6: Node and edge of the cortical area network, CAN. The edge links two areas (A_i, A_j) via a topographic map. In a node inputs from various other nodes are combined to a total stimulus entering the intrinsic operation, Eq. 1. The result is handed on to other areas, sometimes again in a space-variant way.

4 Cortical Area Networks (CAN)

The visual cortex of the primate contains some 15 visual areas which are interconnected via mappings of various type (e.g. [18]). In this section, we propose a framework for modelling the activation dynamics of networks comprised of visual areas as nodes and neural mappings as edges (cf. Table 2 and Fig. 6).

4.1 Nodes

Within a cortical area A_i, a local intrinsic operation β_i is performed, an example of which has been studied in the previous section. β_i may itself be space-variant, as would be necessary to model orientation columns in area 17. The *total stimulus* entering this operation, s_i is composed out of inputs from various other areas, $s'_{1i}, ..., s'_{ni}$. (The order of double indices reflects the flow of excitation, i.e., s'_{ki} corresponds to the path $A_k \rightarrow A_i$.) *Input segregations* as illustrated in Table 2 can be accounted for by space-variant densities of recipient cells c_{ki} with $\sum_{k=1}^n c_{ki} \equiv 1$. E.g., in the case of ocular dominance stripes in area 17, we would have something like (cf. [19]).

$$c_{.,17}(x, y) = \frac{1}{2}(1 \pm \sin \lambda x). \tag{25}$$

In output connections of visual areas, another segregation pattern can be found, in which cells from one spot project to an area a, while cells from a neighbouring spot project to another area b. We therefore include a projection cell density p_{ik} describing the spatial pattern of output segregation. An example of a globally variing projection cell density is given by the retinal ganglion cell density studied in Sect. 2.

4.2 Edges

The edges of the cortical area network are basically topographic mappings formulated in terms of the operator applied to the output distributions e'_{ij}. Since s, s', e and e' are considered spatio–temporal densities of excitation, the equations have to include the area element $|\det J_{\mathcal{R}_{ij}^{-1}}|$.

With these definitions, we can now generalize the constraint of constant cellular magnification formulated for the retino–cortical mapping in eq. 5. For the mapping $\mathcal{R}_{ij}$, we obtain

$$|\det J_{\mathcal{R}_{ij}}(x, y)| = M_{c,ij} \frac{p_{ij}(x, y)}{c_{ij}(\mathcal{R}_{ij}(x, y))}, \tag{26}$$

where the constant $M_{c,ij}$ denotes the cellular magnification in the path $i \to j$. A case where p is constant and c models ocular dominance stripes as in eq. 25 has been studied in [19].

4.3 Network Equations

Putting things together, the network equation of a CAN composed of n nodes $A_1, ..., A_n$ can be obtained in two steps:

1. *Input/Output–Operation* $\alpha_j : \{e_1, ...e_n\} \mapsto s_j$
   This describes, how the *total activites* from all areas are combined to a *total stimulus* in the jth area. In a sense, s_j corresponds to the term net_j used in some neural network models.

$$s_j(\mathbf{x}; t) = \sum_{i=1}^{n} e_i(\mathcal{R}_{ij}^{-1}(\mathbf{x}); t) \left[c_{ij}(\mathbf{x}) p_{ij}(\mathcal{R}_{ij}^{-1}(\mathbf{x})) |\det J_{\mathcal{R}_{ij}^{-1}}(\mathbf{x})| \right] \tag{27}$$

The term in brackets can be collapsed into one space–variant amplification factor. Assuming constant cellular magnification as in eq. 26, eq. 27 reduces to

$$s_j(\mathbf{x}; t) = \sum_{i=1}^{n} e_i(\mathcal{R}_{ij}^{-1}(\mathbf{x}); t) \left[\frac{c_{ij}^2(\mathbf{x})}{M_{c,ij}} \right] \tag{28}$$

2. *Intrinsic Operation* $\beta_j : s_j \mapsto e_j$
   This is simply the intrinsic operation of each area, as described in Sect. 3.

As a simple example, consider the case of *reciprocal feedback* between two areas which can be derived from eq. 27 by setting $n = 2$, $c_{12} \equiv c_{21} \equiv 1$, $c_{11} \equiv c_{22} \equiv 0$, and $\mathcal{R}_{12} = \mathcal{R}_{21}^{-1}$. As was pointed out by van Essen [20], most cortical connections are reciprocal in the sense that if area i projects to area j, the reverse projection exists too. The stronger relation defined here can, e.g., be found for the areas 17 and 18.

In this case, eq. 27 can be simplified by defining a joint mapping Q:

$$Q : A_1 \cup A_2 \mapsto A_1 \cup A_2 \quad ; \quad Q(\mathbf{x}) := \begin{cases} \mathcal{R}_{12}(\mathbf{x}) \text{ for } \mathbf{x} \in A_1 \\ \mathcal{R}_{21}(\mathbf{x}) \text{ for } \mathbf{x} \in A_2 \end{cases} \tag{29}$$

From $\mathcal{R}_{12} = \mathcal{R}_{21}^{-1}$, we have $Q = Q^{-1}$. Furthermore, we assume that for the joint distributions of excitations $e : A_1 \cup A_2 \mapsto \mathbf{R}$, we have a common intrinsic operation $\beta : s \mapsto e$. If the intrinsic operations for A_1 and A_2 are identical, the choice of β is obvious.

354

We finally obtain the network equation for the case of reciprocal feedback to be

$$e(x; t) = \beta(e(e(\mathcal{Q}(x); t))).$$ (30)

With $\mathcal{Q}$ taken to be the identity, fixpoints of this type have been studied by Ermentrout & Cowan [3]. In the reciprocal feedback case with space–variance, more complicated interactions between mapping and intrinsic dynamics can be anticipated.

5 Conclusion

In this paper, we have summarized a number of results and approaches towards a continuous theory of cortical networks. We argue that the continuous approach is appropriate both for anatomical (huge numbers of cells, need for explicit representation of space) and for physiological reasons: The spatio–temporal flow of excitation can and has been studied on a level slightly above that of single cells, i.e. current source density, field potentials, optical recording, etc. In this sense, we hope that the level of description presented here will indeed prove useful for the understanding of pysiological results.

From the point of view of information processing, our approach relates to the idea of *geometrical* information processing which may be traced back to two rather old ideas. These ideas and their originators are:

- *Labeled Line Coding:* The nervous activity itself has no semantic content. Rather, the excited cell determines, what the activation "means" to the brain (Johannes Müller, 1826) [21].

- *Localization of Brain Function:* What information a given neuron codes for, is determined by its location in a neural map. A more global version of this idea goes back to Broca (1865) [22].

Despite the fact that these principles of brain physiology are known for a rather long period of time, a more complete account of geometric information processing is still to be developed.

Acknowledgement Thanks to Klaus Bohrer for providing the simulations presented in Fig 5.

References

[1] W. von Seelen. Informationsverarbeitung in homogenen Netzen von Neuronenmodellen I. *Kybernetik (= Biol. Cybern.)*, 5:133 – 148, 1968.
[2] H. R. Wilson and J. D. Cowan. A mathematical theory of functional dynamics of cortical and thalamic nervous tissue. *Kybernetik (= Biol. Cybern.)*, 13:55 – 80, 1973.
[3] G. B. Ermentrout and J. D. Cowan. A mathematical theory of visual hallucination patterns. *Biological Cybernetics*, 34:137 – 150, 1979.
[4] U. an der Heiden. *Analysis of Neural Networks*. Lecture Notes in Biomathematics 35. Springer-Verlag, Berlin, 1980.

[5] R. J. Tusa, L. A. Palmer, and A. C. Rosenquist. The retinotopic organization of area 17 (striate cortex) in the cat. *The Journal of Comparative Neurology*, 177:213 – 236, 1978.

[6] S. LeVay and D. H. Hubel amd T. N. Wiesel. The pattern of ocular dominance columns in macaque visual cortex revealed by a reduced silver stain. *Journal of Comparative Neurology*, 159:559 – 576, 1975.

[7] J. A. Matsubara, M. S. Cynader, and N. V. Swindale. Anatomical perperties and physiological correlates of the intrinsic connections in cat area 18. *The Journal of Neuroscience*, 7:1428 – 1446, 1987.

[8] H. Wässle, W. R. Levick, and B. G. Cleland. The distribution of alpha type ganglion cells in the cat retina. *The Journal of Comparative Neurology*, 159:419 – 438, 1975.

[9] S. Shipp and S. Zeki. The organization of connections between areas V5 and V2 in Macaque monkey visual cortex. *The European Journal of Neuroscience*, 1:333 – 353, 1989.

[10] H. A. Mallot and K.-P. Hoffmann. Retinotopic mapping functions and density of retinal ganglion cells. In N. Elsner and G. Roth, editors, *Brain – Perception – Cognition (Proc. 18th Göttingen Neurobiol. Conf.)*, page 522, Stuttgart, 1990. G. Thieme Verlag.

[11] H. Wässle, U. Grünert, J. Röhrenbeck, and B. B. Boycott. Cortical magnification factor and the ganglion cell density of the primate retina. *Nature*, 341:643 – 646, 1989.

[12] H. Wässle, U. Grünert, J. Röhrenbeck, and B. B. Boycott. Retinal ganglion cell density and cortical magnification factor in the primate. *Vision Research*, 30:1897 – 1911, 1990.

[13] J. Rovamo and V. Virsu. An estimation and application of the human cortical magnification factor. *Experimental Brain Research*, 37:495 – 510, 1979.

[14] H. A. Mallot. An overall description of retinotopic mapping in the cat's visual cortex areas 17, 18, and 19. *Biol. Cybern.*, 52:45 – 51, 1985.

[15] B. Fischer. Overlap of receptive field centers and representation of the visual field in the cat's optic tract. *Vision Research*, 13:2113 – 2120, 1973.

[16] F. Giannakopoulos. *Nichtlineare Systeme zur Beschreibung geschichteter neuronaler Strukturen.* PhD thesis, Fb. Mathematik, Johannes Gutenberg–Universität, Mainz, 1989.

[17] G. Krone, H. A. Mallot, G. Palm, and A. Schüz. The spatio-temporal receptive field: A dynamical model derived from cortical architectonics. *Proc. Roy. Soc. London B*, 226:421 – 444, 1986.

[18] J. H. R. Maunsell and W. T. Newsome. Visual processing in monkey extrastriate cortex. *Annual Review of Neuroscience*, 10:363 – 401, 1987.

[19] H. A. Mallot, W. von Seelen, and F. Giannakopoulos. Neural mapping and space–variant image processing. *Neural Networks*, 3:245 – 263, 1990.

[20] D. C. van Essen. Functional organization of primate visual cortex. In Alan Peters and Edward G. Jones, editors, *Cerebral Cortex, Volume 3: Visual Cortex*, pages 259 – 329. Plenum Press, New York and London, 1985.

[21] J. Müller. *Beiträge zur vergleichenden Physiologie des Gesichtssinnes.* Leipzig, 1826.

[22] P. Broca. Sur la siège de la faculté du langage articulé. *Bull. Soc. d'anthropol. de Paris*, 6:377 – 393, 1865.

Hierarchical Neural Representations by Synchronized Activity: a Concept for Visual Pattern Recognition

G. Hartmann

Fachbereich 14 Elektrotechnik
Universität - Gesamthochschule - Paderborn
Pohlweg 47-49, D 4790 Paderborn
Germany

Abstract

The architecture of a neural pattern recognition system is described. Parametric mappings allow learning and recognition of objects at different distances. Conditions for proper operation of the system are analyzed and it proves that images are to be hierarchically represented. A representation based on hierarchical verification of continuity provides the tolerance required for matching and allows foveation prior to recognition. This hierarchical representation is efficiently realized on the base of synchronized neural assemblies. Synchronization mechanisms are modelled by mutual short range interconnections. The hierarchical representation of our system is surprisingly similar to the cortical representation of the biological visual system. Model neurons at different levels of the hierarchy behave like cortical neurons at different levels of complexity.

1 Introduction

"First sight" recognition of objects with low and medium complexity is an outstanding feature of the biological visual system. Sequential analysis only takes place, if details of a highly complex object, or objects in a highly complex scene are to be analyzed. The short time for recognition of written syllables, of traffic signs, or of articles for daily use suggests highly parallel strategies on the base of pattern matching.

Another outstanding feature of the biological visual system is its excellent performance in a 3D environment. Invariance against location, orientation, distance and perspective of an object, however, is hardly achieved by some kind of "omnipotent" associative network, and so 3D performance seems to be contradictory to pattern matching.

This contribution is to show first results with our recognition system, providing 3D performance on a pattern matching basis. But before we discuss this system, we should realize the meaning of invariance. It is obviously not the purpose of invariance, to make differently sized objects like cars and matchbox cars indistinguishable. On the contrary, we need information about relative position, orientation, and size of visual structures, as soon as sequential analysis is to be performed. What we really need is not invariance, but "matchability" between a learnt representation of an object and representations of the object at different positions relative to the observer.

Visual systems with moving eyes can easily foveate objects at different positions in the visual field. This mechanism provides "shift invariance", while information about the position of the object is still available from the occulomotor system. However, there seems not really to be "orientation invariance" as long as objects like "p" and "d" or "u" and "n" are correctly recognized as different letters. If necessary, however, we are able to perform mental rotation, and information about the relative rotation is again available. Similarly, we do not confuse cars with matchbox cars, and there seems not to be "size invariance". On the other hand, we are able to perform mental magnification, and again information about the scale factor is available.

The size of the retinal image depends as well on the size of the object as on its distance. While "size invariance" is at least undesirable in 3D recognition, "distance invariance" is obviously helpful. More exactly, if we are able to influence the scale factor of a mental magnification by knowledge about distance, we are able to match an object at different distance. Similarly, we should also be able to influence perspective distortions by knowledge about the line of sight.

Starting from these considerations, we designed a pattern recognition system (fig. 1). Distance invariance and voluntary rotation is provided by "parametric mappings". Foveation is momentarily achieved by shift of the pixel matrix and later by a robot mounted moving camera. Correction of perspective distortions is also investigated but not yet included in the system.

Reliable operation of the system, however, depends on the following conditions: the (retinal) image must be in a well defined centrical position prior to recognition, the distance of the object must be estimated, the background must be seperated from the image of the object, and minor deviations of position, size and orientation must be tolerated. We could show, that hierarchical neural representations fulfill these conditions, and we also could show, that synchronization mechanisms are necessary for hierarchical representations. So the following sections give a discussion of the recognition system and of the parametric mappings, an introduction to hierarchical representations of images, and a detailed description of the underlying synchronization mechanisms. More exactly, we can show that synchronization is not only a highly interesting mechanism, but also an indispensible powerful tool.

2 The recognition system and its parametric mappings

In our experimental recognition system (fig. 1), the orthogonally scanned image is mapped onto a special retina, which is to be discussed below. This retinal area is smaller than the image and so it can be shifted, providing foveation without camera movement. Grey scale as well as colour information is represented by this retinal image, but for shortness discussion of colour processing is omitted. The grey scale information is represented by on-center and off-center neurons at the following layer, and from this some kind of "cortical representation" is formed. At this stage, the image is represented by neurons with oriented receptive fields at different levels of complexity and in different spatial frequency channels [1],[2]. In our system, this representation is a hierarchical structure, strongly depending on synchronization mechanisms. A detailed discussion of this structure is given below, and biological objections against hierarchical cortical structures are considered.

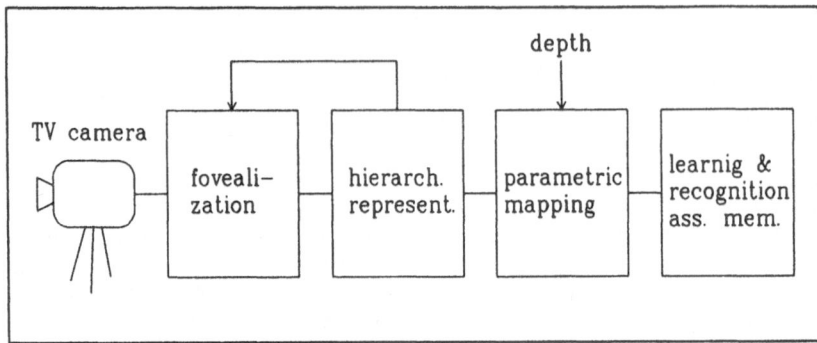

Fig. 1: Block diagramm of the recognition system

In our system (fig. 1), parametric mappings project this hierarchical representation to the input layer of an associative network. These parametric mappings compensate distance and orientation of an object by magnification and rotation of the retinotopic hierarchical representation. Now we can learn the activation pattern, caused by an object at the input layer of the associative network, and we can recognize the object at a different position, if there is information about distance and orientation. The basic idea of a switchable conjunctive mapping controlled by depth information was already described by Feldmann [3], but in detail his approach is very different from our. We confine ourselves to a very simple system, and there are only two open questions. The first question which will be answered in the next section is how to realize parametric mappings. Furthermore, we have to explain the advantage of a hierarchical representation, and the answer to this question will take the rest of this contribution.

The essential mechanism of a parametric mapping does not depend on the input representation and for simplicity we omit the hierarchical representation for a moment. Let the triangular traffic sign in fig. 2 be represented by a layer of neurons, and let the neurons in the dark regions be activated, those in the bright regions be subliminal. The bottom of the triangle is then represented by neuron 1 in the input representation A_1. A topical mapping of A_1 to a layer B of neurons is achieved by an interconnection, activating a triangular subset of neurons in B. Especially, there is to be an interconnection from neuron 1 in A_1 to neuron X in B, both representing the bottom of the triangle. Now we call the complete set of interconnections between A_1 and B a mapping $\mathfrak{M}_1:A_1\rightarrow B$. Of course, a different set of interconnections provides a different mapping, e. g. a mapping $\mathfrak{M}_2:A_2\rightarrow B$, between the source representation A_2 and the target representation B. Again, there is to be a special connection to neuron X in B, representing the bottom of the triangle. But now neuron X is to be acitvated by neuron 2 of the source representation and not by neuron 1. If we are able to switch these connections on and off, we can select $1\rightarrow X$ or $2\rightarrow X$. And if we do this for all the neurons of the target representation, we can switch between $\mathfrak{M}_1:A_1\rightarrow B$ and $\mathfrak{M}_2:A_2\rightarrow B$.

In the example of fig. 2 switching between two input lines of each target neuron, selects one of two mappings with different magnification. But the mechanism is identical for selection between two mappings with different degree of rotation or with different perspective distortion. And obviously, the number of input lines to a target neuron like X is not at all limited to two. With some thousands of input lines we are able to select between some thousands of mappings with slightly different magnification, rotation or distortion. In a neural system this selection is to be controlled by a selecting neural representation S, and the selected mapping depends on the activity pattern of S. Now we are ready to describe a parametric mapping $\mathfrak{M}(S):A{\to}B$ as a mapping selected from a set of mappings by a selecting representation S.

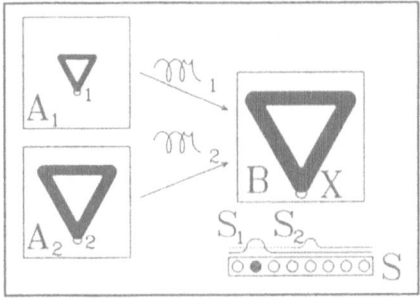 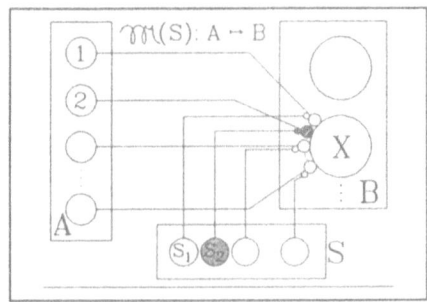

Fig. 2: Selection of scale factor by controlled mapping

Fig. 3: Controlled mappings are easily realized by presynaptic excitatory influence

Biological neurons are excellently equipped for this function. A target neuron may receive some thousands of interconnetions from a source layer and the synapses may be presynaptically influenced. In fig. 3 neuron X in the target representation B receives input from different neurons of source representation A, but only a synapse between neuron 2 and X is presynaptically activated. Presynaptic excitation is due to activity of neuron S_2 of the selecting representation S. As soon as a different neuron, say S_1, is active, source neuron 1 is connected to target neuron X and all the other interconnections are disabled. As all the other target neurons are also influenced by S, this structure performs a parametric mapping $\mathfrak{M}(S):A{\to}B$. For instance this structure is able to provide distance invariance. We only are to represent distance by the activity pattern of S, with S_1 for high distance, S_2 for lower distance and the right most neuron for very short distances.

At the moment this system looks rather like a digital circuitry than like a neural network. In our simulations, however, not only one neuron but an activity peak in S represents distance or orientation. So activity of a source neuron is fed to some neighbouring target neurons and not only to one. This is necessary, because mapping of a discrete grid to a discrete grid with arbitrary scale factor requires interpolation. In a grey scale image this mechanism would cause blurring, but if we go back to our cortical representation, this multiple representation provides overlap between learnt and presented patterns.

Though the principle of this system is quite simple, proper function depends on numerous conditions. A high quality mapping requires an object to be represented by a comparable number of neurons at the source layer and at the target layer. The extended retinal image of a nearby object is to be represented by as much neurons as the small sized retinal image of a more distant object. Consequently, the neural density of our retina is high in the central area and decreases to the periphery. A detailed discussion of this retina which is more complex than the well known log z model, is out of the scope of this contribution.

The function of our system not only depends on the structure of the retina, and additonal conditions for proper function are listed in table 1.

360

Table 1:

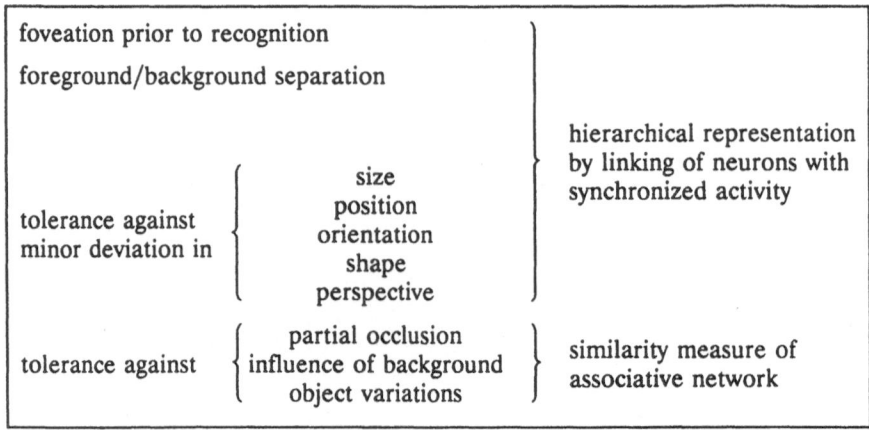

It is very surprising that most of these conditions are fulfilled by hierarchical representations. A detailed description of the hierarchical representation in our system is given in the following section, and I only anticipate three items.

- Our hierarchy is a linking hierarchy. Neurons, representing elements of continuous structures are labelled by synchronization and synchronous neurons are linked. This verification of continuity allows seperation of objects from background (table 1).

- Linked features are explicitly represented by neurons at higher linking levels. In this way continuous objects are represented by "trees". Extended objects are represented by trees growing to high linking levels, while small objects are represented by small trees. Trees of dominant objects have roots at the highest linking levels. Activity of "root" neurons guides foveation in our system prior to recognition (table 1).

- Neurons at increasing linking levels show features of cortical neurons at increasing levels of complexity. One of these features is increasing local tolerance, which is essential in our system. It is almost impossible, to have representations of a presented object and of the learnt object without any deviation in size, position, orientation, shape, and perspective (table 1). This is due to incorrect estimation of distance (size) and orientation, due to incorrect foveation (position) and due to minor variations in shape and perspective of the object. As a consequence of all these effects, there are minor local deviations of oriented line elements and edges. Tolerance against these deviations is achieved in our system by learning and recognition of neural representations at higher levels of "complexity".

The function of our system also depends on a second group of conditions (table 1). We need robustness against partial occlusion of objects, against influences of not correctly seperated parts of the background, or against minor individual differences between objects of one class. These deviations are not predictable and can not be eliminated by an adequate representation. As long as these deviations are small, they are tolerated by the associative network. In our system we use our "Closed Loop Antagonistic Network" [4] with an adjustable similarity measure (vigilance control).

The theory of associative memories, however, is a well known field, and so I want to concentrate on the above mentioned hierarchical representations for shortness.

3 Hierarchical neural representations

When we started our investigations with hierarchical neural representations we tried to realize the linking mechanism by an appropriate interconnection scheme. The result of this approach was a combinatorical explosion. So it was very surprising to recognize, that the linking mechanism is easily realized on the base of synchronization mechanisms. We learnt, that synchronization is not only a highly interesting phenomenon. In our opinion it is an absolutely necessary tool. This conclusion requires an introduction to our hierarchical representation which is subsequently given.

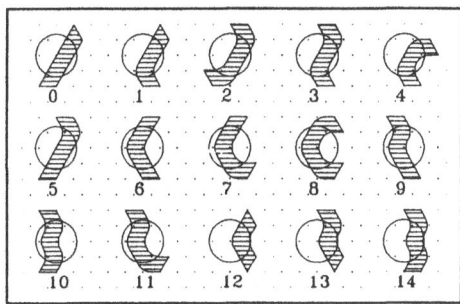

Fig. 4: Oriented receptive fields of model neurons in one of six orientations, reflections omitted.

In our simulations lines and edges are represented by detector neurons with oriented receptive fields. We also encode regions and colour, but we concentrate our discussion on the hierarchical representaion of contours for shortness. In our system the visual field is subdivided to a hexagonal arrangement of subfields. In the following discussion we refer to a linear hexagonal grid, but please note that our non-linear model retina is also hexagonally arranged. Each of these hexagonally arranged subfields is represented by a set of detector neurons with differently shaped and oriented receptive fields. In our terminology we describe these neurons by the type t of contour, to which they are sensitive (edge, bright/dark line). Additionally, we describe them by the shape m and by the orientation φ of the receptive field. A complete set of differently shaped (m) receptive fields is shown by fig. 4 for one orientation φ.

This set of receptive fields is complete and so each contour within a subfield is represented by the activity pattern of the corresponding set of neurons (fig. 5a). Of course, line structures of different width and differently blurred edges need differently sized receptive fields for complete encoding. So we use additional sets of detector neurons $<t,m,\varphi|$ with receptive fields of double (fig. 5b), quadruple and 2^k-fold size. To distinguish these differently sized neurons $<t,m,\varphi|$, we add the size k and write $<t,m,\varphi|k>$. These neurons are similar to the simple cortical neurons and provide a representation of contour structures in different spatial frequency channels k. This representation encodes all the information about contours including an implicit information about continuity.

Continuity becomes explicit by our linking mechanism and a hierarchical representation is formed. In a first step continuity is verified in a "rosette" of seven subfields (fig. 5c). Active neurons in adjacent subfields of a rosette encode a continuous piece of contour if the receptive fields form a continuous sequence.

362

However, there are some tenthousand fitting combinations between some hundred receptive fields per subfield. So it is not very encouraging to represent each of these possible sequences by an appropriate neuron, as linking between sequences of neighbouring rosettes would lead to a combinatorical explosion.

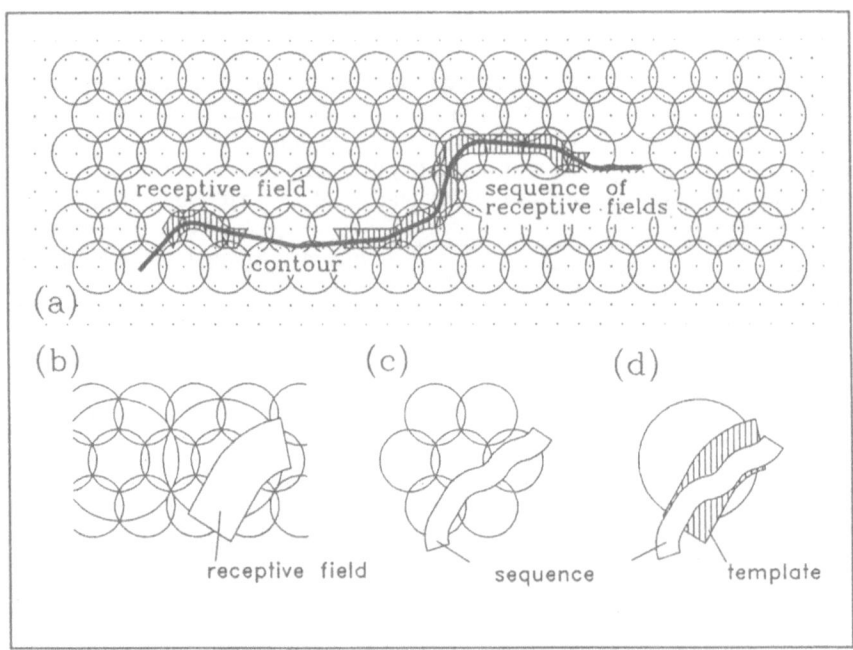

Fig. 5: Receptive fields of neurons form smooth sequences when continuous contours are encoded (a). Continuity is verified in rosettes of seven sub-fields (c). Sequences are enveloped (d) by double sized templates of linking neurons. Linking neurons with double sized templates (d) must not be confused with detector neurons of lower spatial frequency channels with double sized receptive fields (b).

This problem is avoided in our system by a template operation. A set of double sized templates is defined (fig. 5d) and a well defined set of sequences with similar run is enveloped by each template. A linking neuron is assigned to each of these templates now, and not longer to an individual sequence. As soon as detector neurons in a rosette encode a continuous piece of contour, their receptive fields form a sequence, and the linking neuron of the enveloping template is activated.

The shapes of these templates are congruent with the shapes of double sized detector neurons and we can also describe linking neurons by $<t,m,\varphi|$. But we are to distinguish detector neurons with double sized receptive fields (fig. 5b) and neurons at the first linking level $n=1$ which also have double sized fields (fig. 5d). So we write not only the spatial frequency channel k, but also the linking level n to describe a neuron $<t,m,\varphi|k,n>$. In this terminology, the detector neuron ($n=0$) in fig. 5b is called $<t,m,\varphi|k,0>$, while the neuron at the first linking level $n=1$ in fig. 5d is called $<t,m,\varphi|k-1,1>$, as it responds to a continuous piece of contour, encoded by detector neurons with smaller sized fields (k-1).

At the first linking level continuity is again verified within rosettes of seven double sized subfields. Again active neurons $<t,m,\varphi|k,1>$ in adjacent subfields encode a continuous contour if the double sized templates form a continuous sequence. These sequences are again represented by neurons $<t,m,\varphi|k,2>$ at the second linking level $n=2$ with quadruple sized templates. In a similar way, continuity is verified in rosettes of subfields at linking level (n-1) and sequences are represented by activity of neurons $<t,m,\varphi|k,n>$ at the n-th linking level.

Now we are ready to explain that this representation of contour structures by neurons $<t,m,\varphi|k,n>$ fulfills the above mentioned conditions of our recognition system. All the neurons $<t,m,\varphi|k,0>$, $<t,m,\varphi|k,1>$ ... $<t,m,\varphi|k,n>$ describe contour structures in spatial frequency channel k. At the detector level $n=0$, the local position of the contour is most precisely described by ("simple") detector neurons. With increasing n, the local precision decreases due to recursive envelopment by templates. Neurons at increasing linking levels are very similar to cortical neurons at increasing levels of complexity. So representations at higher linking levels by neurons of higher "complexity" provide the required local tolerance, which was one of our conditions for pattern matching.

While local precision decreases at higher linking levels, information about continuity increases. From linking level to linking level continuity is verified within increasing local areas and continuity of increasing structures is explicitly represented. Explicit representation of continuity, however, provides seperation of objects from background and fulfilles another basic requirement for pattern matching.

Finally, the set of active neurons representing a piece of continuous contour at the detector level $n=0$ and the "complex" neuron at level $n=1$ may be seen as a tree. All pieces of an extended contour are represented by trees with leaves $<t,m,\varphi|k,0>$ and roots $<t,m,\varphi|k,1>$. But neurons at the level $n=1$ are linked again and there are trees with leaves $<t,m,\varphi|k,1>$ and roots $<t,m,\varphi|k,2>$. These trees grow to a level n at which all pieces of a contour are linked. So extended contours are represented by neurons $<t,m,\varphi|k,n>$ at high linking levels n, while smaller contours are only represented at low linking levels. In our system foveation is controlled by "complex" neurons. In this way dominant objects are easily selected and foveated. Foveation prior to recognition, however, was also shown to be a condition for pattern matching.

After this short description of the advantages of a hierarchical representation, we are to ask for the interconnection scheme of this network. At first sight it seems very simple and straight forward, to realize the underlying mechanism in two steps. Linking of sequences seems possible by "sequence neurons" which are to be active if and only if neurons in adjacent subfields of a rosette encode a continuous piece of contour (fig. 6). In a second step the template mechanism could be realized by neurons $<t,m,\varphi|k,n+1>$ at the next linking level, if each of these neurons could be activated by all those "sequence neurons", representing fitting sequences (fig. 6).

There are, however, some objections against this model. Neurons would degenerate into logical elements. In fig. 6, the sequence neurons would behave like "and" gates, while the linking neurons $<t,m,\varphi|k,n+1>$ would behave like "or" gates. There would be a very high number of these "sequence neurons" with very elongated receptive fields, but neurons of this type are not found in the biological system. The strongest objection, however, arises from combinatorical considerations. A set of some hundred neurons $<t,m,\varphi|k,n+1>$ at linking level (n+1), representing seven sets of some hundred neurons $<t,m,\varphi|k,n>$ at level n would be driven by a set of some tenthousands of "useless" interneurons (fig. 6).

Of course, we can simulate a network without taking notice of these objections. We also have non-neural implementations [5] of similar hierarchical representations, called Hierarchical Structure Code (HSC). But if the obvious similarity between the different types of cortical neurons and the modelled neurons of our system should be of any biological relevance, there must be a different mechanism. We can show in the next section, that synchronization mechanisms provide a surprisingly simple solution to this problem.

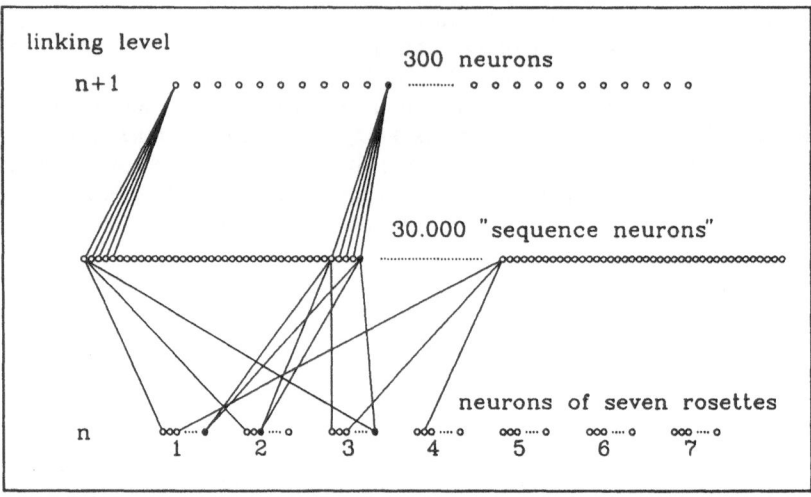

Fig. 6: A straight forward interconnection scheme proves to be extremly inefficient. About 30000 "sequence neurons" are wasted in order to provide 300 linking neurons.

4 Synchronization and hierarchical representation

Ten years ago von der Malsburg [6] has pointed out that temporal labelling would provide a very efficient tool for neural information processing. Freeman [7] reported first evidence of synchronous activity in the olfactory system, and recently Gray and Singer [8] and also Eckhorn and Reitböck [9] found stimulus induced oscillations in the visual cortex. Simulations of synchronization mechanisms are based on two types of models. Schillen and König [10] are modelling coupled oscillators, while Eckhorn [11] and Taylor [12] include leaky integrator model neurons. Some of these models use long range interconnections between synchronized neurons. But for some reasons discussed below, our model is exclusively based on next neighbour interconnections.

Our model neurons are of the well known type described by French and Stein [13]. In detail, the incoming spike signals are multiplied by a synaptic weight and temporally integrated by a leaky integrator. The signals of all the integrators are summed up to yield the membrane potential which is compared with a dynamic threshold. As soon as the membrane potential exceeds the threshold a spike is generated and the threshold is increased by a fixed step. The threshold decays exponentially to its normal value within a refractory period.

To explain the synchronizing mechanism, we restrict our two-dimensional network to a chain for a moment (fig. 7). The neurons are driven by afferent signals at feeding inputs. The synaptic weights at these inputs are relatively small and the time constants are relatively long. As a result, a simple spike does not cause a major change of the membrane potential and activation results from temporal integration over many spikes. In addition to the afferent signals, each neuron receives signals from its next neighbours (fig. 7) at trigger inputs. The synaptic weights at these inputs are higher and a single spike may increase the membrane potential significantly. So a neuron may be stimulated by a single spike at a trigger input if its membrane potential is close to the threshold. In other words, a neuron can only be triggered if it receives signals also at its feeding inputs. A neuron, however, will not be activated only by triggering-signals independend of the rate. This is due to a very short time constant at the triggering inputs, preventing significant temporal integration.

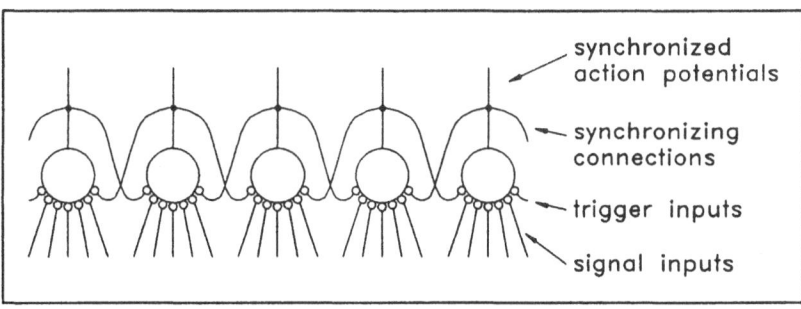

Fig. 7: Mutual synchronizing interconnections in a chain of neurons

At first sight, however, it seems impossible to synchronize a longer chain of neurons by this mechanism. There is a delay between an incoming spike at a trigger input and the resulting spike of the activated neuron. This delay seems to accumulate and to disturb synchronization. Fortunately, this consideration proves to be a fallacy and there is synchronism as soon as refractory behaviour of neurons is included.

Our synchronization mechanism is easily explained by fig. 8. At the ordinate the neuron numbers are plotted in the order of the chain, while time is represented at the abscissa. The circles show the moment of firing and exact synchronism would be represented by circles exactly located on a perpendicular line. For simplicity, we assume that all the neurons have been synchronously active before time zero which is outside the left margin of fig. 8. All neurons receive activity at feeding inputs and so some of them (filled circles in fig. 8) become supraliminal without being influenced by trigger pulses from neighbours. But as soon as these neurons 3, 6 and 10 in our example are activated, they send trigger signals to their neighbours. Neuron 3 triggers its neighbours 2 and 4, neuron 2 triggers neuron 1, and neuron 4 would like to trigger its neighbour 5. But neuron 5 was already activated by neuron 6 and so it is in its absolute refractory period.

In a chain with n neurons, i neurons will fire input-driven and $s = n-i$ will fire due to stimulation. From each of the i input driven neurons, two wave fronts of triggering signals are starting, travelling up and down the chain. A wave front stops as soon as it collides with another front, travelling in the opposite direction. The mean number of neurons, triggered by one wave front is $n/2i$, which is obviously independent of the number n of neurons in the chain. This number $n/2i$ multiplied by the delay between triggering signal and output spike is a good measure for the time interval within which all neurons of a chain are firing.

We adjusted the parameters of our model neurons to values compatible with biological neurons. The total input rate, summed up over all feeding inputs of one neuron was 200 spikes/second. The increase of membrane potential was adjusted to 4 mV per spike at a feeding input and 10 mV per spike at a trigger input. The time constant was 30 ms at feeding inputs and 2 ms at trigger inputs. The delay time between a triggering spike and a stimulated spike was adjusted to 1ms. With these parameters we immediately achieved good synchronization. With different parameter settings we could show that the synchronization effect is not limited to a small parameter space.

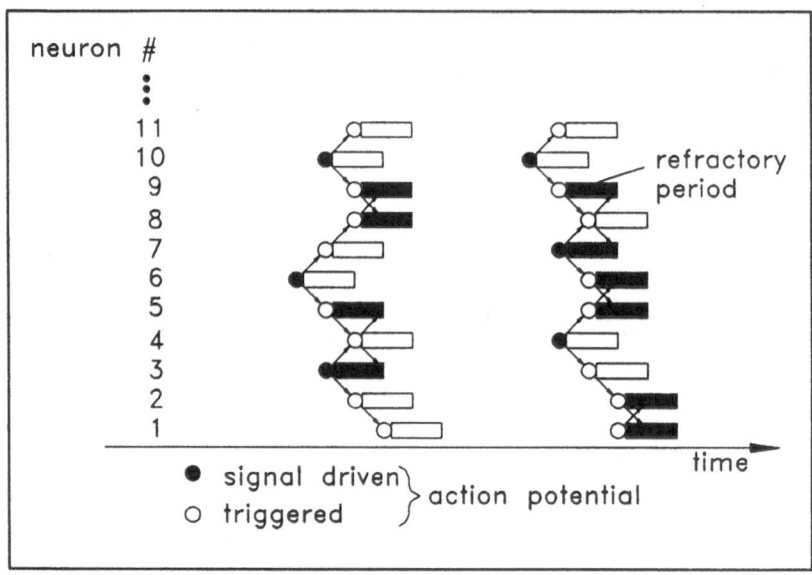

Fig. 8: Synchronisation in a chain of mutually interconnected neurons

Now we are ready to return to our two dimensional problem and to show that the previously described mechanism remains valid. We simulated a small visual field with 16x16 hexagonally arranged subfields (compare fig. 5). Each of these subfields is again represented by detector neurons $<t,m,\varphi\,|\,k,0>$ with differently shaped oriented receptive fields. In our simulations we simplified the feeding inputs and we also reduced the complexity of the detector set by omitting detectors with highly curved receptive fields. We added, however, the interconnections necessary for synchronization.

Suppose a bright line is running through subfield A, B, C, D, E, F, G in fig. 9. The line shall fit to the receptive fields of neuron 1, 2, 3, 4, 5, 6, and 7 so that these neurons are excited. As in our chain configuration, neuron 1 and 2, 2 and 3, and all the other adjacent pairs shall be mutually interconnected. As we have seen in the last chapter, all the neurons of this chain will synchronize their spikes.

Now we change the input pattern to a slightly different contour encoded by the neurons 1, 2, 8, 9, 10 and 7 (fig. 9). In this case neuron 2 must be connected with neuron 8 instead of 3 and similarly neuron 7 with neuron 10 instead of 6. Of course it is simple to add all the new interconnections 2-8, 8-9, 9-10, and 10-7. But we are not allowed to remove the old interconnections as long as we want to present the old pattern again. The problem is not to achieve synchronism in the new chain, the problem is to ensure that synchronization is not disturbed by the additional interconnections due to the old pattern.

This is easily proved in two steps. If our new line runs through the receptive fields of neurons 1, 2, 8, 9, 10 and 7, the neurons in the "dead branch" of the chain (3, 4, 5, 6) receive no signals at feeding inputs. According to our parameter setting these neurons can not be activated by spikes at trigger inputs. So our first conclusion shows that neurons in the "dead branch" remain subliminal, though some of them (3 and 6) receive trigger signals. If, however, neurons in the "dead branch" remain subliminal, we easily conclude that they can not send spikes to the "active branch", disturbing synchronization.

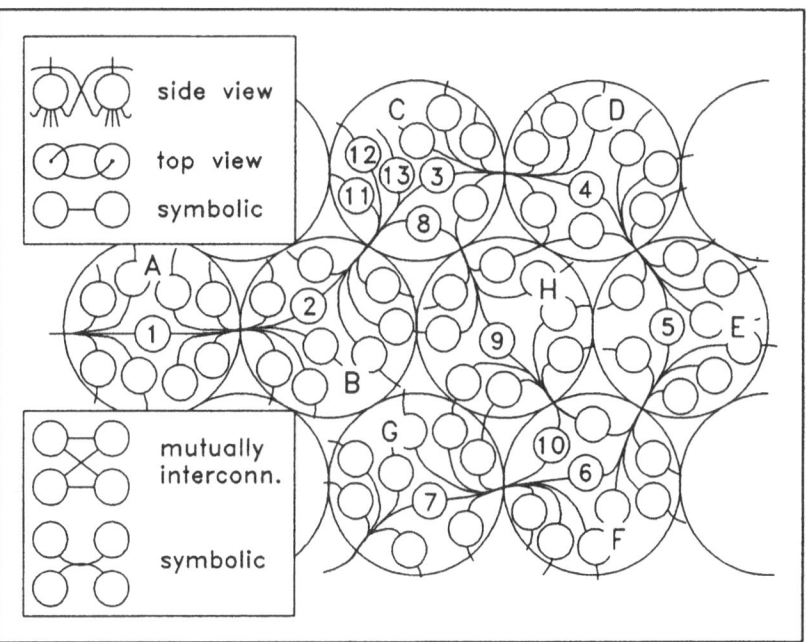

Fig. 9: Synchronistion mechanism in a two dimensional visual field. Neurons of adjacent subfields with fitting receptive fields are mutually connected.

Of course, patterns in our visual field are not restricted to two different lines, and we need a tremendous number of differently combined chains to represent all these contours. It is the advantage of our distributed synchronization mechanism that all these chains are realized by a simple interconnection scheme. In our model synchronization exclusively depends on next neighbour interconnections and these are limited to pairs of neurons in adjacent subfields. More exactly, each neuron of a subfield must be connected to all neurons with fitting receptive fields. If all neurons with fitting receptive fields are mutually interconnected, also those neurons will always be connected which are activated by an arbitrary continuous contour. As we have proved above, all the other interconnections outside the activated chain can not disturb synchronization. In simulations we presented arbitrary continuous contours activating up to 1337 neurons. Synchronization was as good as in the case of one dimensional chains.

This synchronous response to continuous contours is due to the special interconnection scheme between trigger inputs of matching neurons. Simulations show that these interconnections can be organized by unsupervised learning. We presented arbitrary continuous contours to the network, and allowed the weights at the trigger inputs to change according to a Hebbian-like rule. The general idea is to start with a complete mutual interconnection between all the trigger inputs of neurons in adjacent subfields and to increase the weights of simultaneously active pairs [14]. As the synchronizing interconnections are exclusively local, we restricted the network to a group of seven subfields. The resulting weights were copied to the other subfields at the end of the learning period.

Sometimes synchronization is synonymously used with feature linking. We prefer to regard synchronism as a non-physical labeling of linkable features which proves to be very advantageous for our actual linking mechanism. In the preceding section we tried to achieve the linking mechanism of our hierarchical representation in two steps by a "physical" interconnection (fig. 6) and we ended up with a combinatorical explosion. Now we are ready to show that our two step linking mechanism is easily realized in one step, if linkable features are "non-physically" labeled by synchronized activity.

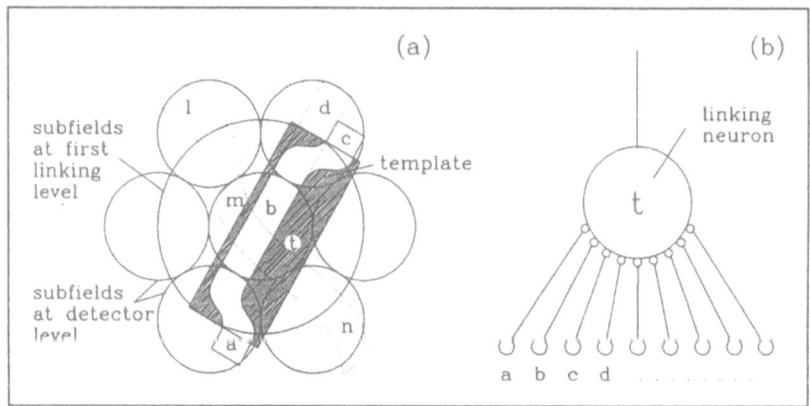

Fig. 10: Neuron t performs linking as well as the tempate operation (b) if all those neurons a, b, c, d, ... are interconnected, which may be part of a sequence within the template (a) of neuron t.

The one step implementation of our linking mechanism is shown by fig. 10 . The receptive fields of neurons a, b and c form a sequence and these neurons at the detector level $|k, n = 0>$ are acitvated and synchronized by a corresponding contour. The receptive fields of these neurons are enveloped by the double sized template of neuron t and this neuron is activated by the incoming synchronized signals of neurons a, b and c (fig. 10b). Though neuron t represents the sequence a, b, c it must not be confused with a "sequence neuron" in fig. 6. Neuron t in fig. 10 has hundreds of imputs from different neurons forming sequences. As an example, t also becomes active if a continuous contour excites neurons a, b and d. This is correct as the receptive fields of a, b and d form another sequence enveloped by the template of neuron t. In our new architecture (fig. 10), not only neurons a, b, c and d provide input to neuron t, but all those neurons of the rosette belonging to sequences within the template of neuron t. So neuron t is already the linking neuron at the first linking level $|k,n=0>$.

Without synchronized activity at the detector level this simple interconnection would fail. If only activity of three neurons at $|k,0>$ would be sufficient to activate t, e. g. activity of a, b and c, then neuron t could also be activated by a, c and d (fig. 10). This is obviously wrong, however, as the receptive fields of a, c and d form not a sequence. If the activity at the detector level is synchronized by continuous contours, neuron t is able to verify continuity. In the case of synchronous input activity the increments at the membrane potential of neuron t pile up and t responds with a spike after a short delay. As neuron t provides a spike for each triple of synchronized spikes, neuron t itself is synchronized to the detector neurons. If the input to t is not due to a continuous contour, e. g. if a, c and d are active, there is no "pile up" at the membrane potential and neuron t remains subliminal.

As the linking neurons are synchronized to the detector neurons, there is also synchronism at the first linking level between all those neurons, linking parts of continuous contour. So neurons at the first linking level $|k,1>$ are linked to neurons at the second linking level $|k,2>$ by exactly the same mechanism (fig. 10) by which detector neurons at level $|k,0>$ are linked to neurons at level $|k,1>$. Generally spoken, a hierarchical representation of continuous contour structures at different linking levels $|k,n>$ is easily achieved, if linkable features are "labelled" by synchronization. The interconnection scheme is uniform for all the linking layers and very simple compared with the scheme of fig. 6.

5 Conclusion

The preceding sections deal with technical and also biological aspects of pattern recognition. From an engineer's point of view we can regard our system as a small contribution to the rapidly growing research in the field of artificial neural networks. We sketch the complete architecture of a system between camera and associative memory and we show that proper operation crucially depends on a hierarchical neural representation of images.

The architecture of our system is based on a special interpretation of invariance in the biological visual system. Biological mechanisms like presynaptic control or synchronization play an essential role in our implementation. But in the true sense of the word our system is not a model of the biological system. There are, however, two results asking for a biological interpretation.

Firstly, the neurons at different linking levels of our hierarchical representastion are remarkably similar with cortical neurons at different levels of complexity. In our system neurons at different linking levels are absolutely necessary and there is the question whether neurons of different complexity play a similar role in the biological system. Secondly, the only simple way to simulate hierarchical representations was on the base of synchronization. So there is the question whether there is a similar interconnection scheme in the biological system.

We know the objections against a hierarchical cortical interconnection between simple and complex neurons: there is no delay between response of simple and complex cells, and there is evidence that complex neurons receive input from the fast Y-system. In our system, however, there is no significant delay due to the immediate stimulation of higher levels by synchronous spikes. We also have some ideas, how to include fast input signals to complex neurons in our model.

Acknowledgement: This work is supported by a grant (413 5839 -01 IN 105 C/5 of the BMFT

REFERENCES

[1]   Hubel, D. H., Wiesel, T. N.: *Receptive fields of single neurons in the cat's striate cortex.* J. Physiol. 148, 574-579 (1959)

[2]   Maffei, L.: *Spatial frequency channels: neural mechanisms.* In: Handbook of Sensory Physiology, vol. 8, Springer, 39-66 (1978)

[3]   Feldmann, J. A.: *A functional model of vision and space.* In: M. R. Arbib and A. R. Hanson (Eds.): Vision, Brain, and Cooperative Computation, MIT Press 531-562 (1987)

[4]   Hartmann, G.: *Learning in a closed loop antagonistic network.* In: Artifical Neural Networks, T. Kohonen et al. (Eds.), Elsevier Science Publishers, 239-244 (1991)

[5]   Hartmann, G.: *Recognition of hierarchically encoded images by technical and biological systems.* Biol. Cybern. 57, 73-84 (1987)

[6]   von der Malsburg, C.: *The correlation theory of brainfunction.* Internal report 81-2, Dpt. Neurobiology, Max Planck Institute for Biophysical Chemistry (1981)

[7]   Freeman, W. J.: *Mass action in the nervous system.* Academic Press New York (1975)

[8]   Gray, C. M., Singer, W.: *Stimulus specific neuronal oscillations in the cat visual cortex: a cortical functional unit.* Soc. Neurosc. abstr. 404.3 (1987)

[9]   Eckhorn, R. et al.: *Coherent oscillations: a mechanism of feature linking in the visual cortex.* Biol. Cybern. 60, 121-130 (1988)

[10]   Schillen, T. B. and König, P.: *Stimulus - dependent assembly formation of oscillatory responses: I. Synchronization, II. Desynchronization.* Neural Computation 3(2) (1991)

[11]   Eckhorn, R. et al.: *Feature linking via stimulus-evoked oscillations: Experimental results from cat visual cortex and funcional implications from a network model.* Proc. IJCNN89, IEEE, 1.723-1.730 (1989)

[12]   Mannion, C. L. T. and Taylor, J. G.: *Coupled excitable cells.* To appear in NCM'90: Developments in Neural Computing. C. L. T. Mannion and J. G. Taylor (eds.) Springer (to appear)

[13]   French, A. S., Stein, R. B.: *A flexible neuronal analog using integrated circuits.* IEEE Trans. Biomed. Eng., 17, 248-253 (1970)

[14]   Hartmann, G. and Drüe, S.: *Self organization of a network linking features by synchronization.* In: Parallel Processing in Neural Systems and Computers, R. Eckmiller, G. Hartmann and G. Hauske (Eds.), Elsevier Science Publishers 361-364 (1990)

AUTHOR INDEX